THE EUROPEAN UNION AND GLOBAL EMERGENCIES

This collection of essays analyses the European Union's involvement in global emergencies from a law and policy perspective. Bringing together leading academics and officials from the European Union institutions, the book offers an expert account of the theoretical and practical issues the EU faces when dealing with global emergencies. The subjects covered are highly topical and include the financial and debt crisis, regional security and the fight against terrorism, public health and food scares, human trafficking and energy security.

Volume 26 in the series Modern Studies in European Law

Modern Studies in European Law

Recent titles in this series:

Unfair Contract Terms in European Law: A Study in Comparative and EC Law
Paolisa Nebbia

Energy Security: The External Legal Relations of the European Union with Major Oil and Gas Supplying Countries *Sanam S Haghighi*

EU Criminal Law *Valsamis Mitsilegas*

Effective Judicial Protection and the Environmental Impact Assessment Directive in Ireland *Áine Ryall*

Network-Based Governance in EC Law: The Example of EC Competition and EC Communications Law *Maartje de Visser*

Legitimacy in EU Cartel Control *Ingeborg Simonsson*

Mixed Agreements Revisited: The EU and its Member States in the World
Edited by Christophe Hillion and Panos Koutrakos

Reflexive Governance: Redefining the Public Interest in a Pluralistic World
Edited by Olivier De Schutter and Jacques Lenoble

The Impact of EU Law on Minority Rights *Tawhida Ahmed*

Direct Investment, National Champions and EU Treaty Freedoms: From Maastricht to Lisbon *Frank S Benyon*

The Cyprus Issue: The Four Freedoms in a Member State under Siege
Nikos Skoutaris

For the complete list of titles in this series, see 'Modern Studies in European Law' link at www.hartpub.co.uk/books/series.asp

The European Union and Global Emergencies

A Law and Policy Analysis

Edited by

Antonis Antoniadis

Robert Schütze

and

Eleanor Spaventa

• HART •
PUBLISHING

OXFORD AND PORTLAND, OREGON
2011

Published in the United Kingdom by Hart Publishing Ltd
16C Worcester Place, Oxford, OX1 2JW
Telephone: +44 (0)1865 517530
Fax: +44 (0)1865 510710
E-mail: mail@hartpub.co.uk
Website: http://www.hartpub.co.uk

Published in North America (US and Canada) by
Hart Publishing
c/o International Specialized Book Services
920 NE 58th Avenue, Suite 300
Portland, OR 97213–3786
USA
Tel: +1 503 287 3093 or toll-free: (1) 800 944 6190
Fax: +1 503 280 8832
E-mail: orders@isbs.com
Website: http://www.isbs.com

British Library Cataloguing in Publication Data

Data Available

ISBN: 978-1-84946-082-8

Typeset by Columns Design XML Ltd, Reading
Printed and bound in Great Britain by
TJ International Ltd, Padstow, Cornwall

Foreword

The first decade of the twenty-first century has been marked by a series of emergencies – terrorism, wars and rebellions; natural and man-made disasters; and the destabilisation of the world's financial and economic foundations. The climate, the safety of maritime areas and even whole countries, and energy and food supplies are under threat. Europe is affected by them all in human, political and economic terms.

At the time of writing this Preface, the damage to the nuclear power plant at Fukushima has put in issue once again the wisdom of relying on nuclear power as an answer to Europe's over-reliance on fossil fuels. Almost contemporaneously the fire of dissent lit in Tunisia threatens to destabilise regimes throughout the Maghreb (a term that used at one time to embrace Andalusia, Sicily and Malta) emphasising that, for Europe, the Mediterranean is truly the 'middle sea'. Quite apart from the toll of human suffering that Europe must play its part in alleviating, the effect of these new developments on the world's financial and economic stability is wholly unpredictable.

In the media coverage of these global crises, and the many others with which we have been confronted since the heady days of 1989, the European Union figures hardly at all. The larger Member States play a part but they parade their disagreements in public while claiming the credit for any success. They hardly even try to present a united front to the rest of the world. Some observers are pleased that this is so, since it supports their belief that a political union was never more than a pipe dream and a rather dangerous one at that. Others lament the fact that it should be so, but accept that the workings of the EU and the scale of its successes do not lend themselves to simple explanations.

The reality is that the workings of the EU are necessarily complex because it is a novel experiment in continental governance developed against a background of ever more complex and dangerous global events. So we need to know whether the EU's constitutional machinery is fitted to meet these challenges. Do we indeed know what the challenges are and what has already been done to face them? These are the fundamental questions to which this book seeks to provide some at least of the answers.

The book is the product of a very lively conference at Durham University organised by the Durham European Law Institute of which I have been privileged to serve as a member of its Board. The resulting papers have now been brought together within an overall structure that is clearly explained in the Editors' Introduction. They deserve very close study, not least by those who believe that the EU is toothless and impotent. I hope and believe that the book will contribute to a better public understanding of the challenges and the ways in which the EU seeks to meet them.

Sir David Edward
Edinburgh, March 2011

Acknowledgements

In 2009, the Durham European Law Institute organised a series of events generously funded by the European Commission Representation in the United Kingdom under the theme of 'The EU and Global Emergencies'. The project included a seminar series, a public lecture, a public debate and an international conference which was held in Durham on 8–9 May 2009. We are grateful to the European Commission, the Durham European Law Institute, and the Durham Law School for their generous financial and logistical support. We are also grateful to all those who contributed to the success of the project and in particular to Tom Allen, then Head of School; Michelle Zang, Annegret Engel and Nadine Zipperle, for helping with the organisation of the conference; and to Julie Platten for her invaluable organisational skills. We are of course indebted to all conference participants and especially to those who presented a paper and to those who agreed to chair the sessions. Finally, we would like to thank the staff at Hart Publishing, and in particular Rachel Turner, for their patience and professionalism.

Antonis Antoniadis
Robert Schütze
Eleanor Spaventa

Contents

List of Contributors

Antonis Antoniadis is a Legal Officer in the Office of the European Ombudsman, a Lecturer in Law at Durham Law School, Durham University and has served as the Deputy-Director of the Durham European Law Institute.

Alessandra Arcuri is Associate Professor, Department of International Law and Rotterdam Institute of Law and Economics, Erasmus School of Law, Erasmus University of Rotterdam.

Steven Blockmans is the Head of the Department of Research at the TMC Asser Institute (The Hague) and a Visiting Professor at the University of Leuven.

Peter Cameron is the Director of the Centre for Energy, Petroleum and Mineral Law and Policy, University of Dundee, and a Professor of International Energy Law and Policy, as well as an honorary professorial fellow at the University of Edinburgh Europa Institute.

Tim Corthaut is a Post-doctoral Researcher and Project Manager at the Leuven Centre for Global Governance Studies, University of Leuven.

Marise Cremona is Professor of European Law, European University Institute.

Holly Cullen is the Winthrop Professor of Law, University of Western Australia.

Alan Dashwood is Professor Emeritus of European Law at the University of Cambridge and Fellow Emeritus of Sidney Sussex College, Cambridge.

Daniela Gauci is a Legal Adviser in the Legal Service of the European Parliament.

Caoimhín MacMaoláin is a Lecturer in Law, School of Law, Trinity College Dublin.

Gilles Marhic is a Legal Adviser in the Legal Service of the Council of the European Union.

Robert Schütze is a Reader in Law at Durham Law School.

Eleanor Spaventa is a Reader in Law at Durham Law School, the Director of the Durham European Law Institute, and a Professor of European Law at the College of Europe, Natolin.

Steven Sterkx is Research Coordinator of the Leuven Centre for Global Governance Studies and a Lecturer on the History of European Integration, University of Leuven.

Ramses Wessel is Professor of the Law of the European Union and other International Organizations, Centre for European Studies, University of Twente.

Eric White is a Legal Adviser in the Legal Service of the European Commission.

Jan Wouters is Jean Monnet Chair *Ad Personam* 'EU and Global Governance', Professor of International Law and International Organizations and the Director of the Leuven Centre for Global Governance Studies and the Institute for International Law, University of Leuven.

Table of Cases

Canada

European Court of Human Rights

European Court of Justice

Alphabetical

Chronological

Permanent Court of International Justice

United Kingdom

United States of America

WTO

Table of Legislation

Canada

European Union

Common Positions

Decisions

Directives

Joint Actions

Recommendations

Regulations

Resolutions

Germany

United Kingdom

Statutory Instrument

United States of America

Table of Conventions, Treaties, etc

Introduction: the European Union and Global Emergencies

BY AND LARGE, modern societies face three major types of crisis:[1] political crises, such as wars or rebellions; or natural disasters, such as floods or earthquakes; or economic crises, a type of emergency which has become more prominent in contemporary society.[2] How should a legal order deal with such emergencies? Constitutional orders are designed to consolidate solutions to social problems. What if this social order is challenged—internally or externally—to such an extent that its 'ordinary' principles appear inadequate?

Two constitutional options are possible: a 'relativist' or an 'absolutist' approach.[3] The 'relativist' approach accepts that the ordinary constitutional principles may not apply in emergency situations and can be suspended in times of crisis. This approach has informed German constitutional thought. It found expression in Article 48 of the Weimar Constitution,[4] and the current German Constitution provides an extensive 'emergency constitution' that will abrogate the ordinary constitutional principles in times of crisis.[5]

[1] There are different possible typologies. For example, the Canadian Constitution distinguishes four types of emergencies: 'public welfare', 'public order', 'international' and 'war' emergencies; *cf* (Canadian) Emergencies Act 1985 (c 22—Supplement IV).

[2] CL Rossiter, *Constitutional Dictatorship: Crisis Government in the Modern Democracies* (New York, Harcourt, Brace & World, 1963) 6.

[3] On the distinction between 'absolutist' and 'relativist' views, see: J Lobel, 'Emergency Power and the Decline of Liberalism' (1988–89) 98 *Yale Law Journal* 1385. For a different typology, see: O Gross and F Ní Aoláin, *Law in Times of Crisis* (Cambridge, Cambridge University Press, 2006), distinguishing between 'accommodation' models, 'business-as-usual' models, and 'extra-constitutional' models.

[4] On the use of Art 48 of the Weimar Constitution, see: CL Rossiter, *Constitutional Dictatorship* (n 2) especially chs III–V. The abuse of emergency powers during the Weimar Republic led to the suspension of the the 'relativist' constitutional approach under the early Bonn Constitution. *Cf* CG Schweitzer, 'Emergency Powers in the Federal Republic of Germany' (1969) 22 *Western Political Quarterly* 112.

[5] The 'emergency constitution' is placed in a separate title within the German Constitution and was designed for the 'state of defence'. It provides, inter alia, for special constitutional principles that allow an extension of the legislative powers of the federation (Art 115c GC) and a shortened legislative procedure for urgent bills (Art 115d GC). For an argument in favour of an 'emergency constitution' in the United States, see: B Ackermann, 'The Emergency Constitution' (2004) 113 *Yale Law Journal* 1029.

By contrast, the 'absolutist' approach has informed the United States of America.[6] It considers the constitution as a 'law for all seasons';[7] yet, this does not prevent the legislator from adopting 'emergency legislation'.[8] In the words of the Supreme Court: 'While emergency does not create power, emergency may furnish the occasion for the exercise of power.'[9]

While not a state, the European Union may face one of the three emergency types identified above, either within or outside its borders. In this respect, if the above typology of constitutional approaches were to be applied to it, the Union legal order would be posited nearer the 'absolutist' constitutional approach, which implies the absence of an 'emergency constitution'. The EU legal order nonetheless offers a variety of constitutional and legislative tools to deal with internal or external emergencies. From the very beginning, the European (Economic) Community expressly recognized special emergency powers.[10] Moreover, the 'ordinary' powers under Articles 100 and 235 EEC served as the legal basis, within an emergency context, to develop a monetary as well as an environmental policy.[11] This adaptability to emergencies could already be seen in 1974, when the (then) European Communities faced a global economic emergency—the oil crisis:

> Recognizing the need for an overall approach to the internal problems involved in achieving European unity and the external problems facing Europe, the Heads of Government consider it essential to ensure progress and overall consistency in the activities of the Communities and in the work on political cooperation. The Heads of

[6] See also: G Winterton, 'The Concept of Extra-Constitutional Executive Power in Domestic Affairs' (1979–80) 7 *Hastings Constitutional Law Quarterly* 1, 40: 'It [the US Constitution] was framed by men who had experienced war. They wrote a document which recognized that the nation would be faced with problems of war, invasion, insurrection, rebellion and domestic violence, and they gave Congress and the President power to deal with them. The suggestion that, if and when these vicissitudes arise, the Constitution should be suspended, because it was not intended to operate in times of crisis, is not only factually incorrect, but subversive of the system of constitutional democracy practiced in the United States.'

[7] In *Ex parte Milligan*, the US Supreme Court thus held that 'The Constitution of the United States is a law for rulers and people, equally in war and in peace' and therefore applied 'at all times, and under all circumstances': *Ex Parte Milligan* 71 US 2 (1866), 120.

[8] J Ferejohn and P Pasquino, 'The Law of the Exception: A Typology of Emergency Powers' (2004) 2 *International Journal of Constitutional Law* 210, 215: 'Advanced democracies do not necessarily need to use constitutional powers when confronting emergencies. They often prefer to deal with emergencies through ordinary legislation. Such legislation may delegate a great deal of authority to the executive and may be enacted for temporary periods. And there may be a sense that the legislation is in some ways exceptional. But, however unusual it may be, emergency legislation remains ordinary within the framework of the constitutional system[.]'

[9] *Home Building & Loan Association v Blaisdell* 290 US 398 (1934), 426.

[10] The 1958 EEC Treaty recognised specific exceptions to the normal constitutional principles in the context of the free movement of capital (*cf* Art 73 EEC), state aids (Art 92(2) and (3) EEC), and the common commercial policy (Art 115 EEC).

[11] J Usher, 'The Gradual Widening of European Community Policy on the Basis of Articles 100 and 235 of the EEC Treaty' in J Schwarze and HG Schermers (eds), *Structure and Dimension of European Community Policy* (Baden-Baden, Nomos, 1988) 25.

> Government have therefore decided to meet, accompanied by the Ministers of Foreign Affairs, three times a year and, whenever necessary, in the Council of the Communities and in the context of political cooperation ... These arrangements do not in any way affect the rules and procedures laid down in the Treaties ...
>
> With a view to progress towards European unity, the Heads of Government reaffirm their determination gradually to adopt common positions and coordinate their diplomatic action in all areas of international affairs which affect the interests of the European Community. The President-in-Office will be the spokesman for the Nine and will set out their views in international diplomacy. He will ensure that the necessary concertation always takes place in good time ... The Heads of Government consider it necessary to increase the solidarity of the Nine both by improving Community procedures and by developing new common policies in areas to be decided on and granting the necessary powers to the Institutions.[12]

The birth of the European Council, an institution not envisaged in the Rome Treaty, represented a pragmatic mixture of intergovernmentalism and supranationalism. It soon provided significant impetus to the supranational Community, particularly relevant at times of crisis.

The (reformed) European Union legal order builds on the limited Union emergency constitution.[13] Article 78(3) TFEU, for example, offers a special legal basis for provisional measures '[i]n the event of one or more Member States being confronted by an emergency situation characterised by a sudden inflow of nationals of third countries'. Another example may be found in Article 122 TFEU, which provides, in paragraph 1, for appropriate measures 'if severe difficulties arise in the supply of certain products, notably in the area of energy', and, in paragraph 2, for Union financial assistance to a Member State 'in difficulties or . . . seriously threatened with severe difficulties caused by natural disasters or exceptional occurrences beyond its control.' Beyond the Treaties, provision for emergency situations is made widely in EU legislation.[14] A good illustration for this 'legislative' approach is Article 5(a)(6) of the Comitology Decision, which provides a special 'emergency procedure' for the adoption of executive legislation in times when urgent action is needed.[15]

With the above in mind, the aim of this edited collection is to provide an overview of the Union's limited emergency constitution. The objective of this book is not to provide a comprehensive treatise on the Union's emergency powers and policies. This book identifies and discusses certain constitutional horizontal

[12] European Council, 'Communiqué of the meeting of heads of Government of the Community' (1974) 12 *Bulletin of the European Communities* 7–12.

[13] Special exceptions are made in the Treaty on European Union (Arts 30(2), 41 and 42(7) TEU) as well as in the Treaty on the Functioning of the European Union (Arts 78(3), 213 and 218 TFEU).

[14] *cf* Council Regulation 1224/2009 establishing a Community control system for ensuring compliance with the rules of the common fisheries policy [2009] OJ L343/1, especially Art 108 entitled 'Emergency Measures'.

[15] Council Decision 1999/468 laying down the procedures for the exercise of implementing powers conferred to the Commission [1999] OJ L184/23 as amended by Council Decision 2006/512 [2006] OJ L200/11.

questions, such as the Union's competences, instruments and procedures. Indisputably, the Union's constitution is better understood when tested in specific policy contexts. This is because of the existence of policy-specific emergency provisions in the Treaties and the measures which have been taken in accordance with 'ordinary' constitutional principles. The book is not intended to remain purely theoretical. The emergency provisions of the Treaties have, on many occasions, been tested in practice, and a practical perspective should complement the theoretical analysis.

To achieve these objectives, the book is divided into three parts: Constitutional Challenges (Part I); Thematic Challenges (Part II); and The Perspective of the Institutions (Part III). Part I analyses the basic parameters of the Union constitutional framework in dealing with global emergencies. It addresses common features of the Union's emergency constitution such as the perennial questions on EU competences, instruments, and procedures. Part II deals with the specific contexts, such as armed conflict, terrorism, the financial and debt crisis, energy security and food safety, within which the Union emergency constitution has been tested and developed. In this regard, the relevant contributions not only address the substantive content of EU policy, but they also examine context-specific constitutional challenges as they arise. Part III gives the perspective of the Union institutions and provides a practical flavour on how constitutional and substantive policy considerations are taken into account by those who handle such emergencies when they occur.

Chapter one provides an overview over the constitutional landscape created by the Treaties. To start with, Marise Cremona addresses the crucial questions concerning the Union's competences and instruments in emergency situations. Based on the principle of enumerated powers, the Union is not all-competent. It needs to base its actions on a legal basis that will determine the scope and nature of its powers. On the basis of its express 'emergency powers', the EU developed four main instruments to coordinate its response to global emergencies; in particular, the author analyses: (a) the Humanitarian Aid Regulation, (b) the Stability Instrument, (c) the Civil Protection Mechanism and (d) the crisis management missions within the framework of the Common Security and Defence Policy. However, the Union has equally utilised 'non-emergency powers' in emergency situations, and the second part of Cremona's contribution is dedicated to the constitutional potential offered by them.

Having regard to the Union's competence in various crisis situations, chapter two explores the constitutional issues arising from competence 'conflicts' when responding to global emergencies. Disagreements about competence to act in a given field of external relations are indeed a familiar feature of legal and political life in the Union, and as Alan Dashwood insists, 'they need to be managed sensibly, in order to minimise delays in decision-making', especially in situations such as global emergencies, 'where a timely response is of the essence'. Dashwood's chapter comments on the changes in the post-Lisbon constitutional order that are likely to have a bearing on future conflicts of competence, especially between the relevant TFEU competences and the Union's competence under the CFSP.

Internal or global emergencies often are the 'hour of the executive'. The slowness and complexities of the parliamentary procedure seem ill-equipped to meet emergencies. Emergencies require quick and strong action. The legislator will thus often delegate powers to the executive to—temporarily—deal with the crisis. However, many legal orders recognise constitutional limits to such a delegation. Is there a non-delegation doctrine in the Union legal order? What are the constitutional limits to delegated powers; and if there are limits, will they depend on the identity of the delegee? In chapter three, Robert Schütze analyses the constitutional principles restricting delegations of power to the European institutions, European agencies and international bodies, and the Member States. Europe's non-delegation doctrine is shown to be differential and flexible. The Union legal order thereby allows for wide regulatory powers to be delegated to the Commission as long as essential policy choices are constitutionally reserved to the Union legislature.

The book then moves to the thematic challenges starting with the Union's role in security emergencies in its neighbourhood. In chapter four, Steven Blockmans and Ramses Wessel examine the contribution of the Union to the resolution of armed conflicts on its borders in light of the European Security Strategy. Their principal question is: 'What kind of role can and should the European Union play to peacefully settle disputes in its neighbourhood?' Set against the background of the international legal framework for the peaceful settlement of disputes, their contribution pays special attention to the scope and limits of the European Neighbourhood Policy. The Union's role in the resolution of the conflict over South Ossetia and Abkhazia is thereby taken as a case study. They convincingly argue for a new *unitary* vision in the EU's approach to de facto states in the area of wider Europe.

Eleanor Spaventa looks at another global emergency: the terrorism threat, which is both a threat in itself and a threat for established fundamental rights principles. The author focuses on the practice of drawing lists of suspected terrorists and evaluates, from a fundamental rights perspective, the changes which have occurred as a result of judicial and legislative intervention. Despite the many improvements to the listing regimes, both at UN and EU level, the situation is still highly problematic, not least because of lack of judicial oversight at UN level; and, because of the unwillingness of the European courts to engage with substantive issues as to whether there is sufficient evidence to define those listed as terrorists. And yet, some mild optimism might for once be appropriate, especially in relation to the EU's own regime, where recent rulings of the general Court have significantly curtailed the discretion of the Council.

Article 194(1)(b) TFEU entrusts the Union to 'ensure security of energy supply'. Peter Cameron looks, in chapter six, at 'energy security', that is, the economic and social risks inherent in a dependence on imports of oil and gas.

While he admits that 'very few emergencies have ever materialised', he argues that 'the risks to energy security in the EU have increased significantly in the past decade'. The role of law in providing the basis for 'energy security' has thereby been little appreciated, despite the fact that a number of legal instruments were tried and tested by the Russo-Ukrainian gas disputes of 2006 and 2009. However, the latter fuelled an extensive debate on the legal approaches to avoid future energy emergencies through extensive monitoring and regulatory activities by the European Commission.

The book then shifts to economic crises. In chapter seven, Wouters, Sterkx and Corthaut discuss the 2008 financial crisis which exposed the fragility and weaknesses of the global financial system. Nevertheless, it has triggered a global response, principally within the framework of the revitalised G-20, and led to the reform of global financial governance. This chapter pays particular attention to the position, role and representation of the European Union in the changing system of financial governance and the international financial institutions. Building on the Union role and contribution during the financial crisis, the contribution reflects on the impact of the changes which were brought about by the Treaty of Lisbon.

Moving to the 2010 debt crisis, in chapter eight Antonis Antoniadis examines the specific measures taken to deal with the Greek crisis as well as the general measures to defend the Euro and to appease the financial markets. The contribution argues that the emergency measures at issue pose a number of interesting questions as regards the construction of the EU economic constitution, from both internal and external perspectives. The chapter also looks at the EU institutional architecture in economic governance as it emerges from the combined effect of the entry into force of the Treaty of Lisbon and the emergency measures taken to counteract the debt crisis.

Food safety represents another major challenge and is examined in the next two contributions. In chapter nine, Caoimhín MacMaoláin traces the development of rapid alert systems, crisis management procedures and the European Food Safety Authority in the BSE crisis of the 1980s. The current policy and legal framework contributed to the development of a crisis-centred approach in EU food law. This constitutes an important shortcoming as such but also because it channelled the focus of the EU in a specific direction. Food-borne diseases and contamination may have devastating consequences and it is important for the EU to shift its attention from 'crisis control' and dealing with 'emergencies' addressing ongoing concerns related to the nutritional value and the wholesomeness of food.

Alessandra Arcuri moves from the Union context to that of the World Trade Organization (WTO). Chapter ten explores the different theoretical models in risk analysis in the interpretation of the main legal concepts of the Sanitary and Phytosanitary (SPS) Agreement, namely, the quantitative-risk model and holistic-risk model. She concludes that the Appellate Body of the WTO seems to have a marked a paradigm shift to choose the holistic-risk model in the analysis of the key concepts of the SPS Agreement. This shift implies that WTO members can more easily include cultural and socio-economic considerations in the process of setting their food safety standards. This is crucially important for the EU, and should be welcomed, given that the EU has often argued for a more comprehensive approach in risk analysis.

In the final contribution to the thematic part, Holly Cullen looks at one of the plights of our times, the trafficking in human beings, and engages in an extensive and critical analysis of the EU response to such an emergency. Cullen's discussion of the progress and shortcomings of the EU's approach are contextualised with reference to international conventions, and especially to the Council of Europe Convention on Human Trafficking.

The last part of the book offers insights into EU action on the ground in cases of global emergency, thanks to contributions from members of the Institutions (Council, the Commission and the European Parliament) who have to respond to global emergencies. Many of the issues touched upon in this Part have been explored in other contributions; and yet, as the reader will note for herself, the insight from these three contributions on the workings and perspectives of those who have to react to emergencies, whether foreseeable or not, is unique. In this respect, Part III highlights the importance, for an effective (and efficient) response to global emergencies, of elements as diverse as the availability of manpower; of budgetary resources; of negotiating structures; and, of course, of an institutional mechanism allowing the Union to react swiftly whilst also respecting both institutional balance and allocation of competences.

In chapter twelve, Gilles Marhic provides us with a detailed account of how the Crisis Management Missions operate and the challenges they face, from staffing and chain of command issues, to matters concerning association of third parties and co-operation between the UN and the EU in crisis management. The contribution then addresses in detail the changes introduced by the Lisbon Treaty.

We then turn to the Commission's view on other tools and instruments developed by the Union to deal with a different set of global emergencies. Thus, Eric White, after having briefly reviewed the safeguard action and having contributed to the discussion about crisis management and its financing, addresses in more detail those challenges that affect directly Union citizens as well as the global community at large. White provides an analysis of the role of the precautionary principle in relation to food safety and environmental emergencies; he then turns briefly to the challenges arising from climate change and, topically, from the financial and economic crisis.

Finally, Daniela Gauci looks at the external aid measures in response to emergency situations. The chapter provides a detailed analysis of the available instruments from the perspective of the European Parliament as a co-decider and includes both the negotiations with the Commission and the Council which led to their adoption and the issues governing their implementation. The contribution also reflects on the role of the European Parliament in the post-Lisbon era and offers an interesting perspective on the new comitology regime.

Part I

The European Union and Global Emergencies: Constitutional Challenges

1

The EU and Global Emergencies: Competence and Instruments

MARISE CREMONA

I INTRODUCTION

THE FIRST PART of this book will consider the constitutional dimension of the EU and global emergencies, and in this chapter I will discuss the competence of the EU to act in global emergencies, and the different instruments it has at its disposal. To start with, we should remind ourselves of something that is perhaps obvious: the EU does not have unlimited power, it can act only where it has been given the competence to do so. As the Treaty of Lisbon says—in this as in so much else, restating the pre-existing position:

> The Union shall pursue its objectives by appropriate means commensurate with the competences which are conferred upon it in the Treaties.[1]

And:

> The limits of Union competences are governed by the principle of conferral. The use of Union competences is governed by the principles of subsidiarity and proportionality.
>
> Under the principle of conferral, the Union shall act only within the limits of the competences conferred upon it by the Member States in the Treaties to attain the objectives set out therein. Competences not conferred upon the Union in the Treaties remain with the Member States.[2]

More than this, when it acts, the Union has to choose the appropriate power or competence on which to base its actions; the different bases of competence (or legal bases) may carry different procedural requirements and allow different types of action. In the context we are discussing here, we need also to remember

[1] Art 3(6) TEU. In this chapter, the abbreviation 'TEU' used after a Treaty article refers to the Treaty on European Union in the version in force after 1 December 2009, while 'TFEU' refers to the Treaty on the Functioning of the European Union. The abbreviation 'EC' after a Treaty article refers to a provision of the European Community Treaty in the version in force until 30 November 2008; similarly 'EU' refers to an article of the Treaty on European Union in the version in force until that date.

[2] Art 5(1) and (2) TEU.

that the Union is constrained in terms of resources. Happily, it cannot just decide to spend its limited resources on whatever it wants; there must be a provision in the budget for that type of action and a financial instrument establishing the basis on which money can be spent. So in responding to a global emergency the Union cannot just be driven by need, or even politics, it needs to think about competence and resources. And it needs to make sure that what it does is coherent with what its Member States are doing and with the response of other agencies.

In this contribution, I am going to focus on the competence issue. What powers does the Union have to react to global emergencies? My purpose is not to go into a great deal of detail about each instrument since other contributions will discuss specific types of action, but rather to give an idea of the range of tools that are available for the EU and how its response 'toolkit' is structured. First, let us think about different types of global emergency:

- The 'classic' emergency caused by a natural disaster on a global scale: the Indian Ocean Tsunami, earthquakes, a volcanic eruption, famine.
- An emergency response to a man-made disaster: the Chernobyl nuclear explosion, a terrorist attack, the needs of populations uprooted by war and civil conflict.
- Global health emergencies: bird flu, swine fever, BSE.

Emergencies like these have certain characteristics: they happen suddenly without warning and require urgent action; they are not chronic, they do not represent an ongoing problem or structural state of affairs, although these may lead to an emergency. These characteristics suggest that in terms of instruments:

- We should exclude ongoing policy programmes such as development cooperation, which may be said to address the structural problems which may themselves lead to emergencies.
- We require a 'stand-by' capability that can be activated quickly.
- We need instruments that are geared to temporary relief, although they will hand over to other instruments in the longer term and smooth linkage is important.

Emergencies like these do not know boundaries, they may affect EU Member States as well as non-Member countries. As far as the EU is concerned we can identify a shift: initially the EU was mainly concerned with emergency response to overseas disasters. Member States were expected to deal with their own natural and man-made disasters, perhaps with offers of bilateral assistance but no concerted EU-level response. However since the mid-1990s, in a trend which has accelerated since 2000, we can see a tendency to expect an EU-level response to emergencies *within* the EU, and therefore the growth of strategies and plans at EU level to deal with possible future emergencies—a terrorist attack, a natural disaster, the financial crisis. Three new clauses in the Treaty of Lisbon sum up this development.

First, for overseas emergencies, the provisions relating to external action contain a new clause on humanitarian assistance to people in third countries, Article 214 TFEU:

1. The Union's operations in the field of humanitarian aid shall be conducted within the framework of the principles and objectives of the external action of the Union. Such operations shall be intended to provide ad hoc assistance and relief and protection for people in third countries who are victims of natural or man-made disasters, in order to meet the humanitarian needs resulting from these different situations. The Union's measures and those of the Member States shall complement and reinforce each other.
2. Humanitarian aid operations shall be conducted in compliance with the principles of international law and with the principles of impartiality, neutrality and non-discrimination.
3. The European Parliament and the Council, acting in accordance with the ordinary legislative procedure, shall establish the measures defining the framework within which the Union's humanitarian aid operations shall be implemented.
4. The Union may conclude with third countries and competent international organizations any agreement helping to achieve the objectives referred to in paragraph 1 and in Article 21 of the Treaty on European Union.
   The first subparagraph shall be without prejudice to Member States' competence to negotiate in international bodies and to conclude agreements.
5. In order to establish a framework for joint contributions from young Europeans to the humanitarian aid operations of the Union, a European Voluntary Humanitarian Aid Corps shall be set up. The European Parliament and the Council, acting by means of regulations in accordance with the ordinary legislative procedure, shall determine the rules and procedures for the operation of the Corps.
6. The Commission may take any useful initiative to promote coordination between actions of the Union and those of the Member States, in order to enhance the efficiency and complementarity of Union and national humanitarian aid measures.
7. The Union shall ensure that its humanitarian aid operations are coordinated and consistent with those of international organizations and bodies, in particular those forming part of the United Nations system.

This article provides a new explicit legal base for humanitarian aid which, as we shall see, has hitherto been conducted under development cooperation powers. A number of features of Article 214 TFEU are worth highlighting. First, the article covers 'ad hoc relief' directed at 'people in third countries'; it is an external measure designed for emergencies (natural or man-made disasters), rather than ongoing long-term assistance, which would fall under either Articles 208 or 212 TFEU. Second, although an express competence is given to the Union in this field enabling it to develop a common policy, this is not a competence which will have a pre-emptive effect on the Member States: as the Treaty puts it, 'the exercise of that [Union] competence shall not result in Member States being prevented from exercising theirs'.[3] Third, humanitarian aid is conducted in accordance with 'the

[3] Art 4(4) TFEU.

principles of impartiality, neutrality and non-discrimination' (paragraph 2); therefore, although it is also conducted within the framework of the EU's general principles and objectives relating to its external action,[4] it is not subject to conditionality. Fourth, this is clearly Union action, but there is an emphasis on coordination and complementarity with Member State action and indeed with the action of other international organizations. The High Representative for Foreign Affairs and Security Policy (HR) has an important role in managing this coordination, both between the EU institutions and between the EU and the Member States. So for example, when the earthquake struck Haiti on 12 January 2010, the High Representative, in coordination with the Spanish Presidency and the European Commission, convened an extraordinary session of the Foreign Affairs Council (Foreign Affairs/Development and Humanitarian Aid) on 18 January 2010 in order to make the first political statements and coordination declarations.[5]

The second new provision introduced by the Treaty of Lisbon is internal in perspective; Article 222 TFEU provides for solidarity between the Member States in the face of natural or man-made disasters and terrorist attack.[6] It states:

> 1. The Union and its Member States shall act jointly in a spirit of solidarity if a Member State is the object of a terrorist attack or the victim of a natural or man-made disaster. The Union shall mobilise all the instruments at its disposal, including the military resources made available by the Member States, to:
> (a) — prevent the terrorist threat in the territory of the Member States;
> — protect democratic institutions and the civilian population from any terrorist attack;
> — assist a Member State in its territory, at the request of its political authorities, in the event of a terrorist attack;
> (b) assist a Member State in its territory, at the request of its political authorities, in the event of a natural or man-made disaster.

[4] As set out in Arts 3(5) TEU and 21 TFEU.

[5] Council conclusions on the earthquake in Haiti, Extraordinary Foreign Affairs Council meeting, Brussels, 18 January 2010, Council doc 5418/10. Initially, the Commission allocated €30 million in humanitarian aid to Haiti, followed by €100 million of non-humanitarian assistance. In total, the aid was to amount to about €200 million. In the course of the subsequent meeting of 25 January 2010 further decisions were taken on the total volume of aid provided by the Member States and the EU amounting to approx. €422 million, and the operational capacity of the EU (including setting up a special office). See 'Haiti: Council agrees coordinated EU response to UN appeal', Press Release: 5686/10. The overall response to the Haiti earthquake crisis provided by the EU and 18 Member States is summarized in the Summary of Assistance Offers for Haiti, available at http://europa.eu/rapid/pressReleasesAction.do?reference=MEMO/10/81&format=HTML&aged=0&language=EN&guiLanguage=en.

[6] Note also Art 42(7) TEU which establishes an obligation to aid and assist in cases where a Member State suffers armed aggression on its territory; an important provision, but outside the scope of this chapter.

2. Should a Member State be the object of a terrorist attack or the victim of a natural or man-made disaster, the other Member States shall assist it at the request of its political authorities. To that end, the Member States shall coordinate between themselves in the Council.
3. The arrangements for the implementation by the Union of the solidarity clause shall be defined by a decision adopted by the Council acting on a joint proposal by the Commission and the High Representative of the Union for Foreign Affairs and Security Policy. The Council shall act in accordance with Article 31(1) of the Treaty on European Union where this decision has defence implications. The European Parliament shall be informed.
   For the purposes of this paragraph and without prejudice to Article 240, the Council shall be assisted by the Political and Security Committee with the support of the structures developed in the context of the common security and defence policy and by the Committee referred to in Article 71; the two committees shall, if necessary, submit joint opinions.
4. The European Council shall regularly assess the threats facing the Union in order to enable the Union and its Member States to take effective action.

We have here provision for action both by the Union (in paragraph 1) and the Member States (in paragraph 2), coordinated in the Council. In both cases action is taken only at the request of the political authorities of the Member State needing assistance.[7]

A third new provision in the TFEU deals with civil protection. Article 196 TFEU covers action both within the EU and internationally, reflecting (as we shall see) the most recent instruments adopted on civil protection:

1. The Union shall encourage cooperation between Member States in order to improve the effectiveness of systems for preventing and protecting against natural or man-made disasters. Union action shall aim to:
   (a) support and complement Member States' action at national, regional and local level in risk prevention, in preparing their civil-protection personnel and in responding to natural or man-made disasters within the Union;
   (b) promote swift, effective operational cooperation within the Union between national civil protection services;
   (c) promote consistency in international civil-protection work.
2. The European Parliament and the Council, acting in accordance with the ordinary legislative procedure shall establish the measures necessary to help achieve the objectives referred to in paragraph 1, excluding any harmonisation of the laws and regulations of the Member States.

[7] In March 2004, following the terrorist attack in Madrid, the Member States and States which would be acceding on 1 May 2004 adopted a Declaration to the effect that they would act jointly in case of terrorist attack, in the spirit of this Solidarity Clause which was at that stage in the Constitutional Treaty: Declaration on solidarity against terrorism, annexed to the Declaration on Combating Terrorism adopted by the European Council, 25 March 2004. See also Council Regulation 2012/2002/EC establishing the European Union Solidarity Fund [2002] OJ L311/3.

Again, the emphasis is on Union measures which will support, complement and help to coordinate Member State action, but not replace it.[8]

The fact that these three new provisions have been inserted into the Treaties by the Treaty of Lisbon does not mean that the EU did not previously have competence to act. Indeed, these provisions create new explicit legal bases for a practice which has grown up using other Treaty powers. In the following section we will look briefly at the most important instruments.

II THE MAIN INSTRUMENTS

The four main instruments hitherto used by the EU in coordinating its response to different types of global emergency are: (a) the Humanitarian Aid Regulation, (b) the Stability Instrument, (c) the Civil Protection Mechanism and (d) crisis management missions within the framework of the Common Security and Defence Policy (CSDP).

A Humanitarian aid and food aid

Regulation 1257/96/EC on humanitarian aid provides the legal framework for humanitarian aid response.[9] It is based on Article 179 EC (now Article 209 TFEU), thus it has been linked to the Union's development cooperation policy although, as we have seen, the Treaty of Lisbon has added a new explicit legal base for humanitarian aid. Article 1 sets out its scope: to give assistance, relief and protection in case of natural disasters or man-made crises, or similar exceptional circumstances, as well as disaster preparation and prevention operations. Article 2 specifies the EU's objectives in terms of saving and preserving life during emergencies, providing assistance and relief to people affected by longer-lasting crises, financing the transport of aid and logistical support, short-term rehabilitation and reconstruction work, helping to cope with the consequences of population movements caused by natural and man-made disasters including repatriation and resettlement, disaster preparedness, early-warning and intervention systems, and civil operations to protect the victims of fighting or comparable emergencies. Articles 3 and 4 establish the types of action that may be financed, including purchasing goods and equipment, providing housing and shelter, staff costs, training schemes, technical assistance and coordination measures. Speed of response is allowed for by giving the Commission a power to take financing decisions up to €10 million as emergency aid. Longer-term decisions and planning are taken using the committee procedure (regulatory procedure with

[8] Arts 6 and 2(5) TFEU stipulate that civil protection belongs to the category of EU competence in which EU actions support, coordinate or supplement the actions of the Member States 'without thereby superseding their competence in these areas'; nor is harmonisation of Member State laws possible under these provisions (see also Art 196(2) TFEU, cited in the text).

[9] Council Regulation 1257/96/EC concerning humanitarian aid [1996] OJ L163/1.

scrutiny).[10] Within the Commission, the department for humanitarian aid (ECHO) acts on the basis of Regulation 1257/96.[11] It does not itself act on the ground, but rather through NGOs, UN agencies and other international organisations, such as the World Food Programme or the International Committee of the Red Cross; at the same time, the EU's action is not just a question of funding, but includes training, technical assistance, monitoring and coordination. The DIPECHO programme is a policy designed by the European Commission in order to reduce the risk of disaster occurrence and improve preparedness.[12] Despite its predominantly preventive function, specific post-disaster relief actions fulfil a double function and are therefore included in the DIPECHO programme.

In December 2007 the European Consensus on Humanitarian Aid was adopted, a Joint Statement by the Council and the Representatives of the Governments of the Member States meeting within the Council, the European Parliament and the European Commission.[13] As with the European Consensus on Development,[14] this document starts with the recognition that humanitarian aid is a matter of shared competence, and this is reflected in its form: the first part sets out a 'shared vision' applicable to the EU and its Member States, and the second part then discusses in more detail the implementation of policy at the EU level. The 'shared vision' incorporates four fundamental principles for humanitarian aid: humanity, neutrality, impartiality and independence: humanitarian aid is based on need, without discrimination and without any tie to political, military or other objectives.[15] The Consensus also states that humanitarian aid 'is not a crisis management tool'[16]—as we shall see below, crisis management tools may also be used in emergencies, and despite emphasising the 'specific and distinct' principles applying to humanitarian aid, the Consensus also asserts the need for 'coherence and complementarity' with other instruments, including development cooperation, civil protection and crisis management. More generally the Consensus stresses the need for coordination, not only between different EU policies and instruments, but also with other agencies and donors, in

[10] So, for example, with respect to humanitarian aid for the earthquake in Haiti: Commission Decision of 13 January 2010 on the financing of primary emergency humanitarian actions in Haiti (ECHO/HTI/BUD/2010/01000) allocating €3 million; Commission Decision of 3 February 2010 on the financing of humanitarian Actions in the Caribbean (ECHO/-CR/BUD/2010/02000) allocating €19 million; Commission Decision of 4 March 2010 on the financing of humanitarian Actions in the Caribbean (ECHO/-CR/BUD/2010/02000) allocating €90 million.

[11] European Commission Humanitarian Aid Office, http://ec.europa.eu/echo/index_en.htm.

[12] Commission Communication, 'EU Strategy for supporting disaster risk reduction in developing countries' COM (2009) 84 final.

[13] Consensus on Humanitarian Aid [2008] OJ C25/1.

[14] The Council and the Representatives of the Governments of the Member States meeting within the Council, the European Parliament and the Commission, Joint Statement on European Union Development Policy, 'The European Consensus' [2006] OJ C46/1.

[15] See also EU Guidelines on promoting compliance with international humanitarian law [2005] OJ C327/4.

[16] Consensus on Humanitarian Aid (n 13 above) para 15.

particular the central coordinating role of the UN Office for the Coordination of Humanitarian Affairs (UN-OCHA), and pledges support for 'donor best practice'.

Until 2006 food aid was covered by a specific Regulation,[17] also based on Article 179 EC; this was repealed by Regulation 1905/2006, the financial instrument for development cooperation, which says in recital 17:

> Community policy on food security has evolved towards supporting broad-based food security strategies at national, regional and global level, limiting the use of food aid to humanitarian situations and food crises and avoiding disruptive effects on local production and markets, and needs to take into account the specific situation of countries that are structurally fragile and highly dependent on support for food security, in order to avoid a steep reduction of Community assistance to these countries.[18]

Thus currently humanitarian food aid is administered by the Commission on the legal basis of the Humanitarian Aid Regulation, and its focus is on 'food assistance linked to humanitarian objectives for populations affected by crises in emergency contexts'.[19] Non-emergency action on food security has a different, although still development-focused, policy framework.[20] Thus humanitarian food aid is a part of a wider policy framework concerning food security which focuses on combating hunger and malnutrition and effectively contributing to the Millennium Development Goals, and is based on four objectives: (i) increasing availability of food; (ii) improving access to food; (iii) improving nutritional adequacy of food intake; and (iv) enhancing crisis prevention and management.[21] The Commission's Communication on Humanitarian Food Assistance (accompanied by a more operational Staff Working Document) relates to action by the Commission under the fourth of these objectives.[22] The Communication defines food assistance as ensuring the consumption of sufficient, safe and nutritious food in anticipation of, during, and in the aftermath of a humanitarian crisis, when food consumption would otherwise be insufficient or inadequate. Humanitarian food assistance, like all humanitarian aid, is to be provided on the basis of the principles of humanity, impartiality, neutrality and independence. A recent development has been the adoption in December 2008 of a Regulation, also based on Article 179 EC, establishing a facility for a rapid response to soaring food prices in developing countries which is intended to

[17] Council Regulation 1292/96/EC on food-aid policy and food-aid management and special operations in support of food security [1996] OJ L166/1.

[18] Council Regulation 1905/2006 establishing a financial instrument for development cooperation [2006] OJ L348/41.

[19] Commission Communication, 'Humanitarian Food Assistance' COM (2010) 126 final, 2.

[20] Commission Communication, 'EU policy framework to assist developing countries in addressing food security challenges' COM (2010) 127 final.

[21] See 1996 Rome Declaration on World Food Security and World Food Summit Plan of Action.

[22] COM (2010) 126 final (n 19 above). See also Council Conclusions on Humanitarian Food Assistance of 10 May 2010, Brussels, Council doc 9654/10.

address the period between emergency food aid and medium- to long-term development cooperation on food security.[23] Since existing instruments were stretched to their limit, 'it is necessary to adopt a specific financing facility, complementary to existing external financing instruments, to adopt urgent and supplementary measures that address rapidly the consequences in developing countries of the present situation of volatile food prices.'[24]

B Stability Instrument

The Stability Instrument is based on Articles 179 and 181a EC (now Articles 209 and 212 TFEU), covering cooperation with developing and non-developing countries.[25] It replaces a number of other instruments, such as Regulation 381/2001/EC on the Rapid Reaction Mechanism,[26] Regulation 2130/2001 on operations to aid uprooted people in Asian and Latin American developing countries,[27] and Regulation 2258/96 on rehabilitation and reconstruction operations in developing countries.[28] The Stability Instrument is designed to work in two contexts:

(a) in a situation of crisis or emerging crisis, to contribute to stability by providing an effective response to help preserve, establish or re-establish the conditions essential to the proper implementation of the Community's development and cooperation policies;

(b) in the context of stable conditions for the implementation of Community cooperation policies in third countries, to help build capacity both to address specific global and transregional threats having a destabilising effect and to ensure preparedness to address pre- and post-crisis situations.[29]

We are here concerned mainly with the first of these contexts, and the types of assistance that the EU may provide are detailed in Article 3. They include:

— Support for the establishment and the functioning of interim administrations mandated in accordance with international law, support for measures necessary to start the rehabilitation and reconstruction of key infrastructure,

[23] Council Regulation 1337/2008/EC establishing a facility for rapid response to soaring food prices in developing countries [2008] OJ L354/62 Art 1(1). See further the contribution by Daniela Gauci in this volume.

[24] Council Regulation 1337/2008/EC (n 23 above) recital 12.

[25] Council Regulation 1717/2006/EC establishing an instrument for stability [2006] OJ L327/1. On the purpose and history of this Regulation, see further the contribution by Daniela Gauci in this volume.

[26] Council Regulation 381/2001/EC creating a rapid-reaction mechanism, [2001] OJ L 57.

[27] Council Regulation 2130/2001/EC on operations to aid uprooted people in Asian and Latin American developing countries [2001] OJ L287.

[28] Council Regulation 2258/96 on rehabilitation and reconstruction operations in developing countries [1996] OJ L306/1.

[29] Regulation 1717/2006/EC (n 25 above) Art 1(2).

housing, public buildings and economic assets, as well as essential productive capacity, and for the re-starting of economic activity.

— Support for socio-economic measures to address the impact of sudden population movements, including measures addressing the needs of host communities in a situation of crisis or emerging crisis.
— Support for measures in response to natural or man-made disasters and threats to public health in the absence of, or to complement, Community humanitarian assistance.

The Commission may adopt Exceptional Assistance Measures in a situation of crisis under Article 3 'where the effectiveness of the measures is dependent on rapid or flexible implementation'; such measures may last up to 18 months. It may also adopt Interim Response Programmes of longer duration, but measures under Article 3 of the Stability Instrument are essentially intended to be short-term. There is an emphasis on complementarity: with EU action taken under the CFSP; with other instruments, eg humanitarian aid and development cooperation; and with Member States' action. As with humanitarian aid, there is no human rights conditionality attached to Union action under the Stability Instrument.

The instruments considered so far mainly concern financial assistance of various kinds, although DG ECHO does have an operational element. What if more is needed than funding international aid agencies?

C Civil Protection

Both the instruments considered so far have dealt with emergencies in third countries. Civil protection programmes and plans, on the other hand, increasingly cover emergencies both inside and outside the EU. Although Article 3(1)(u) EC provided that 'the activities of the Community shall include … measures in the spheres of … civil protection', until the Treaty of Lisbon, there was no explicit legal basis in the Treaties for civil protection measures. Action could be taken on the basis of the Treaty provisions on the environment: Article 174 EC (now Article 191 TFEU) includes among the objectives of EC environmental policy, 'promoting measures at international level to deal with regional or worldwide environmental problems'. As an example, the Convention on the Transboundary Effects of Industrial Accidents was concluded by the EC on the basis of Article 175 EC.[30]

[30] Council Decision 98/685/EC. See also Council Directive 96/82/EC on the control of major-accident hazards involving dangerous substances [1996] OJ L10/13.

For more general measures, Article 308 EC (now Article 352 TFEU) had to be used. A Decision was adopted on this legal basis in 2001,[31] which has been used to respond to a range of disasters both inside and outside the EU,[32] including floods in Central Europe (2002), France (2003) and Hungary and Poland (2010), the earthquakes in Algeria (2003), Iran (2003), Morocco (2004) and Chile and Haiti (2010), the forest fires in France and Portugal (2003, 2004) and in southern Europe (2007) as well as the Indian Ocean Tsunami in 2004 and the oil spill in the Gulf of Mexico (2010). The Tsunami provoked a reappraisal and revision of existing instruments,[33] and two instruments were adopted in 2007: the revised Civil Protection Mechanism,[34] and a financial instrument.[35]

The Decision establishing a revised Civil Protection Mechanism is based on Article 308 EC (now Article 352 TFEU) and Article 203 Euratom. Its scope is defined in Article 1(2):

> The protection to be ensured by the Mechanism shall cover primarily people but also the environment and property, including cultural heritage, in the event of natural and man-made disasters, acts of terrorism and, technological, radiological or environmental accidents, including accidental marine pollution, occurring inside or outside the Community, taking also into account the special needs of the isolated, outermost and other regions or islands of the Community.[36]

Whereas Union humanitarian assistance is largely based on cooperation with international agencies, the Civil Protection Mechanism's function is to coordinate the actions and resources of the Member States. As explained by the Commission:

> Civil protection is about immediate relief in the first hours and days of a disaster. Like EC humanitarian aid, its purpose is to save lives and alleviate the effects of a disaster during the first days. It differs from EC humanitarian aid, however, in four respects: civil protection assistance can address the environmental consequences of disasters as well as their humanitarian impact; civil protection assistance is provided through teams, experts and equipment provided by the Governments participating in the Mechanism, rather than through the humanitarian organisations (United Nations

[31] Council Decision 2001/792/EC, Euratom establishing a Community mechanism to facilitate reinforced cooperation in civil protection assistance interventions [2001] OJ L297/7. See also Council Decision 1999/847/EC establishing a Community action programme in the field of civil protection [1999] OJ L327/53.

[32] Commission, 'Improving the Community Civil Protection Mechanism' (Communication) COM (2005) 137.

[33] ibid.

[34] Council Decision 2007/779/EC, Euratom establishing a Community Civil Protection Mechanism [2007] OJ L314/9, replacing Decision 2001/792/EC, Euratom (n 31 above).

[35] Council Decision 2007/162/EC establishing civil protection financial instrument, replacing Decision 1999/847/EC (n 31 above).

[36] Council Decision 2007/779/EC, Euratom (n 34 above) Art 1(2).

specialised agencies, Red Cross organisations and NGOs) used by ECHO; civil protection assistance may be delivered both inside and outside the EU, and the Mechanism can be used also as a tool for facilitating and supporting CFSP crisis management operations.[37]

The Civil Protection Mechanism includes the establishment of a Monitoring and Information Centre (MIC) and a Common Emergency Communication and Information System (CECIS), the establishment and training of intervention teams, and sharing equipment and transport. The mechanism for coordination differs depending on whether the emergency is within or outside the EU. Within the EU, coordination is carried out by the requesting Member State;[38] outside the EU, coordination of the EU response is the responsibility of the Presidency (political and strategic coordination, including political relations with the third country) and the Commission (operational coordination).[39] Where the emergency is linked to conflict, then the Council may decide to operate within the framework of CSDP crisis management.[40] The MIC will coordinate with both ECHO (ie with the EU's humanitarian response to the emergency) and with the UN OCHA (Office for the Coordination of Humanitarian Affairs).[41] The Civil Protection Mechanism is supported by a financial instrument which covers preparation and preparedness within the EU and disaster response both inside and outside the EU.[42] It is designed to apply only where other instruments (such as the Stability Instrument,[43] the Regulation on Humanitarian Aid,[44] and the Decision on terrorism[45]) do not. As far as disaster response is concerned, the instrument applies 'to actions to assist with the response to the immediate consequences of a major emergency regardless of its nature, including the response to accidental marine pollution emergencies through the Mechanism, inside or outside the Community, where a request is made for assistance in accordance with the Mechanism.'

Recent 'high-profile' disasters (if one can use that term) where the Civil Protection Mechanism has been used include the earthquake in Haiti and the Deepwater Horizon oil spill in the Gulf of Mexico. The EU's response to the crisis in Haiti involved a number of teams, including urban search and rescue (USAR) teams, medical teams and supplies, shelter and water sanitation. In addition to

[37] COM (2005) 137 (n 32 above) p 3 (footnote omitted).

[38] Council Decision 2007/779/EC, Euratom (n 34 above) Art 7.

[39] ibid, Art 8.

[40] See further below.

[41] See Exchange of letters between UN OCHA and the Commission of the European Communities concerning their cooperation in the framework of disaster response, 27–28 October 2004.

[42] Council Decision 2007/162/EC (n 35 above).

[43] See n 25 above.

[44] See n 9 above.

[45] Council Decision 2007/124/EC, Euratom establishing for the period 2007 to 2013, as part of General Programme on Security and Safeguarding Liberties, the Specific Programme Prevention, Preparedness and Consequence Management of Terrorism and other Security related risks [2007] OJ L58/1.

Member State resources the EU used the financial instrument to co-finance a water purification unit and an advanced medical post. In June 2010 the US requested EU assistance in providing equipment to prevent the spread of the oil in the Gulf of Mexico: the request was received by the MIC, which put it out to the Member States, who responded with offers of equipment which could then be coordinated by the MIC.[46]

The Counter-terrorism Strategy of the EU incorporates a Civil Protection dimension. Objective 5 of the EU Plan of Action on Combating Terrorism is 'To enhance the capability of the European Union and of Member States to deal with the consequences of a terrorist attack',[47] and this is reflected in the Counter-terrorism Strategy adopted by the European Council in December 2005, one of whose four elements is 'respond' (the others being: prevent, protect, pursue): 'To prepare ourselves, in the spirit of solidarity, to manage and minimise the consequences of a terrorist attack, by improving capabilities to deal with: the aftermath; the co-ordination of the response; and the needs of victims.'[48] The revised Civil Protection Mechanism specifically mentions acts of terrorism as one of the potential causes of emergency requiring a Union response,[49] and this is, as we have seen, reflected also in Article 222 TFEU (the solidarity clause):

> [T]he response systems in place to manage the consequences of natural disasters may also be used to alleviate the effects on citizens in the aftermath of a terrorist attack. Our response to any such events should make full use of the existing structures, including the Civil Protection Mechanism, which the EU has developed to respond to other major European and international crises.[50]

As already mentioned, counter-terrorism has a specific financial instrument and therefore the general instrument for Civil Protection will not apply.[51]

D CSDP: Petersberg tasks and crisis management

The CFSP/CSDP envisages both civilian and military action in the field of crisis management. Under Article 43(1) TFEU the CSDP is to include humanitarian and rescue tasks, tasks of combat forces in crisis management, including peace-making and post-conflict stabilisation. Civil protection has been identified as one

[46] See IP/10/727.

[47] European Union Plan of Action on Combating Terrorism adopted by the European Council of 17–18 June 2004, updated June 2005.

[48] EU Counter-terrorism Strategy, Council doc 14469/4/05, REV 4, p 3.

[49] See text at n 36 above.

[50] EU Counter-terrorism Strategy (n 48 above) para 32. See also Revised European Union Solidarity Programme on the Consequences of Terrorist Threats and Attacks, adopted by the Council 2 December 2004, Council doc 15480/04.

[51] Council Decision 2007/124/EC, Euratom (n 45 above).

of the four priority areas of civilian crisis management.[52] To give some idea of the current scale of these capabilities, Member States have committed 579 civil protection experts and 4445 staff for intervention teams; these are the current capabilities under the 2008 Headline Goal:[53]

- 2 or 3 assessment and/or coordination teams, capable of being mobilised around the clock, and consisting of 10 experts, who could be dispatched within 3 to 7 hours;
- Intervention teams of up to 2000 persons for deployment at short notice;
- Additional or more specialised means which could be dispatched within 2 to 7 days depending on the particular needs of each crisis.[54]

A new Civilian Headline Goal 2010 has been agreed.[55] Included among the priority objectives is 'strengthening coherence and synergies between ESDP missions and other European Union instruments',[56] and indeed it is striking that civil protection is both a CSDP objective and operationalised through a former First-Pillar instrument. The Civil Protection Mechanism may be used in CSDP crisis management missions and the Commission has gone so far as to say that it 'will continue to work with the Council to ensure that the Mechanism fully meets the needs of future operations under the CFSP.'[57] The basis for this is a Joint Council–Commission Declaration of 2003, which sets out the procedures for the use of the Civil Protection Mechanism in CFSP (civilian crisis management) operations:

> Where the Commission receives a request from a third state for civil protection assistance outside the Community, it will, in addition to forwarding the request to civil protection contact points in the Member States and States participating in the Community Mechanism, immediately inform the Presidency … If the Presidency considers that the assistance requested might fall within EU crisis management, it will so inform Member States and the Commission. In those cases the Presidency, following consultations with the Member States and the Commission in the appropriate Council bodies, may establish that the assistance requested falls within EU crisis management and may request, on behalf of the Council, civil protection assistance under the Community Mechanism, either to launch an EU crisis management operation or to add a civil protection component to a pre-existing EU crisis management operation.[58]

[52] Four priority areas of civilian crisis management were defined by the European Council at Feira in June 2000: police, strengthening of the rule of law, strengthening civilian administration and civil protection.

[53] Council doc 15863/04.

[54] Final Report on the Civilian Headline Goal 2008, Council doc 14807/07.

[55] General Affairs and External Relations Council, 19 November 2007, Council doc 14823/07. See also Presidency Report to the European Council, 'Reinforcing the European Union's emergency and crisis response capacities', 15 June 2006, Council doc 10551/06.

[56] Council declaration on strengthening capabilities, 11 December 2008, Council doc 104676.

[57] COM (2005) 137 (n 32 above) 11.

[58] Joint Council–Commission Declaration of 29 September 2003, Council doc 10639/03.

In addition, EU military resources may be used in implementing the Civil Protection Mechanism. The Council adopted in May 2004 the modalities for making the military database available to the Civil Protection Mechanism.[59] This database is of military assets and capabilities relevant to the protection of civilian populations against the effects of terrorist attacks, and includes procedures for the use of military means in the framework of the Mechanism in case of terrorist attacks inside the Union. In 2006 the Council adopted a General Framework for the use of Member States' military and military chartered transportation assets and ESDP coordination tools in support of EU disaster response.[60] The Consensus on Humanitarian Aid envisages the possible exceptional use of military resources for humanitarian aid, but is cautious, recognising the need to ensure that the humanitarian principles (neutrality, impartiality and non-discrimination) are not undermined:

> Under very specific conditions, humanitarian aid may draw upon military assets, notably for logistical and infrastructure support mainly in the context of natural disasters … In order to avoid a blurring of lines between military operations and humanitarian aid, it is essential that military assets and capabilities are used only in very limited circumstances in support of humanitarian relief operations as a 'last resort', i.e. where there is no comparable civilian alternative and only the use of military assets that are unique in capability and availability can meet a critical humanitarian need … The EU reaffirms that a humanitarian operation making use of military assets must retain its civilian nature and character. This means that, while military assets will remain under military control, the humanitarian operation as a whole must remain under the overall authority and control of the responsible humanitarian organization.[61]

The Treaty of Lisbon preserves a distinction between CFSP/CSDP powers and other Union competences, while at the same time allocating overlapping competences. Thus Article 43 TEU includes humanitarian and rescue tasks and crisis management among the CSDP tasks, while Articles 196, 214 and 222 TFEU on civil protection, humanitarian aid and solidarity respectively, fall outside the provisions on the CFSP/CSDP. The combined application of these different CFSP and non-CFSP instruments is made possible, despite the Treaties' insistence on maintaining a separation,[62] by the nature of the EU's non-CFSP instruments: direct financial and technical support and coordination of Member State resources and response.

[59] Council Conclusions on Strengthening the overall civil protection capacity in the European Union, 17 May 2004, Council doc 11549/04.

[60] Council doc 8976/06. See also Reinforcing the EU's emergency and crisis response capacities — Emergency and crisis coordination arrangements, 24 February 2006, Council doc 6747/06.

[61] See n 13 above. There are UN Guidelines on the use of Military and Civil Defence Assets in Humanitarian Operations.

[62] The complete separation resulting from the Pillar structure introduced by the Treaty of Maastricht has disappeared; nevertheless according to Art 24(1) TEU the CFSP 'is subject to specific rules and procedures'; and Art 40 TEU provides that the implementation of the CFSP on the one hand and of other Union competences on the other 'shall not affect' each other.

III USING NON-EMERGENCY POWERS IN EMERGENCIES

In addition to these specific 'emergency' or 'crisis' instruments, some emergencies require the use of powers designed for 'normal' situations: agriculture, imports and exports, food safety, state aids. Here we will look briefly at a few examples relating to food safety and health security.

A Food safety

The European Union has clear competence to deal with food safety emergencies, through the Common Agricultural Policy (CAP), its exclusive competence for trade policy and its competence to adopt measures relating to the internal market with respect to the marketing of foodstuffs.[63] Two examples will illustrate the point.

First, a food emergency of non-EU origin, the explosion at the Chernobyl nuclear power station in 1987. Following the incident, the Council adopted, on the basis of Article 113 of the EEC Treaty (then the legal basis for the common commercial policy, now Article 207 TFEU), a regulation on imports of agricultural products.[64] The release for free circulation of certain agricultural products originating in non-member countries was subjected to compliance with maximum permitted levels of radioactive contamination. The regulation required the Member States to verify compliance with those levels and for that purpose provides for a system for the exchange of information centrally organised by the Commission. In the event of non-compliance with those maximum permitted levels, the regulation established the requisite measures to be taken, including prohibiting the import of the products in question. Greece challenged the legal basis of the regulation on the grounds that it was not a trade measure, but rather a public health measure in response to the nuclear accident.[65] The Court held that:

> according to its objective and its content, as they appear from the very terms of the regulation, the regulation is intended to regulate trade between the Community and non-member countries; accordingly it comes within the common commercial policy within the meaning of Article 113 of the EEC Treaty.[66]

The fact that the measure also concerned public health and environmental protection did not take it outside the CCP.

[63] See generally Opinion of the European Economic and Social Committee on Health security of agricultural and food imports [2009] OJ C100/60.

[64] Council Regulation 3955/87/EEC on the conditions governing imports of agricultural products originating in third countries following the accident at the Chernobyl nuclear power-station [1987] OJ L371/14.

[65] Case C-62/88 *Greece v Council* [1990] ECR I-01527.

[66] ibid, para 16.

Second, a home grown food emergency, BSE. At first, action was taken under legislation based on the CAP and internal market powers (then Articles 43 and 100 EEC), as it directly involved intra-Community trade.[67] The Commission decision imposed restrictions on exports of live cattle from the UK to other Member States, and has been amended many times. The current regulation on the other hand dates from 2001 and is based on Article 152(4)(b) EC (now Article 168(4)(b) TFEU) as a public health measure.[68]

B Health security

Health emergencies are more complex in terms of competences, since the EU's powers in relation to health are limited, but it does have relevant competence under Article 168(1) TFEU (formerly Article 152(1) EC); the final phrase of this provision, which expressly refers to serious cross-border threats to health, was added by the Treaty of Lisbon:

> Union action, which shall complement national policies, shall be directed towards improving public health, preventing physical and mental illness and diseases, and obviating sources of danger to physical and mental health. Such action shall cover the fight against the major health scourges, by promoting research into their causes, their transmission and their prevention, as well as health information and education, and monitoring, early warning of and combating serious cross-border threats to health.

Examples of EU action in this field include surveillance of communicable diseases,[69] the establishment of a European Centre for Disease Prevention and Control,[70] and the establishment of a Health Security Committee.[71] As in other

[67] Commission Decision 89/469/EEC concerning certain protection measures relating to bovine spongiform encephalopathy in the United Kingdom [1989] OJ L225/51. This was based on a Council Directive which gave the Commission the power to act: Council Directive 64/432/EEC on animal health problems affecting intra-Community trade in bovine animals and swine [1964] OJ P121/1977.

[68] Council Regulation 999/2001 laying down rules for the prevention, control and eradication of certain transmissible spongiform encephalopathies [2001] OJ L147/1. On food safety generally see Council Regulation 178/2002/EC laying down the general principles and requirements of food law, establishing the European Food Safety Authority and laying down procedures in matters of food safety [2002] OJ L31/1, which is based on agriculture, internal market, trade and public health legal bases.

[69] Council Decision 2119/98/EC setting up a network for the epidemiological surveillance and control of communicable diseases in the Community [1998] OJ L268/1.

[70] Council Regulation 851/2004/EC establishing a European Centre for Disease Prevention and Control [2004] OJ L142/1.

[71] The Health Security Committee was established in 2001; see Commission Communication to the Council on transitional prolongation and extension of the mandate of the Health Security Committee in view of a future general revision of the structures dealing with health threats at EU level, COM (2006) 69, and Council conclusions of 22 February 2007 on the Health Security Committee. The HSC coordinated the Member States' response to the H1N1 influenza (swine flu) pandemic in 2009: see Council conclusions of 30 April 2009. For HSC activities September 2007–October 2009 see Annex to Commission Staff Working Document, 'Health Security in the EU and Internationally' SEC (2009) 1622 final.

fields of emergency response, the emphasis is on communication and coordinating the actions of the Member States in the framework of international coordination efforts, in this case in particular the WHO's International Health Regulations[72] and the Global Health Security Initiative (GHSI). In a recent Working Document the Commission argued for an improved EU policy framework on global health 'which will address wider areas on global equity, coherence, governance, knowledge.'[73] This would include not only pandemics and terrorist-related health threats (bioterrorism and chemical, biological and radionuclear (CBRN) threats) but also climate change and health systems in developing countries.

IV CONCLUSIONS

A What legal bases and competences have been used?

Humanitarian aid has used development cooperation competence and now has its specific legal basis; the Stability Instrument uses competence for development cooperation and general cooperation with third countries; CSDP civilian crisis management powers have been used. All these are external powers. Other external powers such as the Common Commercial Policy can be used to deal with emergencies as well as 'ordinary' situations.

The food safety and health emergencies, in contrast, used largely internal powers, not designed specifically for emergencies. The EU has taken specific control measures for BSE, but in the case of public health risks in general the emphasis is on coordination of Member State responses (as with swine fever, for example). Where environmental protection is the focus, then the same legal basis can be used for both internal and external measures. Broader civil protection action, intended to cover emergencies both within the EU and overseas, needed the use of the residual power provision, Article 308 EC (and its equivalent in the Euratom Treaty) until the Treaty of Lisbon created a specific legal base (Article 196 TFEU). The Treaty of Lisbon also introduces a 'solidarity clause' (Article 222 TFEU) for action where a Member State is the object of a terrorist attack or the victim of a natural or man-made disaster.

The EU now has a broad range of powers at its disposal to cover a range of different types of emergency. In many cases the underlying legislation gives the Commission power to act quickly (eg to allocate funds, or to prohibit a particular import), or (as with the financial crisis and state aids) the Commission has sufficient discretion to respond flexibly. Smooth cohesion between different

[72] Council conclusions of 16 December 2008 on health security, Council doc 16515/08. The International Health Regulations (IHR 2005) entered into force on 15 June 2007; available on http://whqlibdoc.who.int/publications/2008/9789241580410_eng.pdf.

[73] Commission Staff Working Document, 'Health Security in the EU and Internationally' SEC (2009) 1622 final, 9.

financial instruments can be an issue (eg the transition from humanitarian aid or the Stability Instrument to development cooperation). On the other hand, the possibility of overlap between the CFSP and other instruments such as the Civil Protection Mechanism does not seem to cause particular problems, perhaps because of the emphasis in both cases on coordination of Member State action.

B Link between internal and external instruments

As we have seen, the EU is involved in emergencies both outside and within the EU. Classic instruments such as humanitarian aid, have an 'external' basis but other instruments can be used as well and more recently we have been seeing an emphasis on the linking of external and internal instruments:

> The Community's response to the tsunami illustrated the wealth of instruments at its disposal to address disasters and crisis. It showed that in addition to the relevant external relations instruments, many internal policy instruments can be mobilised in a coordinated way to strengthen the overall response. These include not only the Community Civil Protection Mechanism, but also programmes in the field of research, information society and justice, liberty and security and fisheries. The strength of the Community response lies in its ability to integrate the capabilities built up under its internal policies with the measures delivered under its specialised instruments for external action. A further dimension is brought by the military and civilian capabilities being developed under the Common Foreign and Security Policy.[74]

The new clauses introduced by the Lisbon Treaty further blur the distinction between internal and external action. In the case of civil protection (Article 196 TFEU), the same instrument may be used for both, although the procedures will be different. The solidarity clause (Article 222 TFEU) raises the issue of the relationship between internal and external instruments in a different way: although this provision concerns only the Member States, it is somewhat surprisingly placed in Part V of the TFEU, with the provisions on the EU's external action. As Grevi has pointed out, at the time of the drafting of the Constitutional Treaty the solidarity clause was in fact linked to the requirement of solidarity in foreign policy matters—expressions of which are now found in Articles 24(2) and (3), 31(1) and 32 TEU—and represents a bridge between internal and

[74] Commission, 'Reinforcing EU Disaster and Crisis Response' (Communication) COM (2005) 153. This was a post-Tsunami evaluation. See also Commission, 'Reinforcing the Union's Disaster Response Capacity' (Communication) COM (2008) 130 final, 3: 'boundaries between internal and external disasters are increasingly blurred .... Often the same instruments—in particular civil protection assets—are deployed by the Community and Member States to respond to the same needs within the Union and beyond EU borders.'

external security.[75] This dual dimension is also reflected in the institutional arrangements for the implementation of the clause in paragraph 3, which involve both the Commission and the High Representative for Foreign Affairs and Security Policy, and both internal and external security committees.[76]

C What is the added value of EU action?

As we have seen, the emphasis of EU action in global emergencies has been on coordination and on facilitating communication between the Member States themselves and between Member States and international agencies. Does the EU have a more significant role than as a convenient information clearing house or control centre? This is too large a question for this contribution, and perhaps this volume as whole may help to answer it. The Commission sees the key to be integration between the different phases of disaster response: risk assessment and forecasting, prevention, preparedness, response and recovery. It would like to see the Monitoring and Information Centre (MIC) become an operational centre for civil protection intervention.[77]

The Consensus on Humanitarian Aid[78] lists five ways in which the EU, it argues, has comparative advantage and added value:

- First, a global presence: a network of field experts located world-wide, working out of field offices, including regional support offices, plus its extensive network of Union Delegations.
- Second, with the support of Member States, ensuring coherence in Union policies, in particular at the meeting points between Union policies in the area of humanitarian aid, development, food security, public health and human rights.
- Third, promoting good humanitarian practice.
- Fourth, the EU often has a comparative advantage in being able to intervene in politically sensitive situations more flexibly.
- Fifth, in facilitating coordination, between its own activities and those of the Member States, with other donors and the UN system.

Two of these points are about coherence and coordination—with other Union policies, and with the Member States and other agencies/donors. The EU's stress on the primary role of the UN (especially the UN OCHA) is a good thing. But

[75] G Grevi, 'The Common Foreign, Security and Defence Policy' in G Amato, H Bribosia and B de Witte (eds), *Genèse et Destinée de la Constitution Européenne: Commentaire du traité établissant une Constitution pour l'Europe à la lumière des travaux préparatoires et perspectives d' avenir* (Brussels, Editions Bruylant, 2007) 818.

[76] TFEU Art 222(3).

[77] Commission, 'Reinforcing the Union's Disaster Response Capacity' (Communication) COM (2008) 130 final, 6.

[78] See n 13 above.

this is one of the ongoing challenges—the EU offers a potential for greater coherence but at the same time it is a complex additional 'player', itself adding to the risk of incoherence. A specific aspect of that challenge is the relationship between the former Three Pillars, which Alan Dashwood discusses in the next chapter.

2

Conflicts of Competence in Responding to Global Emergencies

ALAN DASHWOOD

I INTRODUCTION

DISAGREEMENTS BETWEEN THE different institutions of the EU or between the institutions and the Member States about competence to act in a given field of external relations are a familiar feature of legal and political life in the Union. If such conflicts are only to be expected in a complex constitutional entity based on the principle of conferred powers,[1] they need to be managed sensibly, in order to minimise delays in decision-making. The threat that turf-wars represent to effective external action by the Union is most evident in situations such as global emergencies, where a timely response is of the essence.

The principle of conferral, as it is called in the Treaty of Lisbon (TL), has been preserved, indeed strengthened, under the regime of the amended Treaties;[2] and so has its corollary, the drafting technique of specific attribution by way of power-conferring provisions ('legal bases') that identify, either alone or in combination with other provisions, and in varying degrees of detail, the nature and scope of activities the Union is being authorised to undertake, the decision-making procedure to be followed by the responsible Union institution(s), and sometimes also the form(s) of legal instrument that may be used.[3] As a result of successive Treaty amendments culminating in the TL, a collection of legal bases relating expressly to different forms of external action is now available to the

[1] In Opinion 2/94 [1996] ECR I-1759, the Court of Justice famously remarked that the 'principle of conferred powers must be respected in both the internal action and the international action of the Community' (para 24).

[2] Art 5(1) and (2) of the amended TEU.

[3] It was further noted in Opinion 2/94 that 'The Community acts ordinarily on the basis of specific powers which, as the Court has held, are not necessarily the express consequence of specific provisions of the Treaty but may also be implied from them' (n 1 above, at para 25). The qualification 'ordinarily' was presumably a reference to the possible creation of supplementary powers under the provision which, after amendment, is now found in Art 352 TFEU (ex Art 308 EC). The Court's carefully chosen language indicates that implied powers, no less than express ones, arise pursuant to 'specific provisions of the Treaty'.

Union, which enable it, in principle, to mount a response to global emergencies of almost any nature. In the reconfigured Treaty structure, the legal bases more particularly relevant for this purpose are to be found in two places: within the new Part Five of the TFEU, which brings together provisions authorising and organising action by the Union in the external sphere that were formerly scattered around the EC Treaty, and more specifically in its Title III on cooperation with third countries and humanitarian aid; and among the specific provisions on the common foreign and security policy (CFSP) in Chapter 2 of Title V of the amended TEU.

In this contribution, I focus on the competence issues which, experience suggests, are the most likely to be encountered when the Union is considering its reaction to a global emergency. The discussion is divided up as follows. I begin by commenting on changes in the post-Lisbon constitutional order that may have a bearing on future conflicts of competence. I go on to consider the scope for such conflicts between relevant TFEU competences, and afterwards between those competences and CFSP competence. I then make some suggestions about the way in which conflicts between TFEU and CFSP competences can be managed. Finally, I summarise my thoughts on the subject in a brief conclusion.

II STRUCTURAL CHANGES

It may be helpful to recall *in limine* certain changes wrought by the Treaty of Lisbon in the constitutional order of the EU, which have a bearing on the present discussion.

First and foremost, the 'Three Pillars' of the pre-Lisbon Union have been replaced by an integral constitutional order based jointly on the amended TEU and the EC Treaty, born again as the TFEU.[4] Nevertheless, the CFSP remains sharply differentiated from other areas of external policy in which the Union is authorised to act. This is clear from the location of the chapter containing specific provisions relating to the CFSP in Title V of the TEU, isolated from the legal bases for external action in Part Five of the TFEU, as well as from the fact that CFSP competence is treated in Title I of the TFEU as distinct from the categories of competence defined by Articles 2 to 6 of that Treaty; and also from the particularity of the institutional and procedural arrangements applicable to the CFSP, which is explicitly noted in Article 24(2), second subparagraph of the TEU. The choice between a TFEU and a CFSP legal basis is, therefore, still

[4] The intention to establish such an order now seems clear to me, notably in the light of Art 1, third para of the amended TEU and Art 1 TFEU. Initially, I was inclined to think that the TL had simply reduced the Three Pillars of the former Union structure to two. See my evidence to the House of Lords Constitution Committee, 6th Report of Session 2007/2008 (HL Paper 84) 16.

potentially a more contentious issue for the Commission, the Council and the Member States, than the choice between legal bases that are all found in the TFEU.

A second change is the establishment of a common list of objectives for the Union's external action. The list is found in paragraph (2) of the new Article 21 of the amended TEU, among the general provisions on external action in Chapter 1 of Title V of that Treaty. The Union is enjoined by paragraph (3) of the Article to pursue those objectives 'in the development and implementation of the different areas of [its] external action covered by this Title and by Part Five of the [TFEU], and of the external aspects of its other policies'. It would seem, therefore, that, whatever the field of external action in question, all or any of the listed objectives are capable in principle of bearing some degree of relevance to the exercise of Union competence. Manifestly, however, the objectives cannot all bear the same degree of relevance to all the external competences of the Union, since such conflation would subvert the principle of conferral; and it would be incompatible with the retention in the amended Treaties of specific legal bases for international action by the Union, let alone the creation of new legal bases.[5] Article 21 TEU cannot, therefore, be understood to absolve the institutions from determining the correct legal basis for any external action it is proposed the Union should take, by applying the principles laid down for this purpose in the case law;[6] though the Article may well make the task of the institutions more difficult in some instances.

A third change is the abolition of the hierarchy that formerly existed between Community competences pursuant to the EC Treaty ('the First Pillar'), on the one hand, and Union competences for the CFSP pursuant to Title V TEU ('the Second Pillar') and for police and judicial cooperation in criminal matters pursuant to Title VI TEU ('the Third Pillar'), on the other. The indications as to the primacy of the First Pillar found in the common provisions of the pre-Lisbon TEU (the reference in the former Article 1, third paragraph to the Union's being 'founded on the European Communities'; the objective stated in the former Article 2, first paragraph, fifth indent, 'to maintain in full the *acquis communautaire* and build on it'; and the requirement imposed on the institutions by the former Article 3, first paragraph as to 'respecting and building upon the *acquis communautaire*') have not been replicated in the amended Treaties. Most importantly for present purposes, the former Article 47 TEU, interpreted by the Court of Justice as protecting the EC Treaty against 'encroachment' by the TEU (in the sense that, if a measure were capable of being adopted under one of the legal bases in the EC Treaty, it must not be adopted under a Second- or Third-Pillar legal basis[7]), has been replaced by the new Article 40 TEU, which makes clear that CFSP competences and the Union's other competences are to enjoy equal

[5] Notably, Art 214 TFEU on humanitarian aid. See below.

[6] The principles, and relevant authorities, are recalled below.

[7] See the discussion of the *ECOWAS* case, below.

protection against each other. The first paragraph of the new Article provides that 'the implementation of the [CFSP] shall not affect the application of the procedures and the extent of the powers of the institutions laid down by the Treaties'; while the second paragraph provides that 'Similarly, the implementation of the policies listed in those Articles shall not affect the application of the procedures and the extent of the powers of the institutions laid down by the Treaties for the exercise of the Union's competences under this Chapter'. Conflicts over the choice between a CFSP legal basis or a TFEU legal basis can thus no longer be resolved by giving the latter automatic primacy.

III THE SCOPE FOR CONFLICT BETWEEN RELEVANT TFEU COMPETENCES

In this subsection I consider the scope there may be for conflict between the three legal bases provided for by Title III of Part Five of the TFEU, relating respectively to development cooperation, to economic, financial and technical cooperation with third countries (which, for convenience, I call 'general cooperation') and to humanitarian aid. The aim is to assess the degree of precision with which the action the Union has been authorised to undertake is defined, so as to determine the extent of any possible overlap, and whether such overlap would be liable to result in disputes about the choice between legal bases.

Development cooperation is the subject of Articles 208 to 211 TFEU. Article 208 TFEU provides in its first paragraph that 'Union policy in the field of development cooperation shall be conducted within the framework of the principles and objectives of the Union's external action'. The list of objectives in Article 21(2) TEU includes, under point (d), 'to ... foster the sustainable economic, social and environmental development of developing countries, with the primary aim of eradicating poverty'. The second paragraph of Article 208 TFEU adds nothing of substance, stating in its first sentence that 'The Union's development cooperation policy shall have as its primary objective the reduction and, in the long term, the eradication of poverty.' The paragraph goes on to provide that 'The Union shall take account of the objectives of development cooperation in the policies that it implements which are likely to affect developing countries', without giving any more precise indication as to what those objectives might be.

The former Article 177(1) EC appears, at first sight, to have been somewhat more circumstantial. It provided:

1. Community policy in the sphere of development cooperation ... shall foster:
   - the sustainable economic and social development of the developing countries, and more particularly the most disadvantaged among them,
   - the smooth and gradual integration of the developing countries into the world economy,
   - the campaign against poverty in the developing countries.

2. Community policy in this area shall contribute to the general objective of developing and consolidating democracy and the rule of law, and to that of respecting human rights and fundamental freedoms.

...

However, the failure of Article 208 TFEU to mention integration into the world economy or the development and consolidation of democracy, the rule of law and respect for fundamental rights can be explained by the references to those matters under, respectively, points (e) and (b) of Article 21(2) TEU. Bearing in mind that Article 208 TFEU has to be read together with Article 21(2) TEU, the only significant difference between the old and the new definitions of the scope of development cooperation policy is the fact that 'environmental development' is now expressly mentioned.

General cooperation is the subject of Articles 212 and 213 TFEU. Article 212(1) provides:

> Without prejudice to the other provisions of the Treaties, and in particular Articles 208 to 211, the Union shall carry out economic, financial and technical cooperation measures, including assistance, in particular financial assistance, with third countries other than developing countries. Such measures shall be consistent with the development policy of the Union and shall be carried out within the framework of the principles and objectives of its external action ...

Elements of that definition not found in the former Article 181a EC are the express references to the possibility of the Union's providing 'assistance, in particular financial assistance' (in other words, direct money transfers, including by way of balance of payments aid); and to the fact that the envisaged cooperation is with third countries other than developing countries.

The drafting of Articles 208 and 212 TFEU makes explicitly clear that the competences the Articles respectively confer upon the Union are intended to be mutually exclusive. They are, effectively, parallel competences relating to cooperation with different categories of international partners—developing countries and all other third countries. In principle, therefore, no overlap of competences is possible, though there may conceivably be disagreement as to whether a given third country counts as 'developing'.

Under the EC Treaty as last amended by the Treaty of Nice, there was no specific legal basis for humanitarian aid or emergency aid. Authorisation for any action the Community might be minded to take in responding to humanitarian crises was found in an extensive interpretation of the Community's competence for development cooperation.[8] This choice of legal basis appears questionable: the notion of 'cooperation' might be thought to imply a long-term relationship between the Community/Union and the third countries in question, an issue to

[8] Council Regulation 1257/96/EC concerning humanitarian aid [1996] OJ L163/1, was adopted on the basis of the then Art 130w EC (post-Amsterdam, Art 179 EC), the legal basis for development cooperation.

which I return below. At all events, the gap—if such it was—has now been filled by the Treaty of Lisbon. Included under point (g) in the list of objectives in Article 21(2) is that 'to … assist populations, countries and regions confronting natural or man-made disasters'. Competence to conduct operations in the field of humanitarian aid is now specifically conferred by Article 214 TFEU. The substantive scope of the competence is defined in these terms: humanitarian operations 'shall be intended to provide *ad hoc* assistance and relief and protection for people in third countries who are victims of natural or man-made disasters, in order to meet the humanitarian needs resulting from such situations'.[9]

That wording is very broad. The causes of the disaster to be relieved may be natural, such as floods, drought, earthquakes, volcanic eruptions, tsunami; or they may be man-made, such as civil war and the displacement of populations (as in Darfur), state failure (as in Somalia), systematic misgovernment (as in Zimbabwe). A specific limitation is that Article 214 TFEU is a legal basis for aid to third countries: disaster relief in Member States is one of the objects of the solidarity clause in Article 222 TFEU. Other requirements seem designed to draw a dividing line between humanitarian aid and other forms of external action. The purpose of the aid must be to provide '*ad hoc* assistance and relief and protection'; in other words, it should comprise measures that immediately and specifically address the effects of the disaster in question, as compared to longer-term remedies such as improving infrastructure and promoting better governance. Also, the effects to be countered must be ones that give rise to 'humanitarian needs', such as for food, water, shelter and medical supplies and treatment, rather than, for instance, the need to restore or maintain peace and security.

Given that conducting humanitarian aid operations was formerly treated as a branch of development cooperation policy, there must be a possibility of overlap between the two fields of competence; and presumably, in the case of natural or man-made disasters in countries other than developing countries, also between competence for humanitarian aid and competence for general cooperation. At first sight, there might appear to be very little likelihood that such overlap would result in conflicts of competence, since the same procedure for internal decision-making (the European Parliament and the Council acting in accordance with the ordinary legislative procedure) is prescribed by Article 214(3) TFEU as by, respectively, Article 209(1) and Article 212(2) TFEU. However, closer consideration of the three provisions reveals a significant difference between them. Whereas Article 209(1) refers to adopting 'the measures necessary for the implementation of development cooperation policy', and Article 212(2) TFEU to adopting 'the measures necessary for the implementation of [general cooperation]', Article 214(3) TFEU empowers the European Parliament and the Council to 'establish the measures defining the *framework* within which the Union's

9 Art 214(1) TFEU, second sentence.

humanitarian aid operation shall be implemented'.[10] I interpret the difference in wording as meaning that, while co-decision is the prescribed procedure for implementing measures on development cooperation and general cooperation, in the case of humanitarian aid it is required only for the establishment of a 'framework' organising the implementation of individual operations; this leaves open the possibility for the Union legislator to prescribe a less onerous adoption procedure than co-decision for deciding upon individual humanitarian aid operations, which would almost certainly entail a diminished role for the European Parliament.[11] Would there, then, be an incentive for the Parliament to favour action under the legal bases for development cooperation and general cooperation, in preference to that for humanitarian aid? Perhaps in theory, but the risk of conflict as to the choice between these legal bases appears slender, since any simplification of the implementation procedure for humanitarian aid could only have been achieved with the agreement of the Parliament itself.

IV THE SCOPE FOR CONFLICT BETWEEN TFEU AND CFSP COMPETENCES

Chapter 2 of Title V of the amended TEU, which contains specific provisions on the CFSP, follows immediately after the chapter laying down general provisions on the Union's external action, including the common objectives listed in Article 21(2). This juxtaposition evidently led the authors of the defunct Constitutional Treaty to conclude that it would be redundant to provide a list of objectives specific to the CFSP, similar to those set out in the former Article 11(1) TEU,[12] and that far from compelling logic must have been accepted by their successors, who drafted the Treaty of Lisbon. Article 23 of the amended TEU says that 'The Union's action on the international scene, pursuant to this Chapter, shall be guided by the general provisions laid down in Chapter 1', but the same applies to the whole gamut of EU external action. The only textual indication of the substantive scope of the CFSP is found in the extraordinarily wide terms of Article 24(1), first subparagraph of the amended TEU, which provides:

> The Union's competence in matters of common foreign and security policy shall cover all areas of foreign policy and all questions relating to the Union's security, including the progressive framing of a common defence policy that might lead to a common defence.

I have noted elsewhere that the definition brings together the introductory phrase of the former Article 11(1) and the opening sentence of the former Article 17(1) TEU, adopting the extensive concept of security policy found in the latter

[10] Emphasis added.

[11] See generally D Gauci's contribution to this same volume.

[12] *cf* Arts III-292 and III-294 of the Constitutional Treaty.

provision.[13] However, I argued that the omission of the five indents found in the former Article 11(1) could not have been intended to enlarge the scope of the CFSP, so as literally to cover '*all* areas of foreign policy',[14] as these would be understood in the Member States. It was, and remains, my view that the competence conferred by this chapter of the amended TEU applies to 'foreign policy' in a specific sense, namely the political, security and defence aspects of external relations, as distinct from their social, economic or environmental aspects. I still find compelling the two reasons I put forward to support that view. In the first place, the TL, following the style of the Constitutional Treaty, has introduced the new comprehensive term, 'external action', to express the full range of the Union's competence in the external sphere; 'foreign policy' is just one element of such action. Secondly, as I indicated above, it is very clear that, in the new constitutional order of the TL, the competence conferred on the Union in CFSP matters has been conceived as different in kind from the categories of competence defined by Articles 3 to 6 of the TFEU, including the external relations competences provided for in Part Five of the Treaty.[15]

On an interpretation that was alert to the letter of the primary law, as well as to the principle of conferral, there might not be a very grave risk of conflict between available TFEU and CFSP competences, when the Union's response to a global emergency was in question. If *ad hoc* measures were called for, to meet humanitarian needs resulting from natural or man-made disasters, the right legal basis would obviously be Article 214 TFEU. CFSP competence would have to be invoked for any action with a political or security dimension; this might, for instance, involve peace-making or peace-keeping operations, monitoring a cease-fire, maintenance of law and order, collection of weapons, destruction of stockpiles of weapons, bringing pressure to bear upon third country regimes (including by means of restrictive measures that would need to be implemented pursuant to Article 215 TFEU) or monitoring elections or referenda. The legal bases for development cooperation or general cooperation would only come into play once an emergency had been brought under control, in order to organise the long-term relationship between the Union and the third country (or countries) concerned, by way of measures that were, respectively, designed to foster 'sustainable economic, social and environmental development' or were 'economic, financial and technical' in character.

Such an understanding might be thought to have underlain the adoption in 2001 of Council Regulation 381/2001 creating a rapid-reaction mechanism.[16] Recital (1) of the preamble to the Regulation recalled that various forms of aid

[13] In my contribution, entitled 'Article 47 TEU and the relationship between first and second pillar competences', to Dashwood and Maresceau (eds), *Law and Practice of EU External Relations* (Cambridge, Cambridge University Press, 2008) (hereinafter, *Dashwood and Maresceau*) 102.

[14] Emphasis added.

[15] ibid. See also the discussion of the scope of the Union's CFSP competence at pp 73–75.

[16] Council Regulation 381/2001/EC [2001] OJ L57/5.

and cooperation activity were being undertaken by the Community in different parts of the world, while recital (2) noted that the aims of such programmes were liable to be 'jeopardised or directly affected by, inter alia, the emergence of situations of crisis or conflict, by impending or ongoing threats to law and order, to the security and safety of individuals'. Recital (4) stated:

> Accordingly, it is important that provision be made for a mechanism that will underpin existing Community policies and programmes and enable the Community to take urgent action to help re-establish or safeguard normal conditions for the execution of the policies undertaken, in order to preserve their effectiveness.

It seems clear from those recitals, and from the choice of Article 308 EC as the legal basis for Regulation 381/2001, that the creation of the rapid-reaction mechanism was considered necessary in order to achieve an objective beyond the scope of the Community's competence for development cooperation.

In contrast, the basing of Regulation 1257/96 concerning humanitarian aid upon Article 130w EC (equivalent to the present Article 209 TFEU), which I have remarked upon,[17] showed willingness on the part of the EU legislator to take a broad view of the relationship that 'cooperation' entails.[18] Similar elasticity was shown in the interpretation of the socio-economic objectives of development as extending to action against anti-personnel landmines.[19]

This loosening of the EU legislator's conception of development cooperation reached its furthest point (to date) in 2006, with the adoption of Council Regulation 1717/2006 establishing an Instrument for Stability.[20] As I have noted elsewhere,[21] the Commission's original proposal was for a Regulation based on Article 308 EC, which would have allowed financial and technical assistance to be provided by the Community in furtherance of objectives manifestly within the exclusive competence of the Union under the CFSP, such as the preservation of peace and strengthening of international security. After difficult negotiations lasting more than two years, the Regulation was finally adopted in November 2006 as one authorising 'development cooperation measures, as well as financial, economic and technical cooperation measures with third countries',[22] and having

[17] See n 8 above.

[18] See also Council Regulation 2130/2001/EC on operations to aid uprooted peoples in Asian and Latin American developing countries [2001] OJ L287/3. This was adopted as a development cooperation measure, based on what had by then become Art 179(1). It provided for the implementation of a programme of support and assistance to uprooted people, which must provide for the basic needs of those persons from the time a humanitarian emergency subsides to the adoption of long-term solution to resolve their status.

[19] Council Regulation 1724/2001/EC concerning action against anti-personnel landmines in developing countries [2001] OJ L234/1. This had Art 179(1) EC as its legal basis. The companion measure, Council Regulation 1725/2001/EC concerning action against anti-personnel landmines in countries other than developing countries [2001] OJ L234/6, was based on Art 308 EC, since Art 181a had not yet been inserted into the Treaty.

[20] Council Regulation 1717/2006 [2006] OJ L327/1.

[21] *Dashwood and Maresceau* (n 13 above) 86–87.

[22] Council Regulation 1717/2006 (n 20 above) Art 1 (1).

Article 179(1) and Article 181a as joint legal bases. The aims of the Regulation, to be pursued '[i]n accordance with the objectives of such cooperation and within its limits as laid down in the EC Treaty', are identified by Article 1(2) as falling into two broad categories:

(a) in a situation of crisis or emerging crisis, to contribute to stability by providing an effective response to help preserve, establish or re-establish the conditions essential to the proper implementation of the Community's development and cooperation policies;
(b) in the context of stable conditions for the implementation of Community cooperation policies in third countries, to help build capacity both to address specific global and transregional threats having a destabilising effect and to ensure preparedness to address pre- and post-crisis situations.[23]

The situation referred to under (a) is further clarified by Article 3(1) of the Regulation as comprising 'a situation of urgency, crisis or emerging crisis, a situation posing a threat to democracy, law and order, the protection of human rights and fundamental freedoms, or the security and safety of individuals, or a situation threatening to escalate into armed conflict or severely to destabilise the third country or countries concerned'. Article 3(2) then sets out in concrete detail a long list of the forms of technical and financial assistance that may be undertaken in such situations. A similar list of the forms of assistance that may be undertaken pursuant to the Regulation in the context of stable conditions for cooperation is provided by Article 4.

As indicated by the words that I have italicised in points (a) and (b) of Article 1(2), the rationale for the adoption of Regulation 1717/2006 as a measure organising a particular aspect of the Union's cooperation policies in third countries was found in the notion of helping to preserve, establish or re-establish the conditions essential for the implementation of the policies, or to build capacity so that threats to undermine those essential conditions could be addressed. It was sought, in this way, to establish a causal relationship between measures mostly having a political or security-related character, which might have been thought to belong to the domain of the CFSP, and the socio-economic objectives of development cooperation and general cooperation. The problem with this analysis is to identify the degree of proximity in the causal relationship sufficient to justify the choice of legal basis. A criterion so potentially expansive as that of helping to create or maintain conditions for attaining the objectives of cooperation policy makes it difficult to determine the limits of Union competence in this area, with the precision that is necessary in a constitutional order founded on the specific attribution of powers. It is also liable to be applied in an arbitrary way. For example, there is well-nigh universal agreement that trade liberalisation is an indispensable condition for the success of any development

[23] Emphasis added.

strategy; however, it is trite law that the special arrangements that may have to be made in freeing-up trade between the Union and developing countries are an aspect of the common commercial policy, not of development cooperation policy.[24]

The expansive interpretation of the Union's competence for development cooperation (and, by implication, of its competence for general cooperation also) was confirmed by the Court of Justice in the *ECOWAS* case.[25] The dispute in the proceedings concerned the choice of a CFSP measure, Council Decision 2004/833,[26] as the legal instrument for providing financial and technical support for the Moratorium on the Import, Export and Manufacture of Small Arms and Light Weapons, which was an initiative of the Economic Community of West African States (or ECOWAS). The Decision was based upon a Council Joint Action of 2002,[27] which had replaced an earlier Joint Action of 1999,[28] organising the contribution of the EU towards combating the destabilising accumulation and spread of small arms and light weapons. While there had been no challenge to the validity of the Joint Action of 2002 or of its predecessor at the time of their adoption[29] (nor indeed of other implementing Decisions adopted pursuant to those instruments[30]), the Commission sought the annulment of the ECOWAS Decision on the ground that it ought to have been adopted as a Community development cooperation measure. The Court of Justice found that the Decision was designed to further objectives of both development cooperation and the CFSP, and that its content was appropriate for pursuing either set of objectives. That being so, the Court held, the Decision ought to have been adopted under the Community's competence for development cooperation, and it must accordingly be annulled as constituting an 'encroachment' on that competence, contrary to the then applicable Article 47 TEU.[31]

A section of the judgment is devoted to the demarcation of the areas of development cooperation policy and the CFSP respectively. It begins with the

[24] Opinion 1/78 *Natural Rubber* [1979] ECR 2871; Case 45/86 *GSP* [1987] ECR 1493.

[25] Case C-91/05 *Commission v Council* [2008] ECR I-3651. The writer acted for the United Kingdom, which was one of the Member States intervening in the *ECOWAS* case; however, the views expressed in this contribution are exclusively his own. My understanding of the implications of this case has been enhanced by discussing it with colleagues at a round-table that was organised by Professor Marise Cremona at the European University Institute, Florence in December 2009.

[26] Council Decision 2004/833/CFSP of 2 December 2004, [2004] OJ L359/65. Hereinafter, 'the *ECOWAS* Decision' or, where the context permits, 'the Decision'.

[27] Joint Action 2002/589/CFSP [2002] OJ L191/1.

[28] Joint Action 1999/34/CFSP [1999] OJ L9/1.

[29] The issue of the validity of the 2002 Joint Action was raised by the Commission in the *ECOWAS* case, pursuant to Art 241 EC. The plea of illegality was not considered by the Court, since the *ECOWAS* Decision was held to be defective in itself: Case C-91/05 (n 25 above) para 111.

[30] See, in relation to Cambodia, Council Decision 1999/730/CFSP [1999] OJ L294/5; extended and amended by Council Decision 2004/792/CFSP [2004] OJ L348/47; in relation to South East Europe, Council Decision 2002/842/CFSP [2002] OJ L289/1; extended and amended by Council Decision 2004/791/CFSP [2004] OJ L348/46; in relation to Albania, Council Decision 2003/276/CFSP [2003] OJ L99/60.

[31] On the *ECOWAS* case, and for a different view, see D Gauci's contribution in this same volume.

Court's recalling its judgment in *Portugal v Council*[32] as authority for the proposition that 'the objectives pursued by Article 130u of the EC Treaty (now Article 177 EC) are broad in the sense that it must be possible for the measures required for their pursuit to concern various specific matters'.[33] Unfortunately, that brief citation gives a rather misleading impression of the real relevance of the *Portugal* case to the proceedings in *ECOWAS*. The Portuguese Government was contesting the choice of legal basis for the Cooperation Agreement between the Community and India. The Agreement included provisions relating to a range of specific matters identified as falling within the scope of the cooperation—energy, tourism and culture, drug abuse control and intellectual property—and one of the issues in the case was whether the Community's competence for development cooperation would cover all of those matters. The Court held that it did so, but only because of the restricted scope of the provisions in question; they simply identified areas for cooperation, while containing 'nothing that prescribes in concrete terms the manner in which cooperation in each specific area envisaged is to be implemented'.[34] With the evident intention that extravagant conclusions should not be drawn from its finding, the Court explained further:

> The mere inclusion of provisions for cooperation in a specific field does not therefore necessarily imply a general power such as to lay down the basis of a competence to undertake any kind of cooperative action in that field. It does not, therefore, predetermine the allocation of spheres of competence between the Community and the Member States *or the legal basis for implementing cooperation in such a field*.[35]

The lesson I draw from those passages is that, while a development cooperation package may include a general commitment to cooperate in respect of matters for which specific legal bases have been provided elsewhere in the Treaties, any concrete steps to implement such a commitment must be taken under the applicable legal basis. It is a lesson which, in my submission, militated in favour of a CFSP legal basis for the ECOWAS Decision.[36]

The Court of Justice in *ECOWAS* went on to note that Articles 177 to 181 EC referred not only to the socio-economic objectives mentioned in Article 177(1) 'but also to the development and consolidation of democracy and the rule of law, as well as to respect for human rights and fundamental freedoms, in compliance also with commitments in the context of the United Nations and other international obligations'.[37] It then referred to a political text, the Joint Statement by the Council and the representatives of the Governments of the Member States meeting within the Council, the European Parliament and the Commission on

[32] Case C-268/94 *Portugal v Council* [1996] ECR I-6177 ('the *Portugal* case').
[33] *Portugal*, para 37, cited at para 64 of Case C-91/05.
[34] *Portugal*, para 45.
[35] ibid para 47. Emphasis added.
[36] This argument was put to the Court of Justice in *ECOWAS*, but the judgment does not engage with it.
[37] Case 91/05, para 65.

European Union Development Policy, entitled 'The European Consensus', from which it was said to follow 'that there can be no sustainable development and eradication of poverty without peace and security and that the pursuit of the Community's new development policy necessarily proceeds via the promotion of democracy and respect for human rights'.[38] From]those considerations the inference was drawn that:

> While the objectives of current Community development cooperation policy should therefore not be limited to measures *directly* related to the campaign against poverty, it is none the less necessary, if a measure is to fall within that policy, that it contributes to the pursuit of that policy's economic and social development objectives.[39]

Various political texts, including once again 'The European Consensus', were then cited as helping to establish

> that certain measures aiming to prevent fragility in developing countries, including those adopted in order to combat the proliferation of small arms and light weapons, can contribute to the elimination or reduction of obstacles to the economic and social development of those countries.[40]

The Court concluded that a concrete measure designed to combat the proliferation of small arms and light weapons could fall within the scope of the Community's competence for development cooperation, though not where such a measure 'even if it contributes to the economic and social development of the developing country, has as its main purpose the implementation of the CFSP'.[41]

For the Court of Justice, therefore, it is sufficient to justify recourse to the Union's competence for development cooperation that the contemplated measure would be capable of eliminating or of merely reducing obstacles to the attainment of the socio-economic objectives of such cooperation. It seems that a purely abstract risk that such obstacles may exist will satisfy the Court of the need for a counter-measure. What the Court decided in *ECOWAS* with regard to the accumulation and spread of small arms and light weapons would, presumably, apply to any other element of 'fragility' in the political or security situation of a developing country (or other third country).

As we shall see, the replacement of Article 47 TEU by the new Article 40 TEU means that different rules now apply to the management of conflicts between TFEU and CFSP competences; in that respect, the significance of the *ECOWAS* judgment has proved to be short-lived. However, a permanent legacy of the judgment is to have made the occurrence of such conflicts more likely, including when the Union is considering its response to a global emergency, because it has

[38] ibid, para 66. The same passage was cited in Case C-403/05 *European Parliament v Council* [2007] ECR I-9045para 57, as indicating the broad scope of the EC's development cooperation competence.

[39] Case C-91/05, para 67. Emphasis added.

[40] ibid, para 68. The various texts are identified in paras 69 and 70.

[41] ibid, paras 71 and 72.

become virtually impossible to identify a clear line of demarcation between the Union's competence for the CFSP and its TFEU competences for development cooperation and general cooperation.

V MANAGING CONFLICTS OF COMPETENCE

There is settled case law on the rules governing the choice of legal basis, and hence of competence, under which it is appropriate for the Union to act in given circumstances.[42] Familiar as the rules are, it may be helpful to summarise them here:

— The choice of legal basis does not follow from its author's conviction alone but must rest on objective factors, which are amenable to judicial review; such factors include, in particular, the aim and content of the external action that is contemplated.
— If examination of the contemplated action reveals that it pursues two (or more) purposes or has two (or more) components, and if one of these is identifiable as predominant, whereas any others are merely incidental, the action must be founded on a single legal basis, namely that of the predominant purpose and component. To put the point metaphorically, an effort must be made to determine the 'centre of gravity' of the action.
— A dual or multiple legal basis is appropriate only if it is established that the measure in question simultaneously pursues several objectives that are indissolubly linked without any of them being secondary and indirect in relation to the other.

It is, therefore, clear in principle what the competent institutions of the Union have to do, when faced with a choice between exercising CFSP or relevant TFEU competences in reacting to a global emergency. The aim and content of the measure which is contemplated must be carefully considered, to see whether it is predominantly concerned with implementing the CFSP or with implementing the cooperation policies of the Union or a programme of humanitarian aid. The foregoing analysis would suggest that it may not infrequently be difficult to decide, on an objective basis capable of withstanding judicial scrutiny, where the predominant concern (or centre of gravity) of a proposal lies. This may be because, as in *ECOWAS*, the content of the action would be equally appropriate to further CFSP or cooperation objectives. Or it may be because a complex set of measures is called for, none of which can fairly be regarded as incidental to the rest, but which it is nevertheless practically convenient to bring together in a

[42] The principles were initially applied in cases relating to the choice between legal bases in the EC Treaty. See, among numerous authorities, Opinion 2/00 *Cartagena Protocol* [2001] ECR I-9713, paras 22 and 23. As to the choice between First- and Third-Pillar legal bases, see Case C-176/03, *Commission* v *Council* [2005] ECR I-7879, paras 51–53; Case C-440/05 [2007] ECR I-9097, paras 71–73. As to the choice between First- and Second-Pillar legal bases, see the *ECOWAS* judgment, paras 73–77.

coherent package; for instance, in a post-conflict situation, the combination of peace-monitoring with measures to reintegrate former fighters into the civilian population, to undertake mine-clearance and to begin the work of economic reconstruction. In *ECOWAS* the Court of Justice was able to cut the Gordian knot, by ruling that the protection accorded to Community competences pursuant to the then Article 47 TEU meant that the Union's CFSP competence ought to have been left out of account. That simple, if brutal, solution is no longer available, owing to the equal protection that CFSP and TFEU competences now enjoy under Article 40 TEU. The result may have to be the adoption of a joint CFSP/TFEU legal basis (the post-Lisbon equivalent of what used to be called 'cross-Pillar mixity'). However, that may appear in some circumstances to be an unduly cumbersome solution, as it would surely have been in the case of the ECOWAS Decision.

A pragmatic approach, calculated to minimise conflicts of competence in determining the Union's response to global emergencies, would focus on the nature of the action it is proposed to undertake and the means to be deployed for its implementation. The risk of competences overlapping is likely to be confined to emergency situations that can effectively be addressed through the provision of financial or technical assistance; that limits the practical scope for conflict, though the term 'technical' covers a wide range of possibilities. In *ECOWAS* the Court of Justice mentioned, as measures that might fall within CFSP competence, 'the grant of political support for a moratorium or even the collection and destruction of weapons'.[43] The latter example suggests, as a rule of thumb, that CFSP competence should normally be resorted to, where the contemplated action, if performed within a Member State, would entail the exercise of state power. Other considerations would be the necessity for the exercise of political judgment, both at the initial stage and in the course of an operation, and the 'ownership' of the means employed. Such considerations would, for instance, amply justify the organisation as CFSP operations of civilian monitoring missions[44] or of police missions.[45]

It is interesting to note that, in spite of *ECOWAS*, the Council adopted, as a CFSP measure based upon Article 26(2) TEU, a Decision in March 2010 supporting a project that aims to reduce the threat posed to security in the Western Balkans by small arms and light weapons.[46] Considered in the light of its content, the measure, which was limited to providing financial and technical assistance, might perfectly well have had Article 212 TFEU as its legal basis.

[43] Case C-91/05, para 105.

[44] eg Council Joint Action 2008/736/CFSP on the European Union Monitoring Mission in Georgia [2008] OJ L248/26.

[45] eg Council Decision 2010/279/CFSP on the European Union Police Mission in Afghanistan [2010] OJ L123/4.

[46] Council Decision 2010/179/CFSP of 11 March 2010 in support of SEESAC arms control activities in the Western Balkans, in the framework of the EU Strategy to combat the illicit accumulation and trafficking of SALW and their ammunition [2010] OJ L80/48.

However, the preamble to the Decision and its Article 1(1) strongly emphasise its CFSP objectives. This may be contrasted with the ECOWAS Decision, where recital (1) of the preamble implied the existence of a link between the proliferation of small arms and light weapons and the reduction of prospects for sustainable development. The Council appears to have learned the lesson that, if it has good, security-related reasons for an action that might also have been taken in furtherance of cooperation policy, conflict over the choice of a CFSP legal basis can be avoided, by drafting that makes the aims of the measure unequivocally clear.

VI CONCLUSIONS

My brief conclusions are the following. There is no serious risk of conflict in choosing between the competences conferred upon the Union by the three legal bases in Title III of Part Five of the TFEU, which are more particularly relevant for the purpose of organising the Union's response to global emergencies. On the other hand, the expansive interpretation of development cooperation and general cooperation, which has been adopted by the Union legislator and by the Court in *ECOWAS*, together with structural changes brought about by the Treaty of Lisbon, have created an overlap, and hence the potential for conflict, between the relevant TFEU competences and CFSP competence. Nevertheless, there are strategies available that can help minimise such conflicts.

It will be a mark of the success of the new office of the High Representative of the Union for Foreign Affairs and Security Policy, if turf-wars between the institutions over the choice of legal basis for external action by the Union, including with respect to global emergencies, come to be regarded as an aberration of the Union's teenage years.

3

Constitutional Limits to Delegated Powers

ROBERT SCHÜTZE

I INTRODUCTION: EMERGENCIES AND DELEGATED POWERS

THE HISTORY OF the twentieth century has—sadly—shown the 'weaknesses of democracy to meet crises'.[1] The slowness and complexities of the parliamentary procedure seem ill-equipped to meet emergencies. Emergencies require quick and strong action. When on 4 March 1933 President Roosevelt took office, the United States of America was undergoing the biggest economic crisis of the twentieth century: the Great Depression. With millions of Americans unemployed, the new President asked 'for the one remaining instrument to meet the crisis—broad Executive power to wage a war against the emergency'.[2] This led to an explosion of legislative activity, seeing the adoption of the Agricultural Adjustment Act, the Emergency Banking Act, and the National Industrial Recovery Act.[3] The (executive) legislation challenged the 'reserved' powers of Congress and the Supreme Court would eventually strike down the

[1] RA Mauer, 'Emergency Laws' (1934–35) 23 *Georgetown Law Journal* 671, 688.

[2] Inaugural Address of President Roosevelt (4 March 1933) quoted in WE Leutchenburg, *Franklin D. Roosevelt and the New Deal: 1932–1940* (New York, Harper & Row, 1963) 41.

[3] For an overview of the statutes passed in 1933, see NH Josephs, 'The Federal Constitution in Time of Emergency' (1933–34) 11 *New York University Law Quarterly Review* 499. The Agricultural Adjustment Act was enacted on 12 May 1933. Its chief aim was to reduce the agricultural surplus by paying farmers to produce less. The Emergency Banking (Relief) Act was adopted on 9 March 1933. Section 2 of Title I of the Act provided: 'During time of war or during any other period of national emergency declared by the President, the President may, through any agency that he may designate, or otherwise, investigate, regulate, or prohibit, under such rules and regulations as he may prescribe, by means of licenses or otherwise, any transactions in foreign exchange, transfers of credit between or payments by banking institutions as defined by the President, and export, hoarding, melting, or earmarking of gold or silver coin or bullion or currency, by any person within the United States or any place subject to the jurisdiction thereof[.]' Finally, the National Industrial Recovery Act was adopted on 16 June 1933. Section 1 of Title I declared: 'A national emergency productive of widespread unemployment and disorganization of industry'. The most controversial provision was s 3, which stated: 'Upon the application to the President by one or more trade or industrial associations or groups the President may approve a code or codes of fair competition for the trade or industry'. These codes would constitute 'the standards of fair competition for such trade or industry or subdivision thereof'.

heart of the National Industrial Recovery Act as a violation of the non-delegation doctrine. In the words of the Court: 'Congress is not permitted to abdicate or to transfer to others the essential legislative functions with which it is thus vested'.[4]

Is there a non-delegation doctrine in the European legal order?[5] May the Union legislator delegate wide regulatory powers to the Union executive? Are there constitutional limits to delegated powers; and if so, will these limits depend on the identity of the delegee? This chapter wishes to answer these questions in three sections. Section 2 investigates the constitutional limits to delegations of power to two European institutions: the Commission and the Council. Section 3 analyses the (non-)delegation doctrine in relation to 'bodies other than those which the Treaty has established'.[6] We will see here that the European Court established strict substantive limits on delegating powers to European Agencies and has limited delegations of powers to international bodies by emphasising the need for political control mechanisms. Section 4 finally looks at the possibility of delegating powers back to the Member States. Next to a general delegation doctrine within the Union's exclusive powers, a specific form of emergency delegation emerged here in situations of a 'dysfunctional' Union legislator.

II DELEGATING POWERS TO EUROPEAN INSTITUTIONS

The Rome Treaty did not regulate delegations of power. Yet despite a sternly worded Article 7 EC,[7] the treaty makers had anticipated the possibility of a transfer of power from the Council to the Commission. Article 211 EC entitled the Commission to 'exercise the powers conferred on it by the Council for the implementation of the rules laid down by the latter'. On this laconic textual base, the European Community's regime for delegated powers was to be developed.[8]

[4] *ALA Schechter Poultry Corp v United States* 295 US 495 (1935) 529. However, the Supreme Court eventually accepted the 'New Deal'; and in accepting a permanent 'New Deal', the Supreme Court rejected the idea of a temporary 'emergency constitution', *cf* MR Belknap, 'The New Deal and the Emergency Powers Doctrine' (1983–84) 62 *Texas Law Review* 67. This *constitutional* revolution led to significant power changes in the United States. Since 1935 the Supreme Court has apparently not invalidated a single statute on the ground that it delegated too much power to the executive, *cf* G Lawson, 'The Rise and Rise of the Administrative State' (1993–94) 107 *Harvard Law Review* 1231, 1237 (referring to the 'death of the Nondelegation Doctrine'). For the argument that the Supreme Court only 'relocated' the doctrine, see CR Sunstein, 'Nondelegation Canons' (2000) 67 *University of Chicago Law Review* 315.

[5] A preliminary note on terminology: the Lisbon Treaty has introduced a 'formal' or 'procedural' concept of legislation (*cf* Art 289(3) TFEU) and 'delegation' (*cf* Art 290 TFEU). However, this article remains loyal to a 'material' or 'functional' conception of both concepts. The material concept of delegation thus includes 'conferrals' of 'implementing power' under Art 291 TFEU.

[6] Case 9/56 *Meroni & Co, Industrie Metallurgische, SpA v High Authority of the European Coal and Steel Community* [1958] ECR 133, 152.

[7] 'Each institution shall act within the limits of the powers conferred upon it by this Treaty.'

[8] For a brilliant historical analysis of this development, see CF Bergström, *Comitology: Delegation of Powers in the European Union and the Committee System* (Oxford, Oxford University Press, 2005).

The Single European Act codified constitutional practice by amending Article 202 EC. The provision thenceforth clarified that the Council could delegate power to the Commission and thereby 'impose certain requirements in respect of the exercise of these powers'.[9] Alternatively, the Council could 'reserve the right, in specific cases, to exercise directly implementing powers'. This section looks at the constitutional principles that governed delegations of powers under the 'old' Community legal order, before briefly discussing the Lisbon reforms.

A The constitutional rule: delegating powers to the Commission

i Delegations within the European Community legal order

From the very beginning, the EC Treaty had identified the Commission as the principal delegatee of power.[10] The Commission—as an 'executive' authority—would be better able than the Council (and/or Parliament) to quickly adopt the measures. The Court was asked to establish the constitutional parameters of the delegation doctrine in *Köster*.[11] A German farmer had challenged the legality of a legislative system set up by the Commission that established import and export licences for cereals. It was alleged that 'the power to adopt the system in dispute belonged to the Council', which should have acted according to the 'normal' legislative procedure established in Article 37 EC.[12] The Court disagreed:

> Both the legislative scheme of the Treaty, reflected in particular by the last indent of Article [211 EC], and the consistent practice of the Community institutions establish a distinction, according to the legal concepts recognized in all the Member States, between the measures directly based on the Treaty itself and derived law intended to ensure their implementation. It cannot therefore be a requirement that all the details of the regulations concerning the common agricultural policy be drawn up by the Council according to the procedure in Article [37 EC]. It is sufficient for the purposes of that provision that the basic elements of the matter to be dealt with have been adopted in accordance with the procedure laid down by that provision. On the other hand, the

[9] Art 202 (third indent) EC. This chapter will not deal with the—old and new—'political safeguards' attached to a delegation of powers. In the past, Art 202 EC left the specifics of executive rule-making in the hands of the European legislator. Suffice to say that the Council has made extensive use of its power to 'impose certain requirements', setting up a procedural system known as 'Comitology'. The present constitutional regime for Comitology was designed by Council Decision 99/468/EC ([1999] OJ L184/23), as amended by Council Decision 2006/512 ([2006] OJ L200/11).

[10] *cf* Art 155 EEC fourth indent.

[11] Case 25/1970 *Einfuhr- und Vorratsstelle für Getreide und Futtermittel v Köster et Berodt & Co* [1970] ECR 1161.

[12] ibid, para 5.

> provisions implementing the basic regulations may be adopted according to a procedure different from that in Article [37 EC], either by the Council itself or by the Commission by virtue of an authorization complying with Article [211 EC].[13]

In essence, while basic political choices must be made in accordance with the institutional balance prescribed by the EC Treaty, non-essential elements could be delegated and thus adopted by a simpler procedure. This followed from the constitutional scheme of the Treaty, in particular Article 202 EC and the common constitutional traditions of all the Member States. But what was the dividing line between 'basic elements' and 'non-essential' elements? And what was the normative relationship between the 'basic act' and the 'delegated act'?

In *Rey Soda*,[14] the Court tackled the first question. Pointing to the institutional balance between Council and Commission, the Court held that the delegation mandate 'must be interpreted strictly'; yet, despite this limitation, the Court insisted, 'the concept of implementation must be given a wide interpretation'.[15] 'Since the Commission alone is able continually to follow with attention trends in agricultural markets and to act with urgency as the situation requires, the Council may be led in the sphere of the common agricultural policy, to confer on the Commission *wide powers of discretion and action*.'[16] The scope of these—extensive—powers was to be judged in light of the objectives of the enabling act 'and less in terms of the literal meaning of the enabling word'.[17] However, subsequent jurisprudence soon confirmed that there would be three constitutional limitations. First, for 'an enabling provision to be valid, it must be *sufficiently specific*—that is to say, the Council must clearly specify the bounds of the power conferred on the Commission'.[18] Second, 'provisions which are intended to give concrete shape to the fundamental guidelines of Community policy' are beyond delegation.[19] Third, the Commission cannot use its wide implementing powers in one policy area to interfere with the powers of the Council in another.[20]

[13] ibid, para 6. See also: Case 46/86 *Romkes v Officier van Justitie for the District of Zwolle* [1987] ECR 2671, para 16.

[14] Case 23/75 *Rey Soda v Cassa Conguaglio Zucchero* [1975] ECR 1279.

[15] ibid, paras 9–10.

[16] ibid, para 11 (emphasis added).

[17] ibid, para 14.

[18] Case 291/86 *Central-Import Münster GmbH & Co KG v Hauptzollamt Münster* [1988] ECR 3679, para 13. See also: Case C-240/90 *Germany v Commission* [1992] ECR I-5383, paras 41–42 (emphasis added).

[19] *Germany v Commission* (n 18 above) para 37.

[20] Case 22/88 *Industrie- en Handelsonderneming Vreugdenhil BV and Gijs van der Kolk – Douane Expediteur BV v Minister van Landbouw en Visserij* [1989] ECR 2049, paras 16–25: '[I]t follows from the context of the Treaty in which Article [211] must be placed and also from practical requirements that the concept of implementation must be given a wide interpretation . . . However, it must be pointed out that such a wide interpretation of the Commission's powers can be accepted only in the specific framework of the rules on agricultural markets. It cannot be relied upon in support of provisions adopted by the Commission on the basis of its implementing powers in agricultural

What was the normative relationship between the enabling act and the delegated act? In many legal orders, this question is answered by means of a hierarchy of norms. The enabling act is superior to the delegated act. The supremacy of primary over secondary legislation means that the latter cannot amend the former.[21] The Community legal order had not adopted such a clear hierarchical solution. While it principally confirmed the subordinate status of secondary legislation vis-à-vis the enabling act *on which is was based*,[22] this supremacy could be limited where the enabling act expressly allowed the Commission subsequently to amend the basic act.[23] However, the Commission's amendment power for primary legislation would encounter an external limit in the 'basic elements' embodied in that act.[24] Yet the Court has on occasion shown a marked tolerance of executive legislation and allowed for significant amendments of primary legislation.[25] In emergency situations, the Commission may thus have the power to suspend ordinary European law.[26]

matters where the purpose of the provision in question lies outside that sphere but within a sector subject to an exhaustive set of rules laid down by the Council which, moreover, do not confer any implementing powers on the Commission.'

[21] This constitutional rule has exceptions. On so-called 'Henry VIII clauses' in British constitutional law, see A Le Sueur, M Sunkin and J Murkens, *Public Law: Text, Cases, and Materials* (Oxford, Oxford University Press, 2010) 490.

[22] Case 38/70 *Deutsche Tradex GmbH v Einfuhr- und Vorratsstelle für Getreide und Futtermittel* [1971] ECR 145, para 10: 'It cannot be accepted that the said provision altered the system laid down by Regulation No 120/67, especially since Regulation No 140/67, being an implementing Regulation not directly based on Article [37](2) of the Treaty but on the enabling provision of Article 15(4) of Regulation No 120/67, could not have derogated from the provisions of the basic regulation to which it is subordinate.'

[23] Case 100/74 *Société CAM SA v Commission* [1975] ECR 1393, in which the Court confirmed the legality of Art 4 of (Council) Regulation 2496/74 amending the prices applicable in agriculture for the 1974/75 marketing year ([1974] OJ L268/1). This technique has not been overruled by Case C-93/00 *Parliament v Council* [2001] ECR I-10119, see only: Commission Regulation 413/2010 amending Annexes III, IV and V to Council Regulation 1013/2006 on shipments of waste so as to take account of changes adopted by OECD Council Decision C(2008) 156 ([2010] OJ L119/1). The amendment power of secondary legislation is not necessarily confined to provisions in a regulatory annex, but could include changes in the main text of primary legislation, *cf* Case C-417/93 *Parliament v Council* [1995] ECR I-1185.

[24] *cf* Case 230/78 *SpA Eridania-Zuccherifici nazionali et al v Minister of Agriculture and Foresty et al* [1979] ECR 2749, para 8; as well as: Case 46/86 *Romkes v Officier van Justitie* [1987] ECR 2671, para 16: 'an implementing regulation … must respect the basic elements laid down in the basic regulation'. See more recently: Case C-303/94 *Parliament v Council* [1996] ECR I-2943, paras 30–33.

[25] See in particular: Case C-156/93 *Parliament v Commission* [1995] ECR I-2019. The case has led CF Bergström (n 8 above, p 234) to comment on the Court's past position in the following way: 'in a number of rulings the Court struck the balance between the notion of "implementation"—the scope for legislation adopted in accordance with simplified procedures—and "the basic elements"—requiring the use of normal procedures—in such a way as to encourage rather than prevent the Council and the Commission from outflanking the European Parliament.'

[26] For a delegation of power to the Commission to adopt 'emergency measures' in the context of the common fisheries policy, see Council Regulation 1224/2009 establishing a Community control system for ensuring compliance with the rules of the common fisheries policy [2009] OJ L343/1, especially Art 108 entitled 'Emergency Measures': '1. If there is evidence, including based on the results of the sampling carried out by the Commission, that fishing activities and/or measures adopted by a Member State or Member States undermine the conservation and management

ii Delegations after the Lisbon Treaty reforms

What will the constitutional regime for delegated legislation look like after the Lisbon Treaty? The Lisbon Treaty has given new textual foundations to the delegation doctrine. The Treaty on the Functioning of the European Union (TFEU) distinguishes between 'delegated powers' and 'implementing powers'. The former is governed by Article 290 TFEU. The provision confirms that the Union legislature 'may delegate to the Commission the power to adopt non-legislative acts of general application'. Delegated acts will thus have two characteristics: *only* the Commission can henceforth adopt them, and they must be of *general* application.[27] The Lisbon amendments confirm three aspects of the 'old' delegation doctrine. First, Article 290 TFEU retains the hierarchical status of delegated acts: the latter will be able to amend legislative acts and must thus, at least in relation to them, enjoy hierarchical parity.[28] Second, Article 290 TFEU codifies the 'basic elements' principle: the European legislature can only delegate the power to adopt 'non-essential elements of the legislative act'.[29] Finally, Article 290 FEU confirms and elaborates the 'specificity principle': 'The objectives, content, scope and duration of the delegation of power shall be explicitly defined in the legislative act'.

But what will be the difference between 'delegated acts' and 'implementing acts'?[30] The latter are now dealt with in Article 291 TFEU. The provision allows

measures adopted in the framework of multiannual plans or threaten the marine eco-system and this requires immediate action, the Commission, at the substantiated request of any Member State or on its own initiative, may decide on emergency measures which shall last not more than six months. The Commission may take a new decision to extend the emergency measures for no more than six months. (2) The emergency measures provided for in paragraph 1 shall be proportionate to the threat and may include, inter alia: (a) suspension of fishing activities of vessels flying the flag of the Member States concerned; (b) closure of fisheries ...; (h) modification of the fishing data submitted by Member States in an appropriate way.'

[27] In the past, 'implementation' under Art 202 EC comprised both general and specific acts, *cf* Case 16/88 *Commission v Council* [1989] ECR 3457, para 11: 'The concept of implementation for the purposes of that article comprises both the drawing up of implementing rules and the application of rules to specific cases by means of acts of individual application.'

[28] J Bast, 'Legal Instruments and Judicial Protection' in: A von Bogdandy and J Bast (eds), *Principles of European Constitutional Law* (Oxford, Hart Publishing, 2009) 391.

[29] Unfortunately, Art 290 FEU contains two possible definitions of the 'essential elements' doctrine. A first formulation refers to 'non-essential elements *of the legislative act*' (first sentence), while the second formulation is broader and refers to the 'essential elements *of an area*'. This semantic ambivalence may well give rise to an uncertainty that has plagued the concept of 'minimum' standard in the context of complementary competences. There it is unsettled, whether a Member State's power to adopt stricter measures must be viewed against each legislative act or against the policy area in general (*cf* R Schütze, *From Dual to Cooperative Federalism: The Changing Structure of European Law* (Oxford, Oxford University Press, 2009) 272 et seq).

[30] Despite the formal distinction between 'delegated' and 'implementing power', acts adopted under Art 291 FEU are, too, the result of a delegation in a primary act, *cf* CF Bergström (n 8 above) 356. The overlap of the two regimes could have been avoided by confining Art 291 FEU to delegations in non-legislative acts, but this constitutional option was not chosen.

the Union to confer implementing powers on the Commission or — exceptionally — the Council. This provision comes textually closer to Article 202 EC. Implementing acts are not confined to acts of general application and may thus take the form of individual decisions. Implementing acts, it seems, will not be able to amend legislative acts as this function should henceforth be reserved to 'delegated acts'. Strangely, Article 291 TFEU does not mention any constitutional limitations like the 'essentiality principle' or the 'specificity principle'. Did the Member States here assume that the Court's case law would automatically extend to implementing acts?[31] Or, should Article 291 TFEU perhaps not be viewed from a horizontal separation of powers perspective at all?[32] These—hard—questions will soon be battled over in the Union legal order.

B The constitutional 'exception': delegation to the Council

The original Rome Treaty did not consider delegations to the Council a constitutional anomaly. Instead this constitutional option would, with time, develop into a 'full alternative to the delegation of implementing powers to the Commission'.[33] The Single European Act however tilted the balance in favour of the Commission. The (then) newly formulated third indent of Article 202 EC provided that the Council could delegate implementing powers to itself only 'in specific cases'.[34] This identified the Commission as the principal beneficiary of delegated powers.

[31] In this sense: H Hofmann, 'Legislation, Delegation and Implementation under the Treaty of Lisbon: Typology Meets Reality' (2009) 15 *European Law Journal* 482, 488: 'One of the weak points of this non-delegation clause introduced into the new typology of acts is that it is explicitly only formulated for delegated acts under Article 290 TFEU. From a teleological point of view, however, it should also be applicable for the distinction between legislative and implementing acts under Article 291 FEU.'

[32] If Art 291 TFEU is placed within the context of the Union's 'executive federalism', the provision may gain a significantly different meaning, see R Schütze, 'Executive Federalism in the (new) European Union' [2010] 47 *Common Market Law Review* 1385.

[33] K Lenaerts, 'Regulating the regulatory process: 'delegation of powers' in the European Community' (1993) 18 *European Law Review* 23, 34. However, the Court has (occasionally) clarified that the Council could not 'derogate' from its own general acts by means of specific decisions. For example, see Case 119/77 *Nippon Seiko KK and others v Council and Commission* [1979] ECR 1303, para 24: 'The Council, having adopted a general regulation with a view to implementing one of the objectives laid down in Article [133] of the [EC] Treaty, cannot derogate from the rules thus laid down in applying those rules to specific cases without interfering with the legislative system of the Community and destroying the equality before the law of those to whom the law applies.'

[34] This phrase suggested clear guidelines. They would not be given by the (subsequent) Comitology Decisions. K Bradley has indeed heavily criticised the comitology system as failing to respect the wording of Art 202 EC. It 'deprives the requirement that the Council supply detailed reasons for reserving the exercise of implementing powers of its raison d'être'. Under comitology, it is the management or regulatory committee 'rather than the Council, which takes the decision to reserve the implementing powers, in circumstances which do not permit any judicial review' (K St Clair Bradley, 'Comitology and the Law: Through a Glass, Darkly' (1992) 29 *CML Rev* 693, 716).

But how would the European legal order enforce this privileged position? How special would 'specific cases' have to be before the Council could justify a delegation of powers to itself?

Very few constitutional pointers crystallised in the 'old' Community legal order. In *Commission v Council (Budgetary Powers)*, the Court stated that 'after the amendments made to Article [202 EC] by the Single European Act, the Council may reserve the right to exercise implementing powers directly only in specific cases, and it must state in detail the grounds for such a decision.'[35] Did this impose a soft—formal—duty on the Council; or would the Court of Justice establish hard—substantive—limits protecting the executive prerogative of the Commission? In *Commission v Council (Visa Policy)*,[36] the Commission alleged the infringement of Article 202 EC as the Council had reserved implementing power to itself 'improperly *and* without giving adequate reasons for doing so'.[37] This invoked a substantive *and* a formal violation of the delegation doctrine. Substantially, the Commission contested that 'the specific nature of the implementing measures provided for by the contested regulations was such as to justify the exercise of implementing powers by the Council'.[38] Formally, the Commission complained that 'the Council failed to comply with the obligation to state reasons laid down in Article 253 EC'.[39] The Court's answer concentrated on the formal duty to give reasons:

> [T]he Council must properly explain, by reference to the nature and content of the basic instrument to be implemented or amended, why exception is being made to the rule that … it is the Commission which, in the normal course of events, is responsible for exercising that power.[40]

The Court bemoaned that the Council explanations were 'both general and laconic'.[41] However, it justified this explanatory minimalism by reference to the policy area in which the delegation had taken place. In light of the specific constitutional regime for Title VI of the EC Treaty (Visas, Asylum and Immigration)—a regime that provided the Council with more rights than elsewhere in the EC Treaty, 'the Council could reasonably consider itself to be concerned with a specific case'.[42] And because of this constitutional expectation within the specific policy area, the Council had—although in very few words—discharged its formal duty to state the reasons for exercising implementing powers itself. The Court appeared to recognize substantive differences between

35 Case 16/88 *Commission v Council* [1989] ECR 3457, para 10.
36 Case 257/01 *Commission v Council* [2005] ECR I-345.
37 ibid, para 33 (emphasis added).
38 ibid, paras 34–37.
39 ibid, para 38.
40 ibid, para 51.
41 ibid, para 53.
42 ibid, para 59.

policy areas within the European Union. Nonetheless, no clear guidelines on the substantive limits to a delegation of implementing powers to the Council had emerged.

Could the Council delegate power to itself *outside* the constitutional channels established by Article 202 EC? The question was recently discussed in the constitutional review of so-called 'secondary legal bases'.[43] The Council had adopted primary legislation by unanimity (after consulting the European Parliament) to establish 'minimum standards on procedures in Member States for granting and withdrawing refugee status'.[44] Due to disagreement in the Council, no list of third countries to be regarded as safe had been included in the Directive. Instead, Article 29 of the Directive enabled the Council subsequently to adopt—by qualified majority (after consulting the Parliament)—a minimum common list of such safe third countries. This delegation was challenged before the Court.[45] The Council had justified the 'simplified decision-making procedure' *not* by reference to the delegation doctrine, but by invoking the 'practical need to react quickly and effectively to changes in the situation of the third

[43] Case C-133/06 *Parliament v Council* [2008] ECR I-3189. The lack of definitional clarity in this case is appalling. Not only do the Court and its Advocate General constantly refer to 'secondary legislation' when they should be speaking of 'primary legislation' (*cf* R Schütze, 'The Morphology of Legislative Power in the European Community: Legal Instruments and Federal Division of Powers' (2006) 25 *Yearbook of European Law* 91, 105), why could the idea of 'secondary legal basis' not simply have been referred to as an 'enabling provision for secondary legislation'? To make matters worse, the Advocate General tried to find a distinction between the 'delegation of legislative power' and the 'delegation of implementing power' in the EC(!) Treaty by arguing that '[t]he Treaty on European Union [*sic*] does not provide expressly for the delegation of legislative power, only the delegation of implementing powers is provided for in Article 202 EC' (para 26). However, a distinction between a delegation of legislative power and a delegation of implementing power made no sense under the EC Treaty, because of the wide notion of implementing power discussed above. Thus, from the very first paragraph of his analysis, the Advocate General—and the Court—approached the constitutional problem raised in this case from a distorted perspective. This case was simply concerned with the question whether the Council could delegate implementing/legislative power outside the constitutional regime of Art 202 EC.

[44] Directive 2005/85/EC on minimum standards on procedures in Member States for granting and withdrawing refugee status [2005] OJ L326/13.

[45] The case was brought by the Parliament. Why would the Parliament feel excluded under this 'secondary legal basis'? The reason was Art 67(5) of the EC Treaty, which provided that the unanimity plus consultation procedure would be replaced by the co-decision procedure under the condition that 'the Council has previously adopted, in accordance with paragraph 1 of this Article, Community legislation defining the common rules and basic principles governing these issues'. Parliament claimed that this condition had been fulfilled and that it was therefore entitled to co-decision for any legal act based on Art 67 EC. However, this argument only held true for primary legislation adopted directly on the basis of Art 67 EC; it could not hold true for secondary or delegated legislation adopted under the regime of Art 202 EC. Its argument should therefore have been concentrated on the delegation doctrine, especially the 'essentiality principle'. In fact, the reference to the 'political importance' of the designation of safe countries in recital 19 of the preamble of the Directive pointed to the issue being an 'essential element' of the Community scheme. If that road had been taken, the Parliament could have successfully claimed that any delegation—either to the Council or the Commission—would be invalid as parliamentary involvement was, after the adoption of the Directive, required under Art 67(5) EC.

countries in question'.[46] The Court—rightly—started by asking whether the enabling provision could be justified by the delegation doctrine. Noting that 'the Council had the opportunity to apply the third indent of Article 202 EC in order to adopt measures not essential to the subject matter', it found that the Council had not properly discharged its formal duty to explain why it had reserved the implementing power to itself instead of transferring it to the Commission.[47] A proper delegation of implementing power to the Council was thus excluded. The Court then moved to the more general question, whether an institution could, outside Article 202 EC, 'establish secondary legal bases' within primary legislation. It—unsurprisingly—found that this would undermine the institutional balance within the Union and give the European legislator the power to amend the Treaty.[48] The Court thus confirmed the exclusivity of the delegation regime under Article 202 under the EC Treaty.

Has the Lisbon Treaty changed this result? Article 291 TFEU allows the Union to delegate implementing power 'in duly justified cases and in the cases provided for in Articles 24 and 26 of the Treaty on European Union, on the Council'.[49] The constitutional principles analysed above are thus likely to continue, mutatis mutandis, within the 'new' European Union.

III DELEGATIONS TO INTERNAL OR EXTERNAL 'NON-INSTITUTIONAL' BODIES

Legal orders may permit a transfer of governmental tasks to bodies that are not identified as official 'institutions'. These bodies could be national or international bodies. With the rise of the 'administrative state',[50] modern states have increasingly tended to delegate 'regulatory' powers to agencies. 'Open' constitutional orders may even allow delegations of decision-making power to international bodies. This third section analyses the European Union's constitutional limits vis-à-vis both potential delegatees.

A European agencies and the *Meroni* Doctrine

The rise of 'agencies' has been a constitutional phenomenon in the United States since the first half of the twentieth century.[51] The European Union followed this

46 Case C-133/06 *Parliament v Council* (above n 43) paras 31–34.
47 ibid, paras 45–51.
48 ibid, paras 56–58.
49 Art 291(2) TFEU.
50 On this point, see G Lawson, 'The Rise and Rise of the Administrative State' (n 4 above).
51 P Strauss, 'The Place of Agencies in Government: Separation of Powers and the Fourth Branch' (1984) 84 *Columbia Law Review* 573.

trend in the second half of that century.[52] But unlike the American legal order,[53] the European Union would reject the delegation of discretionary powers to agencies.

This constitutional choice was made in *Meroni v High Authority*.[54] The applicant had complained that the High Authority—the 'Commission' within the European Coal and Steel Community—had delegated to an agency 'powers conferred upon it by the Treaty, without subjecting their exercise to the conditions which the Treaty would have required if those powers had been exercised directly by it'.[55] The Court of Justice had little trouble in finding that this could not be done: even if the delegation as such was constitutional, the Community 'could not confer upon the authority receiving the delegation powers different from those which the delegating authority itself received under the Treaty'.[56] A second argument the Court then analysed concerned the constitutional limits to a delegation of powers to agencies as such. While noting that Article 8 ECSC did not provide any power to delegate,[57] the Court nonetheless found that such a constitutional possibility 'cannot be excluded'. It was inherent in the powers of the High Authority 'to entrust certain powers to such bodies subject to conditions to be determined by it and subject to its supervision' if such delegation was necessary for the performance of the Community's tasks. These tasks were set out in Article 3 ECSC—a provision that laid down 'very general objectives', which could not always be equally pursued. The Community thus had to make political choices, and these political choices could not be delegated to an agency:

> Reconciling the various objectives laid down in Article 3 [ECSC] implies a real discretion involving difficult choices, based on a consideration of the economic facts and circumstances in the light of which those choices are made. The consequences resulting from a delegation of powers are very different depending on whether it involves clearly defined executive powers the exercise of which can, therefore, be subject to strict review in the light of objective criteria determined by the delegating authority, *or whether it involves a discretionary power, implying a wide margin of discretion which may, according to the use which is made of it, make possible the*

[52] While a few agencies emerged in the 1970s, there has been a real 'agencification' of the European legal order since the 1990s. Today, almost 40 European agencies exist in the most diverse areas of European law. For an inventory and functional typology of European agencies, see S Griller and A Orator, 'Everything under control?: the "way forward" for European agencies in the footsteps of the Meroni doctrine' (2010) 35 EL Rev 3 (Appendix).

[53] See above n 4.

[54] Case 9/56 *Meroni & Co, Industrie Metallurgische, SpA v High Authority of the European Coal and Steel Community* (1958) ECR 133.

[55] ibid, 146.

[56] ibid, 150.

[57] Art 8 ECSC read: 'The High Authority shall be responsible for assuring the fulfilment of the purposes stated in the present Treaty under the terms thereof.'

> *execution of actual economic policy*. A delegation of the first kind cannot appreciably alter the consequences involved in the exercise of the powers concerned, whereas a delegation of the second kind, since it replaces the choices of the delegator by the choices of the delegate, brings about an actual transfer of responsibility.[58]

This judgment clarified two things. First, a delegation to bodies not mentioned in the Treaties—even 'bodies established under private law'—was constitutionally legitimate. However, such delegations 'can only relate to clearly defined executive powers, the use of which must be entirely subject to the supervision of the High Authority'.[59] This followed from the 'balance of powers which is characteristic of the institutional structure of the Community'. To delegate 'a discretionary power' to 'bodies other than those which the Treaty has established' would render that guarantee ineffective. Subsequent judicial and academic commentary has concentrated on this last passage. *Meroni* came to stand for a constitutional non-delegation doctrine according to which the European institutions could not delegate *any* discretionary power to European agencies.[60]

While this expansive reading may not have been originally intended,[61] constitutional folklore continues to pay homage to a 'Meroni Doctrine'. This constitutional choice has prevented European agencies from exercising *regulatory* powers. They may, at most, be entitled to adopt legally binding individual decisions implementing European norms.[62] But in general, they only assist the Commission in discharging *its* delegated powers. An illustration of this auxiliary character of European agencies can be seen in the European Fisheries Control Agency,

[58] *Meroni v High Authority* (n 54 above) 152 (emphasis added).

[59] ibid.

[60] The most drastic expression of this expansive reading of *Meroni* is Case 98/80 *Romano v Institut national d'assurance maladie-invalidité* [1981] ECR 1241, para 20: 'it follows both from Article [202] of the [EC] Treaty, and in particular by Articles [230] and [234] thereof, that a body such as the administrative commission may not be empowered by the Council to adopt acts having the force of law. Whilst a decision of the administrative commission may provide an aid to social security institutions responsible for applying Community law in this field, it is not of such a nature as to require those institutions to use certain methods or adopt certain interpretations when they come to apply the Community rules.'

[61] In *Meroni* (n 54 above), the Court—repeatedly—referred to the '*wide* margin of discretion' that was delegated to the agency (ibid, 153 and 154; emphasis added). A close historical analysis could thus narrow the ruling to an early expression of the 'basic elements' principle: the High Authority was simply not allowed to delegate *basic* choices to an agency. For a similar reading, see Griller and Orator (n 52 above). The Court has itself (occasionally) signalled its willingness to limit the *Meroni* doctrine to a 'basic elements' doctrine for agencies, see Case C-164/98P *DIR International Film Srl et al v Commission* [2000] ECR I-447; and albeit in a different context, Case C-154–155/04 *R (on the application of Alliance for Natural Health) v Secretary of state for Health* [2005] ECR I-6541, especially para 90.

[62] For an example of an agency of this type, see Office for the Harmonisation of the Internal Market (OHIM) established by Regulation 40/94 on the Community trade mark [1994] OJ L11/1.

established by Regulation 768/2005.[63] Its objective is to establish organisational coordination of fisheries control and inspection activities by the Member States.[64] The Agency shall thereby 'provide the Commission with the necessary technical and administrative support to carry out its tasks'.[65] Of particular interest here are the provisions within the Regulation dealing with emergencies. Where the Commission identifies a 'serious risk to the common fisheries policy, and the risk cannot be prevented, eliminated or reduced by existing means', the Agency shall set up an 'emergency unit'.[66] The function of the emergency unit is defined in Article 17e, which reads:

> Tasks of the emergency unit
>
> 1. The emergency unit set up by the Agency shall be responsible for collecting and evaluating all relevant information and identifying the options available to prevent, eliminate or reduce the risk to the common fisheries policy as effectively and rapidly as possible.
> 2. The emergency unit may request the assistance of any public authority or private person whose expertise it deems necessary to respond to the emergency effectively.
> 3. The Agency shall make the necessary coordination for undertaking an adequate and timely response to the emergency.
> 4. The emergency unit shall, where appropriate, keep the public informed of the risks involved and the measures taken.

The provision reflects the limited role of agencies in the European legal order. Binding emergency measures will have to be adopted by the Commission (or the Council) and the Member States—not the Agency. The central task of the latter is to collect and distribute information and to 'coordinate' the responses by other European or national public authorities. The auxiliary function of the Agency is to help prevent emergencies by means of an effective supervision system.

We encounter similar limitations in the context of the regulation and supervision of financial markets. Reacting to the global financial crisis, the Commission proposed the creation of a 'European System of Financial Supervisors', including a 'European Banking Authority'.[67] The aim of the new Agency is 'to strengthen European supervisory arrangements' by providing 'an early warning of system-wide risks that may be building up and, where necessary, issue recommendations

[63] Regulation 768/2005 establishing a Community Fisheries Control Agency and amending Regulation 2847/93 establishing a control system applicable to the common fisheries policy [2005] OJ L 128/1 as amended by Council Regulation 1224/2009/EC establishing a Community control system for ensuring compliance with the rules of the common fisheries policy [2009] OJ L343/1.

[64] ibid, Art 1. Art 3 specifies the 'mission' and 'tasks' of the Agency and mentions, inter alia, 'to assist the Member States and the Commission in harmonising the application of the common fisheries policy throughout the Community'. This task is further clarified in Art 7 of the Regulation.

[65] ibid, Art 17b.

[66] ibid, Art 17d.

[67] European Commission, 'Proposal for a Regulation establishing a European Banking Authority' COM (2009) 501 final.

for action to deal with these risks'.[68] To fulfil its tasks,[69] the (draft) Regulation would provide the European Banking Authority with a number of powers—including the power to adopt individual decisions in emergency situations.[70] The new agency may even enjoy quasi-regulatory powers—but the *Meroni* boundary would continue to be respected. In the words of the (draft) Regulation:

> As a body with highly specialised expertise, it is efficient and appropriate to entrust the Authority, in areas defined by [Union] law, with the elaboration of draft technical standards, which do not involve policy choices. The Commission should endorse those draft technical standards in accordance with [European] law in order to give them binding legal effect. The draft technical standards have to be adopted by the Commission.[71]

Regulatory tasks would thus continue to remain anchored in the European institutions. A delegation of regulatory powers to a (future) European Banking Agency is thus still regarded as off-limits in the European legal order.

B International bodies and the Opinion 1/76 Doctrine

Despite a common (mis)interpretation,[72] Opinion 1/76 essentially dealt with (internal) constitutional limitations on delegating powers to an (external) international body.[73] The Court had been asked to preview the constitutionality of an international agreement that envisaged the establishment of a Laying-up Fund that was endowed with decision-making powers to implement the objectives of the agreement. The decisions of the Fund were to be generally applicable and binding in all the Member States of the (then) European Union and Switzerland.

[68] ibid, Explanatory Memorandum, 2. The sixth Preamble of the draft regulation further states as follows: 'The Community cannot remain in a situation where there is no mechanism to ensure that national supervisors arrive at the best possible supervisory decisions for cross-border institutions; where there is insufficient cooperation and information exchange between national supervisory authorities; where joint action by national authorities requires complicated arrangements to take account of the patchwork of regulatory and supervisory requirements; where national solutions are most often the only feasible option in responding to European problems, where different interpretations of the same legal text exist. The European System of Supervisors should be designed to overcome these deficiencies and provide a system that is in line with the objective of a stable and single Community financial market for financial services, linking national supervisors into a strong Community network.'

[69] Art 6 of the (draft) Regulation.

[70] ibid, Art 10.

[71] ibid, Preamble 14.

[72] For this point, see R Schütze, 'Parallel External Powers in the European Community: From "cubist" perspectives towards "naturalist" constitutional principles?' (2006) 23 YEL 225, 250 et seq.

[73] Opinion 1/76 (*Inland Waterways*) [1977] ECR 741. The Council had called it the 'essential point' to be settled by the Court (*cf* Opinion 1/76, Council submissions at 750). The following discussion of the ruling focuses on the problems arising from the delegation of decision-making powers to the Laying-up Fund. The agreement also envisaged the creation of a Fund Tribunal and consequently had a judicial dimension too. An extensive discussion of the latter can be found in P Eeckhout, *External Relations of the European Union: Legal and Constitutional Foundations* (Oxford, Oxford University Press, 2005) 206–7.

The Court did not censor the delegation of powers to an external body as such. The Union could 'cooperate with a third country for the purpose of giving the organs of such an institution appropriate powers of decision'.[74] However, the Court found the institutional arrangements set up by the draft agreement problematic: the Fund's Supervisory Board consisted of a delegate from each Member State—with the exception of Ireland—and from Switzerland as well as the Commission. Decisions were to be taken by simple majority; yet, the Commission's role had been reduced to (non-voting) chairman.

Was a delegation of power to *such* an international body possible? A few years earlier, the *ERTA* Court had sounded a warning note: the Council could not decide to leave the supranational channels by its own volition.[75] Each legal base within the Treaty fixed a balance of intergovernmental and supranational elements; and the Member States were obliged to respect this institutional balance for the tasks entrusted to the Union.[76] This was readily admitted by the Council: 'these tasks must be performed by the institutions to which they have been given without their being able in their turn to make [*sic*] them over at will to organs outside the [Union]'.[77] In view of the marginal role played by the Union institutions in the external body it thus concluded:

> [T]he decisions which are taken by the organs of the draft Agreement cannot be considered as the action of the [Union] institutions whatever the influence which they may in fact exert on their adoption. The feature which distinguishes a transfer of powers from a limited delegation is the direct applicability of the decisions adopted by the organs. There is no doubt that the [Union] may, in accordance with the Treaty, enter into international commitments and restrict the exercise of its power. It is however doubtful whether the [Union] may in addition transfer its own powers to external organs.[78]

The Court, after some hesitation,[79] followed this line of argument. Noting that the role of the Union within the international body was 'extremely limited' and

[74] Opinion 1/76, para 5 (emphasis added). The Court denied the legislative quality of the powers transferred, by pointing to their limited scope: 'In fact the provisions of the Statute define and limit the powers which the latter grants to the organs of the Fund so clearly and precisely that in this case they are only executive powers' (ibid, para 16).

[75] Case 22/70, *Commission of the European Communities v Council of the European Communities (European Agreement on Road Transport, ERTA)* [1971] ECR 263, especially para 70: 'Although the Council may, by virtue of these provisions [ie Arts 70 *et seq*], decide in each case whether it is expedient to enter into an agreement with third countries, it does not enjoy a discretion to decide whether to proceed through intergovernmental or Community channels'.

[76] Art 7 EC

[77] Opinion 1/76, Council Submissions, 751.

[78] ibid, 750 (emphasis added).

[79] In order to rescue the terms of the agreement, a draft regulation had been adopted, whose Art 5 was designed to remedy the unconstitutional effects of the Fund's structural arrangements. While acknowledging the effort in the right direction, the Court nevertheless persisted in its negative outlook: 'The Court has examined all aspects of this question and it has duly considered the difficulties which may arise in the search for a practical solution to the problems posed by the organization of a public international institution managed by the Community and a single third

that the 'determinative functions in the operation of the fund are performed by the States',[80] the Court prohibited the arrangement; and this for two reasons. First, the intergovernmental character of the external body meant that several Member States could act 'in place of the [Union] and its institutions in a field which comes within a common policy which Article 3 of the Treaty has expressly reserved to 'the activities of the [Union]'.[81] Second, according to the Court, the agreement discriminated between Member States in a way that was incompatible with the concept of 'common action'.[82] Both constitutional distortions called 'into question the power of the institutions of the [Union] and, moreover, [alterred] in a manner inconsistent with the Treaty the relationships between the Member States'.[83] A delegation of power to the international body must indeed never constitute

> a surrender of the independence of action of the [Union] in its external relations and a change in the internal constitution of the [Union] by the alteration of essential elements of the [Union] structure as regards both the prerogatives of the institutions and the position of the Member States vis-à-vis one another.[84]

In conclusion, Opinion 1/76 set strong constitutional limits to a delegation of legislative powers *outside supranational channels*. However, unlike *Meroni*, the Court's concern was less with the substantive scope of the delegation. Instead, the

country while maintaining the mutual independence of the two partners. Doubtless the specific nature of the interests involved may explain the desire, within the context of organs of management, to have recourse to administrative bodies more directly concerned with the problems of inland navigations. Does this objective justify the creation of a mixed organization in which the presence of national representatives on the supervisory board together with the chairman and the Swiss representative would ensure the defence of the interest of the Community? After considering the arguments for and against, the Court has reached the conclusion that it is no doubt possible to attain an appropriate balance in the composition of the organs of the fund but that this must not result in weakening the institutions of the Community and surrendering the basis of a common policy even for a specific and limited objective. The possibility that the agreement and the Statute, according to the statements of the Commission, might constitute the model for future arrangements in other fields has confirmed the Court in its critical attitude: The repetition of such procedures is in fact likely progressively to undo the work of the Community irreversibly, in view of the fact that each time the undertakings involved will be entered into with third countries. It was for these reasons that an adverse decision finally prevailed within the Court as regards this aspect of the proposal.' (Opinion 1/76, para 14).

[80] Opinion 1/76, para 9.

[81] ibid, para 11.

[82] The Court singled out three distortions that would compromise the 'normal' principles governing the European legal system. Anxious to prevent the Member States from 'sourcing-out' certain task that the Treaty had intended the Community to achieve, the Court declared the following aspects of the international organisation incompatible with the concept of 'common action': (a) the complete exclusion, even voluntary, of a specific Member State (ie Ireland) from the decision-making process within the Fund; (b) the power of certain Member States to take no part in a matter, even if it was falling within a common policy; and (c) the privileged status accorded to certain states at variance with the principles governing the (horizontal) relations between Member States of the Community.

[83] Opinion 1/76, para 10.

[84] ibid, para 5.

ruling concentrated on the political safeguards that the Union wished to have in the decision-making procedure of the international organisation.

IV DELEGATING EUROPEAN POWERS TO THE MEMBER STATES

European constitutionalism accepts the possibility of delegating powers back to the Member States.[85] The doctrine was developed in the context of the Union's exclusive powers,[86] but will—mutatis mutandis—apply in the sphere of legislative exclusivity.[87] Two variants of the delegation doctrine crystallised in the past. The Member States are entitled to act as 'trustees of the Union interest', where European action is needed but not forthcoming. Yet the Union can also delegate powers to the Member States where it could have acted itself.

A The Member States as 'trustees' of the Union

We encounter the—rare—'trustees' phenomenon in *Commission v United Kingdom*.[88] The Court here dealt with the area of marine conservation measures, in which the transfer of powers to the Union was 'total and definitive'. Would the European legislator's failure to act restore to the Member States their power to act unilaterally in this field? The judicial answer was in the negative: 'this is a field reserved to the powers of the [Union], within which the Member States may henceforth act only as trustees of the common interest'.[89] The Member States

[85] For an original doubt, see HP Ipsen, *Europäisches Gemeinschaftsrecht* (Tübingen, JCB Mohr, 1972) 443. But for an express recognition of the possibility of a delegation of powers to the Member States, see now Art 2(1) of the Treaty on the Functioning of the European Union (emphasis added): 'When the Treaties confer on the Union exclusive competence in a specific area, only the Union may legislate and adopt legally binding acts, *the Member States being able to do so themselves only if so empowered* by the Union[.]'

[86] Where the Member States enjoy autonomous national powers, there is no need to 'delegate' European powers back to the Member States.

[87] For an extension of the delegation idea to areas in which the Union intends to totally pre-empt the Member States, see Joined Cases 47/83 and 48/83 *Pluimveeslachterij Midden-Nederland BV* [1984] ECR 1721. Pointing to 'the Council's almost total failure to act', this CMO was not able to function normally (ibid, para 21). The Court, referring to its 'trustee of the common interest' doctrine, added that the exercise of national powers '*must not be regarded as involving the exercise of the Member State's own powers, but as the fulfilment of the duty to cooperate in achieving the aims of the common organization of the market which, in a situation characterized by the inaction of the Community legislature, Article [10] of the (EC) Treaty imposes on them* ... Consequently, the measures adopted by the Member States may only be temporary and provisional in nature and they must cease to be applied as soon as Community measures are introduced' (ibid, paras 22–23, emphasis added). The Court thus projected the idea of the Member States acting as trustees of the common interest—established in its jurisprudence on the conservation of biological resources of the sea—to the agricultural field.

[88] Case 804/79 *Commission v United Kingdom* [1981] ECR 1045.

[89] ibid, para 30.

were thus allowed temporarily to fill a legislative gap left open by a dysfunctional Union legislator.[90] However, they would not act autonomously, but as 'agents' of the Union.

The European Court imposed strict constitutional limits on this arrangement:

> the requirements inherent in the safeguard by the [Union] of the common interest and the integrity of its powers, imposed upon the Member States not only an obligation to undertake detailed consultation with the Commission and to seek its approval in good faith, but also a *duty not to lay down national conservation measures in spite of objections, reservations, conditions which might be formulated by the Commission.*[91]

The national measures are thus subject to ex ante control and may be vetoed by the Union.[92] The trustee doctrine has properly been characterised as an expression of the—implied—power to adopt emergency legislation. This decentralised emergency system has increasingly been codified in European legislation.[93] However, national emergency measures are today no longer viewed as *ersatz* for missing European measures, but are seen to complement a centralised emergency system operated by the Commission.[94]

[90] ibid.

[91] ibid, para 31 (emphasis added).

[92] In the words of the title of the 1981 editorial in the Common Market Law Review: 'Inactivity of the Council: Implied power for the Commission' (ibid 267).

[93] See Art 8 of Regulation 2371/2002 on the conservation and sustainable exploitation of fisheries resources under the Common Fisheries Policy [2002] OJ L358/59, entitled 'Member State Emergency Measures'. The provision states: '1. If there is evidence of a serious and unforeseen threat to the conservation of living aquatic resources, or to the marine ecosystem resulting from fishing activities, in waters falling under the sovereignty or jurisdiction of a Member State where any undue delay would result in damage that would be difficult to repair, that Member State may take emergency measures, the duration of which shall not exceed three months. 2. Member States intending to take emergency measures shall notify their intention to the Commission, the other Member States and the Regional Advisory Councils concerned by sending a draft of those measures, together with an explanatory memorandum, before adopting them. 3. The Member States and Regional Advisory Councils concerned may submit their written comments to the Commission within five working days of the date of notification. The Commission shall confirm, cancel or amend the measure within 15 working days of the date of notification…'

[94] See Art 7 ('Commission Emergency Measures') of Council Regulation 2371/2002 (ibid): '(1) If there is evidence of a serious threat to the conservation of living aquatic resources, or to the marine eco-system resulting from fishing activities and requiring immediate action, the Commission, at the substantiated request of a Member State or on its own initiative, may decide on emergency measures which shall last not more than six months. The Commission may take a new decision to extend the emergency measures for no more than six months … (4) The Member States concerned may refer the Commission decision to the Council within 10 working days of receipt of the notification. (5) The Council, acting by qualified majority, may take a different decision within one month of the date of receipt of the referral.'

B The Delegation Doctrine: from specific authorisation to carte blanche

What are the constitutional conditions imposed on a delegation of powers to the Member States? In *Donckerwolke*,[95] the Court clarified that national measures would only be permissible, in an exclusive competence of the Union, 'by virtue of specific authorisation'.[96] What was meant by the requirement of a 'specific' authorisation? Would the Member States have to obtain permission for each and every legislative act adopted?

In subsequent jurisprudence, the Court rejected a strict interpretation of the delegation doctrine. The epitome of this development is *Bulk Oil*.[97] Within the common commercial policy, the Union legislator had adopted Regulation 2603/69 outlawing quantitative restrictions on exports from the European Union to third countries.[98] According to Article 10 of the Regulation, certain products were not covered by the liberalising measure until such time as the Council had introduced common rules. A Union policy for the export of these products, among them crude oil, would thus only be established by *subsequent* European legislation. In 1981, the United Kingdom had imposed *new* quantitative restrictions on the export of crude oil to certain non-Member countries, in particular Israel. In a tricky commercial dispute between two companies, Bulk Oil had raised the objection that the British measure was void, as the Union had given no specific authorisation for the national law. Article 10 of the Regulation could, accordingly, not be regarded as such an authorisation as the provision only 'legalised' the existing disparities in national commercial policy measures before the end of the transitional period. The United Kingdom contested this and argued that Article 10 represented a 'specific authorisation' in the meaning of the *Donckerwolke* ruling.

In a baffling and curt judgment, the Court accepted the British view. It generously accepted the Council Regulation as satisfying the requirements of a 'specific authorisation'. Article 10 would 'constitute a *specific* authorisation permitting the Member States to impose quantitative restrictions on exports of oil to non-member countries'.[99] The legality of national commercial policy measures, old and new, was thus to be simply reviewed by *reference to the terms of existing European legislation*. The idea of a 'specific authorisation' for each national measure within the scope of an exclusive competence was dismissed.

[95] Case 41/76 *Suzanne Criel, née Donckerwolcke and Henri Schou v Procureur de la République au tribunal de grande instance de Lille and Director General of Customs* [1976] ECR 1921.

[96] ibid, para 32.

[97] Case 174/84 *Bulk Oil (Zug) AG v Sun International Limited and Sun Oil Trading Co* [1986] ECR 559.

[98] Regulation 2603/69 (OJ English special edition: Series V Chapter 1952–72, 71) had been adopted on the basis of Arts 131, 133 and 308 EC. Art 1 of the Regulation provided: 'The exportation of products from the European Economic Community to third countries shall be free, that is to say, they shall not be subject to any quantitative restrictions, with the exception of those restrictions which are applied in conformity with the provisions of this Regulation'.

[99] *Bulk Oil* (n 97 above) paras 32–33 (emphasis added).

Bulk Oil's intelligent argument that an uncontrolled re-delegation of European competences to the national level would violate the exclusive nature of the common commercial policy was rebuked with a simple reference to the discretion the Council enjoyed in this matter.[100]

The reasoning was confirmed in *Fritz Werner Industrie-Ausrüstungen GmbH v Germany*.[101] The case arose over the question whether Article 207 TFEU also covered commercial measures motivated by foreign policy objectives. After an affirmative answer, the Court moved to an analysis of Regulation 2603/69—the same Regulation that had featured in *Bulk Oil*. On this occasion, it was Article 11 of the Regulation, which provided an exception from the general rule of free exportation. According to this provision, 'this Regulation shall not preclude the adoption or application by a Member State of quantitative restrictions on exports on grounds of public morality, public policy or public security; the protection of health and life of humans, animals or plants; the protection of national treasures possessing artistic, historic or archaeological value, or the protection of industrial and commercial property'. Did this legislative recognition of state powers constitute a 'specific authorisation'? The Court response was this:

> [T]he concept of public security within the meaning of Article [36] of the [TFEU] covers both a Member State's internal security and its external security. To interpret the concept more restrictively when it is used in Article 11 of the Export Regulation would be tantamount to authorizing the Member States to restrict the movement of goods within the internal market more than movement between themselves and non-member countries . . . So, the risk of a serious disturbance to foreign relations or to peaceful coexistence of nations may affect the security of a Member State . . .
>
> The answer to the question submitted by the national court must therefore be that Article [207] of the [TFEU], and in particular Article 11 of the Export Regulation, do not preclude national provisions applicable to trade with non-member countries under which the export of a product capable of being used for military purposes is subject to the issue of a licence on the ground that this is necessary in order to avoid the risk of a serious disturbance to its foreign relations which may affect the public security of a Member State within the meaning of Article 11 of the Export Regulation.[102]

This type of reasoning rejected the need for a specific delegation mandate to the Member States. On the contrary, the Court based its analysis on the parallelism between the internal and the external sphere. The justifications found in Article 36 TFEU for restrictions on intra-European trade were simply projected to the external sphere. There was no mention of the need for a 'specific authorisation' to exceptionally allow national measures within the scope of an exclusive Union competence. This represented a de facto recognition of autonomous national

[100] ibid, para 36.

[101] Case C-70/94 *Fritz Werner Industrie-Ausrüstungen GmbH v Federal Republic of Germany* [1995] ECR 3189.

[102] ibid, paras 25, 27 and 29.

power in the commercial policy field. The carte blanche for national commercial policy choices goes well beyond any ordinary constitutional doctrine of delegated powers.

V CONCLUSION: CONSTITUTIONAL LIMITS TO DELEGATING POWERS

When democratic societies face emergencies, they often delegate regulatory powers to the executive. Executive action is quicker and will thus better respond to unforeseen situations rapidly. What are the constitutional limits to a delegation of powers in the European legal order? This chapter has investigated the scope of possible delegations to—respectively—European institutions, other internal or external bodies, and the Member States. The following conclusions could be reached.

The principal delegatee of power within the European legal order is the Commission. The Union legislator can delegate wide discretionary powers to this European institution. However, according to the 'essential elements' principle, basic political choices of the Union are reserved to the legislative branch.[103] Importantly, the European legal order has not adopted a strict hierarchical subordination of delegated legislation. Executive legislation is capable of amending or suspending primary legislation as long as the latter's essential elements remain untouched. The specificity principle constitutes a second constitutional limit. The principle, as codified by the Lisbon Treaty, requires that '[t]he objectives, content, scope and duration of the delegation of power shall be explicitly defined in the legislative act'.[104] In the past, both constitutional principles also limited delegations to the Council. However, since the Single European Act, a third limitation applies here too: a delegation of implementing power to the Council may only occur 'in duly justified cases'.[105] We saw above that the Commission has tried to give this phrase a substantive meaning; yet the European Court of Justice has so far only ruled on the formal obligation to provide reasons for a delegation to the Council.

A stricter non-delegation doctrine applies to bodies that are not European institutions. The *Meroni* doctrine insists that no discretionary powers can be delegated to European Agencies. This view reduces European Agencies to auxiliary organs devoid of the power to make any policy choices. The rigidity of the *Meroni* doctrine lies in its disregard for alternative *political* safeguards that could potentially compensate the substantive prohibition on delegating *political* power. Ironically, this has been the Court's approach as regards a delegation of powers to international bodies. Instead of concentrating on the judicial safeguards, the

[103] This is now codified in Art 290 TFEU (above n 29).

[104] ibid.

[105] Art 291 TFEU.

Court has here insisted that the Union must retain control over the decision-making process within international body. By contrast, the European legal order recognises a generous delegation doctrine in relation to its Member States. While this guarantees quick and localised action in emergency situations, the decentralised solution entails the danger of legal fragmentation.

In conclusion, the European non-delegation doctrine is alive and well. While setting some constitutional limits to delegated powers, it appears flexible enough to allow the European Union quickly to act in local or global emergencies.

Part II

The European Union and Global Emergencies: Thematic Challenges

4

The European Union and Peaceful Settlement of Disputes in its Neighbourhood: the Emergence of a New Regional Security Actor?

STEVEN BLOCKMANS AND RAMSES A WESSEL*

I INTRODUCTION

MOST INFORMED OBSERVERS recognise that the words 'conflict' and 'crisis' are over-used when it comes to the European Union. Similarly, the perceived failure of the EU to punch its weight in both global and regional geopolitics is often criticised. Regrettably, the Union's record in terms of the sustainable resolution of 'frozen', 'simmering' and 'boiling' conflicts, especially those in its neighbourhood, is indeed mixed at best. While the famous and ill-fated declaration of Luxembourg's former Minister of Foreign Affairs, Jacques Poos, that Yugoslavia's violent implosion in 1991 heralded 'the hour of Europe' may have been morally true, it certainly was not politically true. Neither the wars on the territory of the former Yugoslavia, nor more recent conflicts in the EU's neighbourhood, have posed an existential threat to (parts of) the Union. Is it perhaps for this reason that the Member States have almost always failed the test of unity in the EU's efforts to resolve conflicts on its borders?

This chapter examines the contribution of the European Union to the resolution of armed conflicts on its borders. The main frame for this analysis of legal and policy-related aspects of the EU's contribution to conflict resolution will be the European Security Strategy (ESS),[1] with the European Neighbourhood Policy

* Both authors are board members of the Centre for the Law of EU External Relations, www.cleer.eu.

[1] See EU High Representative for the Common Foreign and Security Policy, *European Security Strategy: A Secure Europe in a Better World* (Brussels, 2003), as complemented by the High Representative's *Report on the Implementation of the European Security Strategy—Providing Security in a Changing World*, doc 17104/08 (S407/08), endorsed by the European Council, Presidency Conclusions, doc 17271/08 (CONCL 5), point 30.

(ENP) as a sub-strategy to an integrated approach towards the EU's neighbours to the east and the south of its external borders.[2] The guiding research question will be what kind of role the European Union can and should play to peacefully settle disputes in its neighbourhood and thus to contribute to peace, stability and prosperity, while simultaneously serving its own interest in ensuring that countries on its borders are well-governed.[3] In replicating the language of Article 33(1) of the United Nations Charter (UNC), this contribution is restricted to the analysis of the (potential) use of tools to peacefully settle disputes: 'negotiation, enquiry, mediation, conciliation, arbitration, judicial settlement, resort to regional agencies or arrangements, or other peaceful means.'

In order to answer the research question, this contribution will first sketch the international legal framework for the peaceful settlement of disputes as well as the (new) role and place of the EU in that framework (section II). Then, a quick scan will be made of unresolved and potentially violent disputes in the EU's neighbourhood and an overview will be given of the different sorts of instruments used by the European Union to resolve the 'frozen', 'simmering' and 'boiling' conflicts on its borders. Special attention will be paid to the potential and limits of the ENP as a tool for peaceful dispute settlement. The Union's role in the resolution of the conflict over South Ossetia and Abkhazia will be taken as a separate case study as the outcome of it seems to demand a new approach in the EU's dealings with other de facto states in the area of wider Europe (section III). In this light, some critical observations will be made about the lack of vision emanating from the ENP's spin-offs—the Union for the Mediterranean and the Eastern Partnership (section IV). Some concluding remarks about the need to strengthen the European Union's contribution to peaceful dispute settlement in its neighbourhood and to play its potential role as a new regional security actor will conclude this chapter (section V).

[2] See the Commission, 'European Neighbourhood Policy, Strategy Paper', COM (2004) 373 final. For a list of ENP reference documents, including the Action Plans see http://ec.europa.eu/world/enp/documents_en.htm. In May 2010, the Commission published a rather sobering evaluation of ambitions and activities during the first five years of the ENP. See the Commission, 'Taking stock of the European Neighbourhood Policy' COM (2010) 207.

[3] The term 'neighbourhood' is used here with reference to the countries and territories associated with the ENP. The notion as applied here therefore excludes neighbouring countries whose relations with the EU are governed by other association processes (eg Turkey, Croatia and the Former Yugoslav Republic of Macedonia under the pre-accession process, the rest of the Western Balkans under the Stabilisation and Association Process, Russia, the EEA countries and the micro-states in Western Europe). For a theoretical framework centred on four 'pathways' of impact and its application to five cases of border conflicts in wider Europe (Cyprus, Ireland, Greece/Turkey, Israel/Palestine and various conflicts on Russia's borders with the EU), see the contributions to T Diez, M Albert and S Stetter (eds), *The European Union and Border Conflicts: The Power of Integration and Association* (Cambridge, CUP, 2008). For an analysis of the impact and effectiveness of EU contractual relations on conflict resolution in five ethno-political conflicts in the Union's neighbourhood (Cyprus, the Kurdish question in Turkey, Serbia/Montenegro, Israel/Palestine and Georgia's secessionist conflicts), see N Tocci, *The EU and Conflict Resolution: Promoting Peace in the Backyard* (London/New York, Routledge, 2007).

II THE INTERNATIONAL LEGAL FRAMEWORK FOR EU DISPUTE SETTLEMENT INITIATIVES

A International peaceful settlement of disputes

Ever since the conclusion of the United Nations Charter, the peaceful settlement of disputes has been guided by international rules. In fact, it is fair to say that the settlement of disputes forms the core objective of the post-1945 international legal order.[4] Apart from adjudication procedures, the peaceful settlement of disputes has a number of political or diplomatic means at its disposal, often used in combination, and states have a free choice as to the mechanisms adopted for settling their disputes.[5] In the absence of binding Security Council resolutions, all methods available are operative only with the consent of the particular states. As to the definition of a 'dispute', the textbooks continue to refer to a reference by the Permanent Court of International Justice in the 1924 *Mavrommatis Palestine Concessions (Jurisdiction)* case: 'a disagreement over a point of law or fact, a conflict of legal views or of interests between two persons'.[6] Obviously, this definition is much too broad for our purposes, and we will limit ourselves in this chapter to (potential) armed conflicts.

The above-mentioned instruments of Article 33(1) UNC, returned in the 1970 Declaration on Principles of International Law Concerning Friendly Relations and Co-operation among States:

> states shall accordingly seek early and just settlement of their international disputes by negotiation, inquiry, mediation, conciliation, arbitration, judicial settlement, resort to regional agencies or arrangements or other peaceful means of their choice.[7]

While the obligation to seek settlement of their disputes is thus directed to *states*, 'resort to regional agencies or arrangements' is one of the means available to them. Indeed, this is where regional international organisations may come in and some of those organisations explicitly foresee this role in their constitutive treaties.[8] Thus, Article XIX of the 1963 Charter of the (former) Organization of African Unity already referred to the principle of 'the peaceful settlement of disputes by negotiation, mediation, conciliation or arbitration' and the (current)

[4] *cf* also Art 2(3) UNC: 'All members shall settle their international disputes by peaceful means in such a manner that international peace and security and justice are not endangered.'

[5] See more extensively MN Shaw, *International Law* (Cambridge, Cambridge University Press, 2008) 1010—24. See more in general JG Merrills, *International Dispute Settlement* (Cambridge, Cambridge University Press, 2005) as well as his 'The Mosaic of International Dispute Settlement Procedures: Complementary or Contradictory?' (2007) *Netherlands International Law Review* 361.

[6] PCIJ (1924) Series A no 2, 11.

[7] UNGA Res 2625 (XXV) of 24 October 1970, UN Doc A/8082, GA 25th session 121.

[8] See on the concept of regional arrangements, A Abass, *Regional Organizations and the Development of Collective Security: Beyond Chapter VIII of the UN Charter* (Oxford, Hart Publishing, 2004). *Cf* also ThJW Sneek, 'The OSCE in the New Europe: From Process to Regional Arrangement' (1994) 1 *Indiana International & Comparative Law Review* 1.

African Union created a Peace and Security Council as a 'standing decision-making organ for the prevention, management and resolution of conflicts'.[9] Also the African regional organisations, the Economic Community of West African States (ECOWAS) and the Southern African Development Community (SADC) have been concerned with the peaceful resolution of conflicts in their region on the basis of established extensive mechanisms. Similar dispute settlement mechanisms may be found in regional organisations in other parts of the world. Article 23 of the Charter of the Organization of American States (OAS) provides that international disputes between Member States must be submitted to the Organization for peaceful settlement, and the OAS Permanent Council has played an important role in that area.[10] Similarly the Arab League facilitates—although to a much lesser extent—the settlement of disputes between its members. Indeed, these organisations proclaim themselves as a 'regional arrangement or agency'.[11] In Europe, the European Convention for the Peaceful Settlement of Disputes (Council of Europe, 1957), lays down the agreement that legal disputes are to be sent to the International Court of Justice and that other disputes are to be solved through conciliation and/or arbitration. In addition, mechanisms have been set up within NATO and the Organization on Security and Cooperation in Europe (OSCE). The latter organisation in particular established a number of conventions and mechanisms related to early warning, conflict prevention and crisis management—allowing for instance for the sending of observer and mediation missions to participating states.

The question is to what extent the European Union is in any way comparable to these other regional organisations. In fact, the question seems relevant to what extent the European Union may be seen as a 'regional agency or arrangement', in the sense of Chapter VIII of the UN Charter, which can or may be used by states to settle their disputes. In that respect it is striking that the above-mentioned regional organisations and mechanisms are directed at preventing or solving conflicts between their own members. The purpose of the present contribution, however, is to see what role the EU can and does play in the settlement of disputes between third, albeit neighbouring, countries.

[9] See the Protocol Relating to the Establishment of the Peace and Security Council of the African Union, adopted on 9 July 2002.

[10] See Merrills, *International Dispute Settlement* (n 5 above) 282.

[11] See also C Dominicé, 'Co-ordination between Universal and Regional Organizations', in NM Blokker and HG Schermers (eds), *Proliferation of International Organizations: Legal Issues* (The Hague, Kluwer Law International, 2001) 65–84. *Cf* also G Nolte, 'Die "neuen Aufgaben" von NATO und WEU: Völker- und verfassungsrechtliche Fragen' (1994) *ZaöRv* 95, 107. Nolte pointed to the fact that in the OAS a multinational force to deal with an internal conflict was only based on the *general purposes* of the treaty. There existed a new situation that could not have been foreseen at the time of the conclusion of the treaty. Similarly, the Arab League based troops in Lebanon from 1977–83, the Organization of African Unity in Chad from 1981–82, and the Economic Community of Western African States did the same in Liberia (from 1990).

B A stronger EU–UN relationship?

The relationship between the EU and the UN has been debated extensively over recent years.[12] Following the *Yusuf* and *Kadi* judgments by the Court of First Instance[13] (2005) and the Court of Justice[14] (2008), the legal relationship between UN law and EU law received renewed attention in the academic debate. One of the main issues in these cases was the hierarchy between UN and EU law, and in its ground-breaking judgment of 2008 the ECJ held that 'the obligations imposed by an international agreement cannot have the effect of prejudicing the constitutional principles of the EC Treaty, which include the principle that all Community acts must respect fundamental rights'.[15] This implies that even UN Security Council Resolutions, when implemented by the EU, should not violate the fundamental rights that form a constitutional element of the EU legal order.

Nevertheless, the attention accorded to the United Nations and its principles in the new EU treaties is overwhelming. In fact the United Nations is referred to not less than 19 times in the current EU treaties (including the Protocols and Declarations). Irrespective of the ECJ's judgment in the 2008 *Kadi* case, the EU obviously regards many of its actions as being part of the global governance programme. The United Nations and its Charter are presented as the guiding legal framework for the EU in its external relations. Article 3(5) TEU mentions 'respect for the principles of the United Nations Charter' which are to be pursued by the EU as part of 'the strict observance and the development of international law'. Similar wordings reappear in Article 21 TEU of the general provisions on the Union's external action. In fact, the promotion of 'multilateral solutions to common problems' should be done 'in particular in the framework of the United Nations'. Finally, as reflected in the Preamble to the Treaty on the Functioning of the European Union (TFEU), UN law not only guides the external relations of the Union, but also its association with its overseas countries and territories (compare Articles 198–204 TFEU). The Member States announced that they intended to 'confirm the solidarity which binds Europe and the overseas countries and desiring to ensure the development of their prosperity, in accordance with the principles of the Charter of the United Nations.'

[12] See for example J Wouters, F Hoffmeister and T Ruys (eds), *The United Nations and the European Union: an Ever Stronger Partnership* (The Hague, TMC Asser Press, 2006).

[13] CFI, Cases T-304/01, *Yusuf and Al Barakaat International Foundation v Council and Commission* and T-315/01, *Kadi v Council and Commission*, 21 September 2005. See on these cases: RA Wessel, 'Editorial: The UN, the EU and Jus Cogens' (2006) *International Organizations Law Review* 1–6.

[14] ECJ, Cases C-402/05 P and C-415/05 P, *Yassin Abdullah Kadi* and *Al Barakaat International Foundation v Council* and *Commission*, 3 September 2008. See also the special forum on this judgment in (2008) 2 IOLR and the introduction to this forum: RA Wessel, 'The *Kadi* Case: Towards a More Substantive Hierarchy in International Law', 323–27. More extensively on these issues: C Eckes, *EU Counter-Terrorist Policies and Fundamental Rights: The Case of Individual Sanctions* (Oxford, Oxford University Press, 2010).

[15] Cases C-402/05 P and C-415/05 P (n 14 above) para 285.

In the implementation of the EU Common Foreign and Security Policy (CFSP), a specific provision (Article 34(2) TEU) aims to ensure that CFSP outcomes are also taken into account by EU members in the UN Security Council: 'Member States which are also members of the United Nations Security Council will concert and keep the other Member States and the High Representative fully informed. Member States which are members of the Security Council will, in the execution of their functions, defend the positions and the interests of the Union, without prejudice to their responsibilities under the provisions of the United Nations Charter.' The new Treaty even foresees the possibility of the Union's position being presented not by one of the EU Member States, but by the High Representative of the Union for Foreign Affairs and Security Policy. In that event the Member States which sit on the Security Council shall forward a request to that end to the Security Council. Given the traditionally sensitive nature of the special position of (in particular the permanent) members of the Security Council, this provision can certainly be seen as a further step in facilitating the Union to speak with one voice. Obviously, the ultimate decision to accept a presentation by the High Representative lies in the hands of the Security Council.

In order to prevent these new diplomatic competences of the Union affecting the Member States' own powers, the latter adopted a special Declaration (No 14) during the Lisbon Intergovernmental Conference:

> the Conference underlines that the provisions covering the Common Foreign and Security Policy including in relation to the High Representative of the Union for Foreign Affairs and Security Policy and the External Action Service will not affect the existing legal basis, responsibilities, and powers of each Member State in relation to the formulation and conduct of its foreign policy, its national diplomatic service, relations with third countries and participation in international organisations, including a Member State's membership of the Security Council of the United Nations.

Irrespective of the interpretative character of this type of Declarations they can never be used to evade the actual treaty provisions. The further development will therefore depend on the use by the Member States of the new treaty provisions allowing for a stronger diplomatic representation by the High Representative.

With the coming of age of the EU's Common Security and Defence Policy (CSDP), relations between the EU and the UN have also gained importance in that area. Article 42(1) TEU provides that the Union may use its civilian and military assets missions outside the Union for peace-keeping, conflict prevention and strengthening international security, and again this should be done 'in accordance with the principles of the United Nations Charter.'[16] In fact, the Treaties foresee the possibility of EU missions operating in a UN framework. The preamble of Protocol 10 to the Treaties refers to the fact that 'the United Nations

[16] Similar wordings return in the Protocol (No 10) on Permanent Structured Cooperation established by Art 42 of the Treaty on European Union.

Organisation may request the Union's assistance for the urgent implementation of missions undertaken under Chapters VI and VII of the United Nations Charter.' And Article 1 of the Protocol sees a 'permanent structured cooperation' between able and willing EU Member States in the area of CSDP being necessary 'in particular in response to requests from the United Nations Organisation'. Similarly, UN law forms the legal framework for actions in relation to the new collective defence obligation in Article 42(7) TEU: 'If a Member State is the victim of armed aggression on its territory, the other Member States shall have towards it an obligation of aid and assistance by all the means in their power, in accordance with Article 51 of the United Nations Charter [the provision on (collective) self-defence—SB/RAW].'

Finally, development cooperation (a shared competence between the Union and its Member States) will have to be based on decisions taken by and in other international organisations, including the UN. Article 208(2) TFEU provides that 'The Union and the Member States shall comply with the commitments and take account of the objectives they have approved in the context of the United Nations and other competent international organisations.' The same holds true for humanitarian aid operations, which are to be 'coordinated and consistent with those of international organisations and bodies, in particular those forming part of the United Nations system' (Article 214(7) TFEU).

The extensive references to the UN system as the relevant international legal framework for the EU's external action seem to have reached an all-time high in a special Declaration (No 13) on CFSP, in which the binding nature of UN law *also for the EU as such* is underlined: the Intergovernmental Conference 'stresses that the European Union and its Member States will remain bound by the provisions of the Charter of the United Nations and, in particular, by the primary responsibility of the Security Council and of its Members for the maintenance of international peace and security.' It has been argued that the precise language of this text and the public nature in the context of the Lisbon Treaty may even amount to a unilateral act, which would make it difficult for the EU to argue that it would not be bound by the provisions of the UN Charter in its external operations.[17]

C The EU as a regional agency in the sense of the UN Charter

These (partly) new provisions raise the question of the formal status of the European Union in the global legal framework governing the peaceful settlement of disputes. In that respect the question has been raised to what extent the EU can be seen (and hence *used*) as a regional arrangement or agency in the sense of the

[17] See F Naert, *International Law Aspects of the EU's Security and Defence Policy—with a particular Focus on the Law of Armed Conflict and Human Rights* (Antwerp, Intersentia, 2010) 426.

UN Charter and the Declaration on Friendly Relations.[18] According to Akehurst, 'the difference between an agency and an arrangement would appear to be that an *agency* possesses an institutional superstructure . . . whereas an *arrangement* does not . . . In other words, an agency is simply a more highly developed form of an arrangement'.[19] With regard to the EU, the existence of an 'institutional superstructure' is beyond any doubt. The question, however is, to which extent the institutional structure may also be used to fulfil a role as 'regional agency' is less easy to answer.[20]

In any case, regarding the EU as a regional agency would explain the way in which the Union intends to attain its objective to 'preserve peace, *prevent conflicts* and strengthen international security, in accordance with the purposes and principles of the United Nations Charter' (Article 21(2) TEU).[21] The Union's ambitions in this area are formulated in the so-called 'Petersberg tasks', which are phrased as follows in Article 43 of the post-Lisbon EU Treaty:

> The tasks ... in the course of which the Union may use civilian and military means, shall include joint disarmament operations, humanitarian and rescue tasks, military advice and assistance tasks, conflict prevention and peace-keeping tasks, tasks of combat forces in crisis management, including peace-making and post-conflict stabilisation. All these tasks may contribute to the fight against terrorism, including by supporting third countries in combating terrorism in their territories.

However, the TEU at this moment does not provide any additional clues for the Union to function as a regional agency. Neither did the Treaty expressly claim to fall within the ambit of Chapter VIII UNC. On the other hand, the concept of 'regional arrangements and agencies' is not defined by the Charter, and according to the (former) UN Secretary-General this was intentional:

> The Charter deliberately provides no precise definition of regional arrangements and agencies, thus allowing useful flexibility for undertakings by a group of States to deal with a matter appropriate for regional action which also could contribute to the maintenance of international peace and security. Such associations or entities could include treaty-based organizations, whether created before or after the founding of the United Nations, regional organizations for mutual security and defence, organizations for general regional development or for cooperation on a particular economic topic or function, and groups created to deal with a specific political, economic or social issue of concern.[22]

[18] *cf* L Vierucci, 'WEU: A Regional Partner of the United Nations?' (1993) 12 *WEUISS Chaillot Paper*, who argued that the WEU (at the time the 'military arm' of the EU) could be seen as a regional arrangement.

[19] M Akehurst, 'Enforcement Actions by Regional Organizations with Special Reference to the Organization of American States' (1967) 42 *British Yearbook of International Law* 177. Emphasis added.

[20] See below, section IID.

[21] Emphasis added. The prevention of conflicts was added to the objectives by the Lisbon Treaty.

[22] Report of the Secretary-General, *Agenda for Peace*, UN Doc A/47/277—S/24111.

The Secretary-General at the time even explicitly hinted at the possible 'emergence' of new regional arrangements in Europe:

> [F]or dealing with new kinds of security challenges, regional arrangements or agencies can render assistance of great value. . . . This presupposes the existence of the relationship between the United Nations and regional arrangements envisaged in Chapter VIII of the Charter. The diffusion of tensions between States and the pacific settlement of local disputes are, in many cases, matters appropriate for regional action. The proviso, however, is that efforts of regional agencies should be in harmony with those of the United Nations and in accordance with the Charter. This applies equally to regional arrangements in all areas of the globe, including those which might emerge in Europe.[23]

In its *Agenda for Peace*, the UN thus stressed the need for flexibility in the post-Cold War era, and the purpose of establishing closer links with regional organisations was not to set forth 'any formal pattern of relationship between regional organisations and the United Nations, or to call for any specific division of labour'.[24]

The above-mentioned references to the UN, including the implicit competence in Protocol 10 to the EU Treaties to act in response to a request of the UN to participate in the peaceful settlement of disputes ('the United Nations Organisation may request the Union's assistance for the urgent implementation of missions undertaken under Chapters VI'), indeed point to new characteristics of this organisation.[25] In fact, as we will see, the EU has already been active in assisting the United Nations in a number of operations. Based on this, as well as on the above-mentioned objectives in the EU Treaties, it would be difficult for the EU to deny that it is subject to Chapter VIII UNC, even in the absence of internal conflict management mechanisms.[26] The implications of the acceptance of a new role for the EU as a 'Chapter VIII organisation' are not to be disposed of too easily. According to Article 52 of the UN Charter, the activities of regional arrangements or agencies are to be consistent with the purposes and principles of the United Nations. Moreover, regional arrangements and agencies have a *primary* function in the pacific settlement of local disputes;[27] they shall make every effort in that respect before referring the dispute to the Security Council, but they 'have autonomy in diplomacy, in peaceful settlement, and implicitly in the case of

[23] Report of the Secretary-General on the Work of the Organisation, *Secretary Gen Rep 21*, 1990, 21.

[24] *Agenda for Peace* (n 22 above) 10.

[25] A similar competence to act 'in response to requests from the United Nations Organisation' may be found in relation to the permanent structured cooperation ex Art 42(6) TEU.

[26] See also ND White, 'The EU as Regional Security Actor within the International Legal Order', in M Trybus and ND White (eds), *European Security Law* (Oxford, Oxford University Press, 2007) 329–49.

[27] Local disputes are commonly understood as disputes exclusively involving states which are parties to the regional arrangement or agency. Compare in that respect also Arts 34 and 35 UNC.

consensual peacekeeping, subject to a reporting requirement.'[28] Currently, nothing in the EU Treaties seems sufficient to enable the EU to fulfil this task internally. The Union's policies in this area are primarily (if not exclusively) related to threats to or breaches of the peace within or by states that are *not* members of the EU. This clearly distinguishes the EU from other regional arrangements and agencies, which see as their primary task the settling of disputes among their Member States.[29]

Apart from possibilities for the peaceful resolution of conflicts, the Petersberg tasks foresee the possibility of the EU engaging in peace-*making* operations.[30] As is well-known, the Charter of the United Nations is quite clear on the prohibition on using force (Article 2(4)). Exceptions can be found in the provisions on (collective) self-defence (Article 51) and in actions by the Security Council on the basis of Article 42. In addition, Chapter VIII (Article 53) of the UN Charter allows the Security Council to 'utilize . . . regional arrangements or agencies for enforcement action *under its authority*'.[31] Even for regional arrangements and agencies an authorisation of the Security Council to take enforcement action is necessary.[32]

D New competences and institutional arrangements

The question then is to what extent the new ambitions of the EU are met by actual competences and institutional arrangements.[33] On 18 December 2007 the representatives of the 27 Member States of the European Union signed the Treaty of Lisbon amending the Treaty on European Union and the Treaty establishing

[28] White, 'The EU as Regional Security Actor within the International Legal Order' (n 26 above). Art 54 UNC provides that the Security Council shall at all times be kept fully informed of activities which are undertaken or are being contemplated under regional arrangements by regional agencies for the maintenance of international peace and security. This would include all activities by the EU related to the peaceful settlement of disputes.

[29] ibid.

[30] Peace-*building* activities fall beyond the scope of the present contribution. See on that issue: S Blockmans, J Wouters and T Ruys (eds), *The European Union and Peacebuilding: Policy and Legal Aspects* (The Hague, TMC Asser Press, 2010).

[31] Emphasis added. See also White, 'The EU as Regional Security Actor within the International Legal Order' (n 26 above) 333. Art 53 mentions one exception: measures against renewal of aggressive policy on the part of an enemy state (that is, any state which during the Second World War was an enemy of any signatory of the present Charter). The definition of 'enemy state' highlights the outmoded nature of this provision.

[32] It is interesting to note that Abass, *Regional Organizations and the Development of Collective Security* (n 8 above) xxi nevertheless points to 'a gradual but powerful drive towards a decentralized collective security [as] a process whereby regional organizations assume the legal competence to authorize enforcement actions under their constituent instruments, and beyond the formalistic framework of Chapter VIII'.

[33] See more extensively S Blockmans and RA Wessel, 'The European Union and Crisis Management: Will the Lisbon Treaty Make the EU More Effective?' (2009) 14 *Journal of Conflict and Security Law* 265–308; also published as CLEER Working Paper 2009/1.

the European Community.[34] With its entry into force on 1 December 2009, we have new, consolidated versions of both the EU Treaty (TEU) and the EC Treaty (renamed the Treaty on the Functioning of the European Union—TFEU). Strengthening the Union's role in the world was one of the reasons for the conclusion of the Lisbon Treaty.[35] In addition, Article 8 of the TEU explicitly refers to the Union's relations with the countries in its neighbourhood: 'The Union shall develop a special relationship with neighbouring countries, aiming to establish an area of prosperity and good neighbourliness, founded on the values of the Union and characterised by close and peaceful relations based on cooperation.'

Keeping in mind that a regional agency should have a primary function in the pacific settlement of local disputes, any effective role of the EU as a crisis manager and dispute settler in its neighbourhood calls for speedy and effective decision-making. In that respect the Lisbon Treaty introduced only minor changes. The Council—in its configuration as 'Foreign Affairs Council'[36]—is the key decision-making organ, but, unlike the other Council configurations, is chaired not by Member State representatives, but by the High Representative (HR; currently Baroness Ashton) (Article 18(3) TEU). Also in the new Union unanimity continues to form the basis for CFSP decisions, 'except where the Treaties provide otherwise' (Article 24(1) TEU). In that respect it is interesting to point to the fact that apart from the previously existing possibilities for Qualified Majority Voting (QMV) under CFSP,[37] it is now possible for the Council to adopt measures on this basis following a proposal submitted by the HR (Article 31(2) TEU). Such proposals should, however, follow a specific request by the European Council, in which, of course, Member States can foreclose the use of QMV. In addition QMV may be used for setting up, financing and administering a start-up fund to ensure rapid access to appropriations in the Union budget for urgent financing of CFSP initiatives (Article 41(3) TEU). This start-up fund may be used for crisis management initiatives as well, which would potentially speed

[34] Throughout this contribution, references to provisions of the Lisbon Treaty have been based on the corrected consolidated versions of the TEU and the TFEU, as published in [2010] OJ C83/01.

[35] See more extensively Blockmans and Wessel, 'The European Union and Crisis Management' (n 33 above).

[36] According to Art 16(6) TEU, 'The General Affairs Council shall ensure consistency in the work of the different Council configurations. It shall prepare and ensure the follow-up to meetings of the European Council, in liaison with the President of the European Council and the Commission. The Foreign Affairs Council shall elaborate the Union's external action on the basis of strategic guidelines laid down by the European Council and ensure that the Union's action is consistent.'

[37] These exceptions recur in Art 31(2) TEU and apply as follows: —when adopting a decision defining a Union action or position on the basis of a decision of the European Council relating to the Union's strategic interests and objectives, as referred to in Art 22(1); —when adopting any decision implementing a decision defining a Union action or position; —when appointing a special representative in accordance with Art 33.

up the financing process of operations.[38] Overall, however, it is clear that any action on the part of the EU will continue to depend on the consent of its Member States.

On the other hand, the key role of the Member States is put into perspective on a number of occasions. Before Lisbon, most proposals in the area of CFSP came from Member States, with the Presidency having a particularly active role. Article 30(1) TEU lays down the new general rule that 'Any Member State, the High Representative of the Union for Foreign Affairs and Security Policy, or the High Representative with the Commission's support, may refer any question relating to the common foreign and security policy to the Council and may submit to it initiatives or proposals as appropriate.' It is in particular this new role of the Commission that may trigger new possibilities for the EU in its external affairs, including the peaceful settlement of disputes in its neighbourhood. Whereas the Commission so far has largely refrained from making use of its competence to submit proposals on issues in the area of foreign, security or defence policy (Article 22 TEU), the creation of the competence to submit joint proposals with the HR may enhance its commitment to this area.

This is strengthened by the fact that the person holding the position of HR at the same time acts as a member (and even a vice-president) of the Commission (Article 17, paras 4 and 5). This combination of the functions of HR and Vice-President of the Commission is, without doubt, one of the key innovations of the Lisbon Treaty.[39] The potential impact of this combination on the role of the EU in international affairs lies in the fact that there could be a more natural attuning of different external policies, in particular where borders between policies are fuzzy, such as in crisis management. At the same time, the continued separation between CFSP and other Union issues may very well lead to a need for different legal bases for decisions, and hence for the use of distinct CFSP and other Union instruments. This holds true not only for the outcome of the decision-making process, but also for the process itself, in which sincere co-operation between the Council and the Commission, supported by the HR/VP

[38] See also DG for External Policies of the Union, Policy Department, 'The Lisbon Treaty and its Implications for CFSP/ESDP', Briefing Paper, European Parliament, February 2008, 3. Nevertheless, for some Member States, resort to the EU budget may remain attractive, even if this means delaying the EU's response. See R Whitman and A Juncos, 'The Lisbon Treaty and the Foreign, Security and Defence Policy: Reforms, Implementation and the Consequences of (non-)Ratification' (2009) 14 *European Foreign Affairs Review* 25, 39.

[39] More extensively: C Kaddous, 'Role and Position of the High Representative of the Union for Foreign Affairs and Security Policy under the Lisbon Treaty', in S Griller and J Ziller (eds), *The Lisbon Treaty: Constitutionalism without a Constitutional Treaty?* (Vienna, Springer, 2008) 206. *Cf* also Whitman and Juncos, 'The Lisbon Treaty and the Foreign, Security and Defence Policy' (n 38 above) 32; and J Paul, 'EU Foreign Policy after Lisbon: Will the New High Representative and the External Action Service Make a Difference?' (2008) 2 *Centre for Applied Policy Research (CAP) Policy Analysis.*

and the new and hybrid EU External Action Service,[40] will remain of crucial importance.

Indeed, successful crisis management by the EU depends on successful leadership. Most of the relevant institutional changes in the Lisbon Treaty relate to the position of the High Representative of the Union for Foreign Affairs and Security Policy. The name change reflects the fact that it has become clear that the HR indeed represents the Union and not the (collective) Member States. The HR's competences are clearly laid down in the EU Treaty and form part of the institutional framework. Although the term 'Foreign Minister', which was used in the Constitutional Treaty, has been abandoned, the new provisions make clear that the HR will indeed be the prime representative of the Union in international affairs. Even the President of the European Council (note: not the European *Union*) exercises that position's external competences 'without prejudice to the powers of the High Representative of the Union for Foreign Affairs and Security Policy' (Article 15, para 6(d)). The HR is appointed by the European Council (with the agreement of the President of the Commission) by QMV. This again underlines the HR's role as a person who can act on behalf of the Union and who is perhaps competent to act even in the absence of a full consensus among the Member States. The HR is to 'conduct' the Union's foreign, security and defence policy, contributing proposals to the development of that policy, and presiding over the Foreign Affairs Council (Article 18 TEU). In addition, the HR's de facto membership of the European Council is codified in Article 15 TEU (although strictly speaking it is stated that the HR only 'takes part in the work' of the European Council). The HR is to assist the Council and the Commission in ensuring consistency between the different areas of the Union's external action (Article 21 TEU), and together with the Council, ensures compliance by the Member States with their CFSP obligations (Article 24(3) TEU). All in all, the position of HR has been upgraded to allow for stronger and more independent development and implementation of the Union's foreign, security and defence policy, which—potentially—allows for a more coherent and more effective role for the EU in peaceful dispute settlement in the Union's neighbourhood.

[40] See Council Decision of 26 July 2010 establishing the organisation and functioning of the European External Action Service, *OJ* 2010 L 201/30. For background and analyses, see, for instance, B Crowe, *The Chatham House Report, The European External Action Service: Roadmap for Success* (London, Chatham House, 2008); S Vanhoonacker and N Reslow, 'The European External Action Service: Living Forwards by Understanding Backwards' (2010) EFA Rev 1–18; S Duke, 'Providing for European-level Diplomacy after Lisbon: The Case of the European External Action Service' (2009) *The Hague Journal of Diplomacy* 211–33; S Duke and S Blockmans, 'The Lisbon Treaty stipulations on Development Cooperation and the Council Decision of 25 March 2010 (Draft) establishing the organisation and functioning of the European External Action Service', *CLEER Legal Brief*, 4 May 2010 (available at www.cleer.eu); and C Hillion and M Lefebvre, 'Le service européen pour l'action extérieure: vers un diplomatie commune?', *Fondation Robert Schuman Policy Paper* no 169, 17 May 2010.

III THE EU AND PEACEFUL SETTLEMENT OF DISPUTES IN ITS NEIGHBOURHOOD

A Disputes in the European Union's neighbourhood

The above analysis not only has theoretical value. The Union's neighbourhood is littered with potential and actual flash points for conflict. What follows is a quick overview.

— *Abkhazia* and *South Ossetia*: both breakaway republics are located within the internationally recognised borders of Georgia, as defined in, inter alia, UN Security Council Resolution 1808 of 15 April 2008, supported also by Russia until President Medvedev's decision on 26 August 2008 to endorse the unanimous votes of Russia's Federation Council and State Duma to recognise the independence of the two entities in the wake of the August 2008 war between Georgia and Russia.[41]

— *Nagorno-Karabakh*: the unrecognised but de facto independent and predominantly Armenian republic which, under international law, is officially part of Azerbaijan.[42] The statelet fought a bloody 'war of independence' in the early 1990s. Russia, the US and France, which serve as co-chairs of the so-called 'Minsk Group' under the auspices of the OSCE,[43] are relatively united and have advanced proposals to resolve the conflict between Azerbaijan and Armenia. But both parties to the conflict seem to believe that time is on their side with a status quo. Sporadic fighting should be understood in this context.[44]

— *Transnistria*: the unrecognised but since 1990 de facto independent republic which lies within the internationally recognised borders of Moldova, wedged between the river Nistru and the border with Ukraine.[45] A 1200-strong Russian military contingent has been present in Transnistria since the 1992 ceasefire agreement between Moldova and Transnistria. The status of this contingent is disputed. Russia insists that its troops are serving as peacekeepers authorised under the 1992 ceasefire and will remain until the conflict is fully resolved.[46]

[41] Statement by President of Russia Dmitry Medvedev, 26 August 2008, available at www.kremlin.ru/eng/speeches/2008/08/26/1543_type82912_205752.shtml. See sub-section E, below.

[42] See T Potier, *Conflict in Nagorno-Karabakh, Abkhazia and South Ossetia: A Legal Appraisal* (The Hague, Kluwer Law International, 2001).

[43] EU Member States Germany, Italy, Portugal, the Netherlands, Sweden and Finland are also participating in the process.

[44] See 'Karabakh casualty toll disputed', BBC, 3 March 2008.

[45] In the wake of the August 2008 war in Georgia, Abkhazia and South Ossetia have 'recognised' Transnistria as an independent state, and plan to establish diplomatic relations in return for reciprocal recognition.

[46] 'NATO must recognize Russia's compliance with Istanbul accords', *Interfax*, 14 June 2007.

— *Palestinian territories*: the proposed establishment of an independent state for the Palestinian people in the Gaza Strip, which is currently controlled by Hamas, and parts of the West Bank, which is administered by the Palestinian National Authority, is caught in a protracted negotiation process under US leadership of the Quartet on the Middle East (including Russia, the EU and the UN). The precise borders of this state are subject to debate with Israel. The right of the Palestinian people to a state is recognised by approximately 100 countries.[47] Armed conflict is a daily reality in the region.
— *Western Sahara*: this sparsely populated territory has been on the UN list of Non-Self-Governing Territories since the 1960s, when it was still a Spanish colony.[48] The Western Sahara was partitioned between Morocco and Mauritania in April 1976, with Morocco acquiring the northern two-thirds of the territory. When Mauritania, under pressure from the Polisario Front's independence fighters, which proclaimed the Sahrawi Arab Democratic Republic (SADR) earlier that year, abandoned all claims to its portion in August 1979, Morocco moved in an attempt to occupy that sector. Backed by Algeria, the SADR is a de facto state which currently controls about 20 per cent of the entire territory of Western Sahara which it claims.[49] The republic is currently recognised by 43 states, mostly African, Asian and Latin American countries. It is not a member of the Arab League but has been a full member of the African Union (AU, formerly the Organization of African Unity) since 1984.[50] Morocco is the only African country which is not a member of the AU. Moroccan 'territorial integrity', including Western Sahara, is explicitly recognised by the Arab League and by 25 states.[51] In both instances, recognitions have over the past two decades been extended and withdrawn according to changing international trends. In April 2007, the UN—which has had a peacekeeping force on the ground since 1991—asked the parties to enter into direct and unconditional negotiations to reach a mutually accepted political solution to the conflict.[52] So far, these efforts remain without result.

The EU has not been able to play its role as a regional security actor and sustainably resolve any of these 'frozen', 'simmering' and 'boiling' conflicts on its

[47] Institute for Middle East Understanding (2008), 'How many countries recognize Palestine as a state?', available at http://imeu.net/news/article0065.shtml.

[48] The list is available at www.un.org/Depts/dpi/decolonization/trust3.htm. See further T Whitfield, *Friends Indeed? The United Nations, Groups of Friends, and the Resolution of Conflict* (Washington DC, United States Institute of Peace Press, 2007) 191.

[49] See P Baehr and L Gordenker, *The United Nations at the End of the 1990s* (New York, St Martin's Press, 1999) 129.

[50] See www.africa-union.org/root/AU/memberstates/map.htm.

[51] See 'Arab League supports Morocco's territorial integrity', *Arabic News*, 8 January 1999.

[52] Report of the Secretary-General on the situation concerning Western Sahara, UN Doc S/2007/202, 13 April 2007.

borders. This is not a problem of lack of effort though. EU Special Representatives have been sent to Moldova, the South Caucasus, Georgia and the Middle East by the Union's High Representative and all have been mandated to work towards the peaceful settlement of the respective disputes.[53] ESDP/CSDP missions of various kinds have been deployed: for instance, a police operation to the Palestinian territories (EUPOL COPPS), EU border assistance missions (EUBAM) to Ukraine/Moldova (over Transnistria)[54] and to Rafah (Palestinian territories), a judicial reform mission to Georgia (EUJUST THEMIS)[55] and an EU Monitoring Mission to Georgia (EUMM).[56] Restrictive measures have been adopted to force, eg, the leadership of Transnistria to the negotiating table.[57] Financial and technical assistance has been given to projects in the breakaway regions in Georgia to prevent these societies from falling further behind, economically.[58]

Yet, for all the would-be incentives and restrictive measures listed above, none of these instruments appears as a particularly strong leverage for securing sustainable dispute settlement on the EU's outer periphery. The same observation applies to the European Neighbourhood Policy, which serves as the European Security Strategy's regional sub-set for the neighbouring countries to the east and the south of the Union's borders.

[53] The mandates of these missions are included in the Joint Actions underpinning them. The Joint Actions are available at www.consilium.europa.eu/cms3_fo/showPage.asp?id=268&lang=EN&mode=g.

[54] See sub-section C, below.

[55] And the 'invisible' civilian ESDP operation in Georgia, ie the reinforced EUSR Support Team, comprising a Rule of Law follow-up to EUJUST THEMIS and a Border Support Team, facilitated entirely through European Commission programmes.

[56] For a complete and up-to-date list, see the website of the Council of the EU.

[57] Council Common Position 2008/160 of 25 February 2008 restricting the admission of persons responsible for preventing progress in arriving at political settlement of the Transnistrian conflict [2008] OJ L51/23.

[58] ECHO has been present in Georgia since 1993 to meet the needs of the most vulnerable communities. With the allocation of €2 million for people most affected by the unresolved conflict between Abkhazia and Georgia (internally displaced people, returnees and other vulnerable groups in Abkhazia), the total of the Commission's humanitarian aid funding totalled €104 million for Georgia at the end of 2007. Under the Partnership and Cooperation Agreement with Georgia, TACIS assistance has been granted for small-scale rehabilitation projects in South Ossetia (and Azerbaijani regions 'liberated' from Armenian occupation), such as the restoration of a hydroelectric plant in Inguri (close to Abkhazia). Assistance has also been given through other channels, such as Tempus, Traceca (Transport Corridor Europe-Caucasus-Asia) and Inogate (Interstate Oil and Gas Transport to Europe).

B ENP: Not in itself a dispute settlement mechanism

Since the formalisation of the ENP in 2004,[59] political dialogue with partners has occupied a central place in the EU's relations with its neighbouring countries.[60] However, the ENP's principal contribution to international peace is through the promotion of local democracy, regional cooperation and socio-economic progress, all of which can only indirectly contribute to a more positive climate for peaceful dispute settlement. The former External Relations and ENP Commissioner Benita Ferrero-Waldner admitted as much when she observed that the ENP is 'not in itself a conflict prevention or settlement mechanism'.[61] Nonetheless, the ENP is also premised on a more direct contribution to stability in the EU's neighbourhood. In June 2003, the General Affairs and External Relations Council noted the importance of 'shared responsibility for conflict prevention and conflict resolution' among ENP partners and the EU.[62] In a 15-item list of 'incentives' to implement ENP goals, it prioritised more effective political dialogue and cooperation, intensified cooperation to prevent and combat common security threats, and greater cooperation in conflict prevention and crisis management.[63] The Commission's 2004 ENP Strategy Paper notes a similar ambition and adds specific areas of activity beyond political dialogue, namely 'the possible involvement of partner countries in aspects of CFSP and ESDP, conflict prevention, crisis management, the exchange of information, joint training and exercises and possible participation in EU-led crisis management operations.'[64]

Putting flesh on the bones, the Action Plans envisage 'new partnership perspectives' over a broad range of activities. This includes a commitment by ENP partners to 'certain essential aspects of the EU's external action, including

[59] Commission, 'European Neighbourhood Policy' (Strategy Paper) COM (2004) 373 final. For further details on the ENP, see http://ec.europa.eu/world/enp/index_en.htm. For an academic assessment, see, eg, the contributions to S Blockmans and A Łazowski (eds), *The European Union and Its Neighbours: A Legal Appraisal of the EU's Policies of Stabilisation, Partnership and Integration* (The Hague, TMC Asser Press, 2006); and M Cremona and C Hillion, 'L'Union fait la force? Potential and Limitations of the European Neighbourhood Policy as an Integrated EU Foreign and Security Policy' (2006) 39 *EUI Working Papers, LAW.*

[60] See M Smith and M Webber, 'Political Dialogue and Security in the European Neighbourhood: The Virtues and Limits of 'New Partnership Perspectives' (2008) 13 EFA Rev 73, 77–78.

[61] See B Ferrero-Waldner, 'Political reform and sustainable development in the South Caucasus: the EU's approach', Speech at the Bled Strategic Forum 'Caspian Outlook 2008', SPEECH/06/477, 28 August 2006; and, more generally, B Ferrero-Waldner, Benita, 'The European Neighbourhood Policy: The EU's Newest Foreign Policy Instrument' (2006) 11 *EFA Rev* 139–42.

[62] GAERC, Council Conclusions of 16 June 2003, Press Release no 10369/03 (Presse 166) 33.

[63] ibid.

[64] See COM (2004) 373 (n 59 above), under 'A more effective political dialogue'. Currently, Ukraine is one of five and the only of the ENP countries to have concluded a framework agreement on the participation in EU crisis management operations. In April 2010, the Council authorised the HR to open negotiations with a view to concluding such agreements with another 20 countries, among which were Egypt and Morocco as the only ENP countries. See Council conclusions, 26 April 2010, 8979/10 (Presse 90).

... the fight against terrorism and the proliferation of weapons of mass destruction (WMD), as well as efforts to achieve conflict resolution'.[65] Ferrero-Waldner observed that these Action Plans offered the opportunity for 'deeper political integration [through] more frequent and higher level political dialogue'.[66] This would serve to both strengthen democratic governance in partner states and promote 'our common foreign policy priorities, like making multilateral institutions more effective, and in addressing our common security threats'.[67]

But in spite of these lofty objectives, the reality on the ground remains that, so far, the European Union has been unable to achieve a great deal in its neighbourhood in the sphere of sustainable dispute settlement. This is partly due to the fact that the agenda for the implementation of the ENP's objectives is set by both the EU, on the one hand, and the respective partner country, on the other. Politically sensitive actions to resolve conflict will therefore only be included in the Action Plans if the countries for which they are drawn up agree to them. In practice, the outcome of this political process varies widely. For instance, the Action Plans for Georgia, Israel and the Palestinian territories define several specific priority actions which ought to contribute to the settlement of the disputes over Abkhazia and South Ossetia,[68] and the Middle East conflict respectively,[69] while the one for Morocco does not mention the dispute over the Western Sahara at all.[70] Another problem is that the parties to the existing disputes, as well as the big international players otherwise involved in the dispute settlement mechanisms (eg the US and Russia), simply do not wish to shift negotiations away from the existing platforms (provided for by, eg, the UN and the OSCE) to the relatively new and weak structures of the ENP, where their own roles would be diminished. These attitudes not only thwart the European Union's ambitions at playing a bigger role in the resolution of conflicts over the de facto states in its neighbourhood, they

[65] Commission, 'Commission proposals for Action Plans under the European Neighbourhood Policy (ENP)', COM (2004) 795 final. The Action Plans are 'benchmarked roadmaps' in bringing about needed reforms to bring the neighbours closer to the EU. See J Solana, 'The role of the EU in promoting and consolidating democracy in Europe's East', Address at the Common Vision for a Common Neighbourhood Conference, Vilnius, 4 May 2006.

[66] B Ferrero-Waldner, 'The European Neighbourhood Policy: bringing our neighbours closer', Speech at the 10th Euro-Mediterranean Economic Transition Conference 'Giving the Neighbours a stake in the EU internal market', Brussels, SPEECH/06/346, 6 June 2006.

[67] ibid.

[68] The EU-Georgia Action Plan, under Priority area 6, 'Promote peaceful resolution of internal conflicts', lists seven priority actions.

[69] The EU-Israel Action Plan, at 6, lists eight priority actions to strengthen political dialogue and to identify areas for further cooperation to deal with the Middle East conflict. The EU-Palestinian Authority Action Plan, at 4, declares it a priority action that 'intensified efforts [will be made] to facilitate the peace process and bring about the implementation of the Quartet Roadmap to a permanent two-state solution to the Israeli-Palestinian conflict.'

[70] The EU-Morocco Action Plan, at 1, only declares that 'Cross-border cooperation and shared responsibility for the establishment of an area of peace and stability, including crisis management and the prevention and resolution of conflicts in the region, also form part of the new European neighbourhood policy', and, at 7—under 'actions' (note that the qualifying term 'priority' has been dropped), that the EU and Morocco will 'Contribute to UN regional conflict resolution efforts'.

also continue to undermine bilateral relations with the de jure states implicated in the disputes. As a result, the European Union's institutional involvement in the existing dispute settlement mechanisms on its borders continues to vary widely:

— the EU (represented by the HR/VP) is a full participant in the Quartet for the Middle East conflict;[71]
— the EU participates as an observer in the so-called '5+2 talks' for Transnistria;[72]
— the European Commission has been an observer in the Joint Control Commission for South Ossetia; and
— none of the institutions but individual EU Member States participate in the so-called 'Minsk Group' for Nagorno-Karabakh and the UN Friends of Georgia, the forum which deals with Abkhazia.

C The 'carrot' of EU membership: theoretically only for some ENP countries

The only positive examples of the EU acting as a provider of peaceful dispute settlement pre-date the ENP and relate to another of the EU's transformation processes for neighbouring states: the Stabilisation and Association Process, ie the pre-accession process for the countries of the Western Balkans.[73] In the Western Balkans, the testing ground par excellence of CFSP and ESDP, the European Union, by way of its High Representative, supported by his staff at the Council, was instrumental in brokering a peace deal between the government of Macedonia and the Albanian separatists in Macedonia (FYROM) in 2001 and in hammering out the Belgrade Agreement (2002) to prevent the Federal Republic of Yugoslavia (FRY) from violently falling apart and having a knock-on effect on the precarious balance reached in Kosovo.[74] In both cases, the EU's High Representative—who played a key role in the settlement of the disputes—used the prospect of the conclusion of a Stabilisation and Association Agreement (SAA) and eventual EU membership as a strong lever to persuade the adversarial parties in each country to engage in negotiations to reform the Constitution and establish equal rights for their respective communities. The SAA would establish legal obligations for the countries concerned to approximate their legislation to the EU *acquis* and to cooperate with the other countries of the Western Balkans.

[71] See I Black, 'Israel faces new pressure as Lady Ashton visits Gaza', *The Guardian*, 18 March 2010, and L Harding, 'Quartet blasts Israel over East Jerusalem settlements', *The Guardian*, 19 March 2010.

[72] The five being Russia, Ukraine, OSCE, the EU and the US, the two being Moldova and Transnistria.

[73] Commission, 'Stabilisation and Association Process for Countries of South-Eastern Europe: Bosnia and Herzegovina, Croatia, Federal Republic of Yugoslavia, Former Yugoslav Republic of Macedonia and Albania' COM (99) 235 final.

[74] For backgrounds, analysis and references for further reading, see S Blockmans, *Tough Love: The European Union's Relations with the Western Balkans* (The Hague, TMC Asser Press, 2007) 189–207.

But at the same time it involved the perspective of the establishment of a free trade area between the EU and the countries concerned, provisions on cooperation in a wide range of fields, including justice and home affairs, and the provision of financial assistance to help them achieve the objectives of the SAA.

The alluring promises of the conclusion of an SAA and future membership serve the EU's strategic interests in stability, security and sustainable conflict resolution.[75] Such prospects have helped to increase prosperity and growth opportunities in destitute countries and regions, to improve links with vital transport and energy routes across borders, and to increase the EU's weight in the immediate neighbourhood, as indeed in the world. The consistent implementation of the renewed consensus on enlargement, as defined by the December 2006 European Council,[76] gains importance in the light of recent challenges to stability in the eastern neighbourhood of the EU. While it is clear that the 'carrot' of the prospect of EU membership is lacking in the context of the ENP, those 'European' states that could theoretically fulfil all EU membership conditions mentioned in and attached to Article 49 TEU could perhaps be swayed more easily than their non-European brethren in the ENP to resolve their internal and/or cross-border disputes.[77]

For Moldova, whose 'Europeanness' feeds an aspiration for future EU membership that seeks to overcome the Union's current reluctance to include it in any other group than that for which the prospect of accession to the Union has been excluded, accession negotiations will, in any way, not begin until the situation

[75] There is, however, one notable exception to this success story of 'soft power': Cyprus. For historical backgrounds, political realities and legal analyses, see F Hoffmeister, *Legal Aspects of the Cyprus Problem: Annan Plan and EU Accession* (Leiden, Martinus Nijhoff Publishers, 2006); and M Brus, M Akgün, S Blockmans, et al, *A Promise to Keep: Time to End the International Isolation of the Turkish Cypriots* (Istanbul, TESEV, 2008).

[76] *EU Bulletin*, December 2001, point I.25.1.

[77] According to Art 49 TEU, 'any European state' which respects the values set out in Art 2 TEU (liberty, democracy, respect for human rights and fundamental freedoms and the rule of law) and is committed to promoting them may apply to become a member of the Union. The June 1993 European Council Summit at Copenhagen developed more stringent criteria to measure the level of preparedness of both candidate countries and the EU. EU membership conditionality has been further upgraded into a multi-dimensional instrument geared towards reform and integration of the weak states of the Western Balkans. See F Hoffmeister, 'Changing Requirements for Membership', in A Ott and K Inglis (eds), *Handbook on European Enlargement—A Commentary on the Enlargement Process* (The Hague, TMC Asser Press, 2002); K Smith, 'The Evolution and Application of EU Membership Conditionality' in M Cremona (ed), *The Enlargement of the European Union* (Oxford, Oxford University Press, 2003); C Hillion, 'The Copenhagen Criteria and their Progeny' in C Hillion (ed), *EU Enlargement: A Legal Approach* (Oxford, Hart Publishing, 2004); S Blockmans, 'Consolidating the Enlargement Agenda for Southeastern Europe', in S Blockmans and S Prechal (eds), *Reconciling the Deepening and Widening of the European Union* (The Hague, TMC Asser Press, 2007); and S Blockmans, 'Raising the Threshold for Further EU Enlargement: Process, Problems and Prospects', in A Ott and E Vos (eds), *Fifty Years of European Integration: Foundations and Perspectives* (The Hague, TMC Asser Press, 2009).

regarding Transnistria has been fully resolved.[78] However, such a settlement is impossible without—at the very least—the acquiescence of the Russian government, given its political, diplomatic, economic and military ties with that region.[79] Yet, the 2005 EU-Russia Road Map for a Common Space of External Security is not very detailed as far as it concerns 'the settlement of regional conflicts, *inter alia* in regions adjacent to EU and Russian borders'.[80] Despite the EU's insistence, Russia has not proved ready to engage in a more concrete plan for common action in the shared—and troubled—security space.[81]

While the EU claims to be increasingly involved in the resolution of the conflict over Transnistria, its impact remains rather limited due to the conflict's own dynamics and Moscow's opposition. In March 2005, the Council of the EU appointed Adriaan Jacobovits de Szeged as EU Special Representative (EUSR) for Moldova.[82] The EUSR, who had been a Special Envoy for the Transnistrian conflict for the OSCE Chairman-in-Office under the Dutch Presidency in 2003, was mandated by the EU to (continue to) assist in the resolution of the conflict. One of his tasks is to oversee the activities of the EU Border Assistance Mission (EUBAM) Ukraine/Moldova.[83] This EUBAM was deployed on the Ukrainian/Moldovan border in November 2005, after Commission President Barroso and High Representative Solana received a joint letter by the Ukrainian and Moldovan Presidents inviting the EU to support their efforts in fighting smuggling and trafficking through Transnistria.[84]

As noted above, the EU participates as a mere observer in the so-called '5+2 talks' for Transnistria. This status obviously limits the Union's leverage over the parties to the dispute. While one of the key objectives of the EU-Moldova Action Plan under the ENP is to further support a viable solution to the Transnistria conflict, inter alia by 'consider[ing] ways to strengthen further [the European Union's] engagement',[85] recent developments in Moldova have been frustrating the EU's efforts to settle the dispute in a 'European' way. In a declaration signed

[78] See, eg, O Schmidtke and C Chira-Pascanut, 'The Promise of Europe: Moldova and the Process of Europeanization', in O Schmidtke and S Yekelchyk (eds), *Europe's Last Frontier? Belarus, Moldova, and Ukraine between Russia and the European Union* (New York/Basingstoke, Palgrave Macmillan, 2008).

[79] See S Yekelchyk, 'Out of Russia's Long Shadow: The Making of Modern Ukraine, Belarus, and Moldova', in Schmidtke and Yekelchyk, *Europe's Last Frontier* (n 78 above).

[80] 15th EU-Russia Summit Conclusions, Press release no 8799/05 (Presse 110), 10 May 2005, 39.

[81] According to Nicu Popescu, solving this most 'solvable' of conflicts in the shared neighbourhood would set a positive precedent in building the Common Space of External Security. See N Popescu, 'The EU in Moldova—Settling Conflicts in the Neighbourhood', EUISS Occasional Paper, no 60 (2005) 43.

[82] Council Joint Action 2005/265/CFSP appointing a Special representative of the European Union for the Republic of Moldova [2005] OJ L81/50.

[83] Council Joint Action 2005/776/CFSP, amending the mandate of the European Union Special representative for Moldova [2005] OJ L292/13, and prolonged since then.

[84] See A Skvortova, 'Moldova', in Blockmans and Łazowski, *The European Union and Its Neighbours* (n 59 above) 563–64.

[85] See EU-Moldova Action Plan, 2. At 9–10, five priority actions are listed under this heading.

jointly by the Moldovan President Vladimir Voronin and the Transnistrian leader Igor Smirnov in April 2007, Moldova for the first time recognised the political leadership of the breakaway province as a legitimate entity.[86] And despite the EU's claims to the contrary, Russia tends to consider Kosovo's independence as a precedent for the breakaway regions on its borderincluding Transnistria. Many observers have been critical of Moscow's apparent deviousness in evading any serious peace and reconciliation negotiations, either under UN or OSCE auspices.[87]

D The independence of Kosovo: precedent or excuse?

The argument that Kosovo represents a *casus sui generis* because it has been governed by international sanction for almost a decade after a forceful humanitarian intervention put an end to a situation of internal colonialism, and because an all-inclusive process of international status negotiations proved unsuccessful,[88] represents no legally acceptable justification for breaching standing public international law (on the inviolability of international borders and the prohibition of interference in another state's domestic affairs) and bypassing the UN Security Council as the supreme authority on such matters.[89] However, the recognition of Kosovo as a sovereign and independent state by almost 70 states world-wide (among which were 22 out of 27 EU Member States) does provide evidence that *opinio juris* is shifting from the concept of 'state security' to the notion of 'human security', meaning that a growing body of states considers that, under the given circumstances, human rights and fundamental freedoms of individuals and the principle of external self-determination of peoples should outweigh the orthodoxies of international law.[90] Yet, the consequences of the application of a simplified version of that rationale (eg omitting the condition of lengthy international governance) are potentially harmful, in Kosovo and the EU's neighbourhood, as well as for the international order based on states. Indeed, it did not take long before this liberal interpretation of the traditional concepts of international law backfired on the EU[91] and the US. Contrary to the

[86] Voronin allegedly acted under pressure from the Kremlin. See 'A thaw in the river', *The Economist*, 19 April 2007.

[87] See N Popescu, '"Outsourcing" De Facto Statehood: Russia and the Secessionist Entities in Georgia and Moldova' (2006) 109 *CEPS Policy Brief*.

[88] See M Weller, 'Negotiating the Final Status of Kosovo' (2008) 114 *EUISS Chaillot Paper*; and J Ker-Lindsay, *Kosovo: The Path to Contested Statehood in the Balkans* (London/New York, IB Tauris, 2009).

[89] See M Weller, *Contested Statehood: Kosovo's Struggle for Independence* (Oxford, Oxford University Press, 2009).

[90] See C Borgen, 'Kosovo's Declaration of Independence: Self-determination, Secession and Recognition' (2008) 12 *ASIL Insight*, available at www.asil.org/insights/2008/02/insights080229.html; and the legal commentaries available online at www.kosovocompromise.com.

[91] Also because of the decision of the Council of the EU to dispatch an EU Special Representative, and the Union's biggest rule of law operation to date: see Council Joint Action 2008/124/CFSP of 4

logic applied by Moscow during the final status talks, Russia was quick to switch position and use the West's recognition of Kosovo's independence as a precedent for establishing legal links with the breakaway regions in Georgia.

E Caucasian squabbles: a new 'hour of Europe'?[92]

Judgements about the European Union's reaction to the flare-up of conflict over the breakaway regions of South Ossetia and Abkhazia in August 2008, Russia's incursion into Georgia, and its unilateral recognition of the two de facto states, have varied—from the cartoon of EU leaders held together in a wobbly red jelly on the cover of the *Economist* of 6 September 2008, to the earlier assessment that 'Without the European Union's intervention and rapid reaction on the part of the French president the Russians would already have made Tbilisi theirs'.[93] The reference here is to the diplomatic initiative of Nicolas Sarkozy, who—as holder of the EU's Presidency in the second half of 2008—visited Moscow and Tbilisi, brokered the initial ceasefire agreement on 12 August 2008, and then pushed hard for Russia to observe the terms. In a rare display of unity, the EU Member States followed up at their emergency summit on 1 September—only the third in its history—by sticking together in an unprecedented condemnation of Russian

February 2008 on the European Union Rule of Law Mission in Kosovo, EULEX KOSOVO [2004] OJ L42/92. UNSC Res 1244 (1999), which provided for the interim administration by UNMIK, remained in place due to Russian resistance to other options discussed in the Security Council. Secretary-General Ban Ki-Moon became involved in order to break the deadlock by presenting a six-point plan to the UNSC in a letter on 12 June 2008. On 26 November 2008, the Security Council approved this proposal which provided for the deployment of a status-neutral EULEX under a continued 'UN umbrella', with Resolution 1244 staying in force. This solution had a direct and severe impact on EULEX's mandate: UNMIK would stay in Kosovo and remain the official counterpart for the Serbs. This mainly had repercussions for Kosovo's Serb-dominated north, where UNMIK would continue to play a leading role, thus increasing the risk of a de facto division of the Kosovo territory. See S Keukeleire and R Thiers, 'EULEX Kosovo: Walking a Thin Line, Aiming for the Rule of Law', in Blockmans, Wouters and Ruys, *The European Union and Peacebuilding* (n 30 above).

[92] The focus in this section is on Georgia. As far as the EU's role in peaceful dispute settlement in other parts of the South Caucasus is concerned, the Commission's 2010 ENP regular reports offer a bleak picture of the Union's ability to settle disputes in the neighbourhoood. See, eg, Commission Staff Working Document accompanying the Communication from the Commission to the European Parliament and the Council, 'Taking stock of the European Neighbourhood Policy (ENP)', 'Implementation of the European Neighbourhood Policy in 2009 – Progress Report Armenia', SEC (2010) 516, which highlights the main development in Armenia in 1999, ie the signing of protocols on normalising relations with Turkey in October, mainly through Swiss mediation. However, the ratification procedure stalled after Turkey linked the opening of the border and the establishment of diplomatic relations to progress in peace talks between Azerbaijan and Armenia over Nagorno-Karabakh. Armenia suspended ratification in April 2010, blaming Turkey for the lack of progress. 'The EU was pleased to note Armenia's continued commitment to pursue the process of normalization of Armenian-Turkish relations,' the report said, 'but at the same time expressed concern about the loss of momentum in this process.' In the 'Progress Report Azerbaijan', SEC (2010) 519, the EU merely took note of the 'intensified' attempts to find a settlement over Nagorno-Karabakh.

[93] See J-D Giuliani, 'Editorial: Europe and Russia', *Fondation Robert Schuman Newsletter*, 24 August 2008, available at www.jd-giuliani.eu/en/article/cat-2/101_LEurope-et-la-Russie.html.

aggression.[94] To signal their willingness to act, EU Member States suspended negotiations on the new Partnership and Cooperation Agreement until Russia acted in full compliance with Sarkozy's peace plan. While it was in Russia's own interest to withdraw its forces from the self-declared buffer-zone in Georgia and start a programme of damage control in international relations, Moscow—otherwise used to a squabbling and uncritical EU—will have taken note of Europe's relatively strong reaction; relative, because compared with the tough rhetoric from Washington, the Union's reaction still looked measured. Arguably, the EU's mediating role in the conflict was all the more effective because it was backed by a growling US that openly backed Georgia's President, Mikheil Saakashvili. The Americans found it easier to be firm and critical precisely because they could rely on the EU to do the actual negotiations. The European Union has since supplemented its high-level diplomacy by attempting to mitigate the consequences of the war on the ground. In spite of an Estonian proposal to send a full-fledged ESDP peacekeeping mission to Georgia,[95] foreign ministers eventually authorised a 300-strong European Union Monitoring Mission in Georgia to replace Russian troops in the buffer-zone,[96] and pledged €500 million in aid for the period 2008–10 to help the reconstruction of the devastated Georgian economy.[97] But effectively, the issues of the inaptly named 'frozen conflicts' have been resolved, not in a peaceful manner by the EU but by force by Russia. Both South Ossetia and Abkhazia have been recognised as sovereign and independent states by Moscow, and are heavily dependent on trade with Russia.

Thus, tension and bitterness persisted, not only within the Caucasus, but also between Russia and the West. Many observers, both inside and outside the European Union, looked anxiously eastwards in the belief that Russian efforts to control its 'near abroad' would not stop at the borders of South Ossetia and Abkhazia.[98] Presumably, inaction by the EU and the US would be taken by Russia's zero-sum politicising leadership as an encouragement to move on from the 'success' in Georgia to pursue comparable objectives, tactics and methods in relation to the Russophile regions of Transnistria and the Crimea in Ukraine, and

[94] Presidency Conclusions, Extraordinary European Council, Brussels, 1 September 2008, doc. 12594/08, 11.

[95] See P Runner 'Estonia urges EU peacekeepers for Georgia', *EU Observer*, 5 August 2008.

[96] Council Joint Action 2008/736/CFSP of 15 September 2008 on the European Union Monitoring Mission in Georgia, EUMM Georgia [2008] OJ L248/26 (as amended).

[97] GAERC, Council Conclusions of 15–16 September 2008, Press Release no 13030/08 (Presse 255) 9. See also M Merlingen and R Ostrauskaitė, 'EU Peacebuilding in Georgia: Limits and Achievements', in Blockmans, Wouters and Ruys, *The European Union and Peacebuilding* (n 30 above).

[98] See T Valášek, 'What Does the War in Georgia Mean for EU Foreign Policy?' (2008) *CER Briefing Note*; M Emerson, 'Post-mortem on Europe's First War of the 21st Century' (2008) 167 *CEPS Policy Brief*; and N Popescu, M Leonard and A Wilson, 'Can the EU Win the Peace in Georgia?' (2008) *ECFR Policy Brief*.

to defend 'its' citizens—especially those, it would seem, who have recently been handed a Russian passport—anywhere with crushing force.[99]

With the sense of urgency over the Georgian crisis dissipating, the divisions between EU Member States over how to deal with Russia slowly reappeared.[100] Regrettably, the differences in positions between EU Member States—from the 'new cold warriors' (eg Lithuania and Poland) to Russia's 'Trojan horses' in the EU (eg Bulgaria, Cyprus and Greece)—are so far apart, that building a common framework on EU-Russia relations might provide the ultimate example in defining the lowest common denominator in EU external relations policies and law.[101] The EU will need to continue its debate about why Georgia matters,[102] and what kind of tools it has at its disposal to resolve the Georgian crisis,[103] as indeed the other (potential) conflicts in the neighbourhood shared with Russia. Finally, the EU will need to engage with the big and powerful countries on its borders to resolve the frozen, simmering and boiling conflicts 'in-between'.[104] Therefore, conflicts should always be a key focus of political dialogue with neighbouring countries. The EU should also ensure that the disputes remain on the agenda of dialogues with relevant international organisations and third countries and that it becomes an active participant in those dialogues where it is not.

[99] In the aftermath of the August 2008 Russo-Georgian war, President Medvedev laid down five principles that would guide Russian foreign policy: the primacy of international law; the quest for a multi-polar world; no isolation of Russia; the protection of its citizens; and—last but not least—spheres of influence: 'Russia, just like other countries in the world, has regions where it has its privileged interests.' When asked what these priority regions were, he replied: 'Certainly the regions bordering [on Russia], but not only them.' See P Reynolds, 'New Russian world order: the five principles', BBC News, 1 September 2008.

[100] See, eg, P Runner, 'Lithuania complicates French rapprochement with Russia', *EU Observer*, 7 November 2008; and R Goldirova, 'EU resumes Russia talks, isolating Lithuania', *EU Observer*, 11 November 2008.

[101] ibid. For the conceptualisation and categorisation of EU Member States' positions on Russia-related topics, see M Leonard and N Popescu, 'A Power Audit of EU-Russia Relations' (2007) *ECFR Policy Paper*, 2: 'We have identified five distinct policy approaches to Russia shared by old and new members alike: "Trojan Horses" (Cyprus and Greece) who often defend Russian interests in the EU system, and are willing to veto common EU positions; "Strategic Partners" (France, Germany, Italy and Spain) who enjoy a "special relationship" with Russia which occasionally undermines common EU policies; "Friendly Pragmatists" (Austria, Belgium, Bulgaria, Finland, Hungary, Luxembourg, Malta, Portugal, Slovakia and Slovenia) who maintain a close relationship with Russia and tend to put their business interests above political goals; "Frosty Pragmatists" (Czech Republic, Denmark, Estonia, Ireland, Latvia, the Netherlands, Romania, Sweden and the United Kingdom) who also focus on business interests but are less afraid than others to speak out against Russian behaviour on human rights or other issues; and "New Cold Warriors" (Lithuania and Poland) who have an overtly hostile relationship with Moscow and are willing to use the veto to block EU negotiations with Russia.'

[102] See D Lynch, 'Why Georgia Matters' (2006) 86 *EUISS Chaillot Paper*.

[103] See M Leonard and C Grant, 'Georgia and the EU: Can Europe's Neighbourhood Policy Deliver?' (2005) *CER Policy Brief*; R Asmus, S Cornell, A Herrberg and N Popescu, 'Internationalizing the Georgia-Abkhazia Conflict Resolution Process: Why a Greater European Role is Needed' (2008) *GMF Policy Brief*; and N Popescu, M Leonard and A Wilson, 'Can the EU Win the Peace in Georgia?' (2008) *ECFR Policy Brief*.

[104] See, eg, S Gaenzle, 'The EU-Russia Relations and the Repercussions on the "In-Betweens"', in Schmidtke and Yekelchyk, *Europe's Last Frontier* (n 78 above).

IV VISION …

A … or the perceived lack thereof

The EU's approach in dealing with harder security issues is often perceived by others as weak.[105] Yet, as we have seen in this chapter, the EU's image problem is less related to the scale of its efforts than to inherent structural deficiencies. That is not to say that the efforts developed by the EU could not be strengthened. It goes without saying that, eg, unconvincing (prospects of) benefits, ineffective targeted sanctions, weak mandates for EUSRs and small CSDP missions with limited mandates should be prevented, and amended where already in existence. It is a positive sign that, in the framework of the ENP, for instance, the Commission has indicated to stand ready to develop, together with the Council, further proposals in the field of dispute settlement, using all instruments at its disposal.[106] History will tell whether the war in Georgia in August 2008 was the shock that the European Union needed to get its act together on the European Neighbourhood Policy, energy relations with third countries, and a coherent foreign policy strategy. The first signs, however, give us few reasons to be hopeful. Neither the new Union for the Mediterranean nor the recently launched Eastern Partnership focus much on dispute resolution.[107]

B Union for the Mediterranean: let's agree to disagree and do business instead

Initiated under the French Presidency of the EU on 13 July 2008,[108] the 'Barcelona Process: Union for the Mediterranean' is a community—complete with

[105] See, eg, N Chaban, O Elgström and M Holland, 'The European Union as Others See It' (2006) 11 EFA Rev 245. For more recent figures and clues, see the ongoing survey coordinated by S Lucarelli, 'Research Report: The External Image of the European Union', GARNET Working Paper, no 17 (2007). A first set of data drawn from the survey was published by L Fioramonti and S Lucarelli, 'How Do the Others See Us? European Political Identity and the External Image of the EU' in F Cerutti and S Lucarelli (eds), *The Search for a European Identity: Values, Policies and Legitimacy of the European Union* (London/New York, Routledge, 2008).

[106] Commission, 'A Strong European Neighbourhood Policy', COM (2007) 774 final, 7: 'The Commission will also do all it can to ensure that the potential offered by political dialogue is fully exploited for other issues, such as terrorism, drugs, migratory flows, civil protection, and especially governance. It will continue to promote stability notably through the sustained promotion of democracy, human rights and the rule of law throughout the neighbourhood.'

[107] For issues related to the Black Sea Synergy, see C Weaver, *The EU and the Black Sea: Peace and Stability Beyond the Boundaries?* (2007), available at https://lra.le.ac.uk/bitstream/2381/4093/1/enp%20%26%20black%20sea%20refs.pdf.

[108] See the Joint Declaration of the Paris Summit for the Mediterranean, adopted under the co-presidency of the President of the French Republic and the President of the Arab Republic of Egypt, in the presence of, inter alia, the EU, the UN, the Gulf Cooperation Council, the Arab League, the African Union, the Arab Maghreb Union, the Organisation of the Islamic Conference, and the

institutional structures and headquarters in Barcelona—that unites all EU Member States and all non-EU countries bordering the Mediterranean Sea, plus Mauritania,[109] with the objective of transforming the Mediterranean into 'an area of peace, democracy, cooperation and prosperity'.[110] This strategic ambition is underlined by the agreement among participants 'to continue with renewed dynamism the quest for peace and cooperation, to explore their joint problems and transform these good intentions into actions in a renewed partnership for progress.'[111] However, instead of focusing on dispute settlement, or developing instruments thereto, the founding document of the Union for the Mediterranean only speaks in a more concrete sense of the non-proliferation of weapons. The somewhat vague pledges of partners to 'promote conditions likely to develop good-neighbourly relations among themselves and support processes aimed at stability, security, prosperity and regional and sub-regional cooperation' and to 'consider any confidence and security-building measures that could be taken between the parties with a view to the creation of an "area of peace and stability in the Mediterranean", including the long-term possibility of establishing a Euro-Mediterranean pact to that end', do not reflect a clear vision of the resolution of the conflicts in the Mediterranean region, nor a common will to immediately translate these goals into the necessary hard-hitting tools with which to settle disputes.[112] The Union for the Mediterranean is said to be complementary to both EU bilateral relations with these countries, which will continue under existing policy frameworks such as Association Agreements and the ENP Action Plans, as well as the regional dimension of the EU enlargement policy. In terms of dispute settlement, it is clear that the Union for the Mediterranean will add very little to the weak elements already foreseen in the framework of the ENP.[113] In fact, in the press briefing on the EU's relations with its eastern

World Bank, Paris, 13 July 2008. The Joint Declaration is based on the Communication from the Commission to the European Parliament and the Council, 'Barcelona Process: Union for the Mediterranean', COM (2008) 319 final.

[109] Libya has observer status. The Western Sahara (ie SADR) is not represented.

[110] See Joint Declaration of the Paris Summit for the Mediterranean, 8.

[111] ibid, 9.

[112] ibid, 10. Only the Israeli-Palestinian Peace Process is mentioned by name, with participants to the Paris Summit welcoming the announcement that Syria and Israel initiated indirect peace talks under the auspices of Turkey. Ministers of Foreign Affairs at their Marseille Summit of 3–4 November 2008 stressed, however, 'that the Barcelona Process: Union for the Mediterranean is not intended to replace the other initiatives undertaken in the interests of the peace, stability and development of the region, but that it will contribute to their success.' See Final Statement, 1.

[113] The Final Statement of the Marseille Summit of Ministers of Foreign Affairs of 3–4 November 2008, in its section 'Political and security dialogue' of 'Fields of Cooperation to be pursued in 2009', at 8–9, does not mention *any* concrete effort to resolve the existing conflicts in the region. With regard to the Middle East, the Commission noted in its 'Progress Report Israel', SEC (2010) 520, that there has been no progress in the 'peace process' between Israel and the Palestinians, and that the continued de facto blockade of the Gaza strip by Israel and Egypt has perpetuated a humanitarian crisis there. The EU's border assistance mission has remained on stand-by. In its 'Progress Report occupied Palestinian Territory', SEC (2010) 515, the Commission noted that there has been no progress in talks between Israel and the Palestinians, and that the occupied territories continue to be split in two, with

and southern neighbours over the past five years, European Commissioner Füle for enlargement and ENP bluntly stated that 'The very idea of the Union for the Mediterranean is not to create another framework for political discussions trying to solve the existing conflicts.' As a spin-off of the ENP, the Barcelona-based organisation is instead designed to be a 'project-oriented union, where the secretariat … is expected to put together ideas, investors, experts and to help stamp projects which will bring real benefits to the citizens of the region.'[114]

C Eastern Partnership: new wine, old skins

Proposed by Poland and Sweden on 23 May 2008 as a parallel initiative to the French-inspired Union for the Mediterranean, the Eastern Partnership received broad Member State support in the wake of the Russo-Georgian war at the Extraordinary European Council on 1 September 2008 and was officially launched by the Commission on 3 December of that year.[115] The Eastern Partnership has been heralded by the EU as 'a real step change in relations with our Eastern neighbours, with a significant upgrading of political, economic and trade relations.'[116] While the professed goal is to strengthen the prosperity and stability of Ukraine, Moldova, Belarus, Georgia, Armenia, and Azerbaijan, and thus the security of the EU, with proposals which cover a wide range of bilateral and multilateral areas of cooperation, including energy security and mobility of people, the Eastern Partnership fails to offer concrete innovations in the sphere of dispute settlement.[117] The Partnership talks only in general terms of promoting stability and multilateral confidence-building with the goal of consolidating the sovereignty and territorial integrity of partners, in the sense that it 'should

the West Bank under the control of secular Fatah and the Gaza strip run by Islamist Hamas, with Israel encroaching on both territories. The Palestinian authority, Fatah, has viewed the ENP primarily as a state-building tool and will continue on that path for the foreseeable future. Israel's war on Gaza in December 2008–January 2009 had 'devastating effects' on civilians and 'destroyed' Gaza's economic and institutional structures, the report says. More than 1400 Palestinians, including around 1000 civilians, were killed.

[114] As reported by V Pop, 'Mediterranean union not for conflict resolution, Fuele says', *EU Observer*, 12 May 2010. See also K Pieters, *The Integration of the Mediterranean Neighbours into the EU Internal Market* (The Hague, TMC Asser Press, 2010).

[115] Commission, 'Eastern Partnership', COM (2008) 823/4; and see the accompanying Commission Staff Working Document, SEC (2008) 2974/3.

[116] See the High Representative's 'Report on the Implementation of the European Security Strategy—Providing Security in a Changing World', doc 17104/08 (S407/08) 10.

[117] The Eastern Partnership also failed to satisfy the ambition of future EU membership cherished by some of the six neighbouring countries, most notable Moldova and Ukraine. While the Partnership does not provide them with a promise of EU membership, and is being perceived as a 'triumph of constructive ambiguity', it does put the countries of Eastern Europe on track towards that goal. See M Sadowska and P Swieboda, 'Eastern Partnership—good start, hard labour to come', *demosEUROPA Commentaries and Reports*, 8 December 2008. For a short elaboration of the desire of most Eastern European governments to have ENP á la carte, see N Popescu, 'The EU's Sovereign Neighbours', *ECFR Commentary*, 1 December 2008.

advance political dialogue in fields of common interest and cover specific CFSP and ESDP issues' and that 'Early-warning arrangements should be enhanced, with particular focus on conflict areas.'[118] Here too, therefore, one has to observe that the ENP has not been reinforced with concrete objectives and instruments to engage in conflict resolution on the eastern fringes of the European Union. It would seem that, in spite of the Commission's vow to reinforce the ENP by developing, together with the Council, further proposals in the field of peaceful dispute settlement, the European Neighbourhood Policy has in fact been weakened in this respect.

V CONCLUDING REMARKS

To a great extent, the flagrant lack of common vision on how to tackle and resolve disputes on the borders of the European Union is due to the lack of unity among Member States on how such a strategy should be defined.[119] Indeed, the real test of the EU's effectiveness comes at the level of cohesion among Member States. A Union that is divided, and where the biggest countries pursue their own selfish interests in bilateral deals with powerful neighbouring states, while the smaller Member States stubbornly block decisions defining EU positions and actions to draw attention to their own concerns, will achieve little but derision, both at home and abroad. A European Union that unites around clearly defined objectives will stand a much better chance of playing a stabilising role in the neighbourhood and being taken seriously as an 'honest broker' to settle disputes on its borders.

In the face of strong neighbouring states competing for the Union's 'spheres of influence', internal decision-making procedures in CFSP/CSDP which require unanimity allow one or two EU Member States to block any proposal for conflict resolution carried by the other Member States and have the potential of putting the EU's efforts of dispute settlement out of sync with such conflicts' own dynamics.[120] The CFSP risks of faltering more frequently as splinter groups of Member States that diverge in their opinions about how to resolve conflicts proliferate. In section II(D), we have argued that the post-Lisbon EU Treaties will only be able to counter these difficulties when full use is made of the new institutional arrangements. However, the bottom line remains that the willingness of the Member States to act together through 'their' Union is often missing.

[118] See COM(2008) 823/4 (n 115 above) 10 and SEC (2008) 2974/3 (n 115 above) 3. Both documents also mention integrated border management, including at Eastern Partnership countries' non-EU borders.

[119] Another reason is of course the unwillingness of countries like Morocco to accept outside involvement and define a common strategy for the resolution of what they perceive and present as purely domestic disputes.

[120] See, eg, B Coppieters, 'The EU and Georgia: Time Perspectives in Conflict Resolution', EUISS Occasional Paper, no 70 (2007).

While pragmatism about the fact that only a united EU can tackle most of the security challenges posed by a globalising world should make the Member States mend their ways, it will depend on vision and political leadership whether they will.

But these deficiencies do not absolve the EU and its Member States from attaining the mission statements mentioned at the outset of this contribution. Mismanagement of the ethnic-territorial and constitutional conflicts on its borders could have severe and destabilising consequences for the neighbourhood and the EU alike, including a greater likelihood of political extremism, an increase in organised crime and other illegal economic activities, terrorism, armed conflict and further human displacement. New headline-grabbing violence will bring home to the EU what has been common knowledge in its neighbourhood for some time: the status quo is unsustainable. Another episode of war, however limited, would be devastating for all involved and would amount to a policy failure with damaging implications for the international organisations active in the region, in particular the European Union.

Proponents of a more extensive role for the Union in regional dispute settlement may find reason for some optimism in the ambitions laid down in the new Treaties. Indeed, the extensive number of references to the United Nations seems to reflect a new role of the EU as a regional agency in the sense of Chapter VIII of the UN Charter. Applied to the specific functions of the EU, this new role would turn the EU into (perhaps one of) the regional organisations in charge of peaceful dispute settlement in the region. As we have seen, the logic of Chapter VIII UNC implies that these regional organisations carry a primary responsibility to settle regional disputes. In fact, one could argue that by accepting the role of a 'regional agency', the current neighbourhood becomes part of the 'internal' scope of the EU and disputes in the region are to be considered 'local disputes'.[121]

Despite the difficulties we listed on the basis of past performance of the EU in this area, its new ambitions as well as institutional capabilities reveal the existing potential. The EU includes the assertion of its own identity on the international scene and the promotion of peace, security, progress and international law in Europe, its neighbourhood, as indeed the world, among its principle mission statements.[122] It sports a unique combination of capabilities in the fields of policy, law, economics and security, and it has the money, interest, and even some power to stabilise the roughest of its neighbourhoods. What needs to be found is

[121] *cf* Art 52, para 2 UNC: 'The Members of the United Nations entering into such arrangements or constituting such agencies shall make every effort to achieve pacific settlement of local disputes through such regional arrangements or by such regional agencies before referring them to the Security Council.'

[122] See, eg, the Preamble and Art 3 of the Treaty on European Union (TEU); the 2003 ESS (n 1 above) and the 2004 Strategy Paper on the ENP (n 2 above).

the common political will (how) to deal with the parties to the conflicts. Member States should not lose sight of the fact that because 'their' Union is well placed to stabilise the neighbourhood, they carry a heavy responsibility to see the processes of sustainable dispute settlement through.

5

Counter-terrorism and Fundamental Rights: Judicial Challenges and Legislative Changes after the Rulings in Kadi *and* PMOI

ELEANOR SPAVENTA

I INTRODUCTION

SINCE THE TERRORIST attacks perpetrated against the United States of America on 11 September 2001, counter-terrorism strategy has been prominent in the Western political agenda. The novel nature of the threat, which is not linked to the achievement of a particular political aim against one particular regime, made the perceived (and real) danger more urgent, so as to elevate it to a global (although predominantly Western) emergency. As a result, there has been an increase in the counter-terrorism response both at national and at international level. As part of this response, both the UN and the EU adopted a number of measures aimed at enhancing the effectiveness of counter-terrorism policy, by introducing an element of international and/or regional coordination. This contribution will focus on one type of these measures, the practice of drafting a list of individuals and organisations suspected of having links with terrorism. Those included in the list are subject to several 'precautionary' measures, amongst which is the freezing of all of their assets. Both the UN and EU terrorist lists have been at the centre of much legal controversy, and as a result of legal challenges, significant changes were introduced to the original regimes. Those changes have improved the protection of those listed in these international instruments as well as introducing some transparency; and yet, from a fundamental rights viewpoint, these measures are still highly problematic. In this contribution I will look at these issues; thus, after having given some background information, I will briefly recall the changes introduced in the UN's own regime. I will then focus on the EU regimes (both the UN-derived and the EU-own) to conclude with an assessment of the fundamental rights compliance of the modified regimes.

A Background information

The UN introduced several measures aimed at countering the terrorist threat; amongst these is Resolution 1390(2002), which mandates states to freeze the assets of those individuals identified by the UN Sanctions Committee.[1] Resolution 1390(2002) is one of the 'novel' sanction mechanisms:[2] whilst previously both general sanctions and 'smart' sanctions were aimed at pursuing political goals (such as regime change or change in regime practices), and therefore were targeted at countries and political elites, Resolution 1390(2002) targets individuals and organisations which are deemed to be associated with terrorism, and aims at preventing terrorism also by blocking its funding.[3]

Resolution 1390(2002) was implemented by the Member States directly at EU level.[4] The reason for this is almost self-evident: given the free movement rights in the EU, and especially the free movement of capital rights, implementation at national level might have been significantly less effective, since potential differences in the timing of implementation of the Security Council Resolution might alert those subject to the freezing orders and allow them to move their assets to friendlier shores before the freezing order at national level took effect.[5] Furthermore, as part of the global fight against terrorism, the EU also adopted its own

[1] This is also referred to as the 1267 Committee, as it was created pursuant to UN Resolution 1267(1999).

[2] For an interesting review (which however does not cover the sanctions under discussion here), see A Tostesen and B Bull, 'Are Smart Sanctions Feasible' (2002) *World Politics* 373.

[3] Resolution 1333(2000) is the first example of the use of international sanctions to target specific individuals in this way; the Resolution originally instructed Member States to freeze Usama Bin Laden's, Al-Qaida etc assets because of their role in the terrorist attacks against the US in Kenya and Tanzania. As we shall mention briefly below, the very nature of these sanctions (as well as the power of the UN to identify individuals in this way) is contested.

[4] Common Position 2002/402/CFSP concerning restrictive measures against Usama Bin Laden, members of the Al-Qaida organisation and the Taliban and other individuals, groups, undertakings and entities associated with them and repealing Common Positions 96/746/CFSP, 1999/727/CFSP, 2001/154/CFSP and 2001/771/CFSP [2002] OJ L169/4; implemented by Regulation 881/2002 imposing certain specific restrictive measures directed against certain persons and entities associated with Usama Bin Laden, the Al-Qaida network and the Taliban, and repealing Council Regulation 467/2001/EC prohibiting the export of certain goods and services to Afghanistan, strengthening the flight ban and extending the freeze of funds and other financial resources in respect of the Taliban of Afghanistan [2002] OJ L139/9 (hereinafter 'original Regulation 881/2002'), recently modified by Regulation 1286/2009 [2009] OJ L346/42. The amendments will be the focus of detailed analysis below.

[5] In a way this is still a problem since there is a gap between the decision at UN level and its implementation at EU level; see eg 'Guidelines on implementation and evaluation of restrictive measures (sanctions) in the framework of the EU Common Foreign and Security Policy', 15 December 2009, doc no 17464/09, para 36, where it is stated that the EU should aim to implement the UN Security Council Resolution within 30 days, and within three days in the case of updates to the lists. In both instances, the 'surprise' effect, so treasured by the Council in its submissions to cases before the ECJ, seems to be rather compromised.

terrorist lists identifying individuals and organisations that it considers linked with international and internal terrorism.[6]

Both the UN-derived list and the EU list were adopted through a complex legal mechanism since, pre-Lisbon, the EC did not have a clear competence to adopt sanctions against individuals not connected to a specific 'state'. Thus, Article 301 EC stated that where it was so provided in a Common Position, the Council could interrupt economic relations with one or more *countries*. In this case, the Council could rely on Article 60 EC to take the necessary urgent measures in relation to the movement of capital as regards the third countries concerned. The problem with the terrorist freezing orders was that the individuals and groups identified were often not connected with a specific country, especially after the regime change in Afghanistan. As a result, and to supplement the above competence, the Council relied also on Article 308 EC (the residual competence of the Community) to enact measures that targeted individuals rather than countries, as expressly provided by Articles 301 and 60 EC. However, individuals connected only with intra-EU terrorism were identified in the Common Position (using Third-Pillar competence) but were (and are) not subject to the freezing of funds, since the competence provided in the above-mentioned provisions was deemed not to extend to situations where there was no connection to a third country. The Treaty of Lisbon has introduced in Article 75 TFEU clear competence for the adoption of asset freezing orders against individuals suspected of terrorism and related activities.[7]

Leaving aside the competence issues, the identification of individuals (and organisations) supposedly connected to terrorism as a result of a mere executive decision (whether adopted at UN or EU level) is obviously highly problematic from a legal viewpoint. It risks subverting the division of powers between the branches of governments (and especially between the executive and the judicial branch) which is seen very much as the basis of contemporary Western democracies. The European governments' response to this criticism has been to categorise the freezing of assets as an administrative measure, which therefore does not necessitate the guarantees that are provided for criminal sanctions. And yet, it is not difficult to challenge that argument: even should the freezing of assets be qualified as a mere 'administrative measure', and leaving aside its effects on the right to property which are acknowledged by the Council, it is clear that being defined as a suspected terrorist is not without consequences for those affected by the designation. And not surprisingly, with time both the UN and the Council had to acknowledge, at least partially, the criticisms voiced against the

[6] Common Position 2001/931/CFSP on the application of specific measures to combat terrorism [2001] OJ L344/93, partially implemented by Council Regulation 2580/2001 on specific restrictive measures directed against certain persons and entities with a view to combating terrorism [2001] OJ L344/70.

[7] The new competence has not solved all of the problems since the Commission and the Council on one side, and the EP on the other, seems to take different views of its scope; see pending case C-130/10 *Parliament v Council* on the legal basis of Regulation 1286/2009; see further Spaventa, forthcoming.

system, and introduce some changes with the aim of better protecting the fundamental rights of those suspected of terrorist activity.[8] We shall now analyse the UN and the EU listing regimes, together with the changes which have been introduced in recent years. The contribution will then address the extent to which these changes are sufficient to solve the fundamental rights gap created by the exercise of this type of powers by executives.

II THE UN LISTING REGIME

It has been mentioned above that the identification of those individuals to be included in the UN list is made by the UN Sanctions Committee. The procedure for both listing and de-listing has evolved significantly in the past eight years, not least because of the legal challenges brought within UN Member States as well as in the EU.[9] Originally, listing and de-listing were not much more than executive decisions: at the request of one or more governments, individuals would be placed on the list. Individuals were not necessarily given information as to the reasons for their inclusion in the list; nor could they make representations to challenge the decision directly to the Sanctions Committee, rather having to persuade the Member State of residence or nationality to make representations on their behalf. All assets would be frozen and there was no humanitarian exception. The severity of the regime led the CFI to impose substantial obligations on EU Member States.[10]

[8] It should be noted that there is no UN definition of terrorism, and that of course different states might take very different views on the matter; for a recent very extensive definition of what constitutes material support for terrorism, see the US Supreme Court decision in *Holder, Attorney General et al v Humanitarian Law Project et al*, decision of 21 June 2010, available at www.supremecourt.gov/opinions/09pdf/08–1498.pdf; in the European context, and for a much more cautious approach, see Case C-340/08 *M and Others v Her Majesty's Treasury*, judgment of 29 April 2010, nyr.

[9] See eg in Canada the Federal Court ruling in *Abousfian Abdelrazik v The Minister of Foreign Affairs and the Attorney General* (http://decisions.fct-cf.gc.ca/en/2009/2009fc580/2009fc580.html; see also the report from statewatch in relation to a new legal action initiated by Mr Abdelrazik: www.statewatch.org/news/2010/jun/iclmg-terr-list-challenge.pdf), and generally A Tzanakopoulos, 'United Nations sanctions in domestic courts: from interpretation to defiance in Abdelrazik v Canada (Minister of Foreign Affairs)' (2010) 20 *Journal of International Commercial Law* 249; in the UK, see the Supreme Court's ruling in *A, K, M, Q and G v HM Treasury* (www.supremecourt.gov.uk/decided-cases/docs/UKSC_2009_0016_Judgment.pdf), and *Hay v HM Treasury* (www.supremecourt.gov.uk/decided-cases/docs/UKSC_2009_0016_Judgment.pdf); generally see eg the Eighth Report of the Monitoring Team, 'Report of the Analytical Support and Sanctions Monitoring Team pursuant to Resolution 1735(2006) concerning Al-Qaida and the Taliban and associated individuals and entities', especially para 41; and UN Human Rights Council, 'Report of the Special Rapporteur on the promotion and protection of human rights and fundamental freedoms while countering terrorism' (Scheinin Report) A/HRC/6/17, which is very critical of the listing regime. See also A Tzanakopoulos, 'Domestic Court Reactions to UN Security Council Sanctions', SSRN paper, http://papers.ssrn.com/sol3/papers.cfm?abstract_id=1480184.

[10] See Case T-253/02 *Ayadi* ECR II-2139; this was at a time in which, following the CFI's ruling in *Kadi* but before the ECJ's ruling, the validity of inclusion in the EU-derived list could be challenged

However, things have changed since Resolution 1390(2002) was first adopted: individuals affected can now apply for exceptions for essential expenses;[11] and they can make representation directly to a focus point (soon to be replaced by the Ombudsperson),[12] although the decision relating to de-listing rests with the Sanctions Committee. Furthermore, Resolution 1526(2004) established a Monitoring Team;[13] and Resolution 1617(2005) introduced regular reviews of the lists and the obligation for Member States to provide a statement of reasons with the listing request.[14] Finally, Resolution 1904(2009) provides that an Ombudsperson be created to assist the Sanctions Committee in dealing with requests for de-listing. The Ombudsperson shall be an individual of 'high moral character', 'with high qualifications and experience in relevant fields such as legal, human rights, counter-terrorism and sanctions'. The Ombudsperson 'shall be independent and impartial' and will not receive or seek instructions from governments.[15]

The changes brought to the original listing regime are to be welcomed, and demonstrate the problems underlying the assertion of jurisdiction by the Security Council (through its Sanctions Committee) over the direct identification of individuals for reasons of terrorism prevention, rather than for reasons relating to the political situation in a given country. That said, those changes still fall far short of what is required in communities governed by the rule of law and due process. Thus, independent/judicial oversight of the UN decision to identify someone as a suspected terrorist is still excluded, and in this respect the introduction of the Ombudsperson does not change much. Their role will be limited to assisting the Sanctions Committee: the Ombudsperson will not represent the listed person; they will have no power to oblige states to share information or answer queries; and the decision as to delisting is still taken by the Sanctions Committee. For this reason, even following the changes highlighted above, any meaningful protection might only occur at regional or national level,

only under *jus cogens* principles. The ruling in *Ayadi* has been annulled as a result of the *Kadi* ruling in Case C-403/06 P, judgment of 3 December 2009, nyr.

11 *cf* UN Security Council Resolution 1452(2002) para 1.

12 UN Security Council Resolution 1730(2006).

13 Established by UN Security Council Resolution 1526(2004); for the most recent report, see 'Tenth Report of the Analytical Support and Sanctions implementation Monitoring Team submitted pursuant to resolution 1822(2008) concerning Al-Qaida and the Taliban and associated individual entities', S/2009/502. The report discusses the problems arising from national and regional courts' reactions to the lack of judicial review in relation to the listing decisions, and puts forward several alternatives, amongst which are that of a review panel and that of the creation of an Ombudsperson (accepted in SC Resolution 1904(2009)).

14 *cf* UN Security Council Resolution 1617(2005) especially para 3 *et seq*. The narrative summaries of the reasons for listing are public and can be found at www.un.org/sc/committees/1267/narrative.shtml.

15 Resolution 1904(2009) para 20; see also 'EU Presidency declaration on adoption of Security Council Resolution 1904 (2009): Threats to international peace and security caused by terrorist acts', 18 December 2009, 17681 (Presse 383) 140. The first Ombudsperson is Judge Kimberly Prost. See document SC 9947; www.un.org/News/Press/docs//2010/sc9947.doc.htm.

although, of course, such protection would be extremely limited since a national/regional decision has only effects in that jurisdiction and does not give raise to de-listing at UN level.

Having briefly analysed the UN legal regime, it is now time to turn to the EU-specific problems. We will first analyse the implementation of the UN regime and then turn to the EU regime.

III THE UN–EU LISTS AND JUDICIAL REACTIONS: THE RULING IN *KADI*

The EU implemented UN Security Council Resolution 1390(2002), as well as adopting its own lists of individuals and organisations deemed to be associated with terrorism. In the case of the UN-derived list, the Council adopted Common Position 2002/402,[16] which was then implemented through Regulation 881/2002;[17] the identification of those to be included in the list was done directly at UN level and the Council did not consider it had any discretion in implementing the list. For this reason, unlike in the case of the EU list, the task of updating the list was delegated to the Commission. It is in this context that the Court delivered its *Kadi and Al Barakaat* decision, which we will recall briefly.[18]

Kadi is a rich Saudi businessman who was included in the UN list at the request of the USA. He brought proceedings in front of the General Court (then CFI) seeking the annulment of Regulation 881/2002 on grounds of lack of competence and breach of fundamental rights as protected by the general principles of Union law. The General Court found that the Community had competence to adopt the Regulation, and that the EU judiciary lacked competence to assess the compatibility of a Regulation implementing a UN Security Council Resolution with the general principles of Community law, since that would amount to an indirect review of the lawfulness of the UN Security Council Resolution. However, the Court found that it had jurisdiction to assess the

[16] Common Position 2002/402/CFSP concerning restrictive measures against Usama Bin Laden, members of the Al-Qaida organisation and the Taliban and other individuals, groups, undertakings and entities associated with them and repealing Common Positions 96/746/CFSP, 1999/727/CFSP, 2001/154/CFSP and 2001/771/CFSP, [2002] OJ L169/4.

[17] Regulation 881/2002 imposing certain specific restrictive measures directed against certain persons and entities associated with Usama Bin Laden, the Al-Qaida network and the Taliban, and repealing Council Regulation 467/2001/EC prohibiting the export of certain goods and services to Afghanistan, strengthening the flight ban and extending the freeze of funds and other financial resources in respect of the Taliban of Afghanistan [2002] OJ L139/9 (hereinafter 'original Regulation 881/2002'), recently modified by Regulation 1286/2009 [2009] OJ L346/42.

[18] Joined Cases C-402/05 P and C-415/05 P *Kadi and Al Barakaat v Council* [2008] ECR I-6351, reversing the General Court's decisions in Case T-315/01 *Kadi v Council and Commission* [2005] ECR II-3649; Case T-306/01 *Yusuf and Al Barakaat International Foundation v Council and Commission* [2005] ECR II-3533.

compatibility of the Regulation with *jus cogens*, since those principles also bind the Security Council; it then found that no breach had occurred.[19]

On appeal, the European Court of Justice reversed the ruling;[20] whilst it confirmed (with a slightly different line of reasoning) that the Community had competence to adopt Regulation 881/202, it found that the fact that the Regulation implemented a UN Security Council Resolution did not shelter it from review in relation to Community primary law (including the general principles). The ECJ then found that the Council had breached the applicants' fundamental rights, and in particular their right to effective judicial protection, since it had failed to communicate to the applicants the grounds which justified their inclusion in the list. As a result the applicants could not rebut those grounds, and the Court was in a position in which it could not review whether inclusion was justified. Neither could the Council blankly invoke national/international security to justify the absence of a statement of reasons and of the right to be heard since if (some of the) matters relating to the applicants could not be communicated to them, it was for the Community judicature to find a way to balance the procedural rights of those included in the list and security concerns. For these reasons, the Court found that the Council had breached the applicants' rights to be heard as well as their right to an effective legal remedy. The Court also found that, although as a matter of principle the freezing of assets of suspected terrorists was a proportionate limitation to the right to property,[21] in the case at issue the latter had been breached because the essential procedural guarantees (statement of reasons and right to be heard) had not been respected.[22]

A The repercussions of the *Kadi* ruling: the new regime

The ruling in *Kadi* provided a stand-still period of three months to allow the Community institutions to remedy the procedural breaches that had led to the

[19] Case T-315/01 *Kadi v Council and Commission* [2005] ECR II-3649; Case T-306/01 *Yusuf and Al Barakaat International Foundation v Council and Commission* [2005] ECR II-3533.

[20] Joined Cases C-402/05 P and C-415/05 P *Kadi and Al Barakaat v Council* [2008] ECR I-6351.

[21] The Court also held that the 'freezing measure constitutes a *temporary* precautionary measure which is not supposed to deprive those persons of their property', *Kadi* para 358, emphasis added. It is open to debate whether these measures are really temporary.

[22] The *Kadi* ruling gave rise to a wealth of academic commentary; see eg T Tridimas, 'Terrorism and the ECJ: empowerment and democracy in the EC legal order' (2009) 34 *European Law Review* 103; Halberstam and Stein, 'The United Nations, the European Union, and the King of Sweden: Economic sanctions and Individual Right in a Plural World Order', (2009) 46 *Common Market Law Review* 13; Kunoy and Dawes, 'Plate Tectonics in Luxembourg: the Ménage à trois between EC Law, International Law and the European Convention on Human Rights following the UN Sanctions Cases', (2009) 46 CML Rev 73; A Gattini, 'Annotation of *Kadi*', (2009) 46 CML Rev 213; Griller, 'International Law, Human Rights and the European Community's Autonomous Legal Order: Noted on the European Court of Justice Decision in *Kadi*', (2008) 4 *European Community Law Review* 528; G De Búrca, 'The European Union and the International Legal Order after *Kadi*', *Jean Monnet Working Paper* 1/09, www.jeanmonnetprogram.org/papers/09/090101.pdf; and JH Weiler, '*Kadi*: Europe's Meddling', editorial, (2008) 19 *European Journal of International Law* 895.

annulment of the inclusion of Kadi and Al-Barakaat in the list. The names were then reinserted following the adoption of a statement of reasons.[23] More importantly, the *Kadi* ruling raised issues of a general nature: neither the Common Position nor the Regulation provided for the procedural rights deemed by the ECJ essential to render the Community implementation of the sanctions regime compatible with the general principles of Community law. In order to remedy this, the Council adopted Regulation 1286/2009[24] amending Regulation 881/2002. The new regime introduces some significant changes. It might be recalled that the original framework provided little or no discretion in designating those to be included in the list, so that designation by the Sanctions Committee warranted inclusion in the first list; and the Commission was then empowered to amend (with no procedural requirements) the list on the basis of the determinations of the Security Council or the Sanctions Committee. Regulation 881/2002 was then a mere and almost automatic implementation of Security Council Resolution 1390(2002). Whilst the new regime maintains, as a precondition for listing, that the individual/organisation be designated by the Security Council or the Sanctions Committee,[25] the following changes have been introduced:

— The Commission takes a decision as to the inclusion in the Union list *as soon as* the statement of reasons has been provided by the Security Council.[26]
— If the person/organisation, after having seen the statement of reasons, submits observations, the 'Commission *shall review its* decision' and the result of the review shall be communicated to both the person concerned and the Sanctions Committee.[27]
— When reviewing the decision to include someone in the list, the Commission is assisted by a committee and must follow the procedure provided for in Decision 1999/468, ie the comitology procedure for regulatory acts.
— If the United Nations de-lists a person, the Commission shall amend the Union list accordingly.[28]
— In processing data, the Commission must comply with the data protection Regulation.[29]

[23] Regulation 1190/2008 amending for the 101st time Council Regulation 881/2002 [2008] OJ L322/25.

[24] Council Regulation 1286/2009 amending Regulation 881/2002 [2009] OJ L346/42; consolidated version available at http://eur-lex.europa.eu/LexUriServ/LexUriServ.do?uri=CONSLEG:2002R0881:20091226:EN:PDF.

[25] Art 7(a) Regulation 881/2002 as amended by Regulation 1286/2009.

[26] New Art 7(a)(1) Regulation 881/2002; the statement of reasons is that which is publicly available, see new Art 1. It is difficult to understand how the security concerns of Member States, which form such a big part in the submissions to the various courts, can be reconciled with such public statements.

[27] New Art 7(a)(2) Regulation 881/2002.

[28] Art 7(a)5, introduced by Regulation 1286/2009.

[29] Regulation 45/2001 [2001] OJ L8/1.

At first sight, the new regime seems then to include an element of discretion that was not present in the previous system. Originally the Commission would amend the list on the basis of determinations made by the UN Security Council or Sanctions Committee.[30] In the new regime, if the person or entity involved submits observations, the Commission *must* review its decision. Furthermore, both the observations submitted and the outcome of the review must be communicated to the Sanctions Committee.

However, the Regulation is silent both as to the type of review conducted by the Commission and as to the effect of any positive findings.[31] In relation to the former, it is unlikely (although technically possible) that the Commission will engage in a substantive review, not least since it might not have access to the information (beyond the statement of reasons) that led to listing. Thus, any review will most likely be limited to ascertaining the soundness of formal elements, such as possible cases of mistaken identity.[32] In relation to the latter, it is unclear what would be the outcome of a Commission's decision in favour of the individual who submitted observations. The most likely answer is that the Commission would limit itself to submitting its observations to the Sanctions Committee (and possibly to the Ombudsperson) and wait for the former to take a decision as to continued inclusion in the list. If this were to be true, the main improvement in the fundamental rights protection of those listed would stem from the UN changes,[33] and in particular from the obligation to provide a statement of reasons, rather than from the amendments in the Union regime. And yet, the wording introduced in the amended Regulation might be relevant in that it clearly locates the decision to include someone in the Union list with the Commission. This is important, since it endorses (at least formally) the ruling in *Kadi*, and the vision of the relationship between international and Union law therein espoused. If the decision is to be attributed to the Commission then, of

[30] Art 7 Regulation 881/2002, original version.

[31] No light is shed by the most recent of the Notices for the attention of individuals listed in the Regulation where the Commission clarifies that the individuals concerned can at any time request the UN Committee to reconsider its decision to include them in the list, whilst merely restating that individuals can submit observations and request the grounds for their listing to the Commission. See European Commission, 'Notice for the attention of Nayif Bin-Muhammad al-Qahtani and Qasim Yahaya Mahdi al-Rimi, who were added to the list referred to in Article 2, 3 and 7 of Council Regulation (EC) No. 881/2002 … by virtue of Council Regulation (EU) No 450/2010' [2010] OJ C135/10, especially paras 2 and 4.

[32] The Council does not seem to anticipate any exercise of discretion by the EU institutions in deciding to include or exclude someone from the list implementing the UN Sanctions; see 'Guidelines on implementation and evaluation of restrictive measures (sanctions) in the framework of the EU Common Foreign and Security Policy', 15 December 2009, doc no 17464/09, para 36 *et seq*.

[33] Although of course the changes at UN level might have been influenced, if not driven, by the developments at EU level, and particularly by the *Kadi* ruling.

course, it can be challenged should it violate the general principles of Community law; and such a challenge would not amount to a direct or indirect challenge to the Security Council Resolution.[34]

That said, and as we shall see in more detail below, it is open to debate whether the combination of the amended regime and the *Kadi* ruling is sufficient to afford effective protection to the individuals and organisations listed at UN level. Before doing that we will analyse the EU's own lists and the changes brought about in the past few years.

IV THE EU LISTS—THE RULINGS IN *PMOI*

The EU adopted its own list of suspected terrorists, through Common Position 2001/931 and Regulation 2580/2001. Here, according to Article 1(4) of the Common Position, the task of identifying those to be considered as involved in either intra-EU terrorist activity, or in international terrorist activity, falls upon the Council. A precondition for inclusion in the EU list is that a decision has been taken by a 'competent authority' in respect of the individual/organisations concerned. The competent authority in question is a 'judicial authority', or where judicial authorities have no competence, an 'equivalent' authority. The request to include someone in the list can originate from a state outside the EU, and Common Position 2001/931 can also serve as a vehicle for the implementation of UN sanctions against people who the Security Council has identified as being connected to terrorism. According to Common Position 2001/931 the list needs to be reviewed at least every six months.

The original regime presented several problems from a fundamental rights perspective, such as:

— No duty was imposed on the Council to inform those listed of the reasons for inclusion;[35] nor was there any duty for the Council to hear those who had been included in the list.
— There was no duty to indicate which national authority had taken the original decision.
— The constant updating meant that legal challenges, even when successful, would not be of much use, since they would affect decisions that had already been replaced by new decisions.[36]

[34] In this respect *cf* the US regime, where the executive has discretion as to whether or not to implement the measures provided for by Security Council Resolution 1390(2002); see further DS Meyers, 'The Transatlantic divide over the implementation and enforcement of Security Council Resolutions', http://works.bepress.com/cgi/viewcontent.cgi?article=1000&context=daniel_meyers.

[35] See recently Case C-550/09 *E and F*, judgment of 29 June 2010, nyr, where the Court made clear that lacking a statement of reasons, the decision to include someone in the list is illegal and cannot be relied upon, at least for criminal law purposes.

[36] See eg the *OMPI/PMOI* saga: Case T-228/02 *Organisation des Modjahedines du peuple d'Iran (OMPI) v Council* [2006] ECR II-4665, noted C Eckes, (2007) 44 *CML Rev* 1117; Case T-256/07

— The European Court of Justice lacked jurisdiction on the own-terrorist list since those were identified in a Common Position and there was no competence to enact a Regulation freezing their assets.[37]

These systemic problems were worsened by practice; thus, the list was not always updated within the required 6 months,[38] and the requirement that a judicial authority or equivalent must have taken a decision prior to the inclusion in the list was not always met.[39]

It is within this framework then that the General Court (then CFI) imposed some procedural guarantees for those included in the lists and, in particular, the duty for the Council to state reasons (although in order to maintain the 'surprise effect' such statement can postdate the decision to include someone in the list); the right of the parties to make their views known; the need for the Council to clearly identify which authority had taken the original decision so that those affected could challenge it in front of the relevant national court; the need for one such decision having been adopted and communicated; and the need for the authority to be a 'competent' one according to the provisions of Common Position 2001/931.[40] However, the Court also made clear that national courts/authorities would be primarily responsible for the substantive review over the designation of individuals/organisations as terrorists to be included in the list.[41]

In turn, the Council, slowly and perhaps somewhat reluctantly, established a series of changes, although regrettably those have not been incorporated in either

People's Mojahedin Organization of Iran v Council (*PMOI II*) [2008] ECR II-3019; Case T-284/08 *People's Mojahedin Organization of Iran v Council* (*PMOI III*) [2008] ECR II-3487, noted E Spaventa (2009) 46 *CML Rev* 1239.

[37] Although the Court indicated that the Common Position listing own terrorists might in fact be a decision, see Case C-355/04 P *Segi and Others v Council* [2007] ECR I-1657; see generally E Spaventa, 'Remembrance of Principles Lost: on Fundamental Rights, the Third Pillar and the scope of Union Law' (2007) 26 *Yearbook of European Law* 153.

[38] More than a year elapsed between Council Decision 2006/379 implementing Art 2(3) of Regulation (EC) No 2580/2001 on specific restrictive measures directed against certain persons and entities with a view to combating terrorism and repealing Decision 2005/930/EC [2006] OJ L144/21; and Council Decision 2007/445 implementing Art 2(3) of Regulation (EC) No 2580/2001 on specific restrictive measures directed against certain persons and entities with a view to combating terrorism and repealing Decisions 2006/379/EC and 2006/1008/EC [2007] OJ L58; more recently, at the time of writing (2 July 2010), the Council had yet to adopt a new decision, although the six-month period elapsed on 23 June 2010 (last decision Council Implementing Regulation (EU) No 1285/2009 of 22 December 2009 implementing Art 2(3) of Regulation (EC) No 2580/2001 on specific restrictive measures directed against certain persons and entities with a view to combating terrorism and repealing Regulation (EC) No 501/2009 [2009] OJ L346).

[39] See eg Case T-284/08 *People's Mojahedin Organization of Iran v Council* [2008] ECR II-3487 (appeal pending Case C-27/09 P); see also Case T-341/07 *Jose Maria Sison v Council*, judgment of 30 September 2009, nyr.

[40] See generally the *OMPI/PMOI* saga: Case T-228/02 *Organisation des Modjahedines du peuple d'Iran (OMPI) v Council* [2006] ECR II-4665; Case T-256/07 *People's Mojahedin Organization of Iran v Council* (*PMOI II*) [2008] ECR II-3019; Case T-284/08 *People's Mojahedin Organization of Iran v Council* (*PMOI III*) [2008] ECR II-3487.

[41] *PMOI II* (n 40 above) para 131 *et seq.*

the Common Position or in the Regulation, instead being contained in a plethora of documents and decisions.[42] The main amendments are as follows:[43]

— A duty for the Council to state reasons; the statement of reasons needs to be sufficiently detailed as to allow the Union judicature to conduct a review; in particular, it must clarify how the criteria for inclusion in the list required by Common Position 2001/931 have been met (including terrorist acts committed, nature and identification of national authority, and type of decision taken by it).[44]
— A right for those whose assets have been frozen to make their views known.[45]
— A statement alerting those listed of their rights, including the right to bring review proceedings in front of the European Union judicature.[46]

Furthermore, the Council also created the CP 931 WP, a working party entrusted with the implementation of Framework decision 2001/931,[47] replacing the so-called 'clearing house', an ad hoc forum for the implementation of Framework Decision 2001/931.[48] According to its mandate, CP 931 WP examines and evaluates the information relating to listing and delisting, assessing whether it meets the criteria set out in Framework Decision 2001/931, and makes recommendations for listing and de-listing. In particular, the Working Party (whose meetings are classified), following a proposal of designation by a Member Stare or state party, checks compliance with fundamental rights including effective remedy and fair trial, rule of law, presumption of innocence and double jeopardy.[49]

[42] This also means that their legal value is not always clear and that breach, for instance, of the guidelines, would not entail nullity of the decision.

[43] For the most recent state of play, see generally Council, 'Guidelines on implementation and evaluation of restrictive measures (sanctions) in the framework of the EU Common Foreign and Security Policy', doc no 17464/09; CP 931 WP (COCOP)—'Working Party on implementation of Common Position 2001/931/CFSP on the application of specific measures to combat terrorism', COREPER decision of 27 June 2007—declassified doc no 10826/1/07, see also 'Recommendations for dealing with country-specific EU autonomous sanctions or EU additions to UN sanctions lists,' doc no 7697/07; and 'Restrictive Measures: EU Best Practices for the effective implementation of restrictive measures', doc no 10533/06.

[44] CP 931 WP (COCOP) (n 43 above) para 17 et seq.

[45] ibid, para 20.

[46] ibid, para 20.

[47] ibid; for reasons which are not entirely clear to this author, the Council imposes a two-week deadline from publication of the notice in the OJ for requests concerning the statement of reasons (eg Notice for the attention of Hofstadgroep and Communist Party of the Philippines (including New People's Army —NPA) included on the list provided for in Art 2(3) of Council Regulation 2580/2001/EC [2010] OJ C108/7), although the deadline seems to be non-mandatory, as the notice provides that the parties 'should' request the statement within two weeks.

[48] Unfortunately those documents are classified RESTREINT UE, the lowest security classification, but still unavailable in the public domain; for an account, see declassified Council Document 10826/1/07.

[49] This is progress since the General Court indicated in Case T-228/02 *Organisation des Modjahedines du peuple d'Iran (OMPI) v Council*, [2006] ECR II-4665 that it was not for the Council to assess whether the national decision had been adopted with due regard for fundamental rights.

V COUNTER-TERRORISM AND FUNDAMENTAL RIGHTS: ASSESSING THE CHANGES, EVALUATING THE CHALLENGES

The listing regime has undergone significant changes since it was first established: both the UN and the EU own regimes have improved recognising at least some guarantees for those included in the list, and in particular the right to be provided with a statement of reasons. And yet, from a fundamental rights perspective, and possibly from a more general democratic perspective, both systems are far from satisfactory. We will analyse some of the general issues that affect all listing regimes to then turn to the more specific problems faced by the EU own regime.

A The statement of reasons: a reversal of the burden of proof? The UN and UN-derived system

As mentioned above, the introduction of the right to a statement of reason is one of the main improvements in both the UN and EU systems, the (then) CFI and ECJ having played no small part in achieving the latter result (possibly indirectly also on the UN system). However, it should be noted that whilst the statement of reasons allows those listed to know the grounds which led to their inclusion in the list, there is a danger that they might give rise to a reversal of the burden of proof.

Here, there are two, related problems, which are evident when one looks at such statements:[50] first of all, the information contained therein is rather generic and circumstantial,[51] and usually not based on a judicial ruling; this might be natural, given that such information is public and that the secret services might be wary of disclosing too much, lest disclosure should affect their ongoing investigations. And yet, there is no indication that the suspect be provided with more detailed reasons of the case against them.

Secondly, and this is true also for the EU system, there is a danger that the effect of the statement of reasons is to reverse the burden of proof, so that it is for the accused to prove that the facts alleged against him/her are not true or irrelevant, rather than for the governments to prove their case. Of course, the importance of this second objection depends very much on whether the listing of suspects in an international law instrument, and the ensuing asset-freeze, can be qualified as a measure imposing a criminal or semi-criminal sanction. Here, as

[50] The UN statements are publicly available online (www.un.org/sc/committees/1267/narrative.shtml); and it is upon these public statements that the Commission bases its decision to implement the UN Security Council Resolution. The EU statements, on the other hand, are not publicly available; however, for an example, see Case T-341/07 *Sison v Council*, 30 September 2009, para 5, where the statement of reasons against Mr Sison is reproduced.

[51] For the statement in relation to Kadi www.un.org/sc/committees/1267/NSQI02201E.shtml. It seems that there is a certain element of guilt by association, whereby the sole fact of associating with certain individuals might be extremely relevant in determining whether someone is a suspected terrorist.

noted at the very beginning, the national governments have been adamant that the freezing of assets should be considered as an administrative, or civil law, measure. Thus, for instance in the *PMOI* case, the Council and the United Kingdom argued that since the freezing of assets was not a criminal sanction, then:

> it is the *applicant that bears the burden of adducing proof* of its claim that Decision 2007/445 is vitiated by a manifest error of assessment. In this regard the United Kingdom stresses that that decision enjoys a presumption of lawfulness and that the proceedings in which its validity is challenged are *civil proceedings*, with the result that the burden of proof is borne by the applicant and the *standard of proof required is that applicable in civil cases.* Moreover, the legislation applicable nowhere makes provision for any reversal or mitigation of the burden of proof.[52]

In this case, the General Court did not address the matter whilst admittedly, in the preceding *OMPI* case,[53] it seemed to share the Council's view of the nature of the sanction as administrative. Furthermore, Article 75 TFEU which provides for a general competence to impose asset-freeze measures, clearly defines them as 'administrative measures'. To the writer's knowledge, there is no direct authority to supports or rebut the view that an open-ended asset-freeze is a mere administrative measure; this is also due to the fact that traditionally, asset-freezing orders were adopted as a precautionary measure pending criminal investigation or the adjudication of a civil dispute; or as part of a sanction.

In the case of UN freezing orders, the novelty is the separation between a pending case and the measures; and the fact that unlike 'smart' sanctions, the terrorist listing does not pursue international relations/policy aims. Furthermore, inclusion in the UN list is not a provisional, and technically not even a precautionary, measure. It is an open-ended freeze on the assets of those listed; and the only reason for the listing is the government's suspicion over the individual's or the organisation's involvement in a criminal activity (terrorism).[54] The interference with the right to property is very significant (at the time of writing, some of those listed have been unable to access their funds for more than eight years). The consequences of listing are naturally more far-reaching than just the asset-freeze. To then qualify these measures as mere administrative ones, which therefore escape the guarantees afforded by human rights legislation,

[52] *PMOI II* (n 40 above) para 126, emphasis added.

[53] *OMPI* (n 40 above) para 133: 'Next, the Court recognises that, in circumstances such as those of this case, where what is at issue is a temporary protective measure restricting the availability of the property of certain persons, groups and entities in connection with combating terrorism, overriding considerations concerning the security of the Community and its Member States, or the conduct of their international relations, may preclude the communication to the parties concerned of certain evidence adduced against them and, in consequence, the hearing of those parties with regard to such evidence, during the administrative procedure'.

[54] To the author's knowledge, aside from cases of death or incorrect transliteration of Arab names, no person or organisation has been taken off the UN list.

seems rather expedient to the achievement of what is, at the end of the day, a political will to escape the constraints of the standard judicial process.[55]

B How effective is judicial review? The UN derived system

It has been mentioned that there is no system of judicial review at UN level, rather just a right to make representations to the Ombudsperson. Any meaningful judicial review must therefore be sought at national or EU level; in the *Kadi* ruling, the ECJ asserted jurisdiction over the Regulation implementing the Security Council Resolution and made clear that such Regulation could not escape scrutiny in relation to Union primary law, including fundamental rights as protected by the general principles of Union law. As a result, as we have explained before, the Council amended the Regulation to include some procedural guarantees so as to make the system compatible with Union primary law. However, these are only procedural guarantees: it is as yet unclear whether the Court will be willing to engage in any substantive review of the evidence supporting inclusion in the UN-derived system, and be prepared to quash inclusion if such evidence is insufficient.[56] So far, the Union judicature has been unwilling to engage in the substance of the claims relating to listing (even when dealing with the EU's own list).[57] Indeed, any substantive review would be fraught with difficulties, both procedurally, since the rules of procedure of the Union judicature are ill-equipped to deal with proceedings on these issues,[58] and having regard to the extremely sensitive nature of the evidence presented. Thus, it should be remembered that evidence in relation to those proceedings often originates from a foreign state which might be unwilling (or legally barred) from sharing it in foreign judicial proceedings. So it might be difficult, if not impossible, for the Court to engage in a substantial review of the reasons which led to the listing of the suspect. Other national courts have taken the view that the freezing orders can be upheld only after sufficient evidence has been provided:[59] it would be open to the Court to follow this route. Otherwise, the Court would have to declare that the public summary of the statement of reasons is enough to justify consequences of such magnitude as an open-ended suspension of the right to property.

[55] In relation to the EU own listing, the position is somehow different, and will be analysed in detail below.

[56] Another related issue is whether the standard of proof required would be the criminal law one or not; some light might be shed in the new *Kadi* case, pending case T-85/09 *Kadi v Council*.

[57] See discussion in the next section.

[58] In *Kadi* the Court indicated that it would be prepared to find ways in which to balance the procedural rights of the applicants with the sensitive nature of the evidence in question (para 344).

[59] See eg Turkey.

C The EU lists

In relation to the EU's own list, the problems are similar but the solutions are different, and possibly some real improvements are in sight. It might be recalled that the decision to include an individual or an organisation in the EU list is taken following the decision of a competent authority, ie a judicial authority or equivalent. Initially, and before the intervention of the Union judicature, the listing was characterised by both secrecy and lack of any procedural guarantee. Those listed would not be informed as to why they had been listed; nor would they know which national authority requested their inclusion in the Union list. However, and as briefly mentioned above, the General Court progressively imposed a number of essential procedural requirements for the listing to be compatible with Union law (statement of reasons, including the information about the requesting national authority; and right to be heard). This said, those requirements, welcomed as they might have been, are just procedural requirements; so far, the General Court (and the ECJ) have been unwilling to conduct a review on the substantive reasons that might have led to inclusion in the list. Rather, the General Court indicated that the first and main port of call for those seeking to challenge the substantive grounds for inclusion is the national authority/court.[60] I have argued elsewhere that this 'Pontius Pilate approach' is deeply unsatisfactory, since it is for Union judicature alone to assess the legitimacy of Union acts;[61] and only those who are involved in 'terrorist acts' as defined in Common Position 2001/931 can be included in the list. There is no reason then why the Court should abdicate its interpretative and judicial duty to review whether there is sufficient evidence to include someone or a group in the list.

This said, there might be signs that whilst formally the Court's approach has not changed, the review over whether the formal requirements of Common Position 2001/931 have been met is becoming more intense. Thus, in the *PMOI 2* ruling, the Court finally annulled the inclusion of the PMOI in the EU list since it found that no competent authority for the purposes of Common Position 2001/931 had adopted a decision in relation to the organisation.[62] As a result, the PMOI was struck off the list. More recently, the General Court gave more guidance as to what is to be considered a decision of a competent authority for the purposes of EU law. In the case of *Sison II*,[63] the Council had included Mr

[60] *PMOI I* (n 40 above) paras 131 *et seq.*

[61] E Spaventa, 'Annotation on the *PMOI* cases' (2009) 46 CML Rev 1239.

[62] Originally, the PMOI had been included at the request of the UK; however, following a successful challenge at national level, the PMOI was struck off the UK list; the French authorities then decided to request the listing of the organisation; see Spaventa, 'Annotation on the PMOI cases' (n 61 above) for the details.

[63] Case T-341/07 *Sison v Council*, 30 September 2009. The *Sison* saga has been a long-running affair, starting in 2003 when Mr Sison was included in the list (also following pressure from the USA), and has given rise to several cases: in Case T-47/03, *Sison v Council* [2007] ECR II-73, the Council

Sison in the EU list on two grounds: in reviewing Mr Sison's asylum application, Dutch courts had found that refusal had been legitimate because of Mr Sison's (suspected) involvement with two organisations responsible for several terrorist attacks in the Philippines; and the US had defined him as a 'global terrorist'.[64] The Court proceeded to an extensive analysis of the Dutch rulings and it found that those could not be considered as 'decisions' of competent authorities for the purposes of Union law, since neither rulings contained a condemnation for terrorist attacks; and, there was no decision to initiate investigations or proceedings for a terrorist act. Thus, the Court made clear that a decision for the purposes of Common Position 2001/931:

> must, if the Council is to be able validly to invoke it, form part of national proceedings seeking, *directly* and *chiefly*, the imposition on the person concerned of measures of a preventive or punitive nature, in connection with the combating of terrorism and by reason of that person's involvement in terrorism. That requirement is *not* satisfied by a decision of a national judicial authority ruling only *incidentally* and *indirectly* on the possible involvement of the person concerned in such activity, in relation to a dispute concerning, for example, rights and duties of a civil nature.[65]

Thus, the Court not only takes a narrow interpretation of what constitutes a decision for the purposes of Union law, but also seems to give significant weight to the fact that the national courts/authorities, who had access to the security file on Mr Sison, had taken the decision *not* to open an investigation on Mr Sison or to instigate a prosecution of the applicant. Thus, the Court held that if police or security enquiries are closed without any judicial consequences, the Council must take account of such developments

> which form part of the body of information having to be taken into account in order to assess the situation … To decide otherwise would be tantamount to giving the Council and the Member States the *excessive* power to freeze a person's funds indefinitely, beyond review by any court and whatever the result of any judicial proceedings taken.[66]

decision was annulled on procedural grounds but the General Court also confirmed that it would not go beyond a procedural review (see para 206: 'Because the Community judicature may not, in particular, substitute its assessment of the evidence, facts and circumstances justifying the adoption of such measures for that of the Council, the review carried out by the Court of First Instance of the lawfulness of decisions to freeze funds must be restricted to checking that the rules governing procedure and the statement of reasons have been complied with, that the facts are materially accurate, and that there has been no manifest error of assessment of the facts or misuse of power. That limited review applies, especially, to the assessment of the considerations of appropriateness on which such decisions are based.') In Case T-110/03 *Sison v Council* [2005] ECR II-1429 the Court denied access to documents under Regulation 1049/2001 regarding public access to European Parliament, Council and Commission documents (2001) OJ L145/43 (confirmed in appeal Case C-266/05).

[64] During the course of the procedure, the Council held that the two judicial decisions were the only decisions 'of competent authorities' for the purposes of Common Position 2001/931.

[65] Case T-341/07 *Sison v Council*, para 111; emphasis added.

[66] ibid, para 116; emphasis added.

The *Sison II* ruling might indeed solve most of the problems of judicial protection in relation to the EU by clarifying that the listing at EU level might only be adopted as:

(i) a precautionary measure following the instigation of investigation for terrorist related crime; or
(ii) following judicial findings to the effect that the person or organisation concerned is involved or has been involved in terrorist activity.

The restrictive interpretation of what is a national decision that might trigger inclusion in the list could strike a reasonable balance between the rights of suspects and the need for effective European mechanisms to fight terrorism. This does not mean that *all* problems would be solved, since standards of fundamental rights and judicial protection vary considerably both within and outside the EU.[67] Yet, in the writer's opinion, the *Sison II* ruling signals a true turning point in ensuring the rights of those included in the list. Furthermore, its scope of application should bind the Council also in relation to the list concerning acts of terrorisms internal to the EU, even though for the time being the Court has no jurisdiction over it.[68]

VI CONCLUDING REMARKS

There can be no doubt that the terrorist attacks against the USA first, and Spain and the UK later,[69] have changed the international landscape profoundly. The new terrorist threat, which in many ways is characterised by its borderless and stateless nature, has naturally provoked a significant surge in international, supranational and national action aimed at more effectively countering what is perceived as a global emergency at the top of many a political agenda. And, it is clear that in the era of globalisation, characterised by ease of cross-border movement and ease in communications, a coordinated approach to international terrorism might be essential. Yet, whilst the end is not disputed, the means that have been chosen to achieve it are extremely problematic, and possibly ineffective and even counter-productive.[70] It is in this context that the judicial resistance to

[67] In this respect, and as noted above, the fact that the CP 931 working party also needs to check compliance with fundamental rights at national level before recommending listing is also progress and goes beyond what was suggested by the General Court in the *OMPI* case.

[68] This is at least until such time as a preliminary reference will be made enquiring as to the true nature of the Third Pillar part of the Common Position which, as hinted at by the Court in SEGI, seems to be more akin to a decision.

[69] Of course many other countries (eg Egypt, Pakistan) have suffered similar attacks; and yet there is no denying that as a matter of impact on the geopolitical situation, the attacks against the US first and Europe later are the most significant.

[70] For a detail criticism of the effect of the UN terrorist sanctions see the Scheinin Report (n 9 above).

those measures should be assessed: after all, far from being parochial,[71] such judicial resistance has provided the main impetus for gradual, but steady, change. And, there is no denying that both the UN and the EU systems have improved dramatically. Nevertheless, the situation is far from ideal: in relation to the UN listing, still only national and EU fora can guarantee effective judicial protection, with all the problems that that will entail. That said, it is to be hoped that the Ombudsperson will not shy away from her responsibilities and be willing, when necessary, to apply pressure on the Sanctions Committee and Security Council. It is also to be hoped that the UN Member States will be willing to cooperate fully with the Ombudsperson's requests. As far as the EU is concerned, the extent to which fundamental rights will be effectively protected will depend very much on the Union judicature's willingness to engage in a substantive review of the reasons that led to listing. In this respect, the courts should remember that the improvements to the existing system have been the direct result of the national and European courts' reluctance to provide executives acting in an international forum with a blank cheque in relation to fundamental rights. Refraining from engaging with the problem will not lead to change, nor will it make the problem go away. Finally, in relation to the EU's own listing, we might have reached a point of equilibrium between the need to coordinate anti-terrorist action and the need to ensure that terrorist listing is not used by executives to pursue their own political agendas. For the first time since 2001, a mild optimism seems to be appropriate.

[71] See G De Burca 'The European Court of Justice and the International Legal Order After *Kadi*' Jean Monnet Working Paper 01/09.

6

The EU and Energy Security: a Critical Review of the Legal Issues

PETER D CAMERON

I INTRODUCTION

EVER SINCE ITS inception, the European Union (EU) has been acutely aware of the economic and social risks that accompany its dependence on imports of oil and gas.[1] Energy is a key input for all of the EU economies and is widely used among the industrial, residential and transport sectors. If successful, the present transition to a low carbon economy should reduce the large-scale dependence on fossil fuels. However, the perception of this dependence remains a formative influence on EU external relations policy. It is a volatile factor, in part because of the lack of much theorising about 'energy security'.[2] In practice, the potentially wide-ranging notion of 'energy security' has tended to be defined narrowly in EU debates in terms of the security of supply of fossil fuels from neighbouring states, many of which do not share the EU's liberal democratic values and commitment to a market economy. The risk factor is increased further by the fact that countries such as Russia, Algeria or those in the Middle East region are not amenable to the incentive of future membership of the EU, reducing further the EU's leverage. In the energy sector, other 'security' considerations than supply, such as the guarantee of regular, uninterrupted supplies of energy (electricity mainly) in the context of a liberalising internal market for energy, or in the event of a technical mishap in the EU, have been largely contained.[3] Indeed, very few emergencies have ever materialised, but the risks to energy security in the EU have increased significantly in the past decade, a fact

[1] For example, the Protocol of Agreement between Member States on energy problems in 1964: [1964] OJ 1009; Council doc 1014/67 (decision on Community policy concerning oil and gas).

[2] B Barton, C Redgwell, A Rønne and DN Zillman (eds), *Energy Security: Managing Risk in a Dynamic Legal and Regulatory Environment* (Oxford, Oxford University Press, 2004) 5.

[3] 'The process of market opening in the European Union started at a time with, generally speaking, excess reserve capacity in the system. One of the consequences of market opening and the drive for more efficiency in the sector is a closure of this excess capacity.' DG TREN Note, 'Measures to secure electricity supply,'16 January 2004 (cited in PD Cameron, *Competition in Energy Markets: Law and Regulation in the European Union,* 2nd edn (Oxford, Oxford University Press, 2007) 520. The measures taken to address the possible negative effects of market opening comprised two Directives:

that is reflected in the text of the Lisbon Treaty and Commission proposals for secondary legislation. According to Article 194(1)(b) of the Treaty on the Functioning of the European Union, EU policy on energy 'shall aim, in a spirit of solidarity between Member States, to … ensure security of energy supply in the Union'.[4] Since that was drafted, however, supply and transit risks have further increased with respect to the fuel that has become more strategically sensitive than oil for many Member States: natural gas from Russia. This geopolitical dimension has come to present the gravest threat of short-term disruptions to EU energy supply and a major challenge to the development of legal mechanisms to mitigate that risk. It was dramatically underlined by a single emergency or crisis event in particular: the major interruption of gas flows from Russia to Europe in the early months of 2009.

The role of law in providing the basis for 'energy security' in the EU has been little appreciated, particularly in relation to imports of fossil fuels.[5] Several kinds of law have been tried and tested by the Russo-Ukrainian gas disputes of 2006 and 2009: specifically, an international legal instrument, a regional multilateral instrument involving non-EU states and the EU, and EU law itself. The 2009 emergency (described below), created by a drastic reduction of gas flows across Ukraine to Europe, has precipitated extensive debate and several legal proposals to limit the EU's risks in future years. It will be argued that the failure of the principal multilateral instrument, the Energy Charter Treaty, to deliver energy security, has been offset by a significant increase in the monitoring and regulatory activities of the European Commission as a result of post-crisis EU legal initiatives. These fit into a pattern of increasing willingness of Member States to demonstrate solidarity and accept legal measures to defend what are clearly common interests. This breaks with a long tradition in which Member States have preferred to retain powers to address an emergency at the national level, to be exercised in close cooperation with large energy companies.

II THE ORIGINS OF MULTILATERAL LEGAL COOPERATION

The demise of the Soviet Union in 1991 opened up the possibility of enhancing energy cooperation between the EU and the key energy states in the East. For

Directive (EC) 2005/89 concerning measures to safeguard security of electricity supply and infrastructure investment [2006] OJ L 33/22, and Directive (EC) 2004/67 concerning measures to safeguard security of natural gas supply [2004] OJ L 127/92.

[4] The Treaty of Lisbon amending the Treaty Establishing the European Union and the Treaty Establishing the European Community, Cm 7294 (TSO); Title XX: Energy, Art 176A.1(c) (hereinafter Lisbon Treaty).

[5] A notable exception is the comprehensive overview of EU external relations policy in relation to energy security by SS Haghighi, *Energy Security: the External Relations of the European Union with Major Oil and Gas Supplying Countries* (Oxford, Hart Publishing, 2007). However, this work was completed before the Russo-Ukrainian gas dispute.

practical purposes, this was limited to Russia, Turkmenistan, Azerbaijan and Kazakhstan, as producers, but also Ukraine as the key state for the transit of gas from Russia to the EU. At that time, the idea that such cooperation could be brought about by a broad, multilateral treaty embracing as its parties all of the states of Europe and the former Soviet Union, appeared far from fanciful. It was a time when much collaborative treaty-making appeared possible among nation-states and a new international economic order based on market principles appeared to be imminent. The North American Free Trade Agreement (NAFTA) was emerging, as was the World Trade Organisation (WTO), and from the early 1990s onwards, there was an unprecedented expansion in the conclusion of bilateral investment treaties (BITs) among states. In this context, the EU backed a proposal for an international energy treaty called the Energy Charter Treaty (ECT).

The advantage to the EU of such an international treaty was that it offered the prospect of a set of ground rules for energy trade and transit across a very large common European space. European law itself failed to provide any such guarantees, since it did not bind any of the new states of Central and Eastern Europe at that time. A new multilateral instrument with strong EU support appeared to offer a way of overcoming the limitations of EU law in providing for energy security.

The ECT was signed by some 50 states and the European Communities on 17 December 1994.[6] Its purpose is:

> to establish a legal framework in order to promote long-term co-operation in the energy field, based on complementaries and mutual benefits, in accordance with the objectives and principles of the [European Energy] Charter.[7]

The ECT's scope is wide: in a geographical sense, it is essentially pan-European; in an economic sense, it includes different kinds of market or market-oriented systems; and in a legal sense, it incorporates a wide range of legal commitments, both of the 'hard' and the 'soft' law variety. It entered into force in April 1998, three months after ratification by the required number of 30 states. It has been ratified by all of the EU states and may be seen as part of the *acquis communautaire* or legal order in energy. It has also been ratified by all the new EU Member States (such as Poland and Hungary), and most of the countries in the former Soviet Union, as well as Turkey.

[6] *cf*, Final Act of the European Energy Charter Conference [1998] OJ L69/1, 69/5–69/114. The Treaty and the related Protocol on Energy Efficiency and Environmental Relations entered into force on 16 April 1998, following the deposit of the 30th instrument of ratification on 16 January 1998. See *The Energy Charter Treaty and Related Documents* (Brussels, Energy Charter Secretariat, 1996) (hereinafter ECT). The initiative behind the Treaty lay originally with the Dutch Government's 'Lubbers Declaration' of June 1990.

[7] ECT, Art 2.

The ECT creates rights and obligations in international law for all of its contracting parties.[8] It applies to both East–West and West–East transactions. Its scope comprises 'energy materials and products'. It is principally concerned with the promotion and protection of investment, trade, and the transit of energy goods. Other subjects covered by the ECT are either supportive of the provisions on these matters, or have a lesser significance.

Crucially, the ECT was never ratified by Russia. Its absence limited the scope of the ECT and, more importantly, its authority. In 2009 Russia formally indicated its intention not to ratify the ECT, removing any doubt about its intentions, and with it any last hope that the EU may have had that the ECT might have contributed to the stabilisation by law of the often volatile relations with Russia. A little earlier, on 20 April 2009 President Medvedev of Russia had announced a proposal for an alternative international energy treaty to the ECT which would cover similar subject matter to that in the ECT, but which would have a wider membership and would presumably replace it. The document asserts that the 'existing bilateral arrangements and multilateral legally binding norms governing international energy relations have failed to prevent and resolve conflict situations, which makes it necessary to efficiently improve the legal framework of the world trade in energy resources'.[9] This is a clear reference to the ECT's lack of presence in a number of disputes, such as the transit dispute several months earlier between Russia and Ukraine.

No steps appear to have been taken by the EU to support a successor treaty instrument with Russia with the kind of scope that President Medvedev envisages. However, a more regional approach has indeed been adopted by the EU to address energy and other kinds of security concerns.

[8] The origin of the Treaty lies in a non-binding Declaration signed by 50 states and the European Community three years earlier on 17 December 1991, called the European Energy Charter, based on an initiative of Prime Minister Ruud Lubbers of the Netherlands in 1990. The primary aim of the project was 'to give political support to the democratic process in the former centrally-planned economies. The welfare of these countries' population would benefit from a properly managed supply and from an influx of Western investment attracted by a stable free market system. The resulting improvement in conditions of life would underpin the evolution towards a democratic society.' J Dore and R De Bauw, *The Energy Charter Treaty: Origins, Aims and Prospects* (London, Royal Institute of Int'l Affairs, 1995) 2. The aims of the Charter Declaration were to: improve security of supply; maximise efficiency of production, conversion, transport, distribution, and use of energy; enhance safety; and minimise environmental problems. For a comprehensive collection of materials on the ECT, see TW Waelde (ed), *The Energy Charter Treaty: An East-West Gateway for Investment and Trade* (The Hague, Kluwer International, 1996).

[9] Para 2. The official text in English was published on 21 April 2009. The reference to bilateral 'legally binding norms' is ironic. Russia is a capital exporting country and Russian companies increasingly invest abroad, where they rely upon the familiar legal guarantees in BITs and dispute settlement by international arbitration. The 2009 Russia-Venezuela BIT, for example, contains an arbitration clause with (at the choice of the investor) three options including ad hoc arbitration under UNCITRAL Rules; a state court in the host state; and, for the first time in a Venezuelan BIT, the Stockholm Chamber of Commerce. It also includes a compensation provision in the event of expropriation. See the TDM Knowledge Bank under 'Venezuela'. Available at, www.transnational-dispute-management.com.

III REGIONAL COOPERATION

The regional approach is exemplified by the Treaty establishing an Energy Community for South-East Europe, which was signed on 25 October 2005 in Athens.[10] Initially, it was designed to establish a regional electricity market in South-East Europe. However, from the end of 2005 it was charged with assisting in the creation of a regional gas market. The 34 signatory states are the 25 EU Member States and the Balkan States of Albania, Bosnia and Herzegovina, Bulgaria, Croatia, the Former Yugoslav Republic of Macedonia, Montenegro, Romania, Serbia and UNMIK Kosovo. Moldova, Ukraine and Norway have observer status, while discussions with Turkey on its participation are ongoing.

The basis for the structure of the Energy Community Treaty was the European Coal and Steel Community (ECSC) Treaty.[11] Like the ECSC Treaty, it has its origins in post-war reconstruction and the identification of a key economic sector on which to base a legally binding scheme for cooperation. Although these countries are not members of the EU, the Treaty will act as a vehicle for the gradual transfer to these countries of the *acquis communautaire* in key areas: not only energy, but also competition and environmental matters. The Treaty is also designed to create regional mechanisms that extend into the EU to allow for a deeper integration of local energy markets, especially by means of accelerated infrastructure development.

IV EU ENERGY LAW AND SECURITY

An alternative approach to energy security which the EU has adopted is to take specific legislative measures for application within the EU Member States. However sensible this approach seems, it is one that is likely to provoke opposition from both the energy industry (which fears a new layer of regulation) and many of the Member States (which fear an erosion of their own competences in this area). As a result, the initial version of energy security legislation which emerged with respect to the gas industry in 2004[12] had only a modest impact.

The Directive had three objectives: to establish a common framework in which Member States would define general, transparent and non-discriminatory security of supply policies compatible with the requirements of a competitive internal gas market; to clarify the general roles and responsibilities of the different market players; and to implement specific non-discriminatory procedures to safeguard security of gas supply. It moved away from reliance purely upon Member State

[10] Available at ec.europa.eu/energy/electricity/south_east/treaty_en.htm.

[11] 'The Energy Community Treaty was consciously modelled on the European Coal and Steel Community that is the basis of the European Union'. Commission Press Release MEMO/05/397, 'An integrated market for electricity and gas across 34 European Countries,' 25 October 2005, 2.

[12] Directive (EC) 2004/67 concerning measures to safeguard security of natural gas supply [2004] OJ L127/92 (hereinafter Gas Security Directive).

bodies or industry by establishing a new body with the rather harmless name, the Gas Coordination Group (GCG), and by enhancing the monitoring powers of the Commission. The GCG's aim is to facilitate the co-ordination of security of supply measures at European level in the event of a major supply disruption. It is composed of representatives of the Member States and representative bodies of the industries concerned as well as relevant consumers, with the EU as chair. The detailed workings of the GCG are set out in Article 9. Essentially, the trigger for action is the occurrence of an event that is likely to develop into a 'major supply disruption' for a significant period of time. Such a disruption is defined as a situation where the Union would risk the loss of more than 20 per cent of its gas supply from third countries, and the situation at European level is not likely to be adequately managed with national measures.[13] The foreseeable length of such a supply disruption should cover a significant period of time, which the Directive places at a minimum of eight weeks.[14] Alternatively, Member States may indicate to the Chair of the GCG that an event or events of magnitude and exceptional character have occurred which they consider to be incapable of adequate management with national measures alone.[15] In either case, the Commission shall convene the GCG as soon as possible at its own initiative or at the request of a Member State. Prior to the formal transposition date of the Directive, the GCG was convened to consider the events arising from the suspension of gas deliveries from Russia to Ukraine on 1 January 2006, which resulted in a shortfall in gas deliveries to certain EU Member States.[16] The GCG is also required to examine and, where appropriate, assist the Member States in coordinating the measures taken at national level to deal with major supply disruption.[17]

The Directive expanded the powers of the EU through the introduction of reporting requirements in Article 5. Monitoring is to be carried out by the EU on the basis of the reports it receives, and includes monitoring of new long-term gas supply import contracts from third countries. This may lead the EU to conclude that EU gas supplies will be insufficient to meet foreseeable gas demand in the long-term, and submit proposals as a result.

V THE EMERGENCY

Faced with an emergency, how would these legal instruments work? In 2009 the Russo-Ukrainian gas crisis provided the context in which they could be tested.

[13] ibid, Art 2(2).

[14] ibid, Rec 17.

[15] ibid, Art 9(1).

[16] Due to a dispute between Russia and Ukraine on gas deliveries, Gazprom reduced the flow into pipelines crossing Ukraine by the amount that would otherwise have been for Ukrainian use, leaving it at the level Russia is contracted to supply to its other (EU) customers. However, these customers immediately noticed a fall in their gas supply. Russia blamed this on Ukraine.

[17] Gas Security Directive, Art 9(2). The Group should also exchange information on security of gas supply on a regular basis. Ibid, Rec 15.

On 1 January 2009, Russia suspended gas supplies to Ukraine, but continued transit supplies to the European Union (EU). In practice, this meant that gas supplies from Central Asia via Russia to Ukraine were stopped. On 6 January all supplies to or through Ukraine were suspended, affecting 18 other European countries in the middle of winter. A remarkable feature of this crisis was that once the Ukrainian transport network was closed to deliveries of Russian gas, Naftogaz (the Ukrainian state gas company) reversed the flow of gas in the system, to transport gas from Ukraine's storage facilities in the west to the major consuming areas in the south and east of the country. As one commentator has noted, 'This reversal of one of the world's largest gas transit networks was unprecedented. It seems hard to believe that it could have been undertaken spontaneously, which suggests that, whichever side precipitated the shutdown, Naftogaz' engineers had prepared for it.'[18] When Gazprom, the Russian national gas company, indicated on 12 January that it was prepared to resume gas supplies into part of the pipeline, the offer was not accepted by Ukraine, probably because to have done so would have required it to cease the flow reversal to its large population centres in eastern Ukraine.

The crisis came to an end on 19 January when the respective governments signed an agreement. The crisis would have been more severe if gas demand had not been reduced by the impact of the recession on EU economies. In the event, strategic storage facilities were not used for emergency supplies, and flows of gas were reversed to ensure that supplies were directed where needed, an unusual technical measure. Nonetheless, the crisis dealt a significant blow to the EU Member States' sense of supply security, reminiscent of the Arab oil embargo several decades previously. As a result, it triggered a series of energy security responses that are (with respect to gas at least) more focused than anything that has emerged from the EU in recent years.

In the European Commission's view, the January 2009 gas disruptions:

> resulted in the most serious gas supply crisis to hit the EU in its history, depriving EU Member States of 20% of their gas supplies (30% of imports). Coinciding with a cold spell in many parts of Europe, it demonstrated the vulnerability of the EU and some of its Member States to gas disruption and resulted in important economic repercussions in a number of EU Member States. Within days of the supply interruption of 6 January, a total of 12 Member States and Member Countries of the Energy Community were affected. It was also clear that the interruption could not be resolved by individual EU companies or TSO's alone.[19]

Of course, these dramatic events had a history. The pattern of gas supply and transit and indeed the origins of the recent disputes between Russia and Ukraine have their basis in the joined land-based pipeline infrastructure set up during the

[18] S Pirani, J Stern, and K Yafimava, *The Russo-Ukrainian gas dispute of January 2009: a comprehensive assessment* (Oxford, Oxford Institute of Energy Studies, 2009) 23–24.

[19] Commission, 'The January 2009 gas supply disruption to the EU: an assessment', (Staff Working Document) COM (2009) 363, 8.

time of the USSR. With the collapse of that political system, this unified internal pipeline system for transport and storage of gas was divided into separate ownership among newly independent states, but all of the pipelines had their source in the Russian Federation. This development has created a situation of lasting mutual dependence for as long as Russia seeks to transit gas through Ukraine for sale to Europe, where its customers are willing to pay in hard currency for gas imports and at a level much higher than Russian domestic customers. It is an infrastructure that also binds all other gas producing states, such as Turkmenistan, Kazakhstan and Uzbekistan, to its Russian centre. At present, to reach markets for gas exports, the gas has to be transited through Russian pipelines at rates to be negotiated between the parties. History has also left a legacy of state-owned gas companies, closely controlled by their respective governments, in all of the successor states as the norm in corporate organisation,[20] and a set of problems arising from the subsidised pricing of gas that was common during the Soviet era. Disputes about transit quickly become intensely politicised as a result. In this respect, there are clear differences with the Anglo-American tradition of private ownership in the gas industry, but not with the approach taken in much of continental Europe or even in Germany where a close relationship between the privately owned gas utilities and governments has been evident for many years. Another legacy was the continuation for a number of years of barter practices in gas trade and a degree of opacity that encouraged the establishment of intermediary companies, often with high-level political involvement. These aspects of gas trading have ensured a degree of complexity and controversy among many former communist states, but are especially evident in the gas industries in Ukraine and Russia and their mutual relations.

The strategic character of Ukraine in the post-Soviet transit system cannot be understated. About 80 per cent of the gas which Russia exports to the EU is carried by pipeline across Ukraine, Belarus and Moldova. Of this 80 per cent, as much as 70 per cent of the gas transits Ukraine alone. For Europe as a whole, the stakes are very serious: about 20 per cent of its gas supply passes through Ukraine. The main vehicles for the states' interest in the gas industry are Gazprom (the Russian state gas company) and Naftogaz (Ukraine).

However, the traffic and the management of the revenues is complicated by the fact that each country has a double role: as supplier and transit country (Russia), and consumer and transit country (Ukraine). For the foreseeable future, the revenues accruing to the supplier and the transit country from this traffic are dependent upon the conclusion of mutually satisfactory contractual relationships. The difficulties in achieving this were evident from the interruptions to gas supplies from Russia to the EU in January 2006[21] and again, but more

[20] The state companies may nonetheless represent a reorganised version of the state structures of the Soviet era, with Gazprom being a notable example of this.

[21] For an account of this, see J Stern, *The Russian-Ukrainian gas crisis of January 2006* (Oxford, Oxford Institute of Energy Studies, 2006).

seriously, in January to March 2009.[22] Some of these difficulties lie in the practice of contracting prices and volumes on an annual basis by the companies concerned within a framework set by inter-governmental agreements that involve decision-making by both commercial entities and the respective government (discussed below). This inter-dependence in energy trade and the combination of politics with commercial decision-making have also been evident in relations between Russia and other former Soviet countries, but the volumes of gas traded are much less in such cases, and the number of third parties is far fewer. As a result, they have attracted less attention, but there too in both gas and oil supply and transit, disputes have been evident between Russia and its neighbours involving cut-offs of gas supplies from time to time, such as Belarus in 2004 and 2007 and Ukraine in 2006 and again in 2009.[23]

Another source of complications is the high degree of politicisation of the gas industry in most former Soviet Union countries. Russia and Ukraine are vivid illustrations of this close relationship between company and state. The respective gas companies, Gazprom and Naftogaz, have several features in common. First, the companies responsible for supply, (some, in Russia's case) production and transit are state-owned and subject to fairly tight state control. Many of the contracts for supply and transit are negotiated, and in the event of disputes are managed, at the highest political level: the signature of key contract documents by prime ministers and presidents is often required. Stabilisation in commercial relations has therefore been attempted through the use of inter-governmental agreements. There has been little need for contract stabilisation in the usual sense, although arm's-length arbitration mechanisms are available (not least the ECT, but also contractual mechanisms), but are usually not favoured, and preference is given to the use of diplomacy. Secondly, private investors that contract with either state supplier of gas will find themselves quickly entering a highly politicised arena. In addition to the highly politicised character of decision-making, there is a wide range of countries involved in production as well as supply. For example, the gas that is subject to these contracts is produced and consumed over a wide range of states, including Turkmenistan and Azerbaijan as sources of gas supply and EU and South Eastern European states as consumers of the gas. Thirdly, both companies have since 1991 been engaged in a transition to some form of market-oriented organisation of their business affairs, located firmly within an overall transition of their respective economies. This has

[22] The events are examined in some detail by S Pirani, J Stern and K Yafimava, *The Russo-Ukrainian gas dispute of January 2009* (Oxford, Oxford Institute of Energy Studies, 2009).

[23] A recent example of this is the case of Central Asian countries dependent upon supplies from Uzbekistan. Deliveries to Kyrgyzstan and Tajikistan were suspended in September 2009 when their state gas companies failed to pay outstanding debts of around US$18 million each. This is not the first time that Uzbekistan has taken such action. Inevitably, there are wider national interest considerations that may have influenced its choice of instrument as a response to the indebtedness of its customers. For example, Kyrgyzstan is trying to develop hydro-electricity as a way of reducing its dependence on imported gas, with possible consequences for future sales of water to Uzbekistan.

ensured that commercial issues such as prices, transit tariffs and payments by consumers have been matters of the greatest importance for the economic viability of the respective companies.

VI THE ENERGY CHARTER TREATY AS A SECURITY MECHANISM

The broad aims of the ECT were to depoliticise disputes on transit and facilitate the flows of energy in the event of a dispute. Article 7 contains rules on: non-discriminatory passage with no distinction allowed as to origin, destination or ownership of products or materials; non-discriminatory pricing; absence of unreasonable delays, restrictions or charges; modernisation of infrastructure; non-interruption of transit in case of dispute; and clear dispute and conciliation procedures. In the event of a dispute over transit, it expressly requires in Article 7(7):

> A Contracting Party through whose Area Energy Materials and Products transit shall not, in the event of a dispute over any matter arising from that Transit, interrupt or reduce, permit any entity subject to its control to interrupt or reduce, or require any entity subject to its jurisdiction to interrupt or reduce the existing flow of Energy Materials and Products prior to the conclusion of the dispute resolution procedures set out in Article 7(7).[24]

The teeth required to make such a soft obligation effective are contained in a set of procedural requirements for transit disputes set out in Article 7(7). However, these requirements may only enter into operation when 'all relevant contractual or other dispute resolution remedies previously agreed between the Contracting Parties party to the dispute' or the companies involved in the dispute, have been exhausted. In itself, this is a major limitation to the operation of the ECT provisions on conciliation. Such remedies may be time-consuming, and an interruption to gas supplies may occur and continue in the meantime, without the ECT procedures ever being able to commence. The provision itself is worded in such a way that it is comprehensive: it requires all relevant contractual or other remedies to be exhausted. The highly political character of this kind of gas trade should be recalled here. In addition to (and sometimes instead of) the kind of gas contractual arrangements that are commonly found in gas trade, there will often be protocol instruments or bilateral agreements between the respective governments. Remedies for dispute settlements may be located in a diverse range of documents made between the respective states and state entities. None of them are likely to be activated without the express approval of the respective governments. In particular, the wide range of commercial contracts that increasingly support the gas trade between Russia and Ukraine and their respective state

[24] The only proviso is if there is a specific contractual exemption, or if the conciliator has permitted it.

entities also contain dispute settlement clauses, and so threats to take disputes to international arbitration and seek liquidated damages may also be made as a part of Ukraine's leverage.

The procedural rules allow either of the contracting parties to a dispute to refer the dispute to the Secretary General of the Energy Charter Secretariat (SG) by means of a notification that summarises the matters in dispute. If this happens, the SG shall appoint a conciliator within a period of 30 days. The conciliator then proceeds to seek an agreement between the parties to the dispute to a particular resolution or to a procedure to achieve such a resolution. A 90-day time-limit is imposed on this process, after which period the conciliator 'shall recommend a resolution to the dispute or a procedure to achieve such resolution and shall decide the interim tariffs and other terms and conditions to be observed for Transit from a date which he shall specify until the dispute is resolved'.[25] At this point the decision-making powers of the conciliator resemble the quasi-judicial powers normally associated with an arbitrator. The contracting parties are then required to ensure that the entities under their control, such as Naftogaz and Gazprom, observe any interim decision on tariffs, terms and conditions, for a period of 12 months following the conciliator's decision. Given the strategic economic role which the gas industry has in both the Ukrainian and Russian economies (discussed briefly above), this transfer of sovereign control by contracting states to an individual appointed by an international body seems quite extraordinary, and fraught with risk for the contracting parties concerned.

The key aim of Article 7 was to keep the supply of energy moving while a dispute between the contracting parties or their energy companies was still ongoing. This had clear advantages for the consuming states. For the transit state involved in the dispute, however, the loss of its ability to reduce or to cut off the gas supply would remove at a stroke the leverage that it had vis-à-vis the supplier. Consumers would go on receiving their supplies of gas irrespective of how long the dispute were to last. For a transit state this must appear to be an imbalanced arrangement.

The framework set out in Article 7 of the ECT was to be fleshed out in an additional Protocol, dedicated to transit issues.[26] For a variety of reasons, which need not be gone into here, contracting parties were unable to reach agreement on a final text, and negotiations were concluded some time before the transit disputes between Ukraine and Russia came to a head from 2006 onwards.

If one considers the 2009 gas interruption and the shorter interruption of 2006 in the light of the ECT's provisions on transit, several features are worthy of comment.

[25] Art 7(7)(c).

[26] Art 16 of the draft requires each contracting party to take necessary measures 'to expeditiously restore the normal operation of such Transit' in case of interruption, reduction or stoppage of transit flows. See www.encharter.org/fileadmin/user_upload/document/CC251.pdf.

First of all, in neither case did Ukraine or Russia call on the SG to intervene, or in any other way seek to draw upon the transit principles and procedures in Article 7. The first gas crisis in 2005–06 was a classical conflict between a supplier and a transit country that had arisen in a manner that was envisaged in Article 7(7) of the ECT. Yet the ECT played no role in the resolution of that dispute. This absence was noted in Moscow as a sign of the ECT's lack of teeth or benefits to Russia. In spite of Ukraine's ratification of the ECT, its actions were, on the Russian view, in direct contradiction of the principle in Article 7(6) not to interrupt or reduce the existing flow of energy while dispute resolution procedures were still in progress. They were also in violation of the provisions in the draft Transit Protocol, which Ukraine had supported. This provoked a blunt reaction from Gazprom: 'What kind of document is this? Or should it only be a one-sided document?'[27] The credibility of the ECT's dispute settlement mechanisms suffered as a result of Ukraine's decision to ignore them.

In the second incident (in 2009), the Energy Charter Conference took the initiative. Even though the parties showed no willingness to draw on the Treaty, in January 2009 the conciliation provision was activated by the Energy Charter Secretariat in relation to the dispute about both supply and transit of gas;[28] a conciliator was identified and offered to the parties to assist them in seeking a resolution of the dispute or in developing a procedure for doing so that they would find mutually satisfactory[29]. The conciliator was Mr George Verberg, a former chairman of the International Gas Union and former chairman of Gasunie, the Netherlands national gas company. In the event, neither of the contracting states took up this offer and the dispute was resolved at a high political level without the assistance of a third party. As one commentator has remarked, the events were subject to an 'extreme politicisation'.[30]

In neither of the gas supply interruptions did Ukraine observe the broad principle of non-interruption of existing gas flows set out in Article 7(6) of the ECT, which it had ratified. Given the complexity of the issues and the contractual arrangements involved, it could certainly have provided arguments in defence of its actions. Ukraine was also under no obligation to activate the provisions of Article 7(7). The more specific provisions on conciliation only followed the exhaustion of existing contractual and other remedies, and it could be argued that these had not yet been fully exhausted. Russia's position was quite different:

[27] *Interfax Russian and CIS Oil and Gas Weekly*, 'Gazprom not threatening Europe but seeking new markets' 27 April–3 May 2006 (cited in Pirani, Stern and Yafimava, *The Russo-Ukrainian gas dispute of January 2009*, n 20 above, 430).

[28] 'Russia-Ukraine Gas Dispute: Secretary General Appeals for Conciliation Efforts'. Available at www.encharter.org/index.php?id=21&id_article=167&L=0.

[29] ECT, 'Secretary General Issues Statement on Russia-Ukraine Gas Dispute' 23 December 2008. Available at www.encharter.org/index.php?id=21&id_article=167&L=0.

[30] A Belyi and IG Klaus, 'Russia's Gas Exports and Transit Dispute Resolution under the ECT: Missed Opportunities for Gazprom or False Hopes in Europe?' (2007) 25(3) *Journal of Energy and Natural Resources Law* 205, 206.

it had never formally ratified the ECT, and has since indicated that it has no intention of doing so. The ECT had at best only a provisional application to the Russian Federation. It was therefore unlikely to seek the intervention of the SG, given its long-held position of doubt about the value of the ECT in relation to its energy interests.

VII THE ENERGY COMMUNITY TREATY—IN PRACTICE

The goals of the Energy Community were wide-ranging, and security of supply was implicit in many of them. However, the Russo-Ukrainian gas crisis encouraged the establishment of a Security of Supply Coordination Group (CG) under a Procedural Act in December 2008.[31] This mirrored the GCG set up by the EU under Directive 2004/67/EC. The first meeting of the CG was held in September 2009, and included a lengthy examination of the gas crisis earlier that year.[32] Efforts were made by the gas and electricity industry to ensure that the countries of South and Eastern Europe (SEE) were involved in the new measures to mitigate eventual negative impact of a supply disruption. The question of what additional measures would be required to comply with new EU legislation on this was also raised.

An important feature of the crisis itself was the extent to which the gas industry provided support deliveries to the SEE countries, such as Slovakia, Serbia, Bosnia, Croatia and Slovenia. They argued that the European gas industry was well prepared to tackle external gas supply shortfalls without any explicit measures by the EU.[33] There was no need for an emergency mechanism or regulation, in their view. In practice, none of the major gas markets in the EU were affected by the disruption (Germany, UK, Italy and France), since they managed to obtain gas from other sources. These extra supplies were obtained without any 'security of supply' premium being required. Nonetheless, such supplies to markets were not successful where there were missing pipeline linkages from the West to the East, pointing to a Union dimension in supporting the creation of such linkages. Relations between the industry and the EU were indeed strained following statements made by the EU that EU gas companies could have done a better job, and proposing new legal actions on security of supply.

[31] Procedural Act 2008/02/MC-EnC. Available at www.energy-community.org/pls/portal/docs/296195.PDF.

[32] 'First Security of Supply Group Meeting and Fourth Meeting of the Energy Community Gas Forum: Conclusions' 10–11 September 2009. Available at www.energy-community.org/pls/portal/docs/406193.PDF.

[33] T Horwath (E.ON) 'What worked/what did not work during January '09 Crisis—focus on SEE', 4th Gas Forum, 10 September 2009. Available at www.energy-community.org.

VIII THE PROVISIONS OF EU SECONDARY LEGISLATION TESTED

The European Commission's verdict on the operation of the security provisions of Directive 2004/67 was negative, and it proposed a new legal instrument to replace it. This time, instead of a Directive, it proposed a Regulation to safeguard security of supply.[34] This initiative was broadly supported by the Council and the Parliament, aware that another supply disruption could not be ruled out in the near future.

What the emergency underlined was the regional character of gas markets, dependent as they are on interconnected pipelines. Several Member States are dependent upon the same major pipeline infrastructure, so that each one depends upon the other's actions and consumption. Supply shortages tend to affect a whole region, and it may not be able to manage the disruption by the actions of a single Member State acting alone. The Union dimension of a crisis had become clear.

Several specific inadequacies had been highlighted. There was no specific emergency plan in the EU to deal with short-term supply shortages if market mechanisms or industry and national measures should prove insufficient. Decision-making therefore tended to have an ad hoc character, even in the face of a substantial threat to EU gas supplies. Standards operating at the national level were also, when scrutinised, found to vary widely (what constitutes a 'disruption'), and the roles and responsibilities of market players for security of supply also varied from one Member State to another. Sometimes a Member State relied upon the Ministry to carry out monitoring, sometimes the energy regulator, and in other cases the transmission system operator had responsibility. In the event of a crisis, the question arose as to whether such differences were likely to inhibit cooperation across borders. The threshold set out in Directive 2004/67 for a major disruption in supply or risk of a loss was also deemed to be too high. Shortfalls that did not amount to 20 per cent of imports from third countries for a period of eight weeks might still require a Union response. At the same time, it should be noted that the 2009 emergency was resolved by the use of national measures alone and did not require the intervention of the GCG. However, there was a sense that the GCG, by bringing together Member States, the gas industry and consumers' representatives, provided something positive: a single European voice.[35]

Essentially, the new legal instrument aimed at defining more precisely the roles of the gas industry, Member States and the Union institutions so that they were better able to deal with supply disruptions in the short term and also, importantly, to provide for an expansion of infrastructure in the longer term: 'for measures to be consistent and effective, they have to be prepared well in advance

[34] Proposal for a Regulation of the European Parliament and of the Council concerning measures to safeguard security of gas supply and repealing Directive 2004/67/EC, COM (2009) 363 final.

[35] COM (2008) 769 final, 7.

and to be coordinated at [Union] level'.[36] In considering the appropriate choice of instrument, the Commission took the view that a Regulation was preferable to a Directive, since it was directly applicable to the competent authorities in the Member States, as well as to natural gas undertakings and customers. It also had the advantages of not requiring a lengthy transposition, ensuring clarity and coherence of standards and obligations across the EU and defining directly the participation of Union institutions.

Separately, the EU has renewed efforts to supplement the above with mechanisms for coordination with Russia in the event of a supply disruption. In November 2009 the two parties signed a Memorandum of Understanding (MoU) to reinforce an early warning mechanism that would improve prevention and management in the event of an energy crisis.[37] However, it may be noted that the MoU is not legally binding and expressly states that it creates no rights or obligations under international law. This underlines the difficulties in securing a legal basis for EU energy security with its non-EU energy partners, a problem which the ECT was intended to resolve, but which sadly it did not.

IX CONCLUSION

The approach to energy security taken in this chapter has been to focus on the fortunes of several legal instruments designed to contribute to risk mitigation in this area, and assess how they have fared when tested by a real emergency. There are many other risks that can fall within the scope of 'energy security' and involve different kinds of energy, but with the exception of the oil crisis of 1973 and several electricity outages of limited scope, these risks have not arisen in practice, and an energy emergency has remained a matter of speculation. The Russo-Ukrainian gas dispute of January 2009 was just such an emergency and revealed that the multilateral instrument, the ECT, which the EU had done so much to sponsor in the 1990s was ineffective in addressing the risks created by energy transit through Ukraine. Instead, Member States agreed to support enhanced measures of cooperation and permit EU institutions to take an enhanced role in their implementation. While it is important to treat with caution this development towards a common policy on energy security (national interests continue to be very apparent when there is discussion of new pipeline networks), it is evident that such a trend exists and that it is one that all parties seek to provide with a legal foundation, albeit one that recognises the central role of the energy industry in ensuring energy flows.

[36] ibid, 2.

[37] 'The EU and Russia reinforce the Early Warning Mechanism to improve prevention and management in case of an energy crisis'. European Commission IP/09/1718, 16 November 2009. Available at, ec.europa.eu/energy/international/russia/doc/reports/2009_11_16_ewm_signed_en.pdf.

If the assessment of the ECT appears unduly harsh, it should be placed in its historical setting. At the time the EU supported the conclusion of the ECT, the latest expansion of the EU to the East was still 10 years away. The incorporation of Central and Eastern European states into the EU not only brought them within the ambit of EU law, imposing stricter obligations on them than the ECT, but it also changed the balance of energy security in the EU, giving a significantly enhanced importance to Russian energy imports and to the transit risks from Ukraine. The other event that remained outside of the vision of the ECT drafters was the collapse of Yugoslavia and ensuing war in SE Europe. The shock of the war and devastation had the effect of giving birth to a new regional treaty in the energy sector, which expanded the scope of existing EU law to states that were not yet members. The scope of EU law was therefore dramatically expanded by means of these developments, limiting the advantages of the ECT to the EU's external relations policy. Arguably, they made a large-scale multilateral treaty instrument redundant, while at the same time increasing the urgency with which the EU needed to address its relations with those states on its Eastern borders, Ukraine and Russia. This challenge remains an ongoing one, but it is one that is increasingly being shaped by EU law.

7

The International Financial Crisis, Global Financial Governance and the European Union

JAN WOUTERS, STEVEN STERKX AND TIM CORTHAUT

I INTRODUCTION

THE FINANCIAL CRISIS that hit the world in 2008 has resulted in the worst global economic performance since World War II. In 2009, world output—measured by Gross Domestic Product (GDP) in Constant Prices—dropped by 0.60 per cent: the first time since World War II a decline in global output has occurred. Moreover, the crisis has proven to a truly global one, affecting advanced, emerging and developing economies at the same time. In comparison to an average growth rate of more than 6 per cent between 2000 and 2008, emerging and developing economies witnessed a growth of 2.39 per cent in 2009. The European Union (EU)'s output plunged by 4.08 per cent in 2009, which represents an even sharper decline than the average drop of 3.16 per cent in the group of advanced economies. In the same year, the world's trade volume of goods and services fell by 10.66 per cent.[1] In the EU, the crisis has given rise to a substantial increase of unemployment. In 2009, the overall unemployment rate in the EU-27 reached 8.9 per cent, a 1.9 per cent rise compared to 2008, putting an end to four consecutive years of declining unemployment.[2] It is expected that the rise of EU unemployment will continue throughout 2010 and possibly 2011.

The crisis has triggered a global response: world leaders—for the most part in the framework of the revitalised Group of Twenty (G20)—have held several meetings to discuss and agree on a global plan for recovery and the reform of global financial governance. The first part of this chapter addresses the format and outcome of these deliberations, while the second part focuses particular attention on the position and role of the EU in global financial governance.

[1] IMF, World Economic Outlook Database, April 2010, www.imf.org.

[2] Eurostat, Updated Unemployment Statistics, 29 July 2010, http://ec.europa.eu/eurostat.

Finally, the chapter discusses the changes brought about by the Treaty of Lisbon, and assesses whether they will strengthen the EU's performance on the global scene.

II ACTORS IN THE GLOBAL RESPONSE

A The revitalisation of G20: a global 'playmaker'?

Spurred by the financial crisis that started in September 2008 in the United States, President Bush convened a meeting of the leaders of the G20 nations. On 15 November 2008, they held a meeting in Washington DC to address the challenges posed by the financial crisis and the resulting downward turn of the global economy. In the ensuing Declaration, two overall priorities were set: the restoration of global growth, and the much needed reform of global financial governance—with the aim of preventing a similar crisis happening again.[3] Reform would be based on five common principles, to be implemented by means of an action plan.[4] These principles are: strengthening of transparency and accountability; enhancing sound regulation; promoting integrity in financial markets; reinforcing international cooperation (among regulators and relevant authorities); and—last but not least—reforming the international financial institutions (IFIs). The implementation of the latter principle would include the reform of the Bretton Woods institutions, ie the International Monetary Fund (IMF) and the World Bank, in order to increase their legitimacy—in particular by raising the voice and representation of emerging economies and developing countries—and effectiveness, as well as the expansion of the membership of the Financial Stability Forum (FSF) and other standard-setting bodies. Also, it was agreed that the IMF should be given a key role, both in terms of available resources and surveillance authority, in responding to the crisis.

1 Origins and composition

Perhaps a more remarkable feature than the content of the Washington deliberations and their outcome—from a governance perspective at least—is the fact that the G20 meeting was held, for the very first time, at the level of Heads of State and Government. Although the Group of Twenty was created in 1999, in response to the Asian financial crisis of the late 1990s, meetings between 1999 and 2008 had only taken place at the level of finance ministers and central bank

[3] Washington Declaration, Summit on Financial Markets and the World Economy, 15 November 2008.

[4] Washington Action Plan, Action Plan to Implement Principles for Reform, 15 November 2008.

governors.[5] During that period, multiple calls for G20 summits at leaders' level (at the time, referred to as 'L20') had been made, for the most part with the aim of replacing G8 meetings by a more representative summit constellation.[6] The current crisis has acted as a catalyst for this step to be taken.

Since its creation, the G20 has brought together 'systematically significant' industrialised and developing economies to discuss key issues in the global economy. It is made up of 19 countries and the EU.[7] In addition to these members, the Managing Director of the IMF and the President of the World Bank, along with the chairs of the International Monetary and Financial Committee (IMFC) and Development Committee (DC), also participate in G20 meetings of finance ministers and central bank governors (ex officio). Unlike 'real' international organisations, the G20 is an informal forum or 'club', with no permanent staff of its own and no permanent representatives of its members. Its chair rotates between members, and is selected from a different regional grouping of countries each year.

ii G20 summits

British Prime Minister Gordon Brown followed George W Bush's example and hosted a second G20 summit in London—during the United Kingdom's chairmanship of the G20—on 1 and 2 April 2009.

The London G20 summit set five priorities, much in line with the principles agreed in Washington: restoring growth and jobs, strengthening financial supervision and regulation, strengthening the global financial institutions, resisting protectionism and promoting global trade and investment, and ensuring a fair and sustainable recovery for all. Important decisions, related to the reform of global financial governance, involved the commitment to make available an additional US$1.1 trillion programme of support to restore credit, growth and jobs in the world economy; the establishment of the Financial Stability Board

[5] For an overview of the early functioning of the G20, see JJ Kirton, 'The G20: Representativeness, Effectiveness, and Leadership in Global Governance' in JJ Kirton, JP Daniels and A Freytag (eds), *Guiding Global Order. G8 Governance in the 21st Century* (Aldershot, Ashgate, 2001). The creation of G20 is an initiative of the G7 finance ministers and central bank governors, who at their meeting of 25 September 1999 announced their proposal 'to broaden the dialogue on key economic and financial policy issues among systematically significant economies and promote cooperation to achieve stable and sustainable world economic growth that benefits all.' See Statement of G7 Ministers and Central Bank Governors, 25 September 1999, Washington DC.

[6] M Beeson and S Bell, 'The G-20 and International Economic Governance: Hegemony, Collectivism, or Both?' (2009) 15 *Global Governance* 67, 77; JJ Kirton, 'Toward Multilateral Reform: The G20's Contribution' in J English, R Thakur and AF Cooper (eds), *Reforming from the top: a Leaders' 20 Summit* (New York, United Nations University Press, 2005) 143.

[7] These 19 countries are (in alphabetical order): Argentina, Australia, Brazil, Canada, China, France, Germany, India, Indonesia, Italy, Japan, the Republic of Korea, Mexico, Russia, Saudi Arabia, South Africa, Turkey, the United Kingdom and the United States.

(FSB) as a successor to the FSF, incorporating also all G20 countries; a key role given to the IMF in the field of crisis prevention; and agreement to reform representation at the IFIs.[8]

In more detail, the financial programme included a US$500 billion expansion of the IMF's resources (increasing the IMF's total available resources to US$750 billion), a Special Drawing Rights (SDR) allocation[9] of US$250 billion, at least US$100 billion of additional lending by the Multilateral Development Banks (MDBs), and a pledge to make available US$250 billion to halt the slow-down in trade finance. The expansion of the FSF and its renaming went hand in hand with a strengthened mandate for the new FSB to coordinate all efforts in the field of financial regulation and supervision. The IMF was given a primary role and increased independence with regard to early warning and surveillance. Last but not least, the G20 leaders agreed that emerging and developing countries should have greater voice and representation at the IFIs, with the aim of improving their credibility: in particular, (i) the package of IMF quota and voice reforms already agreed in April 2008 should be swiftly implemented; (ii) the next review of IMF quotas should be concluded by January 2011; (iii) World Bank reforms should be completed by 2010; and (iv) the heads and senior leadership of the IFIs should be appointed through open, merit-based selection processes.

In London, the G20 leaders pledged to meet again and to review progress on their commitments before the end of the year. Hence, a third summit was held in the autumn of 2009, in Pittsburgh, on 24–25 September 2009. At the summit, the Heads of State and Government decided to 'lift' the G20 to the level of 'premier forum for international economic cooperation' (with summits in Canada in June 2010 and in Korea in November 2010, and annual meetings as from 2011), and to launch a 'Framework for Strong, Sustainable and Balanced Growth'.[10] Building on the Washington Action Plan and the London Declarations, the Framework highlighted the need for 'modernising' the architecture for international financial and economic cooperation. With regard to the debate on IFI reform, the Pittsburgh summit added that the G20 members are committed to a shift in IMF quota share 'to dynamic emerging markets and developing countries of at least 5% from over-represented countries to under-represented countries'. Similarly, for the governance of the World Bank, the summit stressed the need for a dynamic formula reflecting 'countries' evolving economic weight and the World Bank's development mission, and generating an increase of at least 3% of voting power for developing and transition countries, to the benefit of under-represented countries'.[11]

[8] See London Summit, Leaders' Statement, 2 April 2009: Declaration on Strengthening the Financial Summit, and Declaration on Delivering Resources through the International Financial Institutions.

[9] These SDR will be allocated to all IMF members, according to their quotas or voting shares.

[10] See Leaders' Statement, The Pittsburgh Summit, 24–25 September 2009.

[11] ibid, paras 20–21.

The most recent G20 summit, held in Toronto on 26–27 June 2010, reaffirmed earlier commitments—among others, the implementation of the Framework for Strong, Sustainable and Balanced Growth—and took note of a 'mutual assessment report' drafted by the G20 finance ministers and central bank governors (assisted by the IMF and World Bank), which underscored the need for 'a more ambitious path of reforms' in order to secure strong and lasting recovery.[12] Reform of the financial sector should rest on four goals: the need for a strong regulatory framework (in particular related to bank capital and liquidity requirements, oversight of hedge funds and credit rating agencies, and accounting standards); effective supervision (with a key task for the FSB—in consultation with the IMF—to draft recommendations); resolution tools for systemic financial institutions in crisis, without taxpayers bearing the burden[13] (also here the FSB is invited to develop policy recommendations); and transparent international assessment (through the IMF and the World Bank) and peer review (through the FSB), including measures addressing 'non-cooperative jurisdictions' and the problem of tax havens and banking secrecy. With regard to the resources and governance of the IFIs, the G20 leaders stressed that they have fulfilled their London summit commitments to mobilise financing (including US$350 billion in capital increases for the MDBs, as such exceeding the commitments made), and that they have endorsed the agreed World Bank voice reforms, increasing the voting power of developing and transition countries by 4.59 per cent since 2008. Concerning IMF reform, however, the G20 leaders merely repeated their promise made in London and Pittsburgh to ensure ratification of the 2008 quota and voice reforms (at the same time stressing, however, that the majority of G20 members have already ratified the reforms), and called for an acceleration of the work that needs to be done on further quota reform. This work was expected to be completed by the Seoul summit on 11–12 November 2010.

iii In search of legitimacy

Together, the G20 members represent more than 85 per cent of global GDP, 80 per cent of world trade (including intra-EU trade), and two-thirds of the world's population. G20 membership includes the most important emerging economies, developing countries and 'representatives' from all regions in the world. This

[12] See the G20 Toronto Summit Declaration, 26–27 June 2010.

[13] In this context, the G20 leaders agreed that the financial sector itself 'should make a fair and substantial contribution towards paying for any burdens associated with government interventions, where they occur, to repair the financial system or fund resolution'. The leaders furthermore acknowledged that 'some countries are pursuing a financial levy', but stressed that this option is only one possible approach out of many, thereby not encouraging the imposition of a so-called 'banking tax' (as promoted by the European members—in particular Britain, France and Germany—of the G20). See the G20 Toronto Summit Declaration, 26–27 June 2010, Annex II on Financial Sector Reform, para 22.

makes the G20 much more inclusive than the G7/8 constellation, which was subject to severe criticism for being illegitimate and unrepresentative.[14] The broad composition of G20 reflects the ongoing power shifts and new political realities in the global economy.[15]

The inclusive character and incorporation of regional viewpoints have led some commentators to recognise the G20 as the best possible forum to tackle global challenges,[16] as well as to wonder whether the G20 signifies the 'death certificate' of G8 summitry.[17] Other assessments are more critical, pointing to the under-representation of the developing world and to the Western 'domination' of G20.[18] In particular Africa, with only one G20 member—South Africa—is under-represented.[19] For this reason, Pascal Lamy, Director-General of the World Trade Organization (WTO), has suggested offering G20 membership to the African Union.[20] In this context, a Brookings report on the functioning of G20 argues that the lack of representation of the developing world has the effect that G20 deliberations do not sufficiently prioritise the development agenda, and that adequate expertise on development issues is currently lacking within the Group.[21] Another concern is that—despite the broad membership and increased influence of emerging economies—the G20 is still a G7-driven forum.[22] In her analysis of G20 summit deliberations, Ngaire Woods finds reasons to believe that the G20 constitutes a final—given their declining power and relative economic weight—attempt of G7-countries to make compromises with emerging economies, rather than a genuine invigoration of inclusive multilateralism.[23] Also G20 expert John Kirton has pointed to the risk of the G20 merely acting as a legitimisation of the G7/8 agenda and outcomes.[24]

[14] See Kirton, 'The G20' (n 5 above) 143.

[15] U Krotz and R Maher, 'Europe in the New World: National Governments and the EU at the G-20' (2009) 39 *Perspectives on Europe*, Council for European Studies 26, 27.

[16] T Renard, 'From the New G20 to a New Multilateral Order' (2010) 12 January *EU Observer*; CJ Bradford, 'G20 Summit: The G Force' (2009) 65 *The World Today*.

[17] K Gnath, 'A Group's Architecture in Flux: The G8 and the Heiligendamm Process' (2010) 6 *EUI Working Papers RSCAS* 9, 9; CJ Bradford and J Linn, 'It's Time to Drop the G8' (2010) *Recovery or Relapse: The Role of the G-20 in the Global Economy*, Global Economy and Development at Brookings 8, 8–9.

[18] M Khor, 'Reality Behind the Hype of the G20 Summit' (2009) 224 *Third World Resurgence* 5, 6; B Muchhala, 'Development-blind G20 Outcome Empowers an Unreformed IMF' (2009) 224 *Third World Resurgence* 14, 15.

[19] E Suruma, 'It's Time for Africa's Voice in the G-20' (2010) *Recovery or Relapse: The Role of the G-20 in the Global Economy*, Global Economy and Development at Brookings 13, 14.

[20] P Lamy, 'L'Union Africaine Doit Siéger au G20' (2009) 2506 *Jeune Afrique*, interview 68, 68.

[21] H Kharas, 'Passing the Development Football from the G8 to the G-20' (2010) *Recovery or Relapse: The Role of the G-20 in the Global Economy*, Global Economy and Development at Brookings 10, 11–12.

[22] *cf* Beeson and Bell, 'The G-20 and International Economic Governance' (n 6 above).

[23] See N Woods, 'Global Governance after the Financial Crisis: A New Multilateralism or the Last Gasp of the Great Powers?' (2010) 1 *Global Policy*.

[24] Kirton, 'The G20' (n 5 above).

We share these concerns, and contend that the G20's success and future will to a large extent depend on whether it will be perceived as genuinely legitimate. Apart from this, the G20 will also have to show it is an effective body, in which all 20 members reach consensus on a common agenda and strong commitments or recommendations. Here, analysts refer to the trade-off between legitimacy and effectiveness: can a forum with 20 members from different regional groupings be effective? Past deliberations have moreover shown that diverging interests not only occur between advanced economies on the one hand, and emerging powers and developing countries on the other. Also within the 'camp' of Western countries, in particular between the United States and European countries, there are conflicting views on how to achieve global recovery (fiscal policy versus debt sustainability) and strong financial markets (weak versus strong regulation and supervision).[25] In our opinion, there should not be such an unavoidable trade-off. So far, the G20 has acted as a deliberative body, not as a centre of decision-making. In this respect, its strength has been to 'put the relevant international organisations to work', and even to reinvigorate their activities—as in the case of the increased surveillance authority given to the IMF. What is important, here, is that the G20—at least for the time being—has the legitimacy to do so. If the G20 can continue to 'steer' existing international organisations, its role in global financial and economic governance will be successful.[26] Its effectiveness, then, will be measured by its ability to make existing organisations and fora implement its recommendations.

iv The G20 in the driver's seat

The G20 has the capacity to act as a global 'playmaker', 'dishing out assists' to the relevant international institutions and bodies in charge of financial and economic governance. In this context we refer to Hillman's challenging proposal to upgrade the G20 to the level of a 'Council of Governors', in particular for the IFIs and the WTO.[27]

However, if the G20 wishes to consolidate its role as a global steering body, we believe that (at least) the following conditions will have to be met. First, the G20 clearly is a crisis-driven forum. It originated—as indicated above, at the level of finance ministers and central bank governors—in the aftermath of the 1997–98

[25] *cf* D Lombardi 'The G-20 Summit Assesses the European Crisis: Finding the Way from Toronto' (2010) *Recovery or Relapse: The Role of the G-20 in the Global Economy*, Global Economy and Development at Brookings 6, 6; E Prasad, 'Back from the Brink, but a Tough Road Still Ahead for the G-20' (2010) *Recovery or Relapse: The Role of the G-20 in the Global Economy*, Global Economy and Development at Brookings 3, 5; T Rajamoorthy, 'The US, the EU and China at the G20 Summit' (2009) 224 *Third World Resurgence* 10, 11.

[26] *cf* T Porter, 'Crisis and the Future of Global Financial Governance: Why International Institutions Matter in the Global Credit Crisis' (2009) 15 *Global Governance* 3.

[27] J Hillman, 'Saving Multilateralism. Renovating the House of Global Economic Governance for the 21st Century' (2010) *Brussels Forum Paper Series*, The German Marshall Fund of the United States, 37.

Asian crisis, and now, in response to the 2008 global financial and economic crisis, it has been 'promoted' to summitry level. Crises have a tendency to act as catalysts for reform.[28] There may therefore be a 'danger' that the G20 at leaders' level—both with regard to its leadership role and its reform agenda—loses momentum as the crisis and the ensuing sense of urgency fade. Also in times of global financial and economic stability, the G20 will have to demonstrate its capacity to lead. Second, and related to the former precondition, the G20 will have to continue to push for governance reform, and for actual implementation of its recommendations. The G20 can only maintain its credibility, in particular vis-à-vis emerging economies and the developing world, when it succeeds in adapting governance rules—relating to voice and representation—to today's political and economic realities.[29] Finally, since its creation, the agenda of G20 has broadened, not merely including strictly financial and economic matters, but also related issues such as energy security and climate change, food security, and development aid. As a global leading forum, the G20 will need to continue the process of widening its agenda, every time there is a need to take position and find consensus on specific events (eg food crises) or ongoing multilateral negotiations (eg trade rounds or the agenda on climate change). The G20 will find increased credibility and legitimacy in adequately responding to global needs.[30]

B Other relevant international institutions and fora

What are the organisations the G20 is 'putting to work', and what is their specific role in global financial governance? We restrict ourselves to those institutions and fora explicitly referred to in G20 summit declarations. The overview in the previous section has already referred to the responsibilities given to the IFIs and FSB, but the G20 has also sought to influence the decision-making process at the WTO, the Organization for Economic Cooperation and Development (OECD), the International Labour Organization (ILO), as well as several standard-setting bodies dealing with financial regulation and oversight.

i The IMF and the World Bank

The IMF, with 187 member countries, has a key role in fostering global monetary cooperation and combating financial crises. In particular, the IMF gives policy advice and loans to assist emerging markets and low-income economies affected

[28] E Helleiner, 'Crisis and the Future of Global Financial Governance: Introduction' (2009) 15 *Global Governance* 1, 1; E Helleiner, 'Crisis and the Future of Global Financial Governance: Reregulation and Fragmentation in International Financial Governance' (2009) 15 *Global Governance* 16, 16.

[29] *cf* B Davis, 'G-20 Urged to Act on Economy' *The Wall Street Journal Europe* (31 March 2010).

[30] *cf* Kirton, 'Toward Multilateral Reform' (n 6 above).

by crisis.[31] As the above overview of G20 summit recommendations shows, the IMF has been given additional authority in the field of monitoring and surveillance, its resources have been 'propped up', and reforms of its governance architecture—in particular the need for quota review—have been announced.

Central to the decision-making process within the IMF is the much-debated quota system. Currently, a member's quota determines (i) the amount of financial resources it contributes to the IMF, (ii) its voting power, (iii) its level of access to IMF financing, and (iv) its share of SDR allocations. IMF members cannot unilaterally increase their quota, as quota reviews must be approved by the IMF Board of Governors and are linked to a formula based on a weighted average of several variables, with a country's GDP—its size within the world economy—having the greatest impact. Major decisions, such as quota reform, require an extraordinary majority of 85 per cent of the votes.[32]

In April 2008, a reform package was adopted by the Board of Governors.[33] This package contained, among other elements, the agreement to adopt a new quota formula, ad hoc quota increases for all 54 countries that would be under-represented under the new quota formula, as well as a commitment to realign quota and voting shares every five years. The next review would have to be decided by 2013.

Today, this reform package is still in need of implementation. For the reform to take effect, the endorsement of 112 members representing at least 85 per cent of total voting power is needed. As indicated above, at the G20 London summit, the Heads of State and Government called for the immediate implementation of the 2008 reform package, and furthermore decided not to wait until 2013 to enact a next quota review. In Pittsburgh, the G20 leaders further committed themselves to a quota shift—to emerging and developing countries—of at least 5 per cent from over-represented to under-represented countries.

In general, quota review is needed to ensure that the quotas of IMF member countries adequately reflect the changes of their positions in the global

[31] However, as the current financial crisis demonstrates, IMF loans are not only used to assist emerging or developing economies hit by crisis. In May 2010, the IMF approved an assistance package designed to stabilise the financial crisis in Greece—a European and 'advanced' economy.

[32] Although the Board of Governors, the highest decision-making body of the IMF, has delegated most of its decision-making powers to the IMF Executive Board, it retains, among other rights, the right to approve quota increases. The Executive Board—composed of 24 Directors (plus the Chair), with the largest economies having their own seat at the table, while most countries are grouped in constituencies—is in charge of the daily business of the IMF. The Executive Board is chaired by the Managing Director, Dominique Strauss-Kahn (in office since November 2007).

[33] LB Smaghi, 'A Single EU Seat in the International Monetary Fund?' in KE Joergensen (ed), *The European Union and International Organizations* (London, Routledge, 2009) 64. The Board of Governors is composed of one governor (usually the minister of finance or the central bank governor) and one alternate governor for each member country. It meets once a year (under normal circumstances), and is advised by two ministerial committees, the IMFC and DC. Major decisions—such as quota review—require an extraordinary majority of 85 % of the votes. Hence, the United States—which has 16.74 % of total voting power—is the only country with the power to block a 'supermajority' on its own.

economy.[34] There is widespread criticism, however, that the 2008 reform package as well as the G20 recommendations are 'too little, too slow'.[35] The result of the reforms not being sufficiently 'radical'—not only with regard to quota shares, but also concerning the broader issue of representation of emerging and developing countries in the Fund's management and staff—is that the IMF will continue to be perceived as a US/West-dominated institution.[36] On a more positive note, it is argued that the IMF—in particular its over-represented, most contributing members—should not impede reform, but welcome it: governance reform will enable the IMF to increase its resources, with emerging economies contributing more in exchange for better representation and voice.[37]

The discussions on the governance of the World Bank, which plays a vital role in providing financial and technical assistance to developing countries with the aim of fighting poverty, are largely similar: the envisaged voting reform is generally deemed too limited, and the representation of developing countries—both in terms of leadership and the capabilities of their staff—is seen as too weak. In contrast with the IMF, the agreed voice reform, namely increasing the voting power of developing and transition countries by 4.59 per cent since 2008—has already been endorsed (*cf* G20 Toronto summit).

ii The Financial Stability Board

The Financial Stability Board (FSB) is the successor to the Financial Stability Forum (FSF), which was established by the G7 finance ministers and central bank governors in 1999 to promote international financial stability through enhanced information exchange and international cooperation in financial market supervision and surveillance.[38] The FSF's prime responsibility was to act as a coordination body for the so-called 'Compendium of Standards', which groups 12 key economic and financial standards that are internationally accepted as important for sound, stable and well-functioning financial systems.[39] Overall implementation of and compliance with these standards, however, has been weak, especially

[34] In this context, the on-going reforms are criticised for not being beneficial to the developing world, in particular Africa (*cf* Suruma, 'It's Time for Africa's Voice in the G-20', n 19 above).

[35] Muchhala, 'Development-blind G20 Outcome Empowers an Unreformed IMF' (n 18 above).

[36] *cf* N Woods, 'The G20 Summit: Saving Globalisation Again?' (2009) 65 *The World Today*; Woods, 'Global Governance after the Financial Crisis' (n 23 above).

[37] *cf* K Barysch, 'The Real G20 Agenda' *CER Insight* (13 March 2009).

[38] The membership of FSF included national financial authorities (central banks, supervisory authorities and finance ministries) from the G7 countries, Australia, Hong Kong, Netherlands, Singapore and Switzerland, as well as the international financial institutions, international regulatory and supervisory groupings, committees of central bank experts and the European Central Bank. Due to its high number of members, including several financial institutions, groupings and committees, the FSF has been described as operating as a 'network of networks'. *Cf* L Mosley, 'Crisis and the Future of Global Financial Governance: An End to Global Standards and Codes' (2009) 15 *Global Governance* 9; B Stokes, 'G-20 Summit Just a Down Payment' (2008) 15 November *National Journal*.

[39] These 12 standards and codes are divided into three categories: Macroeconomic Policy and Data Transparency (Data Dissemination, Monetary Transparency, Fiscal Transparency); Institutional

in emerging economies and developing countries. Besides the heavy reliance on the private sector and the lack of legally binding measures, one of the reasons for the poor implementation and compliance was that the FSF operated as a G7-led initiative without the participation of and input from the developing world and emerging markets.[40]

In response to these deficiencies, and spurred by the financial crisis, the leaders of the G20 decided at the April 2009 London summit to transform the FSF into the FSB, thereby giving a greater role to emerging economies and developing countries. The FSB now includes all G20 countries, with the addition of previous FSF members which do not belong to the G20 (ie Hong Kong, Netherlands, Singapore and Switzerland), Spain, and a total of 12 'international organisations' (including the European Commission and the European Central Bank), standard-setting bodies and other groupings.[41] The FSB has been assigned by the G20 to assess the vulnerabilities affecting the financial system, identify and oversee actions to address them, and promote cooperation and information-sharing.

iii The World Trade Organization

In each of its summit declarations, the G20 has underscored the importance of rejecting protectionism and refraining from raising new barriers to investment or to trade in goods and services. The G20 explicitly called on the WTO, the 153-member international organisation in charge of a common institutional and substantive legal framework for the conduct of trade relations, to monitor the impact of domestic policies on trade and investment, and to report on countries' commitment to an open global economy. In addition, the G20 stated its support for bringing the WTO Doha Development Round 'to a balanced and ambitious conclusion'. Whereas the Pittsburgh declaration still referred to a successful conclusion 'in 2010', the Toronto summit hoped for a conclusion 'as soon as possible'.

With regard to the commitment to avoid protectionism, the G20 has reason to be optimistic. A recent WTO report reviewing trade and trade-related developments from November 2009 to mid-May 2010 concludes that 'despite the severity of the global financial crisis and its widespread impact on economies around the world, governments have largely resisted resort to trade barriers'.[42]

and Market Infrastructure (Insolvency, Accounting, Corporate Governance, Auditing, Anti-Money Laundering, Payment Systems); and Financial Regulation and Supervision (Banking Supervision, Securities Regulation, Insurance Supervision).

[40] *cf* L Mosley, 'Crisis and the Future of Global Financial Governance' (n 38 above).

[41] See www.financialstabilityboard.org.

[42] WTO, Report from the Director-General on Trade-Related Developments, 14 June 2010.

iv The Organization for Economic Cooperation and Development

The subsequent G20 summits have referred to the OECD, an intergovernmental organisation bringing together the governments of 33 countries committed to democracy and the principles of the market economy, in the following context: first, the OECD is invited—together with the WTO—to monitor and report on the commitment of countries to refrain from protectionist measures; second, the OECD—together with other organisations such as the ILO (see below)—is recognised as a pool of expertise on various aspects of economic recovery and growth, in particular issues related to boosting employment (see Pittsburgh and Toronto summit declarations) and banking secrecy (see London summit statement on actions against non-cooperative jurisdictions, including tax havens).[43] The G20 leaders have stated that they will continue to draw on the expertise of the OECD and other relevant organisations, when necessary.

v The International Labour Organization

Analogous to the references made to the OECD, the ILO—a tripartite UN agency bringing together governments, employers and workers of its 183 member states with the aim of promoting decent work throughout the world—is singled out as the expert organisation to deal with the 'human' or 'social' dimension of the crisis. The G20 calls on the ILO to develop training programmes designed to enhance the skills of workers, and explicitly welcomes the 2009 ILO 'Resolution on Recovering from the Crisis: A Global Jobs Pact', which promotes decent work as an essential part of any comprehensive response to the crisis.[44]

vi Standard-setting bodies

As part of its effort to strengthen the financial system, the G20 calls for enhanced regulation and supervision related to various aspects of financial governance. In the field of prudential regulation, the G20 instructed the Basel Committee for Banking Supervision—a forum with 27 member countries for regular cooperation on banking supervision matters—to review the minimum levels of capital, and to develop a global framework for promoting stronger liquidity buffers at financial institutions. In the area of financial reporting and accounting, the G20 leaders stressed the importance of a single set of improved global accounting rules, and called upon the International Accounting Standards Board (IASB)—an independent standard-setting body with 15 members responsible for the development and publication of international financial reporting standards (IFRS)—to further improve its involvement with stakeholders in the framework

[43] *cf* P Gillespie, 'Taxing Matters: The G20 and Offshore Tax Havens' (2009) 224 *Third World Resurgence* 17.

[44] Document no ILC98-Partial-2009–07–0115–1-En.doc; see www.ilo.org/public/libdoc/ilo/2009/109B09_101_engl.pdf.

of an independent standard-setting process. Finally, with regard to the oversight of credit rating agencies, the G20 Heads of State and Government solicited the International Organization of Securities Commissions (IOSCO)—an association (with members from over 100 countries) of organisations in charge of regulating the world's securities and futures markets—to coordinate full compliance with its Code of Conduct Fundamentals.

III THE EUROPEAN UNION IN GLOBAL ECONOMIC AND FINANCIAL GOVERNANCE

The report which the Reflection Group on the Future of the EU 2030 delivered in May 2010 reads as follows:

> As power shifts away from Europe and the United States, the rules of international engagement are themselves being redefined. In this turbulent landscape, the EU can no longer afford to muddle through. It needs to become a driving force in shaping the new rules of global governance, or risk being left behind. To advance purposively, it will also need to champion an international environment that will enable the EU to promote its agenda.[45]

This citation fittingly reflects the challenge the EU is confronted with: if the EU wishes to live up to its leitmotif of 'effective multilateralism'[46] to guide its external relations, it will have to improve its problem-solving capacity in the international arena. In our opinion, a crucial factor here is the EU's ability to organise its performance at the global level in a coherent manner. This section will discuss two aspects of the EU's performance in global economic and financial governance: its representation in the G20 and other relevant organisations, and the EU's internal coordination efforts to arrive at common positions in these fora. The image that will emerge is that of a 'patchwork Europe', as Gstöhl appropriately labels the EU's representation in international institutions.[47] Although membership matters, we do not limit ourselves to the actual formal membership of the EU to international organisations and fora, but will also look at the position of EU Member States, including their duty to reach and defend 'unified positions'.

[45] Project Europe 2030, 'Challenges and Opportunities. A Report to the European Council by the Reflection Group on the Future of the EU 2030', May 2010, 43.

[46] Council of the European Union, 'A Secure Europe in a Better World, European Security Strategy' (Brussels, 2003).

[47] S Gstöhl, '"Patchwork Power" Europe: The EU's Representation in International Institutions' (2009) 14 *European Foreign Affairs Review* 385, 385. *Cf* R Smits, 'International Representation of Europe in the Area of Economic and Monetary Union: Legal Issues and Practice in the First Ten Years of the Euro' (2009) Working Paper at http://195.128.2.97/events/pdf/conferences/emu/RSmits InternationalRepresentationOfEMUpaper.pdf?de5a337d306ac5bda7cc3e70a9bb08bc.

A The EU in the G20

On the European side, membership of the G20 includes four EU Member States—France, Germany, Italy and the United Kingdom—and the EU as such. Symbolically, it is a 'victory' for the EU to be officially included as 'twentieth member'.[48] In comparison, the G8 adds the EU as ninth—ie 'extra'—member. In addition, both Spain and the Netherlands have so far been invited to all four G20 summits, not as official members, but as part of the EU representation or invited guests.[49]

The current situation of European membership and participation to the G20 has added fuel to the debate on 'over-representation' of the EU in global governance. Emerging economies and developing countries, in particular, but also the US, criticise the EU and its Member States for 'dominating' the membership of international organisations and fora by claiming too many seats, a situation which contrasts heavily with the EU's declining (economic) power in the world. At the same time, European voices—in particular the European Commission, the European Parliament and some smaller EU Member States—are not satisfied with the current state of affairs: due to the fragmentation of EU representation in various global governance constellations, Europe risks 'punching below its weight'.[50] The danger for the EU is that 'over-representation'—in terms of the amount of seats and voices—may result in de facto 'under-representation', ie the EU not being able to exert influence according to its economic weight, due to the ineffectiveness of its external representation and communication. Pascal Lamy, in this context, has warned the EU to sharpen its voice at future G20 summits:

> The frank reality is it does not make sense . . . If one European takes the floor on one topic, and then another European takes the floor on the same topic, nobody listens. Nobody listens because either it's the same thing and it gets boring, or it's not the same thing and it will not influence the result at the end of the day ... So the right solution,

[48] *cf* Kirton 'The G20' (n 5 above) 159; Krotz and Maher, 'Europe in the New World' (n 15 above) 27; Renard, 'From the New G20 to a New Multilateral Order' (n 16 above).

[49] In 2008, Spain, the Netherlands and also Poland lobbied for participation at the G20 Washington Summit. France, rotating Presidency of the Council at the time, ceded its 'EU Presidency seats' to Spain and one of its two 'French delegation seats' to the Netherlands. Poland's lobby efforts, however, did not succeed. At the Summit, France, Spain and the Netherlands all acted as members of the EU representation (as the French delegation flag was symbolically replaced by the EU flag). At the 2009 London Summit, Spain participated as rotating Presidency of the Council (it held the Presidency during the first half of 2009), and the Netherlands were invited for the second time. Also in Pittsburgh and Toronto, Spain and the Netherlands were invited to participate.

[50] *cf* former Commissioner for External Relations, Benita Ferrero-Waldner: 'If the EU is to punch its weight in the world we must harness the synergies between all the actors involved. I am looking forward to developing new ways of working to ensure we maximise our leverage and influence in international affairs' (June 2006, in the context of the Commission's Communication on 'Europe in the World: Some Practical Proposals for Greater Coherence, Effectiveness and Visibility').

if I may, is at least to make sure that they speak with one mouth. Not one voice—one mouth—on each topic on the agenda. That would be a great improvement.[51]

Yet, in preparing its participation in the G20 summits, the EU has managed to compensate for this lack of effectiveness by means of unprecedented efforts to coordinate common positions, at the highest political level, ie at the level of Heads of State and Government.[52] Ahead of the 2008 Washington summit, EU leaders—at the 7 November 2008 informal meeting of the Heads of State and Government (with the participation of Commission President José Manuel Barroso)—expressed the unity of the EU Members States in confronting the crisis, and agreed on a number of specific principles and approaches which could be adopted at the G20 summit.

In the run-up to the April 2009 G20 summit in London, the European Commission again played an active role, by means of its Communication for the Spring European Council on 'Driving European Recovery'. This stated that the 'EU must continue to speak with one voice', and that 'the European Union is particularly well-placed to take the lead in proposing concrete solutions that can deliver effective results at global level'.[53] The Commission explicitly referred to the implementation of the European Economic Recovery Plan,[54] which was adopted at the European Council meeting of 11–12 December 2008. These European efforts, in the Commission's view, could serve as an example for global reforms. At the European Council meeting of 19–20 March 2009, the EU Heads of State and Government defined the EU joint position—'agreed language'—for the London summit, and invited the Council and the Commission to ensure appropriate follow-up to the summit.[55] In the summit's aftermath, Joaquín Almunia, then Commissioner for Economic and Monetary Affairs, applauded the G20 summit outcome, and in particular the EU's success in promoting its own agenda at the international level (the 'normative power' of the EU). In his

[51] Quote by Pascal Lamy, WTO Director-General and former EU Trade Commissioner, in the context of the 26–28 March 2010 Brussels Forum (ie the annual high-level conference on transatlantic relations).

[52] Gstöhl, '"Patchwork Power" Europe' (n 47 above) 394. *cf* S Nasra, D Lesage, J Orbie, Jan, T Van de Graaf and M Vermeiren 'The EU in the G8 System: Assessing EU Member States' Involvement' (2009) 45 *EUI Working Papers RSCAS*.

[53] COM (2009) 114 final.

[54] COM (2008) 800 final. For an analysis of the EU's internal reforms, with emphasis on the recommendations of the High-Level Expert Group on EU financial supervision (established by Commission President Barroso on 8 October 2008, and headed by Jacques de Larosière, former IMF director), see—among others—K Lannoo, 'The Road Ahead after de Larosière' (2009) 195/7 *CEPS Policy Brief*; J Pelkmans, *De Rol van de EU in de Financiële en Economische Crisis* (The Hague, Nederlands Instituut voor Internationale Betrekkingen Clingendael, 2009). At the ECOFIN meeting of 7 September 2010, the Council endorsed an agreement with the European Parliament on a reform of the EU framework on financial supervision. The reform involves the creation of a European Systemic Risk Board (ESRB), which will provide macro-prudential oversight of the financial system, and three European authorities for the supervision of the banking, insurance and securities industries. These bodies were planned to be operational as from 1 January 2011.

[55] See European Council, Brussels, 19–20 March 2009, Presidency Conclusions, Annex 1: Agreed language with a view to the G20 Summit in London.

opinion, this was due to the EU's participation as a 'united front'. For Almunia, the crisis has created a window of opportunity for the EU to speak with a single voice.[56]

At the European Council meeting of 18–19 June 2009, EU leaders invited the Council and the Commission to ensure a coordinated EU position for the G20 summit in Pittsburgh, which was finally approved—again using the wording 'agreed language'—at the informal meeting of EU Heads of State and Government of 17 September 2009. After the Pittsburgh Summit, the European Council of 29–30 October 2009 welcomed the progress made, but stressed that—in the context of the agreed Framework for Strong, Sustainable and Balanced Growth—'the IMF and the G20 will have to take fully into account the institutional economic policy set-up of the European Union and the euro area as a whole.' The European Council again called on the Council and the Commission to ensure follow-up and preparation of future G20 meetings.

Finally, with regard to the EU's position for the June 2010 Toronto summit, the European Council referred to the 'Terms of References' earlier agreed upon in preparation of the G20 meeting of finance ministers and central bank governors (Busan, Republic of Korea, 5 June 2010), but added a number of EU priorities, among which were the need for a global system for levies and taxes on financial institutions (see above), a coordinated exit strategy, and progress in the reform of the financial system.[57]

Overall, EU coordination, the institutional framework of which is dealt with below as part of the discussion on the impact of the Lisbon Treaty on EU external action in general and at the G20 in particular, has been rather successful. The EU has managed to arrive at unified positions, and—comparing these positions with the summit outcomes—to influence the G20 agenda and recommendations in a significant way. There is obviously a need to nuance this success, taking into account the informal and deliberative character of the G20, as well as the non-binding nature of its recommendations.

B The EU in the IFIs

All 27 EU Member States are members of the IMF and the World Bank. The EU is not a member while the EU institutions do not actively engage in the work of these organisations. The European Commission has observer status at the Joint IMF/World Bank Development Committee (DC). The ECB is an observer, since 1999, at the meetings of the IMF Executive Board and at the International Monetary Financial Committee (IMFC). On exchange rate issues, the views of the Euro Group are in practice represented by the ECB and/or the Member State

[56] European Commissioner for Economic and Monetary Affairs speaking at a conference organised by the European Commission, 6 April 2009.

[57] European Council, Brussels, 17 June 2010, Conclusions, para 18.

holding the Presidency of the Council/ECOFIN.[58] EU coordination vis-à-vis the IMF takes place both in Brussels, through SCIMF (Sub-Committee on IMF, a substructure of the ECOFIN Council, in charge of long-term planning), and in Washington, through EURIMF (an informal body composed of IMF Executive Directors and other Member States representatives, in charge of day-to-day coordination). As regards the World Bank, EU coordination is handled by the Executive Directors and other Member State representatives.

Representation at the IMF Executive Board—and hence decision-making and voting in the IMF—proceeds through a system of constituencies.[59] The EU Member States—which in total have 32.02 per cent of the votes (compared to the US voting share of 16.74 per cent)—are 'spread' across a variety of 10 constituencies: France, Germany and the UK each have a single chair; Belgium, Italy and the Netherlands lead their respective constituencies, which each include other EU Member States and non-EU countries; the Scandinavian EU Member States are part of a Nordic-Baltic constituency (with rotating chairs); Ireland is part of a constituency chaired by Canada; Spain is part of a constituency with exclusively Latin-American countries (with rotating chairs); and Poland is a member of a constituency led by Switzerland.

EU representation in the IFIs is subject to a debate on over-representation and under-representation, comparable to the criticism on the EU's representation in G20. On the one hand, the combined voting weight of the EU Member States far exceeds the EU's global economic weight, which together with the EU 'dominance' of IFI managing positions (in the Executive Board, the EU Member States currently hold eight out of 24 Director positions), results in a perception that the EU is over-represented. On the other hand, the combined voting weight of the EU Member States is only 'virtual', as mobilising these votes would require the agreement of all states participating in the various constituencies of which the EU Member States are part. Despite having more than 30 per cent of the votes, the EU is a very ineffective actor, which does not—and cannot—succeed in converting its presence into actual influence.[60]

Both problems, ie over-representation and de facto under-representation, however, render it clear that the EU—or at least the euro area—should strive

[58] *cf* LB Smaghi, 'Powerless Europe: Why is the Euro Area Still a Political Dwarf' (2006) 9 *International Finance* 261.

[59] See www.imf.org/external/np/sec/memdir/members.htm. The World Bank is also governed through a similar system of constituencies.

[60] *cf* Smaghi, 'Powerless Europe' (n 58 above); Smaghi, 'A Single EU Seat in the International Monetary Fund?' (n 33 above); Smits, 'International Representation of Europe in the Area of Economic and Monetary Union' (n 47 above).

towards unified representation in the IFIs.[61] Although a more unified representation is most likely to come at the price of conceding a substantial part of the combined voting weight, the voting power left could be put to use in a more effective way.

Progress towards achieving unified representation, however, is slow. Within the EU, proposals for reform—including the creation of a single EU constituency (or a 'euro constituency' to start with)—have been put forward, but so far EU Member States have been generally reluctant to give up their seats in exchange for a single representation.[62] Also smaller Member States, such as Belgium and the Netherlands, which both chair a constituency, show resistance.[63] In the meantime, international pressure—not least in the context of the G20 summits—for the adaptation of the IFI governance structures is mounting.[64]

C The EU in other relevant organisations and fora

The picture of EU representation in the other international organisations and fora is mixed, yet the discussion on over-representation and lack of effectiveness continues. In the FSB, the EU is represented by six Member States—the four big Member States (France, Germany, Italy, UK), together with the Netherlands (which was already an FSF member) and Spain (added as a new member)—as well as by the European Commission and the ECB.[65] As such, with six out of 24 FSB member countries EU Member States, and two out of 12 FSB member organisations or bodies EU institutions, the EU is solidly represented, but in a fragmented way. This fragmentation, even though Member States, in accordance with long-established case law of the Court of Justice, are under a duty to coordinate their positions and loyally defend the Union interest in bodies where

[61] *cf* PC Padoan, 'Europe and Global Economic Governance after the Crisis' in S Micossi and GL Tosato (eds), *The European Union in the 21st Century. Perspectives from the Lisbon Treaty* (Brussels, Centre for European Policy Studies, 2009); LB Smaghi, 'Powerless Europe' (n 58 above).

[62] Reform is supported by both the European Commission and the European Parliament. Former European Commissioner for Economic and Monetary Affairs, Joaquín Almunia, speaking at a conference organised by the European Commission on 6 April 2009, made a plea for consolidation of the EU voice in the IFIs, in particular the IMF, where the EU should strive towards a single seat for the Euro area. *cf* Smaghi, 'Powerless Europe' (n 58 above); Smaghi, 'A Single EU Seat in the International Monetary Fund?' (n 33 above); Smits, 'International Representation of Europe in the Area of Economic and Monetary Union' (n 47 above); Pelkmans, *De Rol van de EU in de Financiële en Economische Crisis* (n 54 above).

[63] *cf* T Van de Graaf, D Lesage, S Nasra, J Orbie and M Vermeiren, 'Van G8 naar G20: Wordt de Stem van Kleine EU-Landen Gehoord?' (2009) 63 *International Spectator* 369.

[64] *cf* Padoan, 'Europe and Global Economic Governance after the Crisis' (n 61 above).

[65] Next to the European Commission and the ECB, the Bank for International Settlements, IMF, World Bank, OECD, Basel Committee on Banking Supervision, Committee on the Global Financial System, Committee on Payment and Settlement Systems, International Association of Insurance Supervisors, IASB and IOSCO are represented as 'international organisations' or 'international standard-setting bodies and other groupings'.

the EU cannot speak for itself,[66] is in practice not compensated for by strong coordination efforts, as for example in the run-up to G20 summits.

In the WTO, the EU is the only international organisation to be one of the 153 full members, along with its 27 Member States. Due to strong internal coordination (with EU positions in the WTO being pre-cooked in the so-called 'Article 133 committee', as it was called before entry into force of the Lisbon Treaty) and the ability to speak with a single voice (the European Commission speaking for the EU at almost all WTO meetings, and acting as an agent of the Member States during trade negotiations), the EU's representation and participation to the WTO is generally considered to be the best available example of how the EU's voice can be heard, ie how a strong presence can effectively be translated into tangible influence.[67]

In contrast with the situation in the WTO, the EU is not a member, but merely an observer at the ILO. The EU Presidency and the European Commission act as 'agents' of the 27 EU Member States, which all have full ILO membership, and issue common statements on their behalf.[68] Coordination, however, is not always successful, and as such, the EU Member States do not always vote in the same way.

In the OECD, 20 EU Member States are represented as full members, and as such 'dominate' OECD membership (there are 33 member countries in total).[69] Furthermore, in a Supplementary Protocol to the OECD Convention, the signatory states decided that the European Commission 'shall participate in the work' of the OECD, thus accommodating the express will of the EU Member States stated in Article 220 TFEU to ensure that the Union shall establish 'all appropriate forms of cooperation' with the OECD. This participation goes well beyond that of a mere observer, and, in fact, gives the European Commission a virtual membership, typically referred to as the status of 'full participant', allowing it to attend all meetings and participate in the work of the OECD on a quasi-equal footing with the OECD Member States. The Commission's representative, however, is self-evidently not entitled to vote when legal acts are being adopted by the Council, the decision-making body of the OECD.

Finally, in international standard-setting bodies such as the IASB or the Basel Committee on Banking Supervision, membership rules vary greatly, and as such, the participation of the EU and its Member States—for the most part EU

[66] See, on the importance of the 'unity' of the external representation and how to achieve it, Opinion 2/91, *Convention No 170 of the International Labour Organization concerning safety in the use of chemicals at work* [1993] ECR I-1061, paras 36–38.

[67] See, inter alia, JL Mortensen, 'The World Trade Organization and the European Union' in KE Joergensen (ed), *The European Union and International Organizations* (London, Routledge, 2009).

[68] *cf* P Nedergaard, 'The European Union at the ILO's International Labour Conferences: A "Double' Principal-Agent Analysis' in KE Joergensen (ed), *The European Union and International Organizations* (London, Routledge, 2009).

[69] The 20 EU Member States are Austria, Belgium, Czech Republic, Denmark, Finland, France, Germany, Greece, Hungary, Ireland, Italy, Luxembourg, the Netherlands, Poland, Portugal, Slovak Republic, Slovenia (since July 2010), Spain, Sweden and the United Kingdom.

Member State nationals who are appointed as members—is very diverse. 'Europe', however, tends to be extremely well represented, in particular in comparison with emerging economies and developing countries.[70] In the IASB, for example, five out of the current 15 members are EU Member State nationals, including the chairman. Furthermore, in the IFRS Interpretations Committee, ie the interpretative body of the IASB, six out of 14 voting members come from EU Member States, and the European Commission acts as an observer. The 'Trustees', who are in charge of appointing the members of the IASB and the Interpretations Committee, consist of 21 members, of which six are EU Member State nationals.[71] The Basel Committee counts nine central banks from EU Member States among its 27 members[72]. While seven of them have introduced the euro as their currency, these states continue to be represented by their respective national banks, with no formal role for either the ECB or the Commission. Yet, given the impact of the proposals on banking supervision rules that the Basel Committee is drafting, Member States are under a duty of loyal cooperation to coordinate their positions with both the Commission and the ECB.

D Towards single voice and unified representation?

The international crisis has exposed several weaknesses of global financial and economic governance. The overview of G20 deliberations and the role of the EU therein, as well as in other relevant organisations and fora, has served to illustrate that today's governance architecture no longer corresponds to global economic realities. In particular the EU's place in this governance architecture—over-represented yet ineffective—is under pressure, both internationally and within the EU.

In its March 2010 Communication on 'Europe 2020', the European Commission draws lessons from the crisis so far. Pertaining to the EU's performance on the global scene, the Commission is confident that the EU still 'adds value', but stresses that 'the EU will influence global policy decisions only if it acts jointly. Stronger external representation will need to go hand in hand with stronger internal co-ordination.'[73]

[70] *cf* KS Brackney and PR Witmer, 'The European Union's Role in International Standards Setting. Will Bumps in the Road to Convergence Affect the SEC's Plans?' (2005) *The CPA Journal*, www.nysscpa.org.

[71] See www.ifrs.org/The+organisation/IASCF+and+IASB.htm.

[72] The members of the Basel Committee are Argentina, Australia, Belgium, Brazil, Canada, China, France, Germany, Hong Kong SAR, India, Indonesia, Italy, Japan, Korea, Luxembourg, Mexico, the Netherlands, Russia, Saudi Arabia, Singapore, South Africa, Spain, Sweden, Switzerland, Turkey, the United Kingdom and the United States; see also www.bis.org/bcbs/.

[73] Commission, 'Europe 2020. A Strategy for Smart, Sustainable and Inclusive Growth' COM (2010) 2020, 6.

In response to international criticism, a scenario for upgrading the EU's external representation—with better coordination in achieving a single voice as a first step, and possibly unified representation at a later stage (in particular in areas where the EU has exclusive competence)—should involve a strategy for 'rationalising' the EU's presence in international clubs, organisations and other bodies.[74] The final section of this chapter will assess whether the Treaty of Lisbon, which is—among other objectives—intended to strengthen the EU's performance on the global scene, succeeds in answering (at least some of) these challenges.

IV IMPACT OF THE TREATY OF LISBON

The external representation of the EU has so far been rather complicated, not only because of the idiosyncrasies of the various international fora, outlined above, but also because of the number of actors that are involved and because of the difficult division of competences between the Union and its Member States, exacerbated by the complexity of the Pillar structure. These vices are not redressed fundamentally by the Lisbon Treaty, even though the desire to have the Union speak with a stronger and more coherent voice is at the heart of the Lisbon reform.

The most obvious change is the disappearance of the Pillar structure. This in turn is the logical consequence of a single European Union with legal personality (see Article 47 TEU) and which is the legal successor to the European Community (but not Euratom) (see Article 1, third indent, *in fine* TEU). The single legal personality is, however, less revolutionary than it sounds. As such, under the old Treaties, the European Community was already explicitly bestowed with legal personality. Moreover, also in respect of the Second and Third Pillars, it became largely accepted, especially after the Treaty of Nice, that for all practical purposes the EU was in a position to conclude international agreements, to take on legal obligations and to enjoy legal rights so as to have functional legal personality as a result of Article 24 of the pre-Lisbon TEU.[75] Effectively, also other international actors, both states and international organisations, proved willing to engage in international agreements with the EU alone, without the patronage of the Member States, even though the latter would—subject to some safeguard mechanisms—also be bound by the agreement. The novelty is then not so much that the Union has legal personality, but that we are left with only one legal person, with express legal personality, and in charge of the totality of the domains that used to be divided over the Union and the European Community and split

[74] *cf* R Gowan, 'The Obama Administration and Multilateralism: Europe Relegated' (2010) 39 *FRIDE Policy Brief.*

[75] K Lenaerts and P Van Nuffel, *Constitutional Law of the European Union* (London, Thomson/ Sweet & Maxwell, 2005) 816–17.

into three Pillars. This should also be reflected in a unified external action, to which effect the second paragraph of Article 21(3) TEU requires the Union to ensure 'consistency between the different areas of its external action and between these and its other policies'. The same provision orders the Council and the Commission, assisted by the High Representative of the Union for Foreign Affairs and Security Policy, to ensure that consistency, and to cooperate to that effect.

In reality, the remnants of the Third Pillar can still be seen in the area of Freedom, Security and Justice, and—more importantly for our purposes—there still is a strong divide between Common Foreign and Security Policy (CFSP) and non-CFSP issues, even though the external action in both fields are governed pursuant to Article 21(3) TEU by the principles laid down in Article 21(1) and 21(2) TEU. Whereas the focus of the G20 is mainly economic, it turns out that there are a number of security-related issues seeping through. While for most states this does not pose major difficulties, as their prime ministers or foreign secretaries are usually deemed to be in a position to speak across the board, regardless of the topic, this is different for the Union, whose external representation varies depending on the subject matter. Accordingly, at G20 summits the EU must be represented by both the President of the European Commission, as under Article 17(1) TEU the Commission 'shall ensure the Union's external representation', but with the exception of the CFSP, and the President of the European Council, who 'shall, at his level and in that capacity, ensure the external representation of the Union on issues concerning its common foreign and security policy' (Article 15(6)(2) TEU). Accordingly, at the June 2010 G20 summit in Toronto—the first such summit after the entry into force of the Lisbon Treaty—Commission President Barroso and European Council President Van Rompuy both attended the meeting on behalf of the Union, with both taking the floor in accordance with a pre-arranged division of labour between the two. If monetary matters are on the agenda, the regime becomes even more complicated, as for the countries of the Eurozone, monetary policy is an exclusive EU competence. The Lisbon Treaty recognises that this also has external consequences, and thus it is provided in Article 138(1) TFEU that the Council—with only the Eurozone countries voting—'*shall* adopt a decision establishing common positions on matters of particular interest for economic and monetary union within the competent international financial institutions and conferences'.[76] However, it is unclear who should represent that position on the ground—Article 138(2) TFEU only provides that the 'Council, on a proposal from the Commission, *may* adopt appropriate measures to ensure unified representation within the international financial institutions and conferences'.[77] That is, provided an agreement can be reached within the Council on such a unified representation, and the forum actually allows for an EU representative to

[76] Emphasis added.
[77] Emphasis added.

appear. The relative informality of the G20 serves here as an advantage, to the extent that it is easier to make ad hoc arrangements. Those arrangements do not hold, however, for the international organisations, such as the IMF or the World Bank, that are steered by G20 policy decisions. Here the absence of a formal role for the European Commission or the European Central Bank results also in a role for the Member States as agents for the EU. While the Member States are in those circumstances under an obligation to act on behalf of the Union in accordance with the principle of sincere cooperation as laid down in Article 4(3) TEU,[78] it is inevitable that this collides with Member States' (views of) rights as long-standing members in their own right of these fora.

The Lisbon Treaty does not, moreover, address in any way the root difficulty behind the complexities of EU external action, ie the problem of mixity. While the EU is competent under Article 216 TFEU to 'conclude an agreement with one or more third countries or international organisations where the Treaties so provide or where the conclusion of an agreement is necessary in order to achieve, within the framework of the Union's policies, one of the objectives referred to in the Treaties, or is provided for in a legally binding Union act or is likely to affect common rules or alter their scope', not much is said about whether the EU is *alone* competent to do so. Admittedly, Article 3(2) TFEU now contains a codification of the case law the ECJ has developed in this respect since the *ERTA* case,[79] indicating that the EU has exclusive competence 'for the conclusion of an international agreement when its conclusion is provided for in a legislative act of the Union or is necessary to enable the Union to exercise its internal competence, or in so far as its conclusion may affect common rules or alter their scope'. However, even though Article 216 TFEU is eerily reminiscent of Article 3(2) TFEU, the truth is that for most domains the conditions are not fulfilled for there to be an exclusive competence, and thus the default position of a shared competence reappears.[80] Yet the drafters of the Lisbon Treaty have failed to specify any rules on how the Member State interest should be represented in those cases, or how the potentially conflicting interests of the Union and the Member States should be reconciled in practice. The result is a constant turf war

[78] Opinion 2/91, Convention *No 170 of the International Labour Organization concerning safety in the use of chemicals at work* [1993] ECR I-1061, paras 36–38; Opinion 1/94 *Agreement establishing the World Trade Organisation* [1994] ECR I-5267, paras 106–09; Case C-246/07 *Commission v Sweden*, judgment of 20 April 2010, nyr. For more, see G De Baere, ''O, where is faith? O, where is loyalty?' – Some thoughts on the duty of loyal cooperation and on the Union's external environmental competences in the light of the *PFOS* case', (2011) 36 *European Law Review*, forthcoming. For a broad analysis of the role of the principle of sincere cooperation in external action, see E Neframi, 'The Duty of Loyalty: Rethinking its Scope through its Application in the Field of External Relations' (2010) 47 *Common Market Law Review* 323.

[79] Case C-22/70 *Commission v Council* [1971] ECR 263. For a discussion, see G De Baere, *Constitutional Principles of EU External Relations* (Oxford, Oxford University Press, 2008) 68–70.

[80] See in this respect R Schütze, 'Lisbon and the federal order of competences: a prospective analysis' (2008) *European Law Review*, 713–14; M Cremona, 'A Constitutional Basis for Effective External Action? An Assessment of the Provisions on EU External Action in the Constitutional Treaty' (2006) 30 *EUI Working Paper* 10–11.

between the European Commission, which seems convinced that the absence of any specific rule should be read as bestowing upon the Commission the default role of representing both the EU interest and the interests of its Member States, and the Council which feels entitled to make separate arrangements for the representation of Member State interests, in particular by reintroducing a role for the Presidency of the Council (which has otherwise no formal role in external relations under the Lisbon Treaty). Furthermore, the situation is even more blurred in those instances, as is often the case in the context of the G20, where there are no formal international agreements to be concluded. There the Treaty is largely silent on how to proceed, confident that ad hoc arrangements will be found, as is mandated by the ECJ as a matter of sincere cooperation.[81]

The institutional novelties of the Lisbon Treaty do not seem of a nature to redress many of the complexities. First, the creation of both a President of the European Council and a High Representative for Foreign Affairs and Security Policy means that there are now two persons to speak on behalf of the Union in CFSP matters, each at their own level. At first glance, their focus on CFSP matters should actually make them also of diminished importance to the economic fora at issue. However, both their roles are blurred in practice. The President of the European Council internally gives impetus to the debate in the European Council on all issues, and so unsurprisingly internationally, at his level, non-CFSP issues will inevitably also come up in fora—such as the G20—that have a very broad focus, so that good coordination with the President of the European Commission is essential. By contrast, the High Representative has also the role of European Commissioner for external relations, and as such she is also charged with the coordination of the non-CFSP external action within the European Commission. Yet, in international fora, the EU should rather be represented by the relevant specialised Commissioners, including the Commissioners for trade, or economic and monetary affairs.

Second, the European External Action Service (EEAS), although potentially a new EU powerhouse, should have little influence over the economic governance. By its terms of reference it is to assist primarily the High Representative for the Foreign and Security Policy, but her duties focus on CFSP issues, not the key economic issues at issue in the various bodies discusses above on which the G20 is currently focusing.[82] The EEAS is, however, also responsible for heading the

[81] Case C-246/07 *Commission v Sweden*, judgment of 20 April 2010, nyr. See in this sense T Corthaut and D Van Eeckhoutte, 'Legal Aspects of EU Participation in Global Environmental Governance under the UN Umbrella' in J Wouters H Bruyninckx, S Basu and S Schunz (eds) *The European Union and Multilateral Governance* (Basingstoke, Palgrave MacMillan, 2011) forthcoming.

[82] See Art 2 of Council Decision 2010/427 establishing the organisation and functioning of the European External Action Service [2010] OJ L 201/30. Whereas that Article also lists as a task of the EEAS to support the High Representative 'in his/her capacity as Vice-President of the Commission for fulfilling within the Commission the responsibilities incumbent on it in external relations, and in coordinating other aspects of the Union's external action', the provision continues by adding 'without prejudice to the normal tasks of the services of the Commission'. This implies that international

Union delegations which, in accordance with Article 221 TFEU, are to be set up in third countries and at international organisations. This raises two new problems. The first one concerns the internal organisation of the delegations, which will be spearheaded by someone from the EEAS, even though the actual policy initiatives falling outside the scope of the CFSP will be dealt with by specialised Commission staff. Secondly, the informal nature of the G20 means that there is no such thing as a Union delegation to the G20. Accordingly, the European Commission could rightly claim that it falls to it to represent the Union in those fora pursuant to its general competences in respect of non-CFSP external action under Article 17 TEU and the division of labour laid down in Article 220(2) TFEU, and not to the EEAS. Nevertheless, the High Representative, in her role as vice-president of the Commission entrusted with the external affairs portfolio, will still be involved in the internal decision-making within the Commission, thus ensuring the overall coherence of the EU external action. And again, to the extent that some of the issues in the G20 may not fall within the exclusive competence of the Union, the issue of who speaks for the Member States arises. The problem is even quite intricate to the extent that some, but not all, Member States are at the table alongside the EU. On EU exclusive competences they must yield to the Commission. On CFSP matters they must yield to the High Representative or the President of the European Council, provided that there is a common position on the issue. On those matters where the Member States within the framework of the Council manage to coordinate their national positions in respect of the issues that formally fall outside the competence of the Union, the principle of sincere cooperation would dictate that the Member States only speak to defend these lines. On all other matters, however, those Member States at the table are in principle free to defend their own interests, probably subject to a duty of sincere cooperation requiring them not to act to the obvious detriment of the Union or other Member States that are unrepresented. Nevertheless, it is clear that those Member States not represented may thus at times be left out of the decision-making, both in the literal sense of not having a seat at the table, but also more broadly in not having their interests being defended by any other party present—neither the EU representatives, nor the other Member States.

V CONCLUSION

This chapter has focused on the international financial crisis that emerged in 2008, the actors in the global response thereto, and the position and role of the EU in the changing system of global financial governance, especially in the light of the Treaty of Lisbon. The latter provides the EU with a new set of actors, most

economic issues, such as the strengthening on rules on banking supervision as discussed above will rather be followed up by the regular Commission services.

notably the President of the European Council, the High Representative/Vice-President of the Commission and the EEAS, who are specifically tasked with making the external action of the European Union more visible. If those new players can find a good *modus vivendi* among themselves and with the European Commission and the Member States, this should result in a more dynamic, visible and coherent external policy. However, the Lisbon Treaty has left much unclear about the external representation, and has failed to address the paralysing problem of a coherent representation of the Union in instances of mixity, as was recently painfully demonstrated in the context of the negotiations on international standards concerning mercury.

Against this background, the representation of the EU in the G20 is an interesting test case, as the informality of the setting, the presence of some, but not all, Member States alongside the Union, and the breadth of the agenda, all make this a potential minefield in a turf war between the Commission, the Council and the Member States. Nevertheless, for now, common sense seems to prevail. If a pragmatic approach is adopted, the representation of the Union after Lisbon will indeed be stronger and more coherent, if only because of the length of tenure of the two main EU actors. If, by contrast, the political will of the Member States to let these two EU representatives speak on their behalf wanes, with more individual Member States seeking backdoor routes into the meetings, or large Member States effectively undermining the EU during G20 meetings and the like, the whole Lisbon reform will but be an empty shell. It is therefore to be welcomed that the European Council on 16 September 2010 re-emphasised that the EU 'must actively contribute through coordinated positions' in the G8 and G20 and that it 'welcome[d] the ambition of the incoming French chairmanship in 2011 to fully use the G20 and G8 to that end.'[83] However, even when the EU manages to bring its own house in order, the intricate arrangements to enable it to fully participate in international fora require quite some openness and creativity on the side of other international organisations and non-EU states. The post-Lisbon external action machinery of the Union will only be fully effective if other international actors are willing to play along. This is not always the case, as was painfully illustrated by the EU's failed attempt to gain the status of enhanced observer at the UN General Assembly in September 2010.[84] Also in international affairs, it takes two to tango.

[83] Conclusions, European Council 16 September 2010, EUCO 21/10, CO EUR 16 CONCL 3, para I.7.a.

[84] The initiative failed when tabled on 12 and 13 September 2010, when a counter-resolution was presented for the EU's resolution to be postponed, and passed by 76 votes to 71. Ironically, the 76 included most of the Africa, Caribbean and Pacific beneficiaries of EU aid.

8

Debt Crisis as a Global Emergency: the European Economic Constitution and other Greek Fables

ANTONIS ANTONIADIS*

I INTRODUCTION

THE ECONOMIC AND Monetary Union is characterised by insufficient checks and balances, encapsulated in the misnomer of the Growth and Stability Pact (GSP).[1] Even before the weakening of the GSP,[2] and depending on the prevailing political and economic conditions, it was envisaged that if a Member State were to face bankruptcy, such bankruptcy might prove contagious, lead to the need for a bail-out, and affect the internal/external strength of the euro.[3] In the first few months of 2010, this, previously unlikely, scenario became probable. The dramatic outlook in the financial press was not inexplicable. It was commonplace that, in the aftermath of the 2008 financial crisis, the world's largest economies committed large amounts in order to

* The opinions expressed in the present contribution are personal and do not necessarily reflect those of the European Ombudsman. The contribution takes account of the developments until 30 July 2010.

[1] See Art 126 TFEU (ex Art 104 TEC). The main texts which comprise the GSP are: Council Regulation 1466/97/EC on the strengthening of the surveillance of budgetary positions and the surveillance and coordination of economic policies [1997] OJ L209/1; Council Regulation 3605/93/EC on the application of the Protocol on the excessive deficit procedure annexed to the Treaty establishing the European Community [1993] OJ L332/7; Council Regulation 1467/97/EC on speeding up and clarifying the implementation of the excessive deficit procedure [1997] OJ L209/6.

[2] In the aftermath of Case C-27/04 *Commission v Council* [2004] ECR I-6649, the GSP was amended by Council Regulation 1055/2005 amending Regulation 1466/97/EC on the strengthening of the surveillance of budgetary positions and the surveillance and coordination of economic policies [2005] OJ L174/1; Council Regulation 1056/2005 amending Regulation 1467/97/EC on speeding up and clarifying the implementation of the excessive deficit procedure [2005] OJ L174/5.

[3] F Amtenbrink and J de Haan, 'Economic Governance in the European Union: Fiscal Policy Discipline versus Flexibility' (2003) 40 *Common Market Law Review* 1075, 1089–95, in particular, 1093.

support the financial institutions and inject liquidity into the market.[4] This, in conjunction with the expansive fiscal policies of the past decade and the economic downturn, led many of them to a dire budgetary position. In this climate, the financial markets started questioning whether certain states would be able to continue servicing their debt. A debt crisis emerged, possessing all the characteristics of a global emergency.[5]

The euro area debt crisis started in Greece. In October 2009,[6] the newly elected Greek government announced that its fiscal position was worse than previously expected.[7] By April 2010, the rising concern about the Greek economy entered the state of alarm. The crisis of confidence became apparent on the financial markets: yield spreads on Greek bonds widened, insurance premiums on credit default swaps rocketed while the Greek economy was being continuously demoted by the international credit-rating agencies. As a result, there was widespread speculation that Greece was going to default on its creditors, or be forced to restructure its debt. Given that Greece could no longer borrow on the financial markets to service its debt, bankruptcy appeared like a self-fulfilling prophecy. Despite the Greek economy counting for only about 2 per cent of that of the euro area, a Greek default could be contagious and likely candidates were identified in Portugal, Ireland and Spain.[8] Even if none of these Member States went bankrupt, an ongoing debt crisis would most likely disrupt the recovery of the global economy from the 2008 financial crisis.[9] The continued survival of the euro was reportedly in jeopardy.[10] In spring 2010, the exchange rate of the euro hit consecutive four year lows against the US dollar.

At the time of writing, a fully fledged EU response to address the debt crisis has not been formed. However, important emergency measures and policy initiatives have been taken, and a clear sense of direction begins to emerge. Two main strands of action may be identified in this respect: first, the emergency measures taken to contain the crisis and, second, the policy initiatives to reform the Union economic governance and prevent such a crisis from happening again in the future. The focus of the present analysis will be on the emergency measures taken by the EU. These may be divided into two categories, which will be examined in

[4] See J Wouters, S Sterkx and T Corthaut, 'The European Union, the International Financial Crisis and Global Governance', ch 7 of this book. For the role of the Commission in the financial crisis, see E White, 'The Constitutional Apparatus of The European Union: The Perspective of The European Commission', ch 13 of this book.

[5] See Introduction of this book.

[6] A timeline of the Greek crisis is available at www.guardian.co.uk/business/2010/may/05/greece-debt-crisis-timeline.

[7] Its budget deficit for 2009 was predicted to reach 12.7% instead of 3.7% originally provided for in its Stability Programme and adjusted to 6% by the previous government.

[8] Together with Greece the four Member States have been referred to in financial reporting under the acronym 'PIGS'. See, Éditorial, 'L'Union économique et monétaire dans la tourmente de déficits publics' (2010) 46 *Revue Trimestrielle de Droit Européen* 1.

[9] 'Volatility persists amid eurozone fears' *Financial Times* (London, 28 May 2010). Olli Rehn, the Economic and Financial Affairs Commissioner, likened Greece of 2010 to Lehman Brothers of 2008.

[10] Niall Ferguson, 'The End of the Euro' *Newsweek*, 7 May 2010.

the corresponding sections: the specific measures taken to deal with the Greek crisis, and the measures taken to defend the euro and appease the financial markets.[11] The overview of the emergency measures raises a number of questions which merit examination from an EU constitutional perspective, excluding any meta-constitutional aspects.[12] The principal question is whether the EU is equipped with the necessary tools to address the challenges caused by an emergency of such timing, nature and intensity. The twin sets of instruments to deal with the Greek debt crisis and the defence of the euro add a layer of complexity to the discussion and pose a number of interesting questions, both as regards the construction of EU economic policy internally and its external dimension. In its final section, the chapter will discuss briefly the institutional architecture of EU economic policy as it emerges from the combined effect of the entry into force of the Treaty of Lisbon and the emergency measures taken to counteract the debt crisis.

II EMERGENCY INSTRUMENTS TO BAIL OUT GREECE: THE FLIGHT OF ICARUS

The Greek crisis is deep-seated. Lax fiscal policy, inadequate responses to mounting imbalances, structural weaknesses and statistical misreporting were contributing factors to the crisis.[13] More precisely, besides the well-known fiscal imbalances and structural weaknesses of the Greek economy, it was revealed, soon after a change of government following general elections, that the budgetary situation in Greece was much worse than expected.[14] In the following months,

[11] In this regard, see, 'Statement of the Heads of State or Government of the Euro area', Brussels, 7 May 2010.

[12] That is, whether its constitution enables the Union to adopt the missing tools. In theory, this is certainly the case, however, in practice, it will be difficult for the following reasons. First, the debt crisis comes at a time when, after a decade-long process of constitutional change there is a common perception driven by constitutional fatigue and, ironically, the financial and debt crisis itself that we have reached some sort of constitutional *finalité* in the EU. A Treaty reform in accordance with the ordinary procedure which will entail specific measures to deal with the emergency in hand must be ruled out. Although it would be premature to pass judgement on the impact of the simplified procedure provided in Art 49(6) TEU, the European Council should be expected to be parsimonious when applying this procedure to anything other than innocuous or inevitable changes. In fact, at the time of writing, the TFEU was amended, subject to approval by the Member States in accordance with their own constitutional requirements, to adjust the number of seats of the European Parliament (see European Council Decision 2010/350 of 17 June 2010 on the examination by a conference of representatives of the governments of the Member States of the amendments to the Treaties proposed by the Spanish Government concerning the composition of the European Parliament and not to convene a Convention [2010] OJ L160/5). An amendment of central provisions of economic policy would also be politically untenable because it might require a referendum in certain Member States.

[13] Commission, 'Reinforcing Economic Policy Coordination' (Communication) COM(2010)250 final.

[14] Eurostat Report on Greek Government Deficit and Debt Statistics, COM(2010) 1 final, available at http://epp.eurostat.ec.europa.eu/cache/ITY_PUBLIC/COM_2010_REPORT_GREEK/EN/COM_2010_REPORT_GREEK-EN.PDF.

the Greek government announced a series of austerity measures, in addition to those already provided in its Stability Programme, in order to regain investor trust.[15] The austerity measures failed to impress the markets.[16] The reaction of the financial markets, which was characterised as opportunistic speculation,[17] meant that the interest rates at which Greece could borrow from the markets rocketed.[18] The downgrading of the Greek debt rating continued, reaching rock bottom at the end of April 2010, when a leading credit-rating agency downgraded Greek debt to 'junk' status.[19]

In view of the persistent readiness of the markets to bank on Greece defaulting, the Greek government tried to mobilise its partners and arrive at a 'European' solution to address the problem. The aim of that effort was not a financial bail-out[20] but a strong political commitment in the form of 'a loaded gun on the table'[21] which would enable Greece to meet its refinancing needs by borrowing from the markets. The Greek government's initiatives met with strong resistance from Germany, which ruled out the option of a bilateral loan.[22] When the (promise of a) financing mechanism became inevitable, Germany insisted on the involvement of the International Monetary Fund (IMF) and its stringent policy conditionality.[23] At first, the involvement of the IMF was not greeted with enthusiasm in the Euro Group;[24] however, it was later acknowledged that the IMF might have a role to play.[25]

The foundations of the Greek bail-out can be traced at the European Council meeting of 25 March 2010.[26] In the statement which followed, the Heads of State

[15] 'Papandreou unveils radical reforms to salvage Greece's public finances' *The Guardian* (Manchester, 14 December 2009). Two further sets of austerity measures were announced on 2 February and 3 March 2010.

[16] Council Decision 2010/291 establishing whether effective action has been taken by Greece in response to the Council Recommendation of 27 April 2009 [2010] OJ L125/50.

[17] Speech by Prime Minister Papandreou before the European Parliament, Brussels, 18 March 2010.

[18] On 1 February 2010, 2-year bond spreads reached 347 basis points; 10-year bond spreads reached 270 basis points. See European Commission, Directorate-General for Economic and Financial Affairs, 'The Economic Adjustment Programme for Greece', Occasional Paper no 61, May 2010, 11.

[19] 'Cuts to Debt Rating Stir Anxiety in Europe' *New York Times* (27 April 2010). On the same day, bond spreads reached unprecedented heights (2-year bond spreads 1552 basis points; 10-years bond spreads 755 basis points).

[20] 'Greece told to make more spending cuts', BBC News, 16 February 2010. Available at http://news.bbc.co.uk/2/hi/business/8517499.stm.

[21] Speech by Prime Minister Papandreou before the European Parliament, Brussels, 18 March 2010.

[22] 'We will not offer Greece a cent': German economy minister deals hammer blow to Athens as rioters attack police on the streets' *Daily Mail* (London, 6 March 2010).

[23] For an excellent comprehensive analysis of the IMF's role in past crises, see AF Lowenfeld, *International Economic Law*, (Oxford, Oxford University Press, 2003) 565–616.

[24] Éditorial, 'L'Union économique et monétaire dans la tourmente de déficits publics' (2010) 46 *Revue Trimestrielle de Droit Européen* 1, 6.

[25] 'Juncker concedes IMF role possible in Greek bail-out' *EU Observer* (22 March 2010).

[26] Available at www.consilium.europa.eu/uedocs/cms_data/docs/pressdata/en/ec/113563.pdf.

and Government of the euro area praised the Greek authorities for the 'ambitious and decisive action' which should allow Greece to regain the full confidence of the markets. The Euro Group reaffirmed its preparedness to take determined and coordinated action, if needed, to safeguard the financial stability in the euro area. To this end, a financing mechanism would be established involving a substantial IMF financing and a majority of European financing and taking the form of bilateral loans from the Member States. The mechanism would be considered as *ultima ratio* and would be conditional on insufficiency of market financing. The financing would be tied to strong conditionality, while setting incentives to Greece to return to the financial markets. Interest rates would not contain any subsidy element.[27] The mechanism would remain inactive until the Greek government requested financial support.

The 'gun on the table' proved insufficient to turn the financial markets around.[28] In a letter sent to the IMF, the European Commission and the European Central Bank (ECB) on 15 April 2010, the Greek government requested discussions to clarify the technical terms on the basis of which the aid would be granted. To this end, a joint IMF/Commission/ECB mission visited Athens from 21 April to 3 May 2010. On 2 May 2010, agreement on the terms of the financing was reached at staff level and, on the same day, the Euro Group took the decision to activate the stability support mechanism.[29] By 18 May 2010, the first instalment was disbursed.[30]

The Greek bail-out takes the following legal form. First, a Memorandum of Understanding (MoU) signed between Greece, on the one hand, and the European Commission, on behalf of those Member States whose currency is the euro, on the other.[31] The MoU outlines the challenges faced by the Greek economy and the policy reforms which need to take place in order to address them, details specific fiscal measures, including the deadline for their introduction and the fiscal benefit they are expected to yield, and sets out the applicable performance criteria and indicative targets. Disbursement of instalments under the loan is made subject to quarterly reviews of conditionality.[32]

[27] Statement by the Heads of State and Government of the euro area, Brussels, 25 March 2010, 1.

[28] It could be said that the markets called the EU's bluff as to whether the gun was actually loaded. On 8 April 2010, the 2-year bond spreads reached 652 basis points, while 10-year bond spreads reached 430 basis points.

[29] Statement by Euro Group, Brussels, 2 May 2010. Available at www.consilium.europa.eu/uedocs/cms_data/docs/pressdata/en/misc/114130.pdf.

[30] European Commission, 'The Economic Adjustment Programme for Greece' (n 15 above).

[31] The MoU comprises a Memorandum of Economic and Financial Policies, Memorandum of Understanding on Specific Economic Policy Conditionality and Technical Memorandum of Understanding.

[32] The MoU is available at www.imf.org/external/pubs/ft/scr/2010/cr10111.pdf.

Second, an Intercreditor Agreement[33] and a Loan Facility Agreement[34] between Greece and the Member States whose currency is the euro.[35] The Agreements provide stability support to Greece in an intergovernmental framework of pooled bilateral loans.[36] The Loan Facility Agreement specifies that the loans are granted in conjunction with funding from the IMF.[37] The Commission takes a coordinating role on behalf of the Member States in consultation with the ECB.[38] The Agreements specify their modus operandi[39] and the applicable interest rate.[40] Among the many interesting features of the Agreements, one can distinguish the choice of English law as the applicable law of the Agreements and the exclusive jurisdiction to the Court of Justice to settle any dispute arising.[41]

Conditionality is ensured by making the support granted to Greece dependent on compliance with the terms to be defined in a Council Decision addressed to Greece in accordance with Articles 126(9) and 136 TFEU *and* the measures set out in the MoU.[42] As far as the first set of conditions is concerned, the Commission submitted a recommendation to the Council one day after the agreement was struck.[43] The Council's Decision of 10 May 2010 provides a mixture of fiscal measures, to include both revenue increases and expenditure cuts, and structural reforms which fully correspond to the requirements of

[33] The English text of these agreements has been retrieved from the Irish Parliament website at www.oireachtas.ie/documents/bills28/bills/2010/2210/b2210d.pdf.

[34] In the Loan Facility Agreement, KfW (Kreditanstalt für Wiederaufbau, a German state-owned banking group) was designated by Germany to act as the lender on its behalf, subject to the instructions of and with the benefit of the guarantee of the Federal Republic of Germany.

[35] The European Commission signed the Agreements on behalf of the euro area Member States.

[36] Art 1(1) of the Intercreditor Agreement.

[37] Third recital of the Loan Facility Agreement.

[38] The Council considered it necessary to clarify that the 'role entrusted to the Commission is limited to the tasks specified in the inter-creditor agreement and not extend beyond tasks associated with the management of the stability support to Greece', Doc 9544/10 (Presse 104) 'Council sets out measures to be taken by Greece to reduce its government deficit', Brussels, 10 May 2010. The Council went on to detail the specific tasks entrusted to the Commission under the Intercreditor Agreement.

[39] The Intercreditor Agreement lays down the provisions concerning disbursement of the loan and its repayment. In particular, Art 3 of the Agreement authorises the Commission to open an account with the ECB, in the name of the lenders. Under the TARGET2 (Trans-European Automated Real-time Gross settlement Express Transfer) system (Decision of the European Central Bank ECB/2007/7 of 24 July 2007 concerning the terms and conditions of TARGET2-ECB, [2007] OJ L237/71) only central banks, European and international organisations could open a cash account with the ECB. Its rules were amended (Decision of the European Central Bank ECB/2010/4 of 10 May 2010 concerning the management of pooled bilateral loans for the benefit of the Hellenic Republic and amending Decision ECB/2007/7 [2010] OJ L119/24).

[40] Pursuant to Art 5 in conjunction with Annex 5 of the Loan Facility Agreement the interest rate is calculated on the basis of the EURIBOR rate plus 300 basis points for the first three years, and 400 for any subsequent period.

[41] Section 14 of the Intercreditor Agreement and section 14 of the Loan Facility Agreement.

[42] Art 3(5)(c) of the Loan Facility Agreement.

[43] Commission, 'Recommandation en vue d'une Décision du Conseil adressée á la Grèce en vue de renforcer et d'approfondir la surveillance budgétaire et mettant la Grèce en demeure de prendre des mesures pour procéder á la réduction du déficit jugée nécessaire pour remédier á la situation de déficit excessif', SEC (2010) 560 final.

specific policy conditionality under the MoU.[44] It comes as no surprise that the measures in the Council Decision and the MoU are identical.

Third, an Agreement between Greece and the IMF in the form of Exchange of Letters.[45] In its Letter of Intent to the IMF requesting financial assistance under the Stand-By Arrangement, the Greek government undertook to fully implement the Council Decision[46] and the MoU.[47] Moreover, it expressed its preparedness to take any further measures that may become appropriate for this purpose. On 9 May 2010, the IMF Executive Board approved the financing under the Stand-By Arrangement.[48] Besides the formal agreement, it should be underscored that the IMF played a dominant role in the drafting of the MoU. In this respect, largely because of Germany's insistence, the IMF was instrumentalised and used as a Damoclean sword in order to achieve enormous fiscal consolidation and promise of structural reform, which could never have been achieved within the framework of EU economic policy coordination alone.

The Greek bail-out is currently in the process of being implemented. The ECB has adopted extraordinary measures to support Greece and its financial institutions.[49] Euro area Member States have ratified the Agreements. A small upset has been caused by Slovakia, which refused to ratify the Agreements.[50] While this has limited impact on the Greek bail-out in economic terms, it is not without political and legal significance.

[44] Council Decision 2010/320 addressed to Greece with a view to reinforcing and deepening fiscal surveillance and giving notice to Greece to take measures for the deficit reduction judged necessary to remedy the situation of excessive deficit, [2010] OJ L145/6.

[45] On the legal status of Stand-By Arrangements see, Lowenfeld, *International Economic Law* (n 23 above) 517–19. It is submitted that Lowenfeld correctly argues that the exchange of letters in question constitutes an international agreement. Should this not be the case, then the Greece–IMF arrangement would be an act in implementation of an agreement of the Member States which predates the entry into force of the Treaties. In such eventuality, the considerations applicable to prior agreements will need to be taken into account. See Art 351 TFEU (ex Art 307 TEC). For an excellent analysis, see R Schütze, 'EC Law and International Agreements of the Member States—An Ambivalent Relationship?' (2007) 9 *Cambridge Yearbook of European Legal Studies* 387.

[46] The Letter of Intent refers to the Council Recommendations of 16 February (Council Decision 2010/190 of 16 February 2010 with a view to ending the inconsistency with the broad guidelines of economic policies in Greece and removing the risk of jeopardising the proper functioning of the economic and monetary union, [2010] OJ L83/65). The Recommendation contains ambitious structural and fiscal reforms but contained no detail of the kind the May 2010 Decision and MoU specify.

[47] IMF Country Report no 10/110, May 2010.

[48] 'IMF Executive Board Approves €30 Billion Stand-By Arrangement for Greece', Press Release no 10/187, May 9, 2010, available at www.imf.org/external/np/sec/pr/2010/pr10187.htm.

[49] Decision of the European Central Bank ECB/2010/3 of 6 May 2010 on temporary measures relating to the eligibility of marketable debt instruments issued or guaranteed by the Greek government, [2010] OJ L117/102.

[50] See 'Slovakia to join EU-IMF fund, reject Greek loan' *EU Observer* (15 July 2010).

III EMERGENCY INSTRUMENTS TO SUPPORT THE EURO: DAEDALUS SHOULD HAVE KNOWN BETTER

The short-term fix of Icarus's wings, namely the Greek bail-out, cannot by itself ensure the viability of the euro area. In fact, the risk of contagion looked increasingly likely in the Member States of the European south. The ink had not dried on the Greek bail-out instruments when the Commission announced, on 8 May 2010, that it would present to the Council a concrete proposal for a European Stabilisation Mechanism to preserve financial stability in Europe.[51] The following day, the extraordinary ECOFIN Council announced that it had agreed on a comprehensive package of measures to preserve financial stability in Europe (European stability mechanism), to include a European Financial Stabilisation Mechanism (EFSM)[52] and a European Financial Stability Facility (EFSF).[53] The total amount earmarked for the operation was set at €500 billion (€60 billion under the EFSM and €440 billion under the EFSF), while provision was made for additional IMF stability support of at least half the total amount.[54]

As regards the EFSM, its development is inspired by an existing mechanism providing medium-term financial assistance to non-euro area Member States in serious balance of payments (BOP) difficulties.[55] Under the BOP Regulation, assistance takes the form of medium-term loans provided by the Commission in conjunction with financing provided by the IMF and other multilateral lenders.[56] Recent experience under the BOP Regulation was in conjunction with funding from the IMF.[57] The assistance aims to ease the external financing constraints and restore the viability of the balance of payments of the beneficiary Member State.

[51] José Manuel Durão Barroso, President of the European Commission, Statement following the meeting of the Heads of States and Government of the Euro Area, SPEECH/10/224, Brussels, 8 May 2010.

[52] Council Regulation 407/2010 of 11 May 2010 establishing a European financial stabilisation mechanism [2010] OJ L118/1 (hereafter the EFSM Regulation).

[53] Terms of reference of the Eurogroup, European Financial Stability Facility, Luxembourg, 7 June 2010. EFSF Framework Agreement, Execution Version, 7 June 2010. Retrieved from www.bundesfinanzministerium.de/nn_83228/DE/Wirtschaft__und__Verwaltung/Europa/20100609-Schutzschirm-Euro-Anlage-1-eng,templateId=raw,property=publicationFile.pdf.

[54] Doc 9596/10 (Presse 108) 'Extraordinary Council meeting, Economic and Financial Affairs', Brussels, 9/10 May 2010, 6.

[55] Council Regulation 332/2002/EC of 18 February 2002 establishing a facility providing medium-term financial assistance for Member States' balances of payments [2002] OJ L53/1. Lending operations are facilitated by the ECB in accordance with Decision of the European Central Bank ECB/2003/14 of 7 November 2003 concerning the administration of the borrowing-and-lending operations concluded by the European Community under the medium-term financial assistance facility [2003] OJ L297/35.

[56] Although no mention of the other lenders is made in the BOP Regulation, such lenders include the EIB, the EBRD or the World Bank, or bilateral assistance from Member States. See 3rd recital of Council Decision 2009/459 of 6 May 2009 providing Community medium-term financial assistance for Romania [2009] OJ L150/8.

[57] Council Decision 2010/183 of 16 March 2010 amending Decision 2009/459/EC providing Community medium-term financial assistance for Romania [2010] OJ L83/19; Council Decision 2009/459 (n 56 above); Council Decision 2009/592 of 13 July 2009 amending Decision 2009/290/EC

The economic policy conditions which need to be met by the Member State in BOP difficulties are agreed by the Commission and the Member State and enshrined in a MoU. Before the disbursement of any instalment under the loan can be made, the implementation of adjustment measures designed to remedy these difficulties needs to be verified.

Compared to the BOP Regulation, the EFSM explodes the scope of financial assistance offered to address not only balance of payments but any kind of financial difficulty. At the same time, it also increases the number of potential beneficiaries to include euro area Member States. Its activation will be in the context of joint EU/IMF support and subject to strong conditionality.[58] A Member State seeking financial assistance under the EFSM shall discuss with the Commission in liaison with the ECB and make an assessment of its financial needs.[59] When granting the loan, the Council will determine the modalities as well as the main policy conditions attached to the support.[60] Such conditions will be detailed in a MoU between the Commission and the Member State concerned.[61] Once the decision on a loan has been made, the Commission shall be authorised to borrow on the financial markets or from credit institutions so as to optimise the cost of funding.[62] The release of funds and subsequent disbursements shall be subject to verification by the Commission that the beneficiary Member State accords with its adjustment programme and the conditions laid down by the Council.[63]

While the EFSM was made immediately available in order to cover any urgent financing needs, the EFSF was established by an intergovernmental agreement of the euro area Member States to provide possible financial assistance to a euro area Member State in difficulty as soon as possible.[64] The EFSF was established in the form of a 'Special Purpose Vehicle' (SPV) and registered as a limited liability company under Luxembourg law.[65] The shareholding of each Member State in the EFSF corresponds to its respective share in the paid-up capital of the ECB.[66] The euro area Member States have concluded a Framework Agreement with the EFSF which details the modalities of this special Member State-backed form of

of 20 January 2009 providing Community medium-term financial assistance for Latvia [2009] OJ L202/52; Council Decision 2009/290 of 20 January 2009 providing Community medium-term financial assistance for Latvia [2009] OJ L79/39.

[58] Sixth and Seventh recitals of the EFSM Regulation.

[59] Art 3(1) of the EFSM Regulation.

[60] Art 3(3) of the EFSM Regulation.

[61] Art 3(5) of the EFSM Regulation.

[62] Art 6(3) of the EFSM Regulation.

[63] Arts 4(2) and 5(2) of the EFSM Regulation.

[64] MEMO/10/173, The European Stabilisation Mechanism, Brussels, 10 May 2010.

[65] www.efsf.europa.eu/index.htm.

[66] Terms of reference of the Eurogroup, European Financial Stability Facility, Luxembourg, 7 June 2010.

stability support.[67] In essence, the EFSF, backed by the guarantees offered by the euro area Member States, will issue bonds and obtain funding on the financial markets.[68] The funds obtained will then be used to provide stability support to a Member State in financial difficulty caused by exceptional circumstances.[69] The financial support to euro area Member States shall be provided by the EFSF in conjunction with the IMF and shall be on comparable terms to the stability support loans advanced by euro area Member States to Greece.[70] The Commission will ensure consistency between EFSF and other operations of assistance to euro area Member States. The Commission, in liaison with the ECB, is also tasked to negotiate the policy conditions attached to any loans provided by the EFSF and to assess compliance with these conditions.[71]

IV EMERGENCY INSTRUMENTS OF EU ECONOMIC POLICY: A PRELIMINARY COMPARISON

The Greek bail-out and the European stability mechanism present many similarities and differences. As regards similarities, it should be noted that, first, the nature of financial assistance is that of medium-term loans. Second, the modalities of financing are similar in terms of interest payable, borrowing and lending operations, administration of the loan etc. Third, they are all subject to conditionality which is agreed between the Member State in difficulty and the European Commission in consultation with the ECB and the IMF and enshrined in a MoU. Fourth, all mechanisms provide for financial support in conjunction with international institutions, predominantly, the IMF.[72]

There are however significant differences in the construction of the Greek bail-out and the EFSM and EFSF. First, the former provides stability support in the form of bilateral loans which come from the coffers of the Member States,[73] while the latter provides for two types of loan: an EU loan under the EFSM and an EFSF loan.[74] Second, the EFSM pays less deference to the IMF than the Greek bail-out and provides that 'the Commission shall examine the possibilities available under the Union financial assistance facility and the compatibility of the envisaged economic policy conditions with the commitments taken by the

[67] EFSF Framework Agreement, Execution Version, 7 June 2010.

[68] Fourth recital of the EFSF Framework Agreement.

[69] Second recital of the EFSF Framework Agreement.

[70] First recital of the EFSF Framework Agreement.

[71] Terms of reference of the Eurogroup, European Financial Stability Facility, Luxembourg, 7 June 2010.

[72] First recital of the EFSF Framework Agreement.

[73] Given their own budgetary positions, the lenders are expected to borrow on the financial markets. An ethical question arises for those Member States which will borrow at a lower interest rate to that they will lend Greece (EURIBOR plus 3%).

[74] In both cases, the Commission and the EFSF will borrow on the financial markets to obtain the necessary funds.

Member State concerned for the implementation of the Council recommendations and Council decisions adopted on the basis of Article 121, Article 126 and Article 136 of the TFEU'.[75]

It is questionable what will happen when the Greek bail-out arrangement runs its course. An early exit from the bail-out would only be conceivable if Greece were able to return to the financial markets earlier than anticipated. If Greece can borrow on the markets, there will be no need to have resort to the EFSM. In theory, it would still be possible, linked, of course, to the political and economic climate at the time when the question is asked but, in view of the temporary character of both the EFSM and the EFSF, such a possibility is slim.[76]

V EMERGENCY INSTRUMENTS OF EU ECONOMIC POLICY: A CRITIQUE

The answer to the question asked in the introduction to this chapter as to whether the EU constitution is equipped with the tools to deal with the debt crisis is simple. Until May 2010, the EU had no mechanism to deal with a debt crisis and could not possibly have one.[77] It could hardly be otherwise, given that the entire edifice of the Economic and Monetary Union is constructed on the basis of a no-deficit–no-debt assumption. Therefore, the availability of a mechanism to deal with debt crisis, which was not supposed to happen in the first place, would represent a Greek paradox.

In this regard, for euro area Member States, stable finances are not simply a Treaty principle (Article 4(3) TEC, before Lisbon) and a rule of economic and monetary policy (Article 119(3) TFEU, after Lisbon) but a *conditio sine qua non* of the monetary union. In order to ensure that the Member States comply with this obligation, EU economic policy comprises three main areas of coordination: broad economic policy guidelines, multilateral surveillance and the excessive deficit procedure.[78] The latter finds expression in the GSP which is intended to ensure budgetary discipline.[79] The GSP contains a variety of measures to achieve

[75] Art 3(8) of the EFSM.

[76] Art 11(2) of the EFSF Framework Agreement provides that the Member States shall liquidate the EFSF after 30 June 2013. In the same vein, Art 9(1) of the EFSM Regulation makes its maintenance subject to the continuation of the exceptional occurrences that justify it.

[77] The emergency measures taken to deal with the debt crisis evince that a crisis resolution mechanism as such is missing in the European Union, and the EU leaders are aware of that. See, 'Statement of the Heads of State or Government of the Euro area', Brussels, 7 May 2010, 3. Also, Olli Rehn European Commissioner for Economic and Monetary Policy Debate on the euro area, Speech/10/217, European Parliament, Brussels, 5 May 2010.

[78] Amtenbrink and de Haan, 'Economic Governance in the European Union' (n 3 above).

[79] Art 126 TFEU. The main texts which comprise the GSP are: Council Regulation 1466/97/EC of 7 July 1997 on the strengthening of the surveillance of budgetary positions and the surveillance and coordination of economic policies [1997] OJ L209/1; Council Regulation 3605/93/EC of 22 November 1993 on the application of the Protocol on the excessive deficit procedure annexed to the Treaty establishing the European Community [1993] OJ L332/7; Council Regulation 1467/97/EC of 7 July 1997 on speeding up and clarifying the implementation of the excessive deficit procedure [1997] OJ

the budgetary discipline objective which escalates to the payment of a fine of an appropriate size.[80]

In parallel, the Treaty lays down rules to ensure that the stable finances principle may not be circumvented or compromised.[81] In a nutshell, the ECB may not provide an overdraft or other credit facility and may not purchase government bonds.[82] In addition, neither the Union[83] nor a Member State[84] nor financial institutions[85] may bail out another Member State. The link between budgetary discipline, the no-bailout clauses and market financing becomes apparent. In essence, 'the prohibition of privileged access to financial institutions . . . forms an essential element of the submission of the public sector in its financing operations to the discipline of the market mechanism and so makes a contribution to the strengthening of budgetary discipline'.[86]

However, even before the common currency was introduced, the efficacy of the existing policy instruments to address major political or economic shocks was questioned.[87] The gist of the argument was that the unavailability of traditional instruments of monetary policy, such as currency devaluation, coupled with tight controls over public finances, left little scope for individual Member States to deal with severe economic disturbances. At the same time, since the ECB makes no overdraft facilities available to the Member States,[88] borrowing on the markets may become more difficult or more expensive, should the Council decide to take any of the measures provided for in the event of non-compliance with the

L209/6; Council Regulation 1055/2005 of 27 June 2005 amending Regulation 1466/97/EC on the strengthening of the surveillance of budgetary positions and the surveillance and coordination of economic policies [2005] OJ L174/1; Council Regulation 1056/2005 of 27 June 2005 amending Regulation 1467/97/EC on speeding up and clarifying the implementation of the excessive deficit procedure [2005] OJ L174/5.

[80] Art 126(11), fourth indent TFEU.

[81] For an overview, K Lenaerts and P van Nuffel, *Constitutional Law of the European Union,* 2nd edn (London, Sweet & Maxwell, 2005) 279–98.

[82] Art 123 TFEU (ex Art 101 TEC). See also, Council Regulation 3603/93 specifying definitions for the application of the prohibitions referred to in Arts 104 and 104b(1) of the Treaty [1993] OJ L332/1. Art 7 of the Regulation states: 'The financing by the European Central Bank or the national central banks of obligations falling upon the public sector vis-à-vis the International Monetary Fund or resulting from the implementation of the medium-term financial assistance facility set up by Regulation (EEC) No 1969/88 shall not be regarded as a credit facility within the meaning of Article 104 of the Treaty.' Regulation 1969/88 to which it refers has been replaced by the BOP Regulation (Council Regulation 332/2002/EC of 18 February 2002 establishing a facility providing medium-term financial assistance for Member States' balances of payments [2002] OJ L53/1).

[83] Art 125 TFEU(1), first sentence (ex Art 103 TEC).

[84] Art 125 TFEU(2), second sentence (ex Art 103 TEC).

[85] Art 124 TFEU (ex Art 102 TEC).

[86] Council Regulation 3604/93/EC of 13 December 1993 specifying definitions for the application of the prohibition of privileged access referred to in Art 104a of the Treaty [1993] OJ L332/4.

[87] F Snyder, 'EMU Revisited: Are We Making a Constitution? What Constitution Are We Making' in P Craig and G de Búrca, *The Evolution of EU Law,* (Oxford, Oxford University Press, 1999) 417, 449–50 and the academic writing quoted there.

[88] Art 123(1) TFEU.

Council Recommendations to reduce the excessive deficit.[89] In this respect, market-induced budgetary discipline might backfire.

It is against this backdrop that the emergency measures taken to counteract the debt crisis should be examined. Inevitably, a political dimension should also be added to the equation. In this respect, one can hardly disagree with the political will to concoct a solution to address the Greek debt crisis, thereby giving tangible meaning to the concept of solidarity, enshrined in several places in the Treaties since the entry into force of the Treaty of Lisbon.[90] However, solidarity is not a constitutional norm (yet) that could render instruments, considered a priori incompatible with the EU constitutional order,[91] less offensive. The present analysis makes no assumptions in this respect.

As mentioned above, the Treaties do not provide the necessary powers to deal with the debt crisis as such. Consequently, it must be determined what powers the Union does have in the domain on economic policy and how those relate to the powers of the Member States. Pursuant to Article 3(1)(c) TFEU, monetary policy is an exclusive competence of the Union. At the same time, EU economic policy enjoys a special status in the competences catalogue of the Treaty alongside employment and social policy. Long before the entry into force of the Treaty of Lisbon, it was argued that EU economic policy is a disguised shared competence.[92] This argument has a stronger claim today having regard to Article 4(1) TFEU which reads: 'The Union shall share competence with the Member States where the Treaties confer on it a competence which does not relate to the areas referred to in Articles 3 and 6.'[93] Economic policy is a Union competence provided for in Articles 2(3)[94] and 5(1) TFEU[95] and hence it is neither an exclusive Union competence nor a complementary competence. Its specificity in relation to the shared competences provided in Article 4 TFEU is also established. It may be inferred that economic policy, alongside employment and social policies, is narrower in scope than the shared competences under the Treaty, the role of the Union being to coordinate national policies. At the same time, it should go beyond the complementary policies and harmonisation should not be excluded. It is only when and in so far as a measure of economic policy, which is

[89] Art 126(11), first indent TFEU.

[90] Art 122 TFEU, Art 222 TFEU and Art 42(7) TEU. See WT Eijsbouts, 'Scratch the Currency and You Will Find the Deal' (2010) 37 *Legal Issues of Economic Integration* 181.

[91] Eijsbouts (n 90 above) states: 'In addition, if, as in these days, the deal is struck at the expense of the existing legal norm, so be it. Each true creation, as the artist tends to know better than the lawyer, is also a violation.'

[92] R Smits, 'The European Constitution and EMU: An Appraisal' (2005) 42 *Common Market Law Review* 425, 430.

[93] Art 3 TFEU deals with exclusive competence and Art 6 TFEU with complementary competences.

[94] 'The Member States shall coordinate their economic and employment policies within arrangements as determined by this Treaty, which the Union shall have competence to provide.'

[95] 'The Member States shall coordinate their economic policies within the Union. To this end, the Council shall adopt measures, in particular broad guidelines for these policies.
Specific provisions shall apply to those Member States whose currency is the euro.'

taken on EU level and which harmonises national law, that the pre-emptive effect of Article 2(2), second sentence TFEU applies.[96] In all other instances, consistently with Article 2(2), first sentence,[97] in the field of EU economic policy, a large measure of competence is vested in the Member States which they are not precluded from exercising either in the Council or outside it.[98] However, the Court's pronouncement in *Bangladesh* that 'the Community does not have exclusive competence in the field of humanitarian aid, and that consequently the Member States are not precluded from exercising their competence in that regard collectively in the Council or outside it' may no longer be extended to fields of shared competence other than those provided in Art 4(3) and 4(4) TFEU.[99]

Let's take stock of the EU competences analysis in the field of economic policy, and move on the analysis of the Greek bail-out which, as mentioned earlier, is based on Member State instruments. In this regard, the euro area Member States took the decision to react to the debt crisis in Greece by means of an Intercreditor Agreement and a Loan Facility Agreement between Greece, on the one hand, and the other 15 euro area Member States on the other.[100] This makes a total of three agreements: the *sui generis* decision of the Member States meeting within the Euro Group formation of the Council to grant the loan, as well as the Intercreditor and Loan Facility Agreements between the Member States. In principle, this is perfectly compatible with the competences analysis above. Inter se agreements of the Member States are permitted in EU constitutional law; they are nevertheless subject to limitations. In this respect, it must be ensured that the inter se agreements do not circumvent the procedure for Treaty amendment, that they respect the institutional framework set by the Treaties and do not affect existing policies.[101]

[96] 'The Member States shall exercise their competence to the extent that the Union has not exercised its competence.'

[97] 'When the Treaties confer on the Union a competence shared with the Member States in a specific area, the Union and the Member States may legislate and adopt legally binding acts in that area.'

[98] Joined cases C-181/91 and C-248/91 *European Parliament v Council and Commission (Bangladesh)* [1993] ECR I-3685, para 16. P Koutrakos, *EU International Relations Law* (Oxford, Hart Publishing, 2006) 155–60. For a criticism of the Court's approach, see, R Schütze, *From Dual to Cooperative Federalism: The Changing Structure of European Law* (Oxford, Oxford University Press, 2009) 320.

[99] In the areas of research, technological development and space, the Union shall have competence to carry out activities, in particular to define and implement programmes; however, the exercise of that competence shall not result in Member States being prevented from exercising theirs.
In the areas of development cooperation and humanitarian aid, the Union shall have competence to carry out activities and conduct a common policy; however, the exercise of that competence shall not result in Member States being prevented from exercising theirs.

[100] Statement by Euro Group, Brussels, 2 May 2010. Available at www.consilium.europa.eu/uedocs/cms_data/docs/pressdata/en/misc/114130.pdf. The present chapter will focus on the latter. See, Schütze, *From Dual to Cooperative Federalism* (n 98 above) 313–20.

[101] B de Witte, 'Future Paths of Flexibility: Enhanced Cooperation, Partial Agreements and Pioneer Groups' in JW de Zwaan, JH Jans and FA Nelissen (eds), *The European Union—An Ongoing Process of Intergration: Liber Amicorum Alfred E. Kellermann* (The Hague, TMC Asser Press, 2004) 141, 148–51. For a more detailed analysis, see, B de Witte, 'Old-fashioned Flexibility: International

There are major question marks in relation to all the three conditions.[102] As outlined above, EU economic policy is constructed on the basis of a no-debt–no-deficit assumption. The only exceptions the Treaty recognises can be found in Article 122 TFEU and concern supply of energy, a natural disaster or exceptional occurrences beyond a Member State's control. It follows that, if debt crisis falls within the scope of Article 122 TFEU, then any financial assistance must be granted via Union channels; if not, it should not be granted at all. By granting financial assistance in the form of pooled bilateral loans, Member States appear to circumvent an explicit prohibition set out in Article 125 TFEU. Moreover, loans at an interest rate, lower than that available to Greece on the financial markets and the acceptance, pursuant to an ECB decision, of Greek debt instruments as collateral, regardless of the rating of the Greek debt,[103] constitute examples of privileged access to financial institutions prohibited by Article 124 TFEU.

Similar, albeit more complex, considerations apply to the EFSF. It must be pointed out however that, only if and when the EFSF exercises its powers, its role as the agent of the financing operations of the Euro area Member States will be fully comprehended. The main difference lies in the absence of the inter se agreements of the Member States. A Framework Agreement has been concluded instead which has been ratified by all euro area Member States with a private body, the EFSF. If financial assistance under the EFSF is requested, a loan agreement will be concluded between the EFSF and the requestor Member State, with policy conditionality agreed in consultation with the Commission and the ECB. As regards its compatibility with the Treaties substantively, the crux of the problem remains, that is, financial assistance to a troubled Member State and privileged access to funds.[104] Constitutionally, it is paradoxical that this *sui generis* private body will be the final arbiter of policy conditionality, including compliance with any Council Recommendations under Article 126 TFEU. Furthermore, the constitutional guarantees offered by the Union institutional framework are also missing.[105]

The EFSM is the only debt crisis emergency instrument to be adopted under the TFEU Treaty. The question of whether the EFSM can sufficiently be based on Article 122(2) TFEU depends on whether the debt crisis constitutes 'exceptional

Agreements between the Member States of the European Union', in G de Búrca and J Scott (eds), *Constitutional Change in the EU—From Uniformity to Flexibility?* (Oxford, Hart Publishing, 2000) 31.

[102] It is immensely ironical that such a constitutional coup d'état took place on the 60th anniversary of the Schuman Declaration, as hinted in Eijsbouts, 'Scratch the Currency and You Will Find the Deal' (n 90 above).

[103] Decision of the European Central Bank ECB/2010/3 of 6 May 2010 on temporary measures relating to the eligibility of marketable debt instruments issued or guaranteed by the Greek government [2010] OJ L117/102.

[104] The guarantee by the Member States ensures that the bonds issued by the EFSF will have an excellent credit rating.

[105] For instance, Art 15 TFEU.

occurrences beyond [a Member State's] control'. It is submitted that the purpose of this provision is to enable the Union to come to the assistance of a Member State in severe difficulties caused in spite of the stable finances dogma, or, maybe, because of it; a systemic interpretation of the provision is therefore required. Albeit an exceptional norm, the inherent dynamism of this provision—'seriously threatened with severe difficulties' — militates in favour of a wide scope of Article 122(2) TFEU. The operation of the mechanism (lending operations, policy conditionality, role of the institutions, relations with the IMF[106]) does not raise additional competence concerns. In fact, the introductory sentence of Article 122 TFEU which reads: 'Without prejudice to any other procedures provided for in the Treaties, the Council, on a proposal from the Commission, may decide, in a spirit of solidarity between Member States' may be interpreted to introduce an exception to all other economic policy restrictions under the Treaty in relation to any financial assistance to a Member State, including, most importantly, privileged access to financial institutions (Article 124 TFEU) and the no-bail-out clause (Article 125 TFEU).

The EFSM lays down common rules on a Union level concerning EU financial assistance to a Member State in financial difficulties. How does this relate to the Greek bail-out package and the EFSF, which cover the same field? In accordance with the principle of pre-emption, outlined above,[107] Member States would be pre-empted from exercising their competences unilaterally, if common rules were laid down by the Union.[108] Consequently, the existence of common rules in the form of the EFSM pre-empt the Member States from bailing-out a Member State in financial difficulty outside the Union framework. In fact, because the Member States have, on this occasion, exercised their competences collectively in the form of an inter se agreement, they should be subject to a stricter pre-emption control.[109] This is because, if Member States agreed to cooperate on a policy initiative which falls within Union competence, they should do so within the Union framework and not the intergovernmental one.[110] A possible argument, influenced by the case law of the Court in the field of development cooperation,[111] that Member States may grant financial assistance in the form of bilateral loans, may not be upheld in the current Treaty framework. As mentioned briefly above, the combined reading of Articles 2(2), second sentence, 2(3) and 5(1) TFEU juxtaposed with Article 4 leads to the following proposition: the Union has the competence to coordinate the economic policies of the Member States and

[106] See next section.

[107] See the text surrounding n 96.

[108] For a detailed analysis see R Schütze, 'Supremacy Without Pre-emption? The Very Slowly Emergent Doctrine of Community Pre-emption' (2006) 43 *Common Market Law Review* 1023.

[109] de Witte, 'Future Paths of Flexibility' (n 101 above) 41–5.

[110] de Witte, 'Future Paths of Flexibility' (n 101 above) 42.

[111] Joined cases C-181/91 and C-248/91 *European Parliament v Council and Commission (Bangladesh)* [1993] ECR I-3685; C-316/91 *European Parliament v Council (EDF)* [1994] ECR I-625.

determine the necessary modalities[112] which shall be exercised by the Council; when the Union exercises its competence in the field, Member States will, unlike research, technological development, space, development cooperation and humanitarian aid, be prevented from exercising their own competences.

In the case at hand, the only question that remains is whether the Greek bail-out package was adopted before the Union had exercised its competence in the form of the EFSM.[113] If common rules were not in place, the Member States could not have been pre-empted from exercising their competence. In such a case, however, Member State action would not be completely unhindered in constitutional terms but would be limited by the duty of cooperation.[114] In the context of EU external relations, the Court has held that Member States ought to abstain from exercising their competences from the moment the Commission was issued directives to negotiate with third countries on the same subject-matter.[115] It is submitted that, mutatis mutandis, the duty of cooperation warrants an interpretation to the effect that Member States should abstain from concluding an inter se agreement if the Union is at the departure point of adopting common rules on the same subject-matter.

Returning to the doctrine of pre-emption, it is clear that Member States may no longer grant financial assistance in the form of an inter se agreement but should do so under the EFSM. Taking a look at the relationship between the EFSM and the EFSF, it should be noted that the EFSF owes its establishment to the Member States' intention to avoid the most important limitation of the EFSM, that is, the amount that could be made available under the latter instrument, an amount clearly insufficient to deal with a debt crisis of such magnitude.[116] Otherwise, the modus operandi of the EFSF, as may be inferred from the Framework Agreement, will not differ from that of the EFSM. In fact, as regards policy conditionality, if a MoU has been agreed between a Member State and the Commission under the EFSM, the same MoU shall be applicable to financing requested under the EFSF.[117] This represents evidence of the awkward symbiosis expected between the EFSM and the EFSF and lends support to the argument that Member States were pre-empted from setting up a private financing channel mirroring the Union one.[118]

[112] I prefer the term 'modalités', taken from the French version of Art 2(3) TFEU, over 'arrangements' in the inelegantly drafted English version.

[113] Agreement on the Greek bail-out was reached first, then the EFSM was adopted, ratification of the Intercreditor and Loan Facility Agreements was swiftly concluded a week later.

[114] Art 4(3) TEU (ex Art 10 TEC); de Witte, 'Future Paths of Flexibility' (n 101 above) 42; E Neframi, 'The Duty of Loyalty: Rethinking its scope through its application in the field of EU external relations' (2010) 47 *Common Market Law Review* 323.

[115] Case C-246/07 *Commission v Sweden*, judgment of 20 April 2010, not yet reported, para 74; Case C-266/03 *Commission v Luxembourg* [2005] ECR I-4805, para 59.

[116] Art 2(2) of the EFSM.

[117] Section 2(1) of the EFSF Framework Agreement.

[118] Schütze, 'Supremacy Without Pre-emption?' (n 108 above) 1040–41 would probably classify this as 'field pre-emption'.

On the basis of the above, it may be concluded that the EFSM comes nearer to satisfying the constitutional limitations set by the Treaties, and constitutes the only instrument which should remain on the Union rulebook, after the crisis is over.

VI EMERGENCY INSTRUMENTS OF EU ECONOMIC POLICY: THE INSIDE LOOKING OUT

The emergency instruments analysed above have in common that they envisage EU and Member State stability support in conjunction with funding obtained from other bodies. The IMF takes a dominant place in the construction of the post-crisis EU economic policy. However, there are numerous legal questions as regards the IMF's role both in procedural and substantive terms.

More specifically, in the case of the Greek bail-out, the rescue package was based on joint EU/IMF funding up to the amount of €80 billion and €30 billion respectively over a period of three years. While Articles 21(1) TEU and 220 TFEU (ex Articles 302 to 304 TEC) provide for the establishment and maintenance of appropriate relations between the European Union and international organisations, this close policy coordination can be difficult to accommodate in such vague diplomatic language.[119]

Furthermore, any future bail-out under the European stabilisation mechanism (EFSM or EFSF) will be funded by the IMF with an amount of up to €250 billion.[120] As mentioned in the previous section, there remains a lot to be surmised about the constitutional orthodoxy of this arrangement. That said, this section addresses the abundant unanswered questions about the relations between the IMF and the European stabilisation mechanism. The first concerns the presumed agreement of the IMF to contribute to such mechanism. Obviously, there does not seem to be any international agreement, even of simplified form, which establishes the IMF consent.[121] A related question is whether such an agreement would be possible, or even, desirable. Moreover, it is questionable whether the contribution of the IMF is a compulsory element of the European stabilisation mechanism even if a Member State would be against its involvement. The ongoing social crisis in Romania, a Member State which received joint financial assistance by the IMF and the EU under the BOP facility,

[119] Twice a year, the Euro Group exchanges views with the IMF on euro-area policies, known as Art IV consultations. In the context of the debt crisis, it should be noted that the Managing Director of the IMF attended several crisis management meetings of the Euro Group and the ECOFIN Council.

[120] Fifth recital to the EFSM Regulation. Given that the amount roughly equals the total subscribed capital of the IMF (SDR 217 billion ≈ €250 billion, see www.imf.org/external/np/sec/memdir/members.htm), the presumption that the IMF would actually approve this level of financial support under the Stand-By Arrangement is astonishing.

[121] Obviously, such undertakings may have been given on the highest political level by the leaders of the IMF members with the highest amount of capital subscription.

represents fresh illustration of how unpopular IMF policy conditionality can be.[122] Third, however unlikely, what if a Member State wishes to ask for support from the IMF and not the EFSM/EFSF?

There is no easy answer to the above questions. To start with, Article 219(4) TFEU (ex Article 111(5) TEC) which provides 'Without prejudice to Union competence and Union agreements as regards economic and monetary union, Member States may negotiate in international bodies and conclude international agreements' seems to be at odds with Article 3(2) TFEU. The most obvious way to reconcile them is to state that '[w]ithout prejudice to Union competence' excludes exclusive Union competence. Any other interpretation would lead to the conclusion of having an exclusive internal Union competence (monetary policy) and a sui generis shared internal competence (economic policy) find external expression in a complementary external competence (economic and monetary policy).

In any event, it is clear that, in the field of economic policy, a Member State may conclude an international agreement, such as an agreement for stability support under the Stand-By Arrangement. From an EU constitutional perspective, however, a euro area Member State should not be allowed to request financial support under the Stand-By Arrangement in the absence of authorisation from the Council. Having regard to the duty of cooperation, it is clear that IMF conditionality has such a profound impact on the economic policy of a Member State that the future direction of EU policy coordination, particularly of euro area Member States, would certainly be affected.[123]

The full agreement of the EU and the IMF on Member State policy conditionality, which is evident in the current conjuncture, may not be presumed in the future. The Greek bail-out package is not static; progress thereunder is subject to quarterly reviews. In its Letter of Intent to the IMF, Greece undertook to take further measures as necessary. Should disagreements arise in the implementation of the Greek bail-out, EU constitutional law and economic and monetary policy risk getting sandwiched between, on the one hand, an agreement between a Member State and the IMF and, on the other, an inter se agreement (the Loan

[122] Council Decision 2009/459 of 6 May 2009 providing Community medium-term financial assistance for Romania [2009] OJ L150/8.

[123] See to this effect, the Opinion of Advocate General Maduro in the *Commission v Austria* and *Commission v Sweden* cases, para 40: 'I wish to make it clear, however, that the problem lies not in the possibility of any future conflict with the Community legislation and its objectives. If every such possibility had to be eliminated there would no longer be a shared competence, but an exclusive one. The problem only arises where the national measures or the international obligations of Member States are liable to jeopardise the effectiveness of possible future Community legislation and, in doing so, *de facto* restrict the freedom which the Treaty confers on the Community to act in those areas. That will depend on the nature of both the national measures or international obligations and the Community competences affected, for example the urgency of the measures to be adopted under such competences.'

Facility and Inter-Creditor Agreements) of the Member States. While, in theory, the primacy of EU law will apply,[124] it would be unwise to test it in practice.

In the interest of ensuring the unity of the Union's identity on the international scene, it would be imperative that the present situation finds remedy in the form of a framework agreement between the EU and the IMF.[125] Broader issues, such as unity of representation in the IMF's Governing Board, may also be addressed within the framework of such agreement,[126] maybe in the form of an attached Code of Conduct.[127] An EU–IMF agreement should be the solution that would formalise the coordination which has already taken place both as regards the Greek bail-out[128] and the European stabilisation mechanism.

Transparency and efficiency militate in favour of such an arrangement. Besides these considerations, it could be argued, on the basis of a competences analysis, that there is a legal requirement to do so. In this respect, the quiver of EU external relations law contains the doctrine of necessity.[129] From a combined reading of Articles 216(1) and 3(2) TFEU it follows that the Union has the competence to conclude an international agreement when it is necessary in order to achieve one of the objectives referred to in the Treaties. Such competence will be exclusive when it is necessary to conclude an international agreement to enable the Union to exercise its internal competence.[130] While the reasons behind the argument that 'it would be difficult to imagine a case in which the objectives of such a loosely co-ordinated economic policy would make it necessary for the Community to enter into international agreements'[131] are perfectly consonant to the circumstances before the crisis, it is argued that the activation of a Stand-By Arrangement with the IMF represents a rare opportunity in which the strict

[124] M Cremona, 'Defending the Community Interest: the Duties of Cooperation and Compliance' in M Cremona and B de Witte (eds), *EU Foreign Relations Law: Constitutional Fundamentals*, (Oxford, Hart Publishing, 2008) 125, 142. See also Case C-308/06 *Intertanko and others* [2008] ECR I-4057, para 52.

[125] Art X of the IMF Articles of Agreement could lend itself as the legal basis from the IMF's perspective.

[126] Art 138 TFEU provides the necessary legal basis for this. Smits, 'The European Constitution and EMU' (n 92 above) 454 also considers such a step necessary.

[127] For a relevant example see the arrangement between the Council and the Commission regarding preparation for Codex Alimentarius Meetings and statements and exercise of voting rights, Annex III to Council Decision 2003/822 of 17 November 2003 on the accession of the European Community to the Codex Alimentarius Commission [2003] OJ L309/14.

[128] Coordination at the implementation of that the Greek bail-out package was exemplary and took the form of joint missions to Greece or joint statements. See, for instance, Joint Statement on Greece by EU Commissioner Olli Rehn and IMF Managing Director Dominique Strauss-Kahn, IP/10/484, Brussels, 2 May 2010.

[129] The doctrine originates in Opinion 1/76 *(Re Laying-up Fund)* [1977] ECR I-741.

[130] A Antoniadis, 'The EU's Implied Competence to Conclude International Agreements after the Reform Treaty: Reformed Enough?' in F Laursen (ed), *The EU in the Global Political Economy*, (Brussels, PIE Peter Lang, 2009) 67, 80–83.

[131] C Zilioli and M Selmayr, *The Law of the European Central Bank* (Oxford, Hart Publishing, 2001) 185.

conditions set by the Court in its case law[132] might actually be fulfilled. Moreover, following the adoption of the EFSM, it follows, in a straightforward application of the *AETR* doctrine,[133] that the Union enjoys a corresponding external competence in this field.[134] The content of such agreement would be limited to the scope of the internal measures,[135] but given the breadth, depth and level of detail of the Council Recommendations to Greece, this should not be too restrictive.[136]

Even in the absence of a framework agreement, inaction or a bilateral agreement between the IMF and an individual Member State does not offer a constitutionally optimal solution to deal with debt crisis in a Member State.[137] In particular, if recourse to the European stabilisation mechanism in conjunction with funding from IMF becomes necessary, then it would be more appropriate for a euro area Member State to make a joint request with the EU for financial assistance under the Stand-By Arrangement from the IMF. Such agreement will share many characteristics of the mixed agreements.

An EU–IMF framework agreement or the EU involvement in requesting activation of the Stand-By Arrangement for a Member State would certainly touch sensitive nerves on many levels. First, the design of EU economic policy, even if this were to be reduced to broad economic policy guidelines, multilateral surveillance and the excessive deficit procedure, would no longer be independent from the IMF. Without necessarily putting a straightjacket on EU economic policy, EU fiscal consolidation would no longer have to take place as a preventive measure to earn the confidence of the financial markets[138] but as a matter of legal obligation. Moreover, an agreement of this kind would inevitably lead de facto to closer economic policy coordination, going, in the medium term, even beyond the recently tabled proposals.

[132] Opinion 1/76 *(Re Laying-up Fund)* [1977] ECR I-741; Opinion 1/94 *(Re WTO)* [1994] ECR I-5267; Case C-466/98 *Commission v UK*, Case C-467/98 *Commission v Denmark*, Case C-468/98 *Commission v Sweden*, Case C-469/98 *Commission v Finland*, Case C-471/98 *Commission v Belgium*, Case C-472/98 *Commission v Luxembourg*, Case C-475/98 *Commission v Austria*, Case C-476/98 *Commission v Germany* (the *Open Skies* cases) [2002] ECR I-9427 and Opinion 1/2003 *(Re Lugano Convention)* [2006] ECR I-1145.

[133] Case 22/70 *Commission v Council (Re ERTA)* [1971] ECR 263.

[134] The unsuccessful codification of the doctrine in Art 216(1) TFEU (implied shared competence) and Art 3(2) TFEU (implied exclusive competence) makes it more likely that such competence will not be exclusive. For an analysis and critique, see, Antoniadis, 'The EU's Implied Competence' (n 130 above) 67–90.

[135] Opinion 1/2003 *(Re Lugano Convention)* [2006] ECR I-1145. For an analysis in the field of EU economic policy, see Zilioli and Selmayr, *The Law of the European Central Bank* (n 131 above) 186. See also Protocol (no 25) on the exercise of shared competence [2008] OJ C115/307.

[136] Council Decision 2010/320 addressed to Greece with a view to reinforcing and deepening fiscal surveillance and giving notice to Greece to take measures for the deficit reduction judged necessary to remedy the situation of excessive deficit [2010] OJ L145/6.

[137] Smits, 'The European Constitution and EMU' (n 92 above) 454–55 makes similar demands already in pre-crisis conditions.

[138] Fiscal consolidation measures were either taken or announced in May 2010 by Spain, Portugal, Italy, the United Kingdom and Denmark.

VII EU ECONOMIC POLICY IN EMERGENCY MODE: THE NEW INSTITUTIONAL ARCHITECTURE

The institutional architecture of the EU economic constitution appears to have gone through transformation in a short period of time as a combined result of the entry into force of the Treaty of Lisbon and the emergency measures taken to deal with the debt crisis.

First and foremost, the Union institutional framework has seen an important addition in the European Council whose status has been formalised by the Treaty of Lisbon. Its remit has been broadly defined 'to provide the Union with the necessary impetus for its development and shall define the general political directions and priorities thereof'.[139] The European Council President is a central figure to coordinate the Union's response and drive the agenda forward. In response to the debt crisis, the President of the European Council has been asked to chair the Task Force on economic governance, a body which was established by the March 2010 European Council and which consists of Member State representatives, the Commissioner of Economic and Financial Affairs, the ECB President and the President of the Euro Group.[140] In fact, the Task Force was entrusted with the task of presenting a crisis resolution framework to the October 2010 European Council.[141]

Second, as regards the Council, the previously informal Council formation of the Member States whose currency is the euro, the Euro Group,[142] has been, since the entry into force the Treaty of Lisbon, formalised.[143] In addition, the ECOFIN Council's role in formulating and adopting the broad economic policy guidelines[144] has been greatly enhanced by the nature of the guidelines issued to a Member State in financial trouble which are unprecedented in terms of reach and intrusiveness.[145] On another point, the EFSM confers on the Council implementing powers to act.[146]

The Commission's role is instrumental in the management of the debt crisis instruments. Subject to subtle differences in each instrument, this role includes the management of all loans under the emergency instruments analysed above, including the promulgation of the agreed policy conditions and the monitoring

[139] Art 15 TEU.

[140] Remarks by H Van Rompuy, President of the European Council, following the first meeting of the Task force on economic governance, PCE 102/10, Brussels, 21 May 2010.

[141] PCE 101/10, Brussels, 20 May 2010.

[142] Annex I to the Conclusions of the Luxembourg European Council, 12 and 13 December 1997.

[143] Art 137 TFEU and Protocol (no 14) on the Euro Group [2010] OJ C115/283.

[144] J Usher, 'The Evolution of Economic and Monetary Union—Some Legal Issues', in A Arnull, PEeckhout and T Tridimas (eds), *Continuity and Change in EU Law: Essays in Honour of Sir Francis Jacobs* (Oxford, Oxford University Press, 2008) 297, 306.

[145] Council Decision 2010/320 of 10 May 2010 addressed to Greece with a view to reinforcing and deepening fiscal surveillance and giving notice to Greece to take measures for the deficit reduction judged necessary to remedy the situation of excessive deficit [2010] OJ L145/6.

[146] Sixth recital of the EFSM Regulation.

of the performance of the Member State in severe difficulty for the duration of the loan. Moreover, the Commission has capitalised on the political environment created by the debt crisis to take a number of legislative initiatives in the field of EU economic policy.

The ECB comes out of this crisis in a very controversial position. On the one hand, its role has been enhanced. On the other hand, however, it appears that the price for this has been to set a question mark on the ECB's independence.[147] In this respect, it should be recalled that the discussion on the status of the ECB has been rigorous and detailed.[148] While the ECB's independence has been juxtaposed to other central banks—most importantly, the Bundesbank—and acclaimed,[149] it appears that full ECB independence is now a memory of the past. The ECB took an active role in the development and management of the Greek bail-out and the European stabilisation mechanism, and, more importantly, provided the necessary supporting measures to guarantee their success. However, in doing so, the ECB appears to have served the will of the Member States in the Euro Group, and not the Treaties. The decision to accept the Greek debt instruments as collateral[150] not only infringes Article 125 TFEU but defies universal financial logic. At the same time, the decision to establish a securities market programme[151] to buy Member State bonds on the secondary market and private bonds in both primary secondary markets also circumvents, in an inelegant manner, the Treaty limitations.[152] These remarkable changes, fuelled by political consensus on the highest level, did not even warrant a Treaty amendment.

Other actors make their presence felt in the Union's economic and monetary architecture. Most importantly, the EFSF represents a novelty whose significance

[147] Art 130 TFEU. See also, Art 7 of Protocol (no 4) on the Statute of the European System of Central Banks and of the European Central Bank [2008] OJ C-115/230.

[148] The theoretical discussion could indeed convince the reader that the ECB enjoys a legally autonomous status and that only certain Treaty obligations actually apply to it. For an academic analysis following Case C-11/00 *Commission v ECB* [2003] ECR I-7147, see C Zilioli and M Selmayr, 'The Constitutional Status of the European Central Bank' (2007) 44 *Common Market Law Review* 355; B Krauskopf and C Steven, 'The Institutional Framework of the European System of Central Banks: Legal Issues in the Practice of the first ten years of its existence' (2009) 46 *Common Market Law Review* 1143. For an earlier treatise, Zilioli and Selmayr, *The Law of the European Central Bank* (n 131 above) 398.

[149] GF Mancini, 'The Euro: A Currency in Search of a State' in Judge GF Mancini, *Democracy and Constitutionalism in the European Union: Collected Essays* (Oxford, Hart Publishing, 2001) 67, 71.

[150] Decision of the European Central Bank ECB/2010/3 of 6 May 2010 on temporary measures relating to the eligibility of marketable debt instruments issued or guaranteed by the Greek government [2010] OJ L117/102.

[151] Decision of the European Central Bank ECB/2010/5 of 14 May 2010 establishing a securities markets programme [2010] OJ L124/8. Pursuant to Art 1 of the Decision, 'Under the terms of this Decision, Eurosystem central banks may purchase the following: (a) on the secondary market, eligible marketable debt instruments issued by the central governments or public entities of the Member States whose currency is the euro; and (b) on the primary and secondary markets, eligible marketable debt instruments issued by private entities incorporated in the euro area.'

[152] Art 123(1) TFEU (ex Art 101 TEC).

it would be premature to assess at this stage. It is not doubted that it will raise questions as regards its relations with the Union's institutions.

VIII CONCLUDING REMARKS

The above analysis demonstrates that the Union now possesses (some sort of) emergency constitution in the field of economic and monetary policy. Its immediate objective is to ensure that the Union is equipped with the instruments to deal with the debt crisis. More important, however, is to ensure that such crisis will not happen again in the future. In this respect, it has been amply understood that the EU may no longer pursue an EMU under which a strong monetary body will be supported by atrophic economic limbs. The manner in which EU economic policy was tested during the debt crisis demonstrates that the distinction is artificial. While further integration may sound as an anathema to some, the debt crisis evinces that this represents the most credible solution.[153] It would not be an exaggeration to state that, as soon as the emergency mode was switched on, the Union economic constitution changed irreversibly.[154]

A stronger economic union is emerging from the ashes of the debt crisis. It is noteworthy that more legislative initiatives have been taken in the field of EU economic governance than ever before. Following a Communication on stronger economic governance[155] and a new Directive on hedge funds, which is currently *ante portas*,[156] the Commission also addressed the issue of credit-rating agencies and the reform of corporate financial governance.[157] More initiatives are coming.[158] In general terms, the coordination of economic policies of the Member States is entering a new era. In many ways, the initiatives already undertaken—and those to follow—reverse the cautious steps taken in the course of Treaty amendment when establishing the competences catalogue in this field.[159]

It seems that, with a couple decades' delay, EU monetary policy paves the way for a broader integrationist strategy. Closer EU coordination will have a great

[153] N Ferguson, 'The End of the Euro' *Newsweek* (7 May 2010).

[154] 'French Minister says bail-out alters EU Treaty' *Financial Times* (London, 27 May 2010). The French Minister to which the title alludes is none other than Pierre Lellouche, France's Europe Minister.

[155] Commission, 'Enhancing Economic Policy Coordination for Stability, Growth and Jobs – Tools for Stronger EU Economic Governance' (Communication) COM (2010) 367/2.

[156] The latest available compromise Proposal for a Directive of the European Parliament and of the Council on Alternative Investment Fund Managers and amending Directives 2003/41/EC and 2009/65/EC can be found in Document 6795/3/10 REV3, 10 March 2010. The proposal represents the Council common position and was sent to the European Parliament on 18 May 2010, Press Release 7500/10.

[157] 'Commission proposes improved EU supervision of Credit Rating Agencies and launches debate on corporate governance in financial institutions', IP/10/656, Brussels, 2 June 2010.

[158] Commission, 'Reinforcing Economic Policy Coordination' (Communication) COM (2010) 250 final.

[159] Smits, 'The European Constitution and EMU' (n 92 above) 431 referring to Kapteyn, 'The EMU and Central Bank: Chances Missed' (2004) 1 *European Constitutional Law Review* 123, 125.

impact in places where the EU currently punches well below its weight, such as (in addition to the IMF) the OECD, the G8 and the G20.[160] The Union should entrust confidence to multilateral institutions but should not be seen as dragging its feet or being unable to take the lead within those.[161]

Now more than ever, however, it is necessary to address grassroots problems too. The continued existence of the euro is not solely dependent on political will and high-level decisions. A populist agenda ran alongside the crisis which was based on fear and intolerance.[162] The wounds left by that campaign are deep, and may be more difficult to repair than the Union's economic troubles. And, if that falters, the fate of Icarus awaits not only the euro, but the Union itself.

[160] For an indication of the direction EU participation takes in these fora, see Informal Meeting of EU Heads of State or Government, Agreed Language for the Pittsburgh G-20 Summit, Brussels, 17 September 2009. See also the contribution from J Wouters, S Sterkx, and T Corthaut, 'The European Union, the International Financial Crisis and Global Governance', ch 7 of this book.

[161] See statement of Extraordinary Meeting of Ministers of Transport, 19 April 2010, related to a European response to the Icelandic volcanic eruption.

[162] Betrüger in der Euro-Familie' *Focus* (22 February 2010).

9

Securing Safety, Controlling Crises: Development and Misapplication of Food Law in the European Union

CAOIMHÍN MACMAOLÁIN

I INTRODUCTION

EUROPEAN UNION LAW and policy on food safety developed in response to a crisis—BSE. As a consequence, EU food law has developed in a 'crisis-centred' way. By this we mean that the most significant legislative and policy developments tend to be related to safety matters, rather than to other important areas of concern, such as quality and nutritional value. In addition to this, much of the decision-making on the regulation of food production and marketing has been brought under the control of the EU institutions. This has taken away the autonomous role of the Member States who, it is here argued, are often best placed to deal with most safety concerns. This has created two problems. First, given that it is the EU that controls food safety, and given that the EU's other aims include the facilitation of the free movement of goods, Member States have been placed in a position whereby they are now unable to take meaningful measures to protect the health of their people from potential food dangers. Second, the focus on 'crisis' and 'emergency' in EU law on food safety leads to very costly interventions where some putative or possible danger from the consumption of food is identified, but prior to any reasonably accurate quantification of consequential risk. As a result, both the EU institutions and the Member States have become over-cautious, resulting in economic costs of billions of euros and countless amounts of wasted food. EU law on food safety is crisis-obsessed.

This chapter commences by tracing the development of EU food law in the post-BSE era.[1] It identifies how the mishandling of that crisis led to the creation of an entirely new approach to the regulation of the food sector. It illustrates how

[1] The BSE crisis has been described as marking 'year zero' for the European Union food regime. See Chalmers, 'Food for thought: Reconciling European risks and traditional ways of life' (2003) 66 *Modern Law Review* 532, 534.

the key features of this new body of EU food laws would primarily be related to safety concerns. New ideas about 'rapid alert', 'crisis management' and 'emergencies' would form the basis of this, leaving little room for other considerations, such as those related to quality and wholesomeness. It is also noted how this has all been based on the mistaken belief that quality and safety and inextricably linked—that if food is safe to eat then it is also of high quality. This is not necessarily the case. The chapter concludes by arguing that EU food law now needs to move away from this over-concern with unlikely risk, towards a more holistic corpus of rules where measures designed to ensure safety, on the one hand, and quality, on the other, are detached. Only if this approach is adopted will other important areas of concern, such as those related to nutrition, be properly addressed.

II DEVELOPMENT OF FOOD SAFETY LAW AND POLICY IN THE EU

While cattle in the UK may have been infected with bovine spongiform encephalopathy (BSE, or 'mad cow disease') as early as the 1970s,[2] it was not until the mid-1980s that the extent of the problem became apparent. By 1987 it had been concluded that cattle had died from BSE infection and that the probable cause of the spread of the disease was the consumption of meat and bonemeal which was made from animal carcasses and incorporated into animal feed. Ten years later, an inquiry into the emergence of BSE and the actions taken to counter its devastating consequences was announced in the UK Parliament. In the intervening period, cases of BSE detected in UK herds had led to the destruction of over 170,000 cattle, and up to 80 deaths from the human variant of the disease, Creutzfeld–Jakob disease (variant CJD).[3] BSE had developed into an epidemic as a consequence of intensive farming practices, in particular the unregulated recycling of animal protein in feed,[4] complicated by the fact that it was not initially believed that the disease was transmissible to humans.[5] It subsequently transpired that it probably could be so transmitted.

It is widely accepted that the BSE crisis was mishandled by those responsible for dealing with it. This was primarily due to: (i) the conflicting evidence about the possible dangers to humans of consuming infected beef; and (ii) the lack of a

[2] Findings of a report to the Minister of Agriculture, Fisheries and Food and Secretary of State for Health. *The BSE Inquiry: The Report* (London, The Stationery Office, 2001).

[3] These statistics are taken from the Findings and Conclusions of the BSE Inquiry Report (n 2 above).

[4] Also a conclusion of the BSE Inquiry.

[5] It was stated at the outset that 'it was most unlikely that BSE would have any implications for human health'. Report of the Working Party on Bovine Spongiform Encephalopathy (Southwood Report) (London, Department of Health/MAFF, 1989).

proper mechanism at European Union level to deal with such a crisis.[6] The result was the introduction of a series of piecemeal responses through the issuing of multiple decisions that altered the types and levels of restrictions on the export of beef and beef products from the United Kingdom. This ultimately resulted in the introduction of a total ban.[7] When the validity of this course of action was challenged, the Court of Justice decided that the introduction of the prohibition on exports from the UK was not beyond the powers of the Commission,[8] and was not disproportionate to the aim pursued.[9] The Court stated in its deliberations on this that:

> Where there is uncertainty as to the existence or extent of risks to human health, the institutions may take protective measures without having to wait until the reality and seriousness of those risks becomes fully apparent.[10]

This position is now enshrined in EU law on health protection.[11] The formalisation of this principle as an element of EU food law is the first significant and lasting legal consequence of the BSE crisis.[12]

Consumer confidence in experts, legislators and regulators was also dented by the BSE crisis. Claims were made that the initial failure to react properly to the emergence of the disease in British herds led to its increased spread between 1987, and the introduction of the full export ban in 1996. It was only then that the link with variant CJD was publicly confirmed. Both the UK authorities and the Commission had been slow to react. Meal bans were introduced in the UK in

[6] Criticism has come from a range of sources, including the European Parliament in its Report of the Temporary Committee of Enquiry on Alleged Contraventions or Maladministration in the Implementation of Community Law in Relation to BSE (as established by EP Decision of 17 July 1996, OJ C239/1) and academics, for example, Vos, 'EU Food Safety Regulation in the Aftermath of the BSE Crisis' (2000) 23 *Journal of Consumer Policy* 227 and Vincent, 'Mad Cows and Eurocrats—Community Responses to the BSE Crisis' (2004) 10 *European Law Journal* 499.

[7] Commission Decision 1996/239/EC on emergency measures to protect against bovine spongiform encephalopathy [1996] OJ L78/47.

[8] Based on Council Directive 1989/662/EEC concerning veterinary checks in intra-Community trade with a view to the completion of the internal market [1989] OJ L395/13, and Council Directive 1990/425/EEC concerning veterinary and zootechnical checks applicable in intra-Community trade in certain live animals and products with a view to the completion of the internal market [1990] OJ L224/29.

[9] Case C-157/1996 *The Queen v Ministry of Agriculture, Fisheries and Food, Commissioners of Customs and Excise, ex p National Farmers' Union and others* [1998] ECR I-2211 and Case C-180/1996 *United Kingdom v Commission* [1998] ECR I-2265. Both judgments were delivered on the same day, 5 May 1998.

[10] ibid, para 63 of the judgment in *National Farmers' Union*, and para 99 of *UK v Commission.*

[11] It could be said that this is the first application of the precautionary principle to EU food law. Prior to this the term was primarily used by EU lawyers in the context of environmental law. For further discussion see: MacMaoláin, 'Using the precautionary principle to protect human health' (2003) 28 *European Law Review* 723.

[12] Now also set out in Art 7 of Regulation 178/2002/EC of the European Parliament and of the Council of 28 January 2002 laying down the general principles and requirements of food law, establishing the European Food Safety Authority and laying down procedures in matters of food safety [2002] OJ L31/1. Discussed in more detail below.

1988, but only on new stocks.[13] Existing stocks could, incredibly, still be used. The first EU response came in 1989, with the introduction of a ban on the export of cattle from the UK that had been born before the date of the meal ban.[14] This was later reduced to a ban on the export of calves under six months old.[15] The export of 'bone-in' beef was limited to that from farms where there had been no BSE in the herd for two years.[16] This was later extended to herds that were BSE-free for at least six years.[17] The link between BSE-infected cattle and the possible transmission by beef consumption to humans as variant CJD was subsequently announced by the UK Spongiform Encephalopathy Advisory Committee (SEAC) in 1996. A decision was immediately introduced as an emergency measure, banning the export of all beef products from the UK.[18] Exports did not resume until 1999, and then only partially.[19]

The European Parliamentary Committee on BSE was highly critical of the way in which the crisis had been handled by the UK authorities and by the Commission.[20] Their criticisms related primarily to the fact that there had been evidence as early as 1990 that the BSE infection could cross species. Adequate further investigation was not carried out into this. Also, from 1990 to 1994 veterinary checks for BSE in the UK were suspended. There was no meaningful legislative intervention by the EU. There were no discussions in Council on the matter either. This was the case despite the fact that the crisis was at its peak at this time.

The lasting consequences for EU food law of the crisis and the way in which it was mishandled, were initially set out in the resultant Green Paper and subsequent White Paper on Food Safety.[21] These policy documents were drafted as a

[13] Bovine Spongiform Encephalopathy Order 1988, SI 1988/1039.

[14] Commission Decision 1989/469/EEC concerning certain protection measures relating to bovine spongiform encephalopathy in the United Kingdom [1989] OJ L225/51.

[15] Commission Decision 1990/59/EEC amending Decision 1989/469/EEC concerning certain protection measures relating to bovine spongiform encephalopathy in the United Kingdom [1990] OJ L41/23.

[16] Commission Decision 1990/261/EEC amending Decision 1989/469 concerning certain protection measures relating to bovine spongiform encephalopathy in the United Kingdom and Decision 1990/200/EEC concerning some additional requirements for some tissues and organs with respect to bovine spongiform encephalopathy [1990] OJ L146/29.

[17] Commission Decision 1994/474/EEC concerning certain protection measures relating to bovine spongiform encephalopathy and repealing Decisions 1989/469/EEC and 1990/200/EEC, [1994] OJ L194/96 and Commission Decision 1994/794/EEC concerning certain protection measures relating to bovine spongiform encephalopathy and repealing Decisions 89/469/EEC and 90/200/EEC, [1994] OJ L325/60.

[18] Commission Decision 1996/239/EC on emergency measures to protect against bovine spongiform encephalopathy [1996] OJ L78/47.

[19] A process started by Council Decision 1998/256/EC of 16 March 1998 concerning emergency measures to protect against bovine spongiform encephalopathy, amending Decision 1994/474/EC and repealing Decision 1996/239/EC [1998] OJ L113/32.

[20] EP Report of the Temporary Committee of Enquiry on Alleged Contraventions or Maladministration in the Implementation of Community Law in Relation to BSE (as established by EP Decision of 17 July 1996, OJ C239/1).

[21] Commission, White Paper on Food Safety. COM (1999) 719.

direct reaction to the shortcomings of existing EU rules on food safety that had become so obvious during the BSE crisis. The use of ad hoc decisions would be replaced by the development of a codified and structured response to any similar future food scare.

A White Paper on Food Safety

The White Paper on Food Safety declared that there was a need for a major review of European Union food law. The disparate nature of existing rules and procedures required the provision of a new framework. A 'farm to fork' system of regulation over the production and marketing of food was to be introduced, ensuring the traceability and control over all stages of food production, right through from the production of animal feed to the final foodstuff for human consumption.

Most importantly, the White Paper noted that the process for transforming scientific advice into legislation or decisions was unsatisfactory. The procedures in place were cumbersome and disparate. There were also too many committees involved in decision-making and a shortage of the resources required to operate them properly. This ultimately led to the creation of the European Food Safety Authority and new framework legislation—the General Food Law Regulation.[22]

B General Food Law Regulation

The Preamble to the General Food Law Regulation notes that recent food safety incidents, most notably the BSE crisis, had demonstrated the need for the establishment of appropriate measures that could be used and applied in emergency situations. The first mechanism that can be resorted to in such situations is the taking of precautionary action, developed by the Court in *National Farmers' Union* and *Commission v UK*,[23] and enacted in EU food law by the Regulation, which states that:

> Where the possibility of harmful effects on health is identified but scientific uncertainty persists, provisional risk management measures necessary to ensure health protection may be adopted, pending further assessment. Any such measures must be proportionate and no more restrictive on trade than necessary.[24]

While this precautionary principle can be resorted to once a risk has become apparent, the introduction of traceability at all stages of food production assists

[22] Regulation 178/2002/EC laying down the general principles and requirements of food law, establishing the European Food Safety Authority and laying down procedures in matters of food safety [2002] OJ L31/1.

[23] Case C-157/1996 *National Farmers' Union* and Case C-180/1996 *United Kingdom v Commission* (n 9 above).

[24] Art 7.

in the identification of which batches of food may present such a risk, as well as identifying at which stage in the production process the risk originated.[25]

The General Food Law Regulation also creates a 'rapid alert system' for any risk to human health that is identified. This system involves interaction and cooperation between the various actors in the regulatory process, including the Member States, the Commission, and the European Food Safety Authority. We discuss the formation and role of the latter body in more detail below. Each of these actors designates a contact point, with the Commission assuming overall responsibility for managing this rapid alert system network.

The rapid alert system works on the basis that any member of the network that has information about a serious risk to human health must immediately notify the Commission of this. This information is then transmitted, again with immediacy, to the other members of the network. Where food or feed that has been the subject of a notification under the rapid alert system has already been dispatched to a third country, then the Commission must inform such countries about this. Member States must inform the Commission of any action that they take under the rapid alert system. This information is then also transmitted to the network. The system may also be opened up to third countries more generally, as well as to international organisations on the basis of reciprocity. The Regulation provides that any information on food borne risks identified under the rapid alert system is generally to be made public.[26]

Another feature of the way in which food crises are to be dealt with under the provisions of the General Food Law Regulation is the response to situations deemed 'emergencies'.[27] Where an identified risk can not be contained by the measures adopted by a Member State, the Commission can suspend the placing of the food in question on the market. This can also be done in the case of foods imported from third countries. The Commission then has 10 working days to confirm, amend, revoke or extend the emergency measures. Where a Member State informs the Commission of the need for emergency measures and the Commission does not act, the Member State may itself introduce interim measures. The Commission then decides whether these measures are necessary.

C European Food Safety Authority

The General Food Law Regulation has, perhaps most significantly, led to the establishment of a permanent authority to oversee aspects of food safety policy throughout the EU. The European Food Safety Authority (EFSA) primarily provides scientific advice and scientific and technical support for the Union's

[25] Art 18.
[26] Art 52.
[27] Art 53.

legislation and policies that impact on food safety.[28] To carry out this role, EFSA collects and analyses data to facilitate the monitoring of risks to health. EFSA opinions, under the terms of the Regulation, serve as the scientific basis for the drafting and adoption of related EU measures. The Authority is designated the 'primary point of reference' on such advice, while also acting as an independent and transparent body that cooperates with competent bodies in the Member States in areas within its remit. EFSA, the Commission and the Member States must cooperate to promote effective coherence between risk assessment, risk management and risk communication.

The scientific opinions of the Authority are provided by the Scientific Committee and the Scientific Panels. The Committee comprises the chairs of the individual panels and six other independent experts. There are panels on additives, additives in feed, plant health, genetically modified organisms, dietetic products, nutrition and allergies, biological hazards, contaminants and animal health and welfare.[29] EFSA issues opinions at the request of the Commission or on its own initiative.[30] The European Parliament and the Member States may also request opinions. However, the data illustrates that the vast majority of opinions are requested by the Commission.[31]

Divergences in opinion between EFSA and other bodies, where these occur, are to be identified and discussed with these other bodies.[32] Where this divergent opinion is that of a Community Agency or Scientific Committee, or a Member State body, then EFSA is obliged to cooperate with this other body with a view to resolving these differences. As has been stated elsewhere, this completely contravenes the principle set out in the Regulation that EFSA is to be the 'primary point of reference' for any such scientific opinion sought.[33]

The European Food Safety Authority commissions studies from independent sources,[34] as well as collecting data to forward to the European Parliament, the Commission and the Member States to assist them in their own decision-making.[35] The Authority searches for data to identify emerging risks.[36] Where a risk to human health is suspected, then the Authority can request additional information on this. As noted above, EFSA also has a role to play in the Rapid Alert System.[37]

[28] Art 22.2.

[29] Art 28.

[30] Art 29.

[31] As analysed by Alemanno, 'The European Food Safety Authority at Five' (2008) 3 *European Food and Feed Law Review* 2.

[32] Art 30.

[33] Alemanno, 'The European Food Safety Authority at Five' (n31 above).

[34] Art 32.

[35] Art 33.

[36] Art 34.

[37] Art 35.

The European Food Safety Authority is required to always act with independence[38] and transparency.[39] Agendas, minutes, opinions (including minority opinions) are all to be made public. The Authority is also obliged, as part of its remit, to develop contacts with consumer groups, producer representatives, processors and other interested parties.[40] There is also a role for third countries in the workings of EFSA, subject to agreements negotiated on this with these countries.[41]

D BSE Regulation

While the primary legislative consequence of the BSE crisis has been the development of a rapid alert system, the construction of a codified emergency measures procedure, the initiation of a traceability scheme and the establishment of the European Food Safety Authority, a new regulation was also introduced to deal with the problems attached to any potential future outbreak of BSE specifically.[42] This regulation requires that a risk analysis be carried out to determine the BSE status of Member States.[43] A state can be classified as 'BSE free', 'BSE provisionally free with no cases', 'low incidence of BSE', or 'high incidence of BSE'.[44] This system can be applied to third countries also. Interested states, both Member States and third countries, apply to the Commission, hoping ultimately to be awarded the status of 'approved for export of live animals or products'.

The BSE Regulation provides that the feeding of ruminants with protein derived from mammals is prohibited.[45] Further restrictions are also to be placed on products of animal origin from countries with a 'high incidence of BSE'.[46] Additional obligations are placed on Member States, who are to ensure that any suspicions of a transmissible spongiform encephalopathy (TSE) are notified to the national competent authority.[47] Movement restrictions are to be put in place for animals in which infection is suspected.[48] Where BSE is suspected, then these restrictions are to be placed on the entire herd, not just individual animals.

38 Art 37.
39 Art 38.
40 Art 42.
41 Art 49.
42 Given that this legislation deals with emergency situations, it has coincidentally been appropriately numbered Regulation 999/2001/EC laying down rules for the prevention, control and eradication of certain transmissible spongiform encephalopathies [2001] OJ L147/1.
43 Art 5.
44 Annex 2 to Regulation 999/2001 (n 42 above).
45 Art 7.
46 Art 9.
47 Art 11.
48 Art 12.

Where the presence of a TSE is confirmed, the animal must be destroyed.[49] The relevant scientific committees are to be consulted on matters that could impact upon public health.[50]

Overall, this regulation was introduced due to the recognised necessity of adopting specific measures for TSEs rather than resorting to a series of decisions based on general animal health directives.[51]

III NEW DIRECTIONS IN THE DEVELOPMENT OF EU FOOD LAW

As previously stated, the primary provisions of EU law on food safety developed in the aftermath of the BSE crisis. As a consequence, the priority for legislators and policy-makers has been on safety, at the expense of other, often more serious and pressing, concerns. This has led to a series of identifiable shortcomings with the current corpus of EU food law.

First, there is too much concern with 'crises', both within the EU institutions and within the Member States. Take, for example, the well-documented scare over dioxin levels in Irish pork in December 2008. Ireland took measures as soon as a potential issue was identified, encouraged by the emergency provisions of the General Food Law Regulation and the atmosphere of caution that exists within EU law on food safety. All pork and pork products were immediately removed from shop shelves. Many were destroyed. All of the pork on sale at the time was, however, perfectly safe to eat. The measures taken were unnecessary. The resultant cost to the Member State was €35 million in the first month alone. Confidence in the pork industry deteriorated and sales fell. The European Food Safety Authority report, issued just a few days after the announcement of the 'potential risk' demonstrated that there was clearly no safety issue.

The real difficulty with a situation such as that created by the presence of dioxins in Irish pork is that in the 'crisis-centred' approach to food safety, contamination limits tend to be set too low. This leads to panic reactions when announcements are made that detected levels of contaminant are 'X' amount of times the permitted level. For Irish pork, the contamination was between 80 and 200 times the permitted level. Yet, there was, in the opinion of EFSA, no identifiable risk to human health. It was declared that consumption of affected pork, all of which was contaminated at the highest level recorded, would have no adverse health effects, even if consumed in large volumes every day for 90 consecutive days.

The second consequence of over-concern with 'crises' is that this leads to inactivity by the EU institutions in other areas, for example in dealing with other food-related health concerns, such as the consequences of a poor diet and, more

49 Art 13.

50 Art 25.

51 Recital 2, Preamble to Regulation 999/2001 (n 42 above).

specifically, obesity. Research shows that the consumption of trans-fatty acids increases the risk of heart disease by 25 per cent.[52] Ten per cent of all health costs in the EU are related to poor diet.[53] In the UK, 18 million sick days were lost from work, there were 30,000 premature deaths and a financial cost to the economy of £2 billion per annum, by 2001.[54] Estimates put the cost to the Irish health service at €70 million by the same date.[55] Despite this, action on tackling obesity within the EU has moved at a relatively slow pace. Individual Member States are prevented from taking their own action to deal with this by EU rules on the free movement of goods. For example, UK attempts to ensure that consumers were properly informed about the nutritional value of food through the introduction of a 'signpost' or 'traffic-light labelling' scheme were frustrated by the fact that any such proposal for inclusion of this on all labels has to remain voluntary. EU law on measures equivalent to quantitative restrictions on imports prevents individual Member States from devising their own forms of food labelling that deviate from the harmonised standard set out in the framework directive.[56] The UK Food Standards Agency (FSA) introduced a voluntary signpost label in March 2006 that producers and/or retailers could choose to use on their products. By July 2006, just four months after the inception of the scheme, 14 different signpost label types, none identical to the FSA model, were being used by retailers and food manufacturers in the UK. A label designed to provide clarity to consumers merely added to the existing confusion.

An EU Green Paper on Obesity was published in 2005,[57] with the White Paper following in 2007.[58] The only legislative proposal arising out of these documents was to keep existing nutrition labelling requirements as they are.[59] Research indicates, however, that many consumers fail to gain any benefit from the current presentation of nutrition information labelling on foodstuffs. There is now also a proposal to incorporate the signpost labelling format, or other similar ones, into the general food labelling provisions.[60] However, the proposal does not go so far as to suggest the introduction of a harmonised scheme, one that would alleviate the difficulties inherent in voluntary labelling disclosures, as shown by the UK

[52] Clarke and Lewington, 'Trans Fatty Acids and Coronary Heart Disease' (2006) 333 *British Medical Journal* 214.

[53] WHO, *European Health Report* (Copenhagen, WHO Regional Publications, 2002).

[54] UK National Audit Office, *Tackling Obesity in England* (London, The Stationery Office, 2001).

[55] Report of the Irish National Taskforce on Obesity, Dublin 2005.

[56] Directive 2000/13/EC on the approximation of the laws of the Member States relating to the labelling, presentation and advertising of foodstuffs [2000] OJ L109/29.

[57] Commission, Green Paper on Promoting Healthy Diets and Physical Activity: a European dimension for the prevention of overweight, obesity and chronic diseases COM (2005) 637.

[58] Commission, White Paper on A Strategy for Europe on Nutrition, Overweight and Obesity Related Health Issues COM (2007) 279.

[59] As set out in Council Directive 1990/496/EEC on nutrition labelling for foodstuffs [1990] OJ L276/40.

[60] Commission, Proposal for a Regulation of the European Parliament and of the Council on the provision of food information to consumers COM (2008) 40.

example discussed above. All that is proposed is that individual Member States may be permitted to implement their own system alongside other EU food labelling requirements.[61]

The link between food contamination and detrimental effects on health is often not proven in food safety cases, yet a high level of interventionist action, both legislative and through the establishment of the European Food Safety Authority, has been taken in relation to these. The link between diet and disease has been proven, yet there is inaction on this.[62] The link between BSE and variant CJD has always been described as 'possible'. There may be some danger from the consumption of the brain and/or spinal cord of affected cattle. In the first 10 years after the detection of BSE in British beef cattle there were 97 recorded deaths from variant CJD in the UK. There were two in France and one in Ireland. The estimated cost was €1 billion in the first year alone, rising to €5 billion by 2000.[63]

The costs, both economic and human, of poor diet tend to be much higher than those related to safety issues. Despite this, meaningful interventionist action is not taken. EU law also prevents Member States from taking legislative responsibility for this, due to the combination of existing harmonised food labelling legislation and EC Treaty rules prohibiting measures equivalent to quantitative restrictions on trade.[64] The EU has assumed control in this area. This prevents, for example, the introduction by Member States of compulsory labelling schemes that clearly identify low value foods to consumers. It also leads to additional confusion and scope for the deception of consumers through the development of voluntary labelling disclosures. The experience of UK efforts to tackle nutrition-related illness through, amongst others, the FSA 'signpost labelling' proposal presents a clear example of this in practice.

The failure to focus on nutrition and quality issues due to over-emphasis on safety in the aftermath of BSE possesses the potential for consequences more devastating than food-borne diseases or contamination generally possess. Reprioritisation at EU level is thus required to redress the current imbalance that exists in the remit of existing EU food laws

IV CONCLUSION

There needs to be a change at EU level from 'crisis control' and dealing with 'emergencies' to instead addressing ongoing concerns related to the nutritional value and the wholesomeness of food. The EU to date has erroneously tended to

[61] Art 34.5 of the Proposal.

[62] See, for example, Greenwald, Clifford and Milner, 'Diet and cancer prevention' (2001) 37 *European Journal of Cancer* 948; and Hu et al, 'Dietary fat intake and the risk of coronary heart disease in women' (1997) 337 *New England Journal of Medicine* 1491.

[63] Buzby and Detwiler, 'BSE: Anatomy of a Crisis' (2001) *Choices* 41.

[64] Arts 28–30 EC (Arts 34–36 TFEU).

see quality and wholesomeness/nutrition as by-products of safety. On such logic, if food is not unsafe it follows that it must also be wholesome. The preamble to the General Food Law Regulation states that the:

> free movement of safe and wholesome food is an essential aspect of the internal market and contributes significantly to the health and well-being of citizens.[65]

However, the issues related to the 'safety' and 'quality' of food must be separated, to ensure that the focus is on both important issues, rather than being on just one of them, safety, presuming that the other, quality, will flow from this.

Full effect now also needs to be given to Article 30 EC on health protection to enable Member States to take their own action where they seek to control what is consumed where this poses a threat to health. Presently, only verifiable dangers to health provide an exception to rules on free movement, as demonstrated, for example, by the reasoning of the Court in the *Bier*[66] and *Milk Substitutes* cases.[67]

Finally, clarity is required on the application of the precautionary principle in EU food law. Scientific opinions presented to the Commission need not be followed,[68] even when presented by 'the primary point of reference', the European Food Safety Authority. When this happens, clear reasoning must be presented to minimise arbitrary decision-making on precautionary grounds. Precautionary action has become too commonplace, leading to the taking of unnecessary, and potentially very serious, action, such as happened in the Irish pork scare. If EFSA opinion were to be sought pre-action rather than post, particularly where almost immediate informed opinion can be provided, then this should become the norm.

The Preamble to the Decision introducing a total ban on the export of beef cattle and products from the UK noted that the action was necessary to counter 'serious concern among consumers' arising out of 'uncertainty'.[69] A shift is now required to move the focus away from pandering to, often unfounded, consumer concerns. The primary considerations that inform the development of EU food law should be evidence based, taken after a demonstration of danger or potential danger. Evidence based concerns surrounding diet and disease are not currently acted upon. The combination of post-BSE safety concerns and support for the free movement of food has led to the development of a body of EU food laws that emphasises safety yet refuses to regulate some of the most unsafe consequences of food consumption.

65 Recital 1, preamble to Regulation 178/2002 (n 22 above).

66 Case 178/84, *Commission v Germany* [1987] ECR 1227.

67 Case 216/1984 *Commission v France* [1988] ECR 793 and Case 76/1986 *Commission v Germany* [1989] ECR 1021.

68 Case T-13/1999 *Pfizer Animal Health SA v Council* [2002] ECR II-3305.

69 Commission Decision 1996/239/EC (n 7 above).

10

Food Safety at the WTO after Continued Suspension: a Paradigm Shift?

ALESSANDRA ARCURI

I INTRODUCTION

ONE OF THE daunting challenges facing the European regulator is food safety. Bovine spongiform encephalopathy (BSE) in beef, salmonella in eggs and listeria in cheese are notorious food scares that have spurred important regulatory changes in the area of food safety, such as those envisaged by the Commission White Paper on Food Safety published in 2000 and the establishment of the European Food and Safety Authority (EFSA) in 2002. Regulating the risks attached to food, however, proves an extremely difficult and controversial task. On the one hand, maintaining food safety is a high priority in Europe; on the other hand, in increasingly integrated markets, food safety regulations often encroach on other states' policies. Disputes between the EU and the US, such as those concerning genetically modified organisms (GMOs) and beef from cattle treated with growth-promoting hormones are evidence of the fact that food safety is rapidly entering the arena of global politics and that Europe needs to take into consideration the limits that international law imposes on its freedom to regulate food.

The World Trade Organization (WTO) is the international body which, allegedly, sets the most prominent boundaries to the national regulator in designing its own food safety laws. This article explores one dimension of the WTO international legal framework relevant for food safety regimes. Rather than looking at individual norms, the article tries to understand what regulatory philosophies are compatible with this international legal regime. This analysis is relevant because it unveils the fact that disputes over particular food safety rules reach beyond the single issues disputed; they are about the values that can be included in the regulatory process.

The agreement that inextricably links EU food law with WTO law is the Sanitary and Phytosanitary (SPS) Agreement, annexed to the WTO. The SPS Agreement strongly encourages WTO Members to follow international standards; if, however they decide to adopt regulatory standards higher than those set at international level, they should base these standards on risk assessment. If

Members do not follow these rules, they may be brought before the WTO quasi-judiciary organs, and if a violation is established, the WTO Dispute Settlement Body (DSB) may authorise complainant Members to impose sanctions, in the form of 'retaliatory measures', on the offending Member. The WTO 'stick' thus hangs like the proverbial sword of Damocles over national risk regulators.

To better understand the type of influence that the WTO may have on national food safety regulation, it is necessary to clarify the meaning of essential concepts in the SPS Agreement, such as 'scientific uncertainty' and 'risk assessment'. The text of the SPS Agreement obviously provides some guidance as to the meaning of these concepts. However, as is often the case with written rules, ambiguities remain in the legal text.

In this regard, the interpretation of some key concepts by the WTO quasi-judiciary organs (i.e., the Panels and the Appellate Body), may offer guidance on the regulatory approach(es) which the SPS Agreement endorses, or at least allows.[1] In other words, the case law on the SPS Agreement provides important information on the regulatory paradigms that Members can follow in designing their national food safety policies.[2]

This article investigates whether the interpretation of concepts such as 'risk assessment' and 'insufficiency of scientific evidence' is consistent throughout the SPS jurisprudence and whether the interpretative choices made by the Panels and the Appellate Body are rooted in different approaches to risk. In this regard, two hypotheses are tested: the first is that, until recently, the interpretation of a number of key concepts in the SPS Agreement was influenced by different and, at times, conflicting approaches to risk (hereafter, the 'juggling hypothesis').[3] With regard to the 'juggling hypothesis', it is postulated that the WTO quasi-judiciary organs are juggling with the core beliefs of different 'knowledge-based groups', a term that this paper defines as a cluster of experts and scholars in the field of risk analysis. The second hypothesis tested examines the question of whether the Appellate Body in *Canada/US—Continued Suspension (Continued Suspension)*[4]

[1] One of the purposes of the WTO dispute settlement system is 'to clarify the existing provisions' of the WTO agreements (Art 3.2 Understanding on rules and procedures governing the settlement of disputes (DSU)).

[2] The scope of this paper is limited to the interpretation developed by the quasi-judiciary organs; a relatively new avenue of research has documented the 'life' of the SPS Agreement beyond dispute settlements. In particular, it is worthwhile mentioning the important work carried out on a daily basis within the SPS Committee. For recent insights on this phenomenon, see ATF Lang and J Scott, 'The Hidden World of WTO Governance' (2009) 20 *European Journal of International Law* 575.

[3] This hypothesis was earlier investigated in A Arcuri, 'Interpreting the concepts of "risk management" and "insufficiency of scientific evidence": juggling between the logics of different knowledge-based groups?' in MC Malaguti, C Dordi, S Di Benedetto and A Alemanno (eds), *Science & Law—Scientific Evidence in International and European Law* (Lecce, Argo Editore, 2009); the sections relating to this hypothesis are partly taken from the mentioned article.

[4] Panel Reports, *Canada—Continued Suspension of Obligations in the EC—Hormones Disputes (Canada/US—Continued Suspension)*, WT/DS320/R, WT/DS321/R, DSR 2008:W; Appellate Body Report, *Canada—Continued Suspension of Obligations in the EC—Hormones Dispute*, WT/DS321/

has shifted towards a 'new paradigm'. In particular, it is examined whether the ideas of one of these knowledge-based groups prevailed.

The main reason to investigate the possible influence of the ideas of different knowledge-based groups on the reports of the WTO quasi-judiciary organs is two-fold. First, panellists and Appellate Body members are generally non-specialists in the field of risk law; yet, the task of interpretation of the SPS Agreement requires them to draw on a clear vision of the problem. Such a vision is plausibly related to the set of beliefs of experts in the field of risk analysis. Second, even though international (quasi-)judiciary organs are not policy-makers, they arguably perform such a role by interpreting concepts enshrined in the treaties. Thus, the relationship between visions of knowledge-based groups and quasi-judicial policy innovation needs to be examined. Eventually, by influencing the interpretation of the SPS Agreement and consequently its substantive content, a knowledge-based group can be seen as a 'source of policy innovation' in the field of risk governance and food safety policy.

In the analysis of these issues, section 2 explains the concept of knowledge-based groups and attempts to identify different knowledge-based groups in the field of risk analysis and governance. Section 3 investigates the 'juggling hypothesis' by examining the different rationales/theories informing the SPS jurisprudence and its relationship with the ideas of the previously identified knowledge-based groups. To this end, a few interpretative issues are selected on the basis of their relevance to the questions studied.[5] Section 4 discusses two significant issues clarified by the Appellate Body in *Continued Suspension*: the role of the 'appropriate level of protection' in risk assessment and in the determination of the sufficiency of scientific evidence; and the question of independence and impartiality of experts. It is further investigated which rationale underpins the Appellate Body reasoning on these issues and whether the Appellate Body has

AB/R, adopted 14 November 2008, DSR 2008:XIV; Appellate Body Report, *United States—Continued Suspension of Obligations in the EC—Hormones Dispute (Canada/US Continued Suspension)*, WT/DS320/AB/R, adopted 14 November 2008, DSR 2008:X.

[5] It must be emphasised that this analysis is not intended to be a complete survey of the whole body of the SPS jurisprudence. Important analysis of the SPS Agreement include: J Pauwelyn, 'The WTO Agreement on Sanitary and Phytosanitary Measures as Applied in the First Three SPS Disputes' (1999) 2 *Journal of International Economic Law* 641; J Scott, *The WTO Agreement on Sanitary and Phytosanitary Measures—Oxford Commentaries on GATT/WTO Agreements* (Oxford, Oxford University Press, 2007); ATF Lang, 'Provisional Measures under Article 5.7 of the WTO's Agreement on Sanitary and Phytosanitary Measures: Some Criticisms of the Jurisprudence so Far' (2008) 42 *Journal of World Trade* 1085; G Shaffer, 'A Structural Approach to WTO Jurisprudence: Why Institutional Choice Lies at the Center of the GMO Case' (2008) 41 *New York University Journal of International Law and Politics* 1; C Foster, 'Public Opinion and the Interpretation of the World Trade Organisation's Agreement on Sanitary and Phytosanitary Measures' (2008) 11 JIEL 427; L Gruszczynski, *Regulating Health and Environmental Risks under WTO Law: A Critical Analysis of the SPS Agreement* (Oxford, Oxford University Press, 2010).

relied on the ideas of one of the two knowledge-based groups. In concluding, the essay draws attention to the importance of these issues for the future of European food safety policy.

II DIFFERENT KNOWLEDGE-BASED GROUPS IN THE FIELD OF RISK ANALYSIS

A Knowledge-based groups and epistemic communities: differences and similarities

A 'knowledge-based group' refers to a cluster of experts and scholars in the field of risk analysis. This concept resembles the one of epistemic community, defined as 'a network of professionals with recognised expertise and competence in a particular domain and an authoritative claim to policy-relevant knowledge within that domain or issue-area'.[6] The similarities of these concepts rest on two sets of ideas. First, as with epistemic communities, the knowledge-based groups of the type identified in this study share core common beliefs (visions) of the same issue-area. Second, similarly to epistemic communities, knowledge-based groups can perform a role of policy coordination or prompt policy evolution.[7]

Despite these similarities, it is appropriate to employ the more generic concept of 'knowledge-based group' because this essay, whilst inspired by the epistemic community scholarship, does not strictly adhere to that methodology. The epistemic community approach, in fact, typically investigates the 'community-dimension' of the experts' networks and the concrete relationships between these networks and (international) policymakers.[8] By contrast, in this chapter, the emphasis is not on the community-dimension of the phenomenon. For the purpose of this analysis, the personal relationships between the members of the group are irrelevant; what matters, is to identify the shared beliefs and their alleged influence on the interpretation of SPS key concepts. Accordingly, this

[6] P Haas, 'Introduction: Epistemic Communities and International Policy Coordination' (1992) 46 *International Organization*, 1, 3. The concept was previously defined by international relations scholar John Gerard Ruggie as follows: 'Epistemic communities may be said to consist of interrelated roles which grow up around an *episteme*; they delimit, for their members, *the* proper construction of social reality' (emphasis in original): JG Ruggie, 'International Responses to Technology: Concepts and Trends' (1975) 29 *International Organization*, 557, 570. For a seminal formulation of the concept of epistemic communities, see also EB Haas, *Beyond the Nation State* (Stanford, Stanford University Press, 1964).

[7] E Adler and P Haas, 'Conclusion: Epistemic Communities, World Order, and the Creation of a Reflective Research Program' (1992) 46 *International Organization*, 367.

[8] For a number of studies endorsing the epistemic community approach and applying it to different fields, see the full volume 46 *International Organization*. The epistemic community approach could also be considered in relation to its method as belonging to new legal realism, because of the inclusion of qualitative field work; for a discussion of new legal realism in international economic law, see G Shaffer, 'A New Legal Realism: Method in International Economic Law Scholarship' in CB Picker, ID Bunn and DW Arner (eds), *International Economic Law: The State and Future of the Discipline* (Oxford, Hart Publishing, 2008).

chapter predominantly employs a textual analysis aimed at understanding the link between the ideas of certain knowledge-based groups and the logic(s) endorsed by the WTO Panels and Appellate Body in interpreting the SPS Agreement. In particular, the analysis focuses on the interpretation of a select number of key concepts of the SPS Agreement: 'risk assessment', 'based on risk assessment' and 'insufficiency of scientific evidence.'

B Identifying two knowledge-based groups

To investigate the 'juggling hypothesis', it is necessary to identify the relevant knowledge-based groups in the field of risk analysis and governance. The scholarship in this field is very rich, and brings together scholars from different disciplines, including economists, sociologists, lawyers, psychologists, political scientists, philosophers of science and others.[9] The wide variety of ideas circulating in this scholarship makes it a difficult and perhaps overly ambitious task to identify groups of scholars that share the same core beliefs. Yet, oversimplifying, two knowledge-based groups of scholars may be identified: the *quantitative-risk logic* and the *holistic-risk logic* groups.[10]

The *quantitative-risk logic* group focuses on a narrow idea of risk: risk is the probability of an event occurring. This probability is almost always calculable, and otherwise techniques to manage uncertainty exist.[11] The preferred policy option is the one which maximises social welfare, more precisely, the one which

[9] One forum where scholars of different disciplines meet is the Society for Risk Analysis (SRA); for an overview of the activities of this society, see the SRA website: www.sra.org/.

[10] The distinction between these two knowledge-based groups is echoed in other treatises. *Cf* E Fisher and R Harding, 'The Precautionary Principle and Administrative Constitutionalism: the Development of Frameworks for Applying the Precautionary Principle' in E Fisher, J Jones and R von Schomberg (eds), *Implementing the Precautionary Principle: Perspective and Prospects* (Cheltenham, Edward Elgar, 2006); A Klinke and O Renn 'A New Approach to Risk Evaluation and Management: Risk-Based, Precaution-Based, and Discourse-Based Strategies' (2002) 22 *Risk Analysis* 1071, 1074. Despite the many similarities between these theories, there are differences in the conceptualisation made by these authors and the one made in the present essay. In the case of Fisher and Harding, the analysis focuses on theories of administrative constitutionalism. With regard to the work of Klinke and Renn, they associate a certain approach directly with decision-making. By contrast, here it is argued that a group of scholars shares the same set of beliefs, and these approaches are not always reflected in a consistent way in the decision-making process.

[11] Delphi method, sensitivity analysis, Monte Carlo analysis, and, more generally, Bayesian updating are techniques commonly used to deal with uncertainty. Richard Stewart discusses this issue and is defending the thesis that cost-benefit analysis can be used under conditions of uncertainty; see RB Stewart, 'Environmental Regulatory Decisionmaking under Uncertainty' in RO Zerbe and T Swantson (eds), *Introduction to the Law and Economics of Environmental Policy: Issues in Institutional Design*—vol 20 Research in Law and Economics (Amsterdam, North Holland, 2002) 71. Against A Arcuri, 'Reconstructing Precaution: Deconstructing Misconception' (2007) 21 *Ethics and International Affairs* 359, 366–68. Also Richard Posner has defended the use of cost-benefit analysis under uncertainty; he has indeed suggested several variations of cost-benefit analysis under conditions of extreme uncertainty, including what he has labeled 'inverse cost-benefit analysis' and 'the tolerable-windows approach;' *cf* RA Posner, *Catastrophe: Risk and Response* (Oxford, Oxford University Press, 2004) 176–87.

maximises net benefits.[12] This group adopts a rational-choice approach to human behaviour as its analytical standpoint. Because risks can always be calculated, risk governance is a process eminently based on the assessment of experts. Also, the disagreement between experts and the layman is commonly attributed to cognitive errors of the latter.[13] This group tends to agree that the process of risk governance requires at least two different steps, one of risk assessment and the other of risk management. Most also agree that in a third phase, a process of risk communication should take place. Last, but not least, this group takes an eminently positivist view of science. In line with these conceptual parameters, these scholars defend a technocratic mode of risk governance.[14] This knowledge-based group is mainly fuelled by economists and legal-economic scholars.[15]

When analysing risk-related questions, the *holistic-risk logic* group emphasises that risk assessment is value-laden and that risks can be properly defined 'only within particular political and cultural contexts'.[16] For this group, risk is a multi-faceted concept where the probability of a hazardous event occurring is not the only relevant feature; other considerations, such as the voluntary/involuntary, equitable/inequitable spread, and the novelty nature of the hazards, are important and contribute to define risk.[17] Science is perceived as complex, entrenched

[12] Representative scholars of this approach are William Kip Viscusi, Cass Sunstein and Richard Posner. Representative works in this area are: WK Viscusi, *Fatal Trade-off: Public and Private Responsibilities for Risk* (New York, Oxford University Press, 1992); CR Sunstein, *Risk and Reason: Safety, Law, and the Environment* (Cambridge, Cambridge University Press, 2002); and Posner, *Catastrophe* (n 11 above).

[13] See for instance, CR Sunstein, *Laws of Fear: Beyond the Precautionary Principle* (Cambridge, Cambridge University Press, 2005) ch 2.

[14] A representative contribution to this line of reasoning is S Breyer, *Breaking the Vicious Circle: Toward Effective Risk Regulation*, (Cambridge, MA: Harvard University Press, 1993).

[15] For an overview of the members of this group see the text and references in nn 11–13 above. Several other scholars may be included in the 'quantitative-risk logic group'; identifying all the scholars that belong to this group is beyond the scope of this chapter. However, in order to give a better idea of the composition of the group, a short selection of works by scholars that can be included in this group is here added: MD Adler and EA Posner, 'Rethinking Cost-Benefit Analysis' (1999) 109 *Yale Law Journal* 165; RW Hahn and CR Sunstein, 'The Precautionary Principle as a Basis for Decision Making' (2005) 2 *Economists' Voice* art 8; available at ssrn.com/abstract=721122; JD Graham, 'Saving Lives through Administrative Law and Economics' (2008) 157 *University of Pennsylvania Law Review* 395.

[16] L Busch, R Grove-White, S Jasanoff, D Winickoff and B Wynne, 'Amicus Curiae Brief Submitted to the Dispute Settlement Panel of the WTO in the case of EC-Biotech' (WT/DS291, 292 and 293) (2004) 15. Available at: http://csec.lancs.ac.uk/wtoamicus/amicus_brief_wto.pdf. Also published as a scholarly article, D Winickoff, et al, 'Adjudicating the GM Food Wars: Science, Risk, and Democracy in World Trade Law' (2005) 30 *Yale Journal of International Law* 81.

[17] A conspicuous number of studies have shown that people often characterise risks on the basis of some of the following qualitative dimensions: risk is voluntarily or involuntarily taken; risk is chronic or catastrophic; it is common or dread; it is known or unknown to those exposed; it is known or unknown to science; it is old or new; it is controllable or uncontrollable by those exposed. A risk that is voluntarily taken is rated as less dangerous than a risk that is involuntarily taken; a chronic risk is feared less than a catastrophic one, and so on. These factors might explain why risk created by nuclear power, which is involuntary taken, catastrophic and dreadful, is considered to be very serious by laymen, in spite of the fact that the probability of dying from nuclear power is very low. In

with uncertainties and its results determined by the endorsement of certain value judgements; in this context some authors explicitly endorse the notion of post-normal science.[18] Within such a framework, public participation is considered central to risk analysis, where a deliberative approach to risk governance appears to be partly the logical consequence of such a vision of risk and science. Members of this knowledge-based group range from philosophers of science, such as Kristin Shrader-Frechette, cognitive psychologists, such as Paul Slovic, to political scientists and lawyers, including the signatories to the *amicus curiae* brief submitted to the Panel in *EC—Biotech.*[19]

It should be noted that the ideas of knowledge-based groups are constantly evolving in light of new knowledge. Accordingly, the core beliefs of knowledge-based groups may change over time due to learning. In turn, the degree of consensus within a knowledge-based group may vary, contributing to the determination of how long a knowledge-based group remains influential.

Within this evolutionary process, it should be stressed that different knowledge-based groups are mutually exposed to the ideas of the others. At times, they use the ideas of the same research school but emphasise different findings. For instance, cognitive psychology has penetrated the set of ideas of both groups in many ways. The *quantitative-risk logic* group has often invoked studies showing the cognitive limitations of the layman, which may lead to the conclusion that more reliance on experts is desirable. By contrast, the *holistic-risk logic* group has paid attention to the results of the studies showing that people

cognitive psychology, this type of research aimed at systematically understanding people's perceptions of risk is also called the 'psychometric paradigm'. On this, see P Slovic, 'Perception of Risk' (1987) 236 *Science*, 280.

[18] M O' Connor, S Faucheux, G Froger, S Funtowicz, and G Munda, 'Emergent Complexity and Procedural Rationality: Post-Normal Science for Sustainability' in R Costanza and O Segura (eds), *Getting Down to Earth: Practical Applications of Ecological Economics* (Washington, DC, Island Press, 1996) 232–33; SO Funtowicz and JR Ravetz, 'Science for the Post-Normal Age' (1993) *Futures* 739.

[19] While this contribution has no pretense to offer a complete coverage of the members of this knowledge-based group, some of its influential members (together with their representative publications) are listed below as an illustration of the group's composition (in alphabetical order): Busch et al, 'Amicus' (n 16 above); EJ Johnson and A Tversky, 'Representation of Perceptions of Risks' (1984) 113 *Journal of Experimental Psychology: General*, 55; P Kane 'There's Method in the Magic' in J Franklin (ed), *The Politics of Risk Society* (Cambridge, Polity Press, 1998); B Rohrmann and O Renn, 'Risk Perception Research—an Introduction' in O Renn and B Rohrmann (eds), *Cross-cultural Risk Perception—A Survey of Empirical Studies* (Dordrecth, Kluwer Academic Publisher, 2000); K Shrader-Frechette, *Risk and Rationality: Philosophical Foundations for Populist Reforms* (Berkeley, University of California Press, 1991); K Shrader-Frechette, 'Reductionist Approaches to Risk' in DG Mayo and RD Hollander (eds), *Acceptable Evidence—Science and Value in Risk Management* (New York, Oxford University Press, 1991); P Slovic, B Fischhoff and S Lichtenstein, 'Characterizing Perceived Risk' in RW Kates, C Hohenemeser, and JX Kasperson (eds), *Perilous Progress: Managing the Hazard of Technology* (Boulder, CO, Westview Press, 1985); Slovic, 'Perception of Risk' (n 17 above); P Slovic, 'Beyond Numbers: A Broader Perspective on Risk Communication and Risk Perception' in DG Mayo and RD Hollander (eds), *Acceptable Evidence—Science and Value in Risk Management* (New York, Oxford University Press, 1991); B Wynne, 'May the Sheep Safely Graze? A Reflexive View of the Expert-Lay Knowledge Divide' in S Lash, B Szerszynski and B Wynne (eds), *Risk, Environment and Modernity: Toward a New Ecology* (London, Sage Publications, 1996).

have different preferences towards risks, such as the so-called psychometric paradigm, implying that the differences between experts and laymen cannot be ascribed to errors only. This traffic of ideas could imply that the outlined knowledge-based groups may further diverge, as the example above shows, but also that they could tend to converge towards a new approach to risk.

III TESTING THE JUGGLING HYPOTHESIS

The juggling hypothesis is used to establish whether the ideas of the outlined knowledge-based groups are reflected in the interpretation of the SPS Agreement by the Panels and the Appellate Body. This section discusses the interpretation of three notions separately: 'risk assessment', 'based on risk assessment' and 'insufficiency of scientific evidence'. From the outset, however, it should be clear that the interpretations of these three notions are interrelated.[20]

A The interpretation of risk assessment as a juggling act

Risk assessment is a key concept of the SPS Agreement. If WTO Members are to adopt SPS measures that differ from international standards, they should base these measures on a risk assessment. But, what exactly is risk assessment? The WTO quasi-judiciary organs were given the opportunity to clarify the meaning of this notion in several cases. In interpreting the definition of Annex A(4) to the SPS Agreement, the Appellate Body, in *Australia—Salmon*, identified two types of risk assessment: (1) risk assessment for quarantine risks and (2) risk assessment for food-borne risks.[21] The former requires an assessment of probability, whereas for the latter it is sufficient to assess the potential of harm. In other words, the calculation of probability is not necessary for risk assessments concerning for

[20] The cases considered for this analysis are the following (listed in chronological order): Appellate Body Report, *EC Measures Concerning Meat and Meat Products (Hormones) (EC—Hormones)*, WT/DS26/AB/R, WT/DS48/AB/R, adopted 13 February 1998, DSR 1998:I, 135; Appellate Body Report, *Australia—Measures Affecting Importation of Salmon (Australia—Salmon)*, WT/DS18/AB/R, adopted 6 November 1998, DSR 1998:VIII, 3327; Appellate Body Report, *Japan—Measures Affecting Agricultural Products (Japan—Agricultural Products II)*, WT/DS76/AB/R, adopted 19 March 1999, DSR 1999:I, 277; Appellate Body Report, *Japan—Measures Affecting the Importation of Apples, (Japan—Apples)*, WT/DS245/AB/R, adopted 10 December 2003, DSR 2003:IX, 4391; Panel Report, *European Communities—Measures Affecting the Approval and Marketing of Biotech Products (EC—Biotech)*, WT/DS291/R, WT/DS292/R, WT/DS293/R, Corr 1 and Add 1, 2, 3, 4, 5, 6, 7, 8 and 9, adopted 21 November 2006, DSR 2006:III–VIII; Panel Reports, *Canada—Continued Suspension of Obligations in the EC—Hormones Disputes (Canada/US—Continued Suspension)*, WT/DS320/R, WT/DS321/R, DSR 2008:XV; Appellate Body Report, *Canada—Continued Suspension of Obligations in the EC—Hormones Dispute*, WT/DS321/AB/R, adopted 14 November 2008, DSR 2008:XIV; Appellate Body Report, *United States—Continued Suspension of Obligations in the EC—Hormones Dispute (Canada/US Continued Suspension)*, WT/DS320/AB/R, adopted 14 November 2008, DSR 2008:X.

[21] AB Report, *Australia –Salmon*, paras 120–21.

food-borne risks.[22] Interestingly, this distinction reflects the two logics discussed above, where the assessment for quarantine risk responds to the quantitative-risk logic, while the risk assessment for food-borne risks responds to the holistic one.

This dichotomous interpretation could simply be the result of a textual interpretation of the letter of the Agreement. However, upon a closer look, such an interpretation is rather an example of 'overtextualism' that lacks a precise rationale. Is the dual reading of the notion of risk assessment as defined in Annex A(4) not the result of a juggling act by the WTO judiciary between the quantitative and the holistic logic? What is, in fact, the practical or theoretical reason for the outlined distinction between quarantine and human health risks? Neither the Panel nor the Appellate Body has provided a clear answer to this question, other than the overtextual interpretation of the letter of Annex A(4).

A closer scrutiny of the way the dual reading of the notion of risk assessment has been further interpreted provides additional support to the thesis that the Panels and the Appellate Body are juggling different visions of risk. Under this dual reading, the calculation of probability appears to be the most important demarcation criterion. However, this criterion has been blurred in practice and serious questions remain as to whether such a calculation is crucial after all. On the one hand, the Appellate Body has unequivocally emphasised the importance of calculating probability and Panels have often concluded that scientific reports did not meet the standard of risk assessment because of the lack of a probability calculation. On the other hand, the Appellate Body has on other occasions downplayed the role of probability.

The cases where the notion of probability has played an essential role will be presented before turning to those cases where the role of probability assessment has been downplayed. The Appellate Body has been explicit in asserting the central relevance of the assessment of 'probability' for quarantine risks: 'A proper risk assessment of this type must evaluate the "likelihood", i.e., the "probability"'.[23] A notable application of this conceptualisation of risk assessment can be found in *EC-Biotech*, where the lack of a probability evaluation has been an important parameter to disqualify several documents produced at the national level as risk assessments. For instance, in the context of the Austrian safeguard measures on T25 maize, the Panel concluded that '*[g]iven the lack of evaluation of likelihood* in the Hoppichler study, we consider that the study does not meet the definition of a risk assessment as provided in Annex A(4), and therefore does not constitute a risk assessment within the meaning of Annex A(4) and Article 5.1'.[24] Similar findings were reached in relation to the studies on the risks attached to Bt-176 maize: 'While the results of these studies may be of

[22] AB Report, *Australia-Salmon*, at fn 69 and para 123; see also a discussion of this issue in L Gruszczynski, 'The Role of Science in Risk Regulation under the SPS Agreement' (2006) EUI Law Working Paper no. 2006/03, available at SSRN: http://ssrn.com/abstract=891114, 14.

[23] AB Report, *Australia-Salmon*, para 123.

[24] Panel Report, *EC-Biotech*, para 7.3046 (emphasis added).

relevance to the assessment of the risks of the potential development of resistance to Bt-176 maize, neither study assesses *the likelihood* of this risk. For this reason, we do not consider that the March 1997 and April 1997 studies meet the definition of a risk assessment as provided in Annex A(4). We therefore consider that these studies cannot be considered risk assessments within the meaning of Annex A(4) and Article 5.1'.[25]

From these cases, the essential role played by probability is evident. It has gone unnoticed, however, that the demarcation between quantitative and qualitative is blurred by a major ambiguity. This problem, paradoxically, originates in *Australia—Salmon* where the Appellate Body ruled that 'the *SPS Agreement* does not require that the evaluation of the likelihood needs to be done quantitatively'; likelihood may be expressed either quantitatively or qualitatively.[26] The exact meaning of such an expression is unclear. If likelihood means probability, it must imply that the analysis is quantitative. If, however, the Appellate Body is satisfied with a qualitative appraisal of risk for quarantine risks, the difference between the first and the second definition of risk assessment hardly becomes defensible. In fact, is assessing that something is possible fundamentally different from assessing that it is a low-probability event? It is fundamentally different *only* when the judgment of low-probability is derived from a quantitative result (eg, 0.05 per cent chance of an event occurring). The ambiguous relation with the notion of probability is puzzling: what is in fact the meaning of equating the concept of likelihood to the one of probability and then being satisfied with a qualitative expression of likelihood? Also, if likelihood can be expressed in qualitative terms, what does the distinction boil down to, in practice?[27]

A possible explanation of the contradictions and the complexity of this interpretative approach is that the Panels and the Appellate Body are juggling the ideas of different knowledge-based groups. On the one hand, there is a tendency to adhere to the quantitative-risk logic by equating the meaning of likelihood to the one of probability. On the other hand, conceding that likelihood may be expressed in qualitative terms seems a concession to the other logic.

In conclusion, the adoption of the dual risk assessment criterion discussed above and the ambiguities attached to the meaning of likelihood are plausibly explained by the attempt of the judiciary organs of the WTO to accommodate the two logics. The juggling of these two logics has led to a form of over-textualism in interpretation and to some ambiguities. In fact, while from a textual point of view one may still try to defend such a dual interpretation of the notion of risk

[25] ibid, para 7.3079 (emphasis added).

[26] AB Report, *Australia-Salmon* para 124.

[27] Perhaps as a result of this confusion, the Panel's reasoning in *EC-Biotech* appears unbalanced. On the one hand several explanations were provided as to why the assessments performed by the EC Member States could not properly be classified as risk assessment. On the other hand, little was said on why the assessment carried out at the European central level could be considered risk assessment. In fact, the Panel report was silent on the fundamental differences between the documents judged to comply with the definition of risk assessment and those that do not meet the standards.

assessment, the rationale underlying it is at best obscure, raising the question: is this act of (unconscious) logic juggling robbing the text of any substance, rather than constructing meaning?

B Based on risk assessment: looking for meanings of a rational relationship

As is well-known, the Appellate Body in *EC—Hormones* has interpreted the concept of 'based on risk assessment' as meaning that there should be a 'rational relationship' between a risk assessment and the SPS measure adopted. Because of the case-by-case approach favoured by the Appellate Body in *EC—Hormones*, the notion of 'rational relationship' remains to be fully fleshed out. Certain scholars consider the test laid down by the Appellate Body as deferential, leaving much discretion to the Members as to the risk management; others as rather strict.[28] The ambiguities in WTO jurisprudence on this issue may explain the differences among these scholars. Not surprisingly, I argue that the juggling act performed by the Panels and the Appellate Body produces these ambiguities.

To follow this reasoning, it is helpful to first understand how the two knowledge-based groups would construe the concept of a rational relationship. The knowledge-based group, following the quantitative-risk logic, would most probably subscribe to the vision that the rational relationship test demands a sort of cost-benefit test. As explained above, this knowledge-based group is mainly composed of mainstream economists and legal-economic scholars. The notion of rationality within this group is generally related to the notion of maximisation under constraints. For a relationship to qualify as rational, the benefits of the sanitary measure adopted must outweigh its costs. While, in theory, this test may not reveal much about the relationship between the SPS measure and risk assessment, in practice, a positive correlation between these two variables may be made. The well-known table produced by economist John Morrall, which compares the cost-per-life saved by different regulations, constitutes an example of how advocates of cost-benefit analysis establish such a correlation.[29] The narrative of the table is that governments tend to adopt extremely costly measures to contain risks that are judged by experts as minimal. This table has indeed been widely used by members of the quantitative-risk community to criticise the logic of regulatory choices. This community would most likely consider an SPS measure, such as an import ban, to be irrational, if experts judged the probabilities of the harm attached to the good at issue to be low.

The group embracing a holistic-risk logic will presumably include more variables in the analysis of a rational relationship, such as the values people attach

[28] For an overview, see Gruszczynski 'The Role of Science' (n 22 above) 19 and literature quoted in its fnn 121–23.

[29] For a critical overview of the wide use of this table by academic scholars, see L Heinzerling, 'Regulatory Costs of Mythic Proportions' (1998) 107 YLJ 1981.

to certain typologies of risk, the way risks are distributed and the ethics underlying certain choices. Accordingly, under this approach, stringent safety measures may be justified even when the risk assessment attaches low probabilities to harmful events.

Having briefly outlined how the two groups would conceptualise a rational relationship, it is useful to examine how the rational relationship test has been applied in practice. In *EC—Hormones*, the Appellate Body made it clear that a rational relationship is a broader notion than merely requiring conformity between 'the scientific conclusions yielded by a risk assessment' and 'the scientific conclusions implicit in the SPS measure'. 'The relationship between those two sets of conclusions is certainly relevant; they cannot, however, be assigned relevance to the exclusion of everything else'.[30] In this wording, one may read the influence of the holistic-risk logic. However, the Appellate Body has further elaborated on the meaning of a 'rational relationship' in *Japan—Apples*, where it adopted an analytical approach resembling a proportionality test.[31] This approach could be considered a reflection of the quantitative-risk logic, according to which a cost-benefit analysis is the most desirable tool for decision-making. Yet, the Appellate Body has also left open the possibility for Members to set their appropriate level of protection at 'zero risk',[32] which is a rather different approach than a proportionality test and arguably conflicting with a quantitative-risk logic.

EC—Biotech offered an alternative to interpret 'rational relationship' in line with the quantitative logic. There, the Panel ruled that 'where a given risk assessment sets out a single opinion, it cannot be reasonably said that an SPS measure is "based on" *that* risk assessment if the relevant SPS measure reflects a divergent opinion which is not expressed in the risk assessment in question' (emphasis in original). The knowledge-based group endorsing the holistic-approach logic would clearly not subscribe to such a view. Following this logic, safety measures may be chosen on the basis of people's preferences even when they conflict with experts' assessment of risk. The *amicus* brief submitted in this case reflects the view that the second knowledge-based group would adopt on this issue, when it states: 'The "rational relationship" test must be understood within the object and purpose of the treaty, which in its preamble reinforces the right of Members to set appropriate levels of protection … Where scientific evidence and public consensus are low, regulators must be allowed to take public value choices into strong consideration when setting the appropriate levels'.[33] By contrast, as discussed above, the group following the quantitative-risk logic, by

[30] AB Report, *EC-Hormones*, para 193.

[31] In particular *cf* AB Report, *Japan—Apples*, paras 144–47 and 162–63. In *EC-Biotech*, the Panel seems to have followed this approach where it has condemned some of the safeguard measures because they were the strictest type of SPS measures.

[32] AB Report, *Australia—Salmon*, para 125.

[33] Busch et al, 'Amicus' (n 16 above) 21.

framing the divergent views between experts and laypeople as the product of the cognitive limitations of laypeople, could well endorse this statement of the Panel.

In *EC—Biotech*, the Panel articulated a reasoning concerning the precautionary principle which sheds new light (or shadow) on the rational relationship concept. The Panel followed the Appellate Body's reasoning in *EC—Hormones* and found that the precautionary principle is reflected in Article 5.7. The Panel, however, went a step further and also saw the principle reflected in the sixth paragraph of the Preamble and in Article 3.3 dealing with the appropriate level of sanitary protection.[34] This means that according to the Panel, the principle could be applied both when scientific evidence is insufficient and thereby risk assessment cannot be performed, but also when risk assessment could be performed. The Panel emphasised in its Report that risk assessments identifying uncertainty can constitute the basis for precautionary measures. In other words, one could infer that even when a risk assessment is favourable, if there is uncertainty, an SPS measure could be justified.

By admitting the theoretical possibility of adopting precautionary measures in cases of scientific uncertainty, the Panel seems to endorse the ideas of the holistic-risk logic, especially, in light of the distinction between insufficiency of scientific evidence and uncertainty previously outlined by the Appellate Body in *Japan—Apples*. According to this distinction the concepts 'are not interchangeable', where 'uncertainty' seems to express a lower degree of ignorance than 'insufficiency'.[35] Thus, granting the possibility of adopting precautionary measures in those cases clearly opens the door to the ideas of the second knowledge-based group. However, as discussed below, the practical implications of this reasoning in terms of applying the precautionary principle are less far-reaching.

First, the Panel emphasises that 'even if a Member follows a precautionary approach, its SPS measures need to be "based on" a risk assessment'. What exactly does the Panel mean by this statement? Does the Panel mean that precautionary measures can result from risk assessments fraught with uncertainty, provided that they are not *too* precautionary? Is the rational relationship to be assessed differently for precautionary measures than for non-precautionary measures? If not, then it is not clear why it would make any sense to allow the theoretical possibility of adopting precautionary measures, when risk assessment is feasible. If so, then the Panel leaves wide open the question of how. Frankly, it is difficult to understand the inner logic of this part of the report. It becomes even more difficult if one considers that the Panel, by concluding that Austria's measure was not sufficiently warranted by the 'favourable risk assessment', has also relied on the argument that 'the European Communities has not identified possible uncertainties or constraints in the risk assessments in question [*sic*]'. This does not seem accurate, however, because as the Panel recalls in its own Reasons

[34] Panel Report, *EC—Biotech*, Panel Report, para 7.87.
[35] AB Report, *Japan—Apples*, paras 183–84.

document, Austria argued that 'the product had not been examined under realistic conditions'. Also, the Opinion of the Scientific Committee on Plants (SCP) regarding the 'Submission for Placing on the Market of Glufosinate Tolerant Corns (Zea Mays) Transformation Event T25' by the Agrevo Company of 10 February 1998, reads: 'Although risks to birds and other non-target species that frequent corn fields are considered to be low *there is no direct data* available from field experimentation' (emphasis added). These notes should suffice to show that at least some uncertainties and constraints were present in the original risk assessment. However, the Panel too easily dismissed the uncertainties and accordingly did not evaluate concretely whether the measures by Austria could be considered precautionary measures.

In short, what the Panel has given with one hand, it has taken away with the other. This apparently contradictory way of reasoning may be due to the fact that the Panel is juggling the two logics; however, the sum of two contrasting logics as applied by the Panel in *EC—Biotech* amounts to something lacking internal coherence.

If *EC—Biotech* is the most notable example where the 'rational relationship' test lacks internal consistency, the above analysis has shown that the interpretation of 'rational relationship' in several SPS cases is still swinging between the quantitative-risk and the holistic-risk logics. This situation has left the meaning of 'rational relationship' rather unclear.

C Insufficiency of scientific evidence

The interpretation of 'insufficient scientific evidence' is a crucial step in the determination of the applicability of Article 5.7 SPS.[36] The seminal case that sheds light on the meaning of 'insufficiency' is *Japan—Apples*, where the AB stated: 'relevant scientific evidence will be "insufficient" within the meaning of Article 5.7 if the body of available scientific evidence does not allow, in quantitative or qualitative terms, the performance of an adequate assessment of risks as required under Article 5.1 and as defined in Annex A to the *SPS Agreement*'.[37] But what is an 'adequate' assessment of risk? Can one assessment be adequate for one country but not for another?

These important questions were raised in *EC—Biotech*. According to the EC, insufficiency of scientific evidence is to be assessed in relation to a Member's appropriate level of protection: 'The sufficiency of scientific evidence cannot be examined in a vacuum, but in relation to the protection goals of the legislators … The lower the level of acceptable risk, the more likely it may be that the legislator

[36] For a detailed discussion of this issue and the state of the art after *EC- Biotech*, *cf* Lang 'Provisional Measures' (n 5 above).

[37] AB Report, *Japan—Apples*, para 179.

may continue to consider ... that the scientific evidence is insufficient'.[38] A *sequitur* of this reasoning is that scientific evidence may be sufficient for one legislator and insufficient for another. The Panel rejected this approach and instead argued that 'relevant scientific evidence is insufficient within the meaning of Article 5.7 if the body of available scientific evidence does not allow, in quantitative or qualitative terms, the performance of a risk assessment as required under Article 5.1'.[39] Because the Panel already found that risk assessment existed for all goods subject to safeguard measures, the case for insufficient scientific evidence was easy to dismiss.

The Panel linked its interpretation of insufficient scientific evidence to the reasoning articulated by the Appellate Body in *Japan—Apples*.[40] Notwithstanding the reasoning of the Panel, because of the specific circumstances of *Japan—Apples*, it is difficult to deduce from the Appellate Body's conclusion that the appropriate level of protection should be divorced from the issue of insufficiency of scientific evidence. Yet, both the Panel in *EC—Biotech* and the Panel in *Continued Suspension* have followed a similar approach that seems to rest on the quantitative-risk logic. As analysed in the next section, in *Continued Suspension* the Appellate Body clarified the issue, marking a shift towards the holistic-risk logic.

IV CONTINUED SUSPENSION: TOWARDS A PARADIGM SHIFT?

In this section, it is contended that in *Continued Suspension* the Appellate Body shifted towards the holistic-risk logic and endorsed the ideas of the second knowledge-based group to a significant extent. This point will be made by looking at two distinct issues addressed in the case: (1) the notion of acceptable level of protection and its bearing on the concepts of risk assessment and insufficient scientific evidence; and (2) the criteria followed to assess the impartiality and independence of experts.

[38] EC first written submission, 179, para 605.

[39] Panel Report, *EC—Biotech*, Panel Report, para 7.3237.

[40] In general, it is true that in *Japan—Apples* the AB established a relationship between the possibility of carrying out risk assessment and the question of when scientific evidence is sufficient/insufficient. However, some important differences in the reasoning of the AB in *EC—Biotech* and *Japan—Apples* should be noted. First, while in the latter, the risk studied is clearly identified by the AB, ie the risk of transmission of fire blight through apples, no specific risk is discussed in the former. In addition, in *Japan—Apples* an independent analysis of the quantity and quality of information available in relation to the risk of fire blight transmission is conducted and in fact the AB withheld the Panel finding that 'not only a large quantity but a high quality of scientific evidence has been produced over the years that describes the risk of transmission of fire blight through apple fruit as negligible', and 'this is evidence in which the experts have expressed strong and increasing confidence'. AB report, *Japan—Apples*, para 180.

A Acceptable level of protection: towards a 'relational' conceptualisation of scientific issues

Perhaps one of the most fundamental issues in the interpretation of the SPS Agreement is the question of the nature of a scientific endeavour. Should risk assessment be conceptualised as independent from social values or should considerations of social values be a legitimate component of risk assessment? This issue has been raised in some SPS cases and was discussed in terms of whether 'the appropriate level of protection' should be taken into account in risk assessment and in the assessment of the sufficiency of scientific evidence. As explained in the previous section, the EC has argued in favour of a conceptualisation of risk assessment shaped by the level of protection. Under this view, societal values and scientific facts become partners. While Panels have rejected such a 'relational' conceptualisation, the Appellate Body in *Continued Suspension* has departed from these Panels' approaches by clarifying this issue as follows:

> The risk assessment cannot be entirely isolated from the appropriate level of protection. There may be circumstances in which the appropriate level of protection chosen by a Member affects the *scope* or *method* of the risk assessment. This may be the case where a WTO Member decides not to adopt an SPS measure based on an international standard because it seeks to achieve a higher level of protection. In such a situation, the fact that the WTO Member has chosen to set a higher level of protection may require it to perform certain research as part of its risk assessment that is different from the parameters considered and the research carried out in the risk assessment underlying the international standard.[41]

This marrying of facts and values by the Appellate Body indicates a shift towards the holistic-risk logic, which rejects an overly rigid separation between science and values.[42] The argument that the holistic-risk knowledge-based group offers the intellectual substrate to support this Appellate Body finding is further corroborated by the words of the authors of the *amicus* brief submitted in *EC—Biotech*: 'If one lesson emerges from the body of social science on risk, it is that reliability and conclusiveness of the science involved in risk assessment are functions not only of the scientific facts, but also of the value commitments of regulators and the public'.[43] Relating risk assessments to the appropriate level of

[41] AB report, *Continued Suspension*, para 534 (emphasis added).

[42] The inclusive approach towards the notion of risk assessment adopted by the Appellate Body is also reflected in the issue of whether to consider questions about the monitoring of the sanitary measures as part of the risk assessment. In this case, in fact, the AB stated that 'the risks arising from misuse or abuse and difficulties of control in the administration of hormones to cattle for growth promotion' could be considered as part of risk assessment. This issue is merely noted here and not further discussed in this section.

[43] See Winickoff, 'Adjudicating the GM Food Wars' (n 16 above). For a similar, if not stronger argument see K Shrader-Frechette, 'Evaluating the Expertise of Experts' (1995) 6 *Risk: Health, Safety and Environment*, 115. Similarly, it has been argued that 'in post-normal science the two categories [fact/values] cannot be realistically separated', Funtowicz and Ravetz, 'Science for the Post-Normal Age' (n 18 above) 751.

protection has at least two very concrete consequences. First, different risk assessments on the safety of the same product could equally qualify as valid for the purposes of Article 5.1 SPS Agreements. These assessments may comply with Article 5.1 while differing in relation to their scope and methodologies, depending on the intended level of protection. Second, there may be situations in which, while a valid risk assessment has been produced by one Member, another Member may find the scientific evidence insufficient to conduct an assessment on the risk of the same product for the purposes of Article 5.7. The Appellate Body reached this conclusion in *Continued Suspension*.[44]

The reasoning of the Appellate Body with respect to these issues moves sharply towards the holistic-risk logic, according to which a plurality of assessments may qualify as 'risk assessment' and consequently pass muster under the SPS Agreement. This does not indicate the presence of a relativistic yardstick; rigorous science would still be a necessary requirement for a risk assessment to qualify as such. Yet, different regulatory objectives may demand the testing of different hypotheses in the practice of risk assessment. Endorsing the vision that 'Values shape the very scientific questions that drive risk assessment'[45] is conceived as perfectly compatible with high scientific standards both by the Appellate Body and by the holistic-risk knowledge-based group.

B Independence of scientific experts and 'the construction of scientific facts'

One of the most salient findings in *Continued Suspension* relates to the selection of the scientific experts. The Appellate Body held that 'The appointment and consultations with Drs. Boisseau and Boobis compromised the adjudicative independence and impartiality of the Panel'.[46] These two experts participated in the Joint FAO/WHO Expert Committee on Food Additives (JECFA)'s evaluation of the safety of the six hormones at issue in *Continued Suspension*. In the Panel's eyes, the experts' affiliation with JECFA was not a reason for doubting their impartiality. The Appellate Body took a diametrically opposite approach and considered the JECFA institutional affiliation of the experts as an important element to cast doubt on the impartiality of the experts. If the descriptive parts of the report are stripped away, the reasoning of the Appellate Body essentially boils down to the idea that institutions where scientists operate may substantially influence their views.

This part of the report attracted some criticism. Sungjoon Cho censored the Appellate Body approach as one of deferentialism that 'tends to come at the

44 AB Report, *Continued Suspension*, paras 685–86.
45 Winickoff, 'Adjudicating the GM Food Wars' (n 16 above) 13.
46 AB Report, *Continued Suspension*, para 481.

expense of science itself'.[47] He further noted: 'The Appellate Body's position seems highly problematic. It might border on an ad hominem argument or on the fallacy of guilt by association'.[48] Is the Appellate Body's finding and underlying reasoning fallacious, as Cho contends? The answer to this question depends on one's own view of science. A positivist image of science, as endorsed by the first knowledge-based group, would lead to a positive answer. However, many members of the second knowledge-based group would probably answer the question negatively, as many of them consider science to be 'socially constructed'.[49]

Against this background it is interesting to read the words of Sheila Jasanoff, an influential scholar of the second knowledge-based group, who has explicitly addressed the issue of appointing independent experts: 'The principal disadvantage … is that the independent experts' own biases could be veiled by the presumption of neutrality that attaches to being appointed by the court. By remaining invisible, these biases could exert undue influence on the fact-finding process'.[50] Is the Appellate Body trying to break the veil of scientific neutrality and root these biases in specific institutions? Another passage in Jasanoff's text evidences the close connection between her approach and the interpretative choices made by the Appellate Body. Here she warned courts that when screening for the biases of party experts they may use 'tests of credibility—whether, for example, the expert has been … a known professional adversary of the person whose work is to be reviewed'.[51] This criterion is very close to the issue decided in *Continued Suspension*. In fact, the work conducted by the contested scientists is at the basis of the international standards that renders the EC risk assessment in need of review. The Appellate Body may have transformed Jasanoff's test of credibility for party experts into a test of independence to be followed by Panels when appointing experts.

That the Appellate Body rests on the idea that science is somehow 'socially constructed' finds further reflection in the fact that the Appellate Body has not

[47] S Cho 'United States: Continued Suspension of Obligations in the EC-Hormones Dispute. WT/DS320/AB/R' (2009) 103 *The American Journal of International Law* 299, 302.

[48] ibid, 302.

[49] For an overview of sociology of science and its possible relevance for lawyers, see S Jasanoff, 'What Judges Should Know about the Sociology of Science' (1992) 32 *Jurimetrics: The Journal of Law, Science and Technology* 345, 354. Let me also emphasise that given the limited scope of this contribution, these notes are merely aimed at indicating a possible link between the Appellate Body interpretation and the ideas of members of this knowledge-based group, rather than demonstrating that all of its members would subscribe to this vision. Equally, it is not the intention of this author to present a survey of the literature and debate on the sociology of science. It suffices to refer to the path-breaking work on this: B Latour and S Woolgar, *Laboratory Life: the Social Construction of Scientific Facts* (Los Angeles, Sage, 1979). A second edition of the book was published by Princeton University Press in 1986 and the word 'Social' was omitted from the title. The reasons for this choice are explained in the postscript.

[50] S Jasanoff, 'Research Subpoenas and the Sociology of Knowledge' (1997) 59 *Law and Contemporary Problems* 95, 116.

[51] ibid 116.

simply looked at the institutional affiliation to infer the potential problems of impartiality; it also considered the institutional positions of the contested scientists and their consequent role in conducting the risk assessment: 'As Chairman, Vice-Chairman, and Joint Rapporteur, they would be expected to have played a significant role in the discussions'.[52] Such a passage reveals the weight that the Appellate Body assigns to social factors in the production of science. The 'scientific facts' are produced in institutions where hierarchy has arguably an impact on the way the discussion/analysis is conducted. The Appellate Body has further critically scrutinised whether having conducted the JECFA work had a concrete influence on the experts' testimony before the Panel: 'Dr. Boisseau's response [to the Panel's questions] shows that he considered JECFA and, in particular, its approach of using ADIs, as the benchmark against which to evaluate the European Communities' risk assessment', and 'For each of the hormones at issue … Dr. Boisseau compared the European Communities' risk assessment with JECFA's conclusions'.[53]

While the Appellate Body makes no explicit reference to it own vision of science, the criteria that it has chosen to screen the impartiality and independence of experts are clearly reconcilable with the holistic-risk approach.

V CONCLUDING REMARKS

This analysis has shown that both the quantitative-risk and the holistic-risk logics seem to have had an influence on the interpretation of the concepts of 'risk assessment', 'based on risk assessment' and 'insufficiency of scientific evidence' given by the Panels and the Appellate Body in past jurisprudence. In *Continued Suspension*, the Appellate Body has arguably taken a turn, whether intended or not, and has rested on the holistic-risk logic in its interpretation of some key concepts. This shift arguably implies that WTO Members can more easily include cultural and socio-economic considerations in the process of setting their food safety standards. Such a change should be welcomed by Europe, that has often argued for a more comprehensive approach. The evidence presented in this essay, however, is inconclusive as to whether a 'paradigm shift' is taking place. In fact, the issues in *Continued Suspension*, whilst noteworthy, are limited.

Several questions remain unresolved. The most significant example in this respect is the dichotomous interpretation of the concept of risk assessment. While apparently justifiable on the basis of a textual reading of the SPS Agreement, on a matter of substance, the dual reading of the concept of risk assessment and the fuzzy qualitative/quantitative distinctions used are rather puzzling. Yet, what becomes clear is that the process of juggling these two logics may lead to internal inconsistencies.

52 AB Report, *Continued Suspension*, para 461.
53 ibid paras 466 and 467.

Is such an interpretative approach desirable and/or sustainable? A first answer to this question is arguably no, because it leads to contradictions. However, if one approaches this question from an evolutionary perspective, not opting for one of these two competing logics could turn out to be a sensible strategy in the short-run. Despite the fact that risk regulation has a long history, its relevance for contemporary societies is possibly much higher now than in the past. Thus, it could be argued that the selection of an appropriate episteme for thinking about food policy (and more generally risk governance) is crucial for the governance of contemporary societies. The issue becomes even more sensitive when the questions are international and, ideally, this episteme should apply to different cultures. The choice of not choosing, or as termed in this paper the juggling of ideas from different knowledge-based groups in the field of risk analysis and governance, might thereby turn out to be a good strategy in a period of transition in which ideas still need to be developed.

A persistent use of two different logics in the long term, however, is not sustainable due to the inconsistencies that are likely to be generated. A further question concerns the future interpretation of the SPS Agreement. The current interpretative choices made by the Appellate Body in *Continued Suspension* seem to suggest a shift towards the holistic-risk logic. Whether this shift will be followed in subsequent jurisprudence remains to be seen.

For Europe, as well as for other WTO Members, it is important to come to terms with the fact that the WTO battlefield does not only determine what particular food safety standards are allowed but, more fundamentally, that it sets the standards of legitimacy for the regulatory philosophy underlying food law.

11

The EU and Human Trafficking: Framing a Regional Response to a Global Emergency

HOLLY CULLEN

I INTRODUCTION

SINCE THE ADOPTION of the Palermo Protocol in 2000, international concern over human trafficking has grown considerably. The EU has adopted a number of measures to assist in the implementation of international law on human trafficking. These measures have been adopted within the policy area of 'freedom, security and justice', thus placing an emphasis on criminal law responses to trafficking. Such an approach has the potential to leave unaddressed the interests of victims of trafficking, particularly children who may be less able to claim their rights or articulate their needs.

While existing EU measures have followed the approach of the Palermo Protocol, the Council of Europe Convention on Action Against Trafficking in Human Beings provides a more victim-focused approach to the problem of human trafficking and is designed particularly for European, rather than global implementation.[1] The 2009 and 2010 proposals for measures to replace the 2002 Framework Decision are moving the EU closer to the approach of the Council of Europe, particularly on victim protection. However, the Council of Europe Convention remains the stricter standard in many areas, as it sets out state obligations in greater detail and grants clearer rights of residence. The most recent EU proposal remains more closely linked to criminal law solutions, while moving away from criminal law as a foundational idea for trafficking policy. Migration control remains a powerful influence on EU policy, preventing the EU from providing a comprehensive range of rights to victims. Nonetheless, the 2009 and 2010 proposals represent a move towards a victim-focused policy, and

[1] CETS 197, opened for signature 16 May 2005, entered into force 1 February 2008. As of 30 May 2010, there were 27 states parties to this treaty. See A Gallagher, 'Recent Legal Developments in the Field of Human Trafficking: A Critical Review of the 2005 European Convention and Related Instruments' (2006) 8 *European Journal of Migration and Law* 163.

therefore a human rights-focused one. The 2009 proposal was not adopted prior to the coming into force of the Lisbon Treaty, requiring a new proposal to be presented under Articles 82 and 83 TFEU. However, the new legal bases for measures on human trafficking require co-decision, thus involving the European Parliament, which is often active in seeking to protect human rights. It remains to be seen whether the Parliament will seek to move EU policy closer to the Council of Europe Convention, and to what extent the new legal bases are seen as permitting a more protection-centred approach.

II IS HUMAN TRAFFICKING A GLOBAL EMERGENCY?

The scope of the prohibition on human trafficking has presented significant problems of definition. Until recently, trafficking was linked to prostitution, in international legal instruments.[2] In the past decade, however, it has been recognised that human trafficking is related to diverse forms of exploitation, not just sexual exploitation.

There are now concerns, on the other hand, that human trafficking is too simplistically linked to contemporary forms of slavery. There is clearly some area of overlap, which was, for example, discussed rigorously by the European Court of Human Rights in *Siliadin v France*.[3] Here, the Court was anxious to distinguish between the different concepts of slavery, servitude and forced labour, all of which are prohibited by Article 4 ECHR. It made reference to the Council of Europe Convention Against Trafficking, and it seems clear on the facts of the case that the applicant had been trafficked as the term is defined in the Convention. Nonetheless, the Court was of the view that the applicant's situation was one of servitude rather than slavery. In a more recent case, *Rantsev v Russia and Cyprus*,[4] the Court went further, declaring that 'trafficking in human beings, by its very nature and aim of exploitation, is based on the exercise of powers attaching to the right of ownership' and therefore always covered by Article 4 ECHR.[5] The use of the phrase 'based on powers attaching to the right of ownership' suggests that the Court considers that trafficking at least in some cases reaches the level of slavery. The Court also decided that the obligations under Article 4 ECHR were broader than those identified in *Siliadin*: 'the duty to penalise and prosecute trafficking is

[2] The International Convention for the Suppression of the White Slave Traffic, 4 May 1910, 1 LNTS 83; International Convention for the Suppression of the Traffic of Women, 11 October 1933, 150 LNTS 431, entered into force 24 August 1934; Convention for the Suppression of the Traffic in Persons and of the Exploitation of the Prostitution of Others, 4 May 1949, 30 UNTS 23, entered into force 21 June 1951.

[3] *Siliadin v France* (2006) 43 EHRR 16. See H Cullen, '*Siliadin v France*: Positive Obligations under Article 4 of the European Convention on Human Rights' (2006) 6 HRLR 585.

[4] *Rantsev v Russia and Cyprus* 2010 ECHR 25965/04.

[5] ibid, para 281.

only one aspect of member States' general undertaking to combat trafficking'.[6] Such obligations include victim protection.[7]

Hathaway has criticised arguments that equate trafficking with slavery, resulting in many forms of slavery being ignored or excluded from the concern of international human rights law,[8] although Gallagher has argued that his definition of slavery is over-broad and his definition of trafficking narrower than it is in practice.[9] Dillon, following Bales, argues that trafficking should be understood as a method to accomplish the aims of slavery, rather than as a synonym for slavery.[10] Arguably, recent definitions of trafficking recognise this by identifying exploitation as the purpose of trafficking rather than as the nature of the act itself.

The first international legal rules concerning human trafficking linked the crime exclusively to prostitution.[11] As late as 1979's Convention on the Elimination of All Forms of Discrimination against Women, human trafficking was thought of solely in relation to prostitution.[12] The Convention on the Rights of the Child was the first international instrument to prohibit human trafficking without any requirement of a link to prostitution.[13]

The main difficulty with the link between human trafficking and prostitution is that it ignores the diverse forms of exploitation to which trafficked persons may be subject.[14] In particular, the use of trafficked workers for forced labour has become increasingly evident,[15] as recognised by the European Court of Human

[6] ibid, para 285.

[7] ibid, paras 286–87. At paras 296–98, the Court found that in the circumstances of the case, the Cypriot police had failed to recognise indications that Ms Rantseva was a trafficking victim and to take appropriate protective actions.

[8] J Hathaway, 'The Human Rights Quagmire of "Human Trafficking"' (2008) 49 *Virginia Journal of International Law* 1. J Quirk, 'The Anti-Slavery Project: Linking the Historical and Contemporary' (2006) 28 *Human Rights Quarterly* 565, 578, also speculates that the term 'slavery' may often be used rhetorically to identify certain human rights abuses as particularly heinous. He does, however, note that the link between human trafficking and slavery has historical precedents and is not merely a recent phenomenon (ibid, 579).

[9] A Gallagher, 'Human Rights and Human Trafficking: Quagmire or Firm Ground?' (2008) 49 *VJIL* 789.

[10] S Dillon, 'What Human Rights Law Obscures: Global Sex Trafficking and the Demand for Children' (2008) 17 *UCLA Women's Law Journal* 121, 165–66.

[11] The International Convention on the Suppression of the White Slave Traffic, 1910; the Convention for the Suppression of the Traffic in Persons and of the Exploitation of the Prostitution of Others, 1949.

[12] Art 6 CEDAW.

[13] Art 35 CRC.

[14] However, Dillon, 'What Human Rights Law Obscures' (n 10 above) 165, argues that a more specific focus on human trafficking for sexual exploitation may be more effective than a broader definition.

[15] See for example, the recent case reported by the International Trade Union Confederation (ITUC) concerning forced labour in Eastern Europe: 'Action Plan for Preventing Future Trafficking Cases in Eastern Europe', 7 April 2010: www.ituc-csi.org/action-plan-for-preventing-future.html?lang=en; the 2008 decision of the Seventh Circuit in the United States, *US v Calimlim* 538 F 3d 706 (7th Cir 2008), concerning servitude and forced labour; the establishment of the Gangmaster Licensing Authority in the United Kingdom; ILO, *The Cost of Coercion* (Geneva, ILO, 2009) para 177.

Rights in *Siliadin*, where the applicant, at the age of 15, was brought to France by means of false representations made to her family and then forced into unpaid domestic service.[16] Concerns about the link between human trafficking and prostitution have also been expressed by advocates for the rights of sex workers, disputing statements which appear to treat all sex workers as trafficked women.[17]

Ultimately, a more detailed approach to the definition of human trafficking is required, rather than simply trying to link trafficking to particular forms of exploitation such as prostitution or slavery. As Quirk notes, trafficking 'covers a spectrum of practices, involving varying degrees of consent, coercion, treatment and autonomy.'[18] Since 2000, the definition regarded as comprehensive and authoritative is that of the Protocol to Prevent, Suppress and Punish Trafficking in Persons, Especially Women and Children, Supplementing the United Nations Convention Against Transnational Organised Crime (the Palermo Protocol).[19] Article 3 sets out the definition, with special rules applicable to children:

> For the purposes of this Protocol:
>
> (a) 'Trafficking in persons' shall mean the recruitment, transportation, transfer, harbouring or receipt of persons, by means of the threat or use of force or other forms of coercion, of abduction, of fraud, of deception, of the abuse of power or of a position of vulnerability or of the giving or receiving of payments or benefits to achieve the consent of a person having control over another person, for the purpose of exploitation. Exploitation shall include, at a minimum, the exploitation of the prostitution of others or other forms of sexual exploitation, forced labour or services, slavery or practices similar to slavery, servitude or the removal of organs;
> (b) The consent of a victim of trafficking in persons to the intended exploitation set forth in subparagraph (a) of this article shall be irrelevant where any of the means set forth in subparagraph (a) have been used;
> (c) The recruitment, transportation, transfer, harbouring or receipt of a child for the purpose of exploitation shall be considered 'trafficking in persons' even if this does not involve any of the means set forth in subparagraph (a) of this article;
> (d) 'Child' shall mean any person under eighteen years of age.

The three elements of the definition are the transfer of a person, use of coercion or deception, and the purpose of the transfer being exploitation. In the case of a child, however, only the first and third elements need be present—there is no necessity of proving that the child (or her parent or guardian) was coerced or

[16] *Siliadin v France* (n 3 above).

[17] B Brooks-Gordon, 'Red mist obscures red light statistics' guardian.co.uk, 3 April 2009.

[18] J Quirk, 'The Anti-Slavery Project: Linking the Historical and Contemporary' (2006) 28 HRQ 565, 576.

[19] 2237 UNTS 319, Annex II, entered into force 25 December 2003. As of 30 May 2010, there are 137 parties to this Protocol. For general discussion of the Protocol, see A Gallagher, 'Human Rights and the New UN Protocols on Trafficking and Smuggling: A Preliminary Analysis' (2001) 23 *HRQ* 975 and S Drew, 'Human Trafficking: A Modern Form of Slavery?' (2002) *European Human Rights Law Review* 481.

deceived. Article 4 of the Palermo Protocol provides that the trafficking must be transnational in nature and must 'involve an organised criminal group'. The Council of Europe Convention on Action Against Trafficking in Human Beings of 2005 uses identical text to the Palermo Protocol, but Article 2 provides that internal as well as international trafficking is covered, and that no link with organised crime need be proven for the Convention to apply.[20] It therefore takes the same basic definition as the Palermo Protocol but extends its scope of application.

Identification of trafficking victims is linked to definitional issues. The Palermo Protocol was adopted at the same time as a Protocol on people smuggling.[21] This led to an unhelpful distinction between people who had been trafficked as innocent victims of crime and people who had been smuggled as criminals. Egan attempts to avoid this problematic language by noting the crucial role of exploitation in human trafficking.[22] This distinction was also difficult to apply in practice.[23] The Council of Europe Convention, in Article 4(e), defines a victim as 'any natural person who is subject to trafficking in human beings as defined in this article'. Importantly, the Council of Europe Convention places clear and detailed obligations on states parties in relation to identification of victims, with special rules for the treatment of children. Article 10 provides that states must adopt laws in this area, and crucially, must train officials in the identification of trafficking victims. Potential victims are not to be removed from the territory of a state party until identification has taken place. Where the potential victim is a child, she shall immediately be given legal representation, and states shall make every effort to identify the child (including her nationality) and if possible to reunite the child with family, where it is in her best interests. Where there is doubt about a potential victim's age, but there are reasons to think she might be a child, then authorities should presume that they are dealing with a child, until the facts are established.

Unsurprisingly, with the continuing confusion over a definition of human trafficking, despite the growing consensus around the Palermo Protocol version, there is no reliable estimate of the number of persons who have been trafficked. The EU itself has no uniform method for data collection on human trafficking, and the potential for reliable statistics is undermined by the fact that EUROPOL uses its own definition of human trafficking and relies on data provided by Member States.[24] One estimate that has been widely quoted is that provided in a

[20] Art 4. The treaty is open to Council of Europe Member States and certain other states (Canada, the United States, Mexico, Japan and the Holy See) plus the European Community. No non-Council of Europe state has signed the Convention to date.

[21] 2241 UNTS 480. Entered into force 24 January 2004. As at 30 May 2010, there were 123 parties to this Protocol.

[22] S Egan, 'Protecting the Victims of Trafficking: Problems and Prospects' [2008] EHRLR 106, 108.

[23] Gallagher, 'Recent Legal Developments in the Field of Human Trafficking' (n 1 above) 166.

[24] I Staiger, 'Trafficking in Children for the Purpose of Sexual Exploitation in the EU' (2005) 13 *European Journal of Crime, Criminal Law and Criminal Justice* 603, 612.

2004 report by the United States Department of State, asserting that between 600,000 and 800,000 people are trafficked annually.[25] This figure was widely criticised as over-broad, and based on politically biased assessments of situations in particular countries,[26] but is no longer used.[27] The ILO, in its 2009 report on forced labour, acknowledged the lack of reliable statistics, and is working on improving the methodology for estimating the number of persons subject to forced labour or trafficking.[28] Furthermore, it criticised the fact that of 25 national action plans on human trafficking reviewed by the ILO, only two were based on statistical data.[29] This move by the ILO is encouraging, particularly in light of its work since the mid-1990s on improving the quality of statistics on child labour.[30]

III THE PALERMO PROTOCOL AND THE COUNCIL OF EUROPE CONVENTION COMPARED—SHOULD WE APPROACH HUMAN TRAFFICKING AS A PROBLEM OF CRIME OR OF HUMAN RIGHTS?

The Council of Europe Convention can be said to build on the Palermo Protocol, but it takes a distinctive approach, moving beyond the exclusive focus on human trafficking as a crime. Both the Palermo Protocol and the Council of Europe Convention assert that their purposes include the protection of victims of trafficking, consistent with the human rights of those victims.[31] However, the substantive provisions of the two treaties differ significantly on this issue. Both treaties require states to establish criminal offences in relation to trafficking and to adopt laws which enable them to take jurisdiction over trafficking offences,

[25] US Department of State, *Trafficking in Persons Report 2004*, 15 and 23: www.state.gov/g/tip/rls/tiprpt/2004. It is worth noting that in the most recent report, ILO figures are quoted instead: US Department of State, *Trafficking in Persons Report 2009*, 7–8: www.state.gov/documents/organization/123360.pdf. The report also cites ILO estimates that the majority of human trafficking is for forced labour.

[26] Dillon, 'What Human Rights Law Obscures' (n 10 above) 131

[27] *Trafficking in Persons Report 2009* (n 25 above).

[28] ILO, *The Cost of Coercion* (n 15 above) para 362.

[29] ibid, para 193.

[30] *Child Labour: Targeting the Intolerable* (Geneva, ILO, 1996) 7–8, indicated that earlier estimates of child labour had been unreliable for several reasons, including inconsistent definitions of childhood. It is worth contrasting this acknowledgement of uncertainty with the most recent global report on child labour, *Accelerating Action Against Child Labour* (Geneva, ILO, 2010) xiii, which highlights that the estimates in the report are based on further refinements of statistical method, and over 60 surveys conducted between 2004 and 2008.

[31] Art 2(b) of the Palermo Protocol states that a purpose of the instrument is 'To protect and assist the victims of such trafficking, with full respect for their human rights.' Art 1(1)(b) of the Council of Europe Convention states that a purpose of the instrument is 'to protect the human rights of the victims of trafficking, design a comprehensive framework for the protection and assistance of victims and witnesses, while guaranteeing gender equality, as well as to ensure effective investigation and prosecution.'

even in some cases when committed outside the territory of the state.[32] Article 15 of the Convention against Transnational Organised Crime requires states to take jurisdiction where the crime was committed on the state party's territory, where the accused or the victim is a national of the state party or where the victim is a stateless person having habitual residence in the state party. It also requires states to adopt the necessary measures to take jurisdiction over an alleged offender who is within their territory where it will not extradite solely on the ground that the alleged offender is a national, and to coordinate actions where several states are investigating or prosecuting the same conduct.

The Council of Europe Trafficking Convention introduces a number of innovations, notably an explicit obligation to establish corporate liability for the offences contained therein.[33] It also goes into greater detail than most concerning sanctions,[34] and sets out that where children are trafficked, this is to be seen as an aggravating factor.[35] The Council of Europe Trafficking Convention, in Article 31, calls on states to establish jurisdiction over trafficking offences where the offence was committed on its territory (including ships and aircraft), where the accused is a national or a stateless person with habitual residence in the state, or whereby the victim is a national of the state. However, states may enter reservations to the acceptance of jurisdiction based on nationality/habitual residence of the accused or nationality of the victim.[36] The principle of prosecute or extradite is applied: states parties are obliged to take the necessary measures to take jurisdiction over offenders present in their territory where they decline to extradite on grounds of nationality.[37]

The Palermo Protocol focuses on criminal justice aspects of victim protection. Some of the gaps in the UN Trafficking Protocol could potentially be filled by soft law, particularly the guidelines prepared by the Office of the High Commissioner for Human Rights on the implementation of the Trafficking Protocol.[38]

The Council of Europe Trafficking Convention goes much further than the Palermo Protocol in its protective measures for victims. It enshrines the principle of non-discrimination, placing it in Article 3, which makes an explicit link between non-discrimination and the protection and promotion of the rights of victims. First of all, states are obliged to ensure that Convention offences can be

[32] See H Cullen, 'The Nature of State Obligations in Relation to Child Labour: Choosing Prosecution Over Protection' in M Bohlander and K Kaikobad (eds), *International Law and Power: Perspectives on Legal Order and Justice* (The Hague, Brill, 2009) 99.

[33] Art 22. This is also followed in the other relevant Council of Europe treaties, the Cybercrime Convention, CETS 185, entered into force 1 July 2004 and the Convention against Sexual Exploitation and Abuse of Children, CETS 201, will enter into force 1 July 2010.

[34] Arts 23–25.

[35] Art 24(b).

[36] Art 31(2). In other respects, Art 45 of the Convention precludes reservations.

[37] Art 31(3).

[38] Recommended Principles and Guidelines on Human Rights and Human Trafficking, Report of the United Nations High Commissioner for Human Rights to the Economic and Social Council, E/2002/68/Add 1, especially Guideline 6 on protection and support for trafficked persons.

prosecuted without the requirement of a victim complaint.[39] Protection of victims and their families from retaliation,[40] and protection of their privacy during court proceedings are also required.[41] In both contexts, the Convention obliges states to take into account the special needs of child victims. Other special protections for children include the protections noted above in the context of identification of victims; special protection for the privacy of child victims (Article 11(2)); access to education (Article 12(1)(f)); protection of their best interests in the investigation process; non-repatriation if this is not in their best interests (Article 15(7)); provision of accommodation, education of health care appropriate to their special needs and rights (Article 12(7)); and protection of their best interests in the context of issuing and renewing residence permits (Article 14(2)).

Of the two treaties, only the Council of Europe Convention, in Article 15, provides for rights in relation to compensation of victims, including the right to be informed about compensation procedures and to be given legal assistance in this area. States must establish the legal remedies for victims to claim compensation from traffickers, and must take steps to guarantee compensation, such as the establishment of a special fund.

In the area of prevention obligations, the difference between an anti-crime approach and a human rights approach is particularly evident.[42] In the Council of Europe Convention, the measures which states are expected to take range from technical (research and information programmes; international coordination) to redistributive (social and economic initiatives and training programmes),[43] to the providing adequate means of legal migration. The latter obligation is somewhat weakened by an emphasis on the provision of information concerning the avenues of legal migration.[44] The Palermo Protocol, Article 9, obliges states to 'endeavour' to introduce preventative measures. The ILO in its 2009 report on forced labour recognises the need for preventative strategies 'including the targeting of poverty reduction programmes and development resources at the communities most in need.'[45] A report by UNICEF and Terre des hommes on prevention strategies concerning the trafficking of children in southeastern Europe recommended debriefing children who have been trafficked and a form

[39] Art 27.

[40] Art 28

[41] Art 30.

[42] J Berman and C Friesendorf, 'EU Foreign Policy and the Fight Against Human Trafficking: Coercive Governance as Crime Control' (2008) 13 *European Foreign Affairs Review* 189, argue that a focus on crime control and immigration security issues is ill-adapted to combat the complexity of the human trafficking phenomenon, and that an approach that also addresses needs for protection and prevention is required. They argue for 'a comprehensive approach, involving development, gender, ethnicity, human rights, labour [and] migration' (ibid, 195).

[43] The UN Trafficking Protocol uses similar language, but this is one of the areas where states need only 'endeavour' to act.

[44] Art 5(4).

[45] ILO, *The Cost of Coercion* (n 15 above) para 388.

of strategic parallelism—meaning that those seeking to prevent child trafficking must be wherever potential traffickers are, at both the recruitment and exploitation ends of the process.[46] This requires the development of international networks aimed at protecting children from traffickers. It is worth noting that neither of these reports regards the prosecution of the users of trafficked children as a prevention strategy. The UNICEF/Terre des hommes report did recommend targeted information campaigns for potential users of children trafficked for sexual exploitation, but not further criminalisation.[47]

On residence rights for victims of trafficking, the Palermo Protocol only obliges states to 'consider' granting residence rights. In the Council of Europe Convention, where there are reasonable grounds to consider that a person is a trafficking victim, the person must be given a 30-day reflection period without threat of expulsion.[48] Thereafter, victims should be given a renewable residence permit where their personal circumstances merit it or (the more likely scenario) where they are cooperating with the police.[49] Italy, unusually, allows for unconditional residence rights.[50]

Repatriation rights are found in the Palermo Protocol,[51] and in the Council of Europe Trafficking Convention. Article 16 of the Council of Europe Convention, however, provides that children should not be repatriated if it is not in their best interests—only they are entitled to a risk assessment in relation to being returned to their country of origin.[52]

IV EU MEASURES ON COMBATING TRAFFICKING

EU policy-making on human trafficking pre-dates the Palermo Protocol, but more recent measures have followed the Palermo Protocol.[53] The first measure adopted by the EU was the 1997 Joint Action on trafficking in human beings,[54] which was replaced by the 2002 Framework Decision,[55] the current legislation in

[46] M Duttridge, *Action to Prevent Child Trafficking in South Eastern Europe* (Geneva, UNICEF and Terre des hommes, 2006) 67–68.

[47] ibid, 68.

[48] Art 13.

[49] Art 14. In the case of child victims, their best interests must be considered when granting or renewing a residence permit. Askola, *Legal Responses to Trafficking in Women for Sexual Exploitation in the European Union* (Oxford, Hart Publishing, 2007) 111, notes that in trafficking trials, defence lawyers have argued that the granting of residence permits to witnesses amounts to a bribe or payment for their testimony, and seek to undermine their credibility before the court on this basis.

[50] ILO, *The Cost of Coercion* (n 15 above) para 179.

[51] Palermo Protocol (n 19 above) Art 8.

[52] Gallagher, 'Recent Legal Developments in the Field of Human Trafficking' (n 1 above) 180.

[53] T Obokata, 'Trafficking in Human Beings: A Critical Appraisal' (2003) 40 *CML Rev* 917, 919–22, provides an overview of EU measures to 2002.

[54] Council Joint Action 97/154/JHA concerning action to combat trafficking in human beings and sexual exploitation of children [1997] OJ L63/22.

[55] Council Framework Decision 2002/629/JHA on combating trafficking in human beings [2002] OJ L203/1.

force. The Framework Decision is focused exclusively on the criminal process. Provision for protection for victims is minimal, particularly in relation to adult victims.[56] Gallagher indeed notes that the Framework Decision is less protective of victims' rights than the previous Joint Action.[57] The Joint Action calls for victim and witness protection, residence rights, repatriation and, albeit in a very general way, and subject to local law, appropriate services for victims.[58] Of course, it is important to note that the obligations placed on Member States by a Joint Action are weaker than by a Framework Decision, which is intended to create binding obligations—which means that Member States are less likely to agree to strongly worded obligations in a Framework Decision. One area in which the Framework Decision goes further than the Palermo Protocol, and is more detailed than the Joint Action, is in making explicit that legal entities such as corporations may be prosecuted, and providing for penalties including the winding-up of corporations involved in human trafficking.[59] The EU's policies on human trafficking have tended to be directed very strongly towards the criminal justice issues of trafficking. Human rights considerations have been addressed only weakly, for which the EU has been criticised.[60]

A crucial feature of EU law which may limit the EU's capacity to commit to a human rights approach to human trafficking is the scope of EU competences, both before and after Lisbon. The legal bases for existing measures, and for the proposals issued in 2009, are treaty provisions on cooperation in police and criminal justice matters. Specifically, Articles 29, 31(1)(e) and 34(2)(b) EC have been used. In order for these to be valid legal bases, the 'centre of gravity' of the EU measure must remain within the listed bases.[61] Article 29 lists 'preventing and combating … trafficking in persons' as a means by which the objective of providing 'citizens with a high level of safety within an area of freedom, security and justice' will be achieved. Article 31(1)(e) states that common action on judicial cooperation in criminal matters shall include 'progressively adopting measures establishing minimum rules relating to the constituent elements of criminal acts and to penalties in the fields of organised crime, terrorism and illicit drug trafficking.' It is worth noting that human trafficking is not specifically mentioned here. Presumably it is to be included, as foreseen by the Palermo Protocol, within the area of criminal acts in the field of organised crime. Article 34(2)(b) stipulates that the Council shall act unanimously (with no consultation

[56] ibid, Art 7.

[57] Gallagher, 'Recent Legal Developments in the Field of Human Trafficking' (n 1 above) 167.

[58] Council Joint Action 97/154/JHA (n 54 above) Title II, paras F and G.

[59] Council Framework Decision 2002/629/JHA (n 55 above) Arts 4 and 5. Council Joint Action 97/154/JHA (n 54 above) Title II, para A(c), also calls on Member States to provide for the liability of legal persons.

[60] See for example, Obokata, 'Trafficking in Human Beings' (n 53 above).

[61] The phrase 'centre of gravity' is used by the Court of Justice to describe the selection of the most appropriate of rival legal bases—whether a particular subject matter is essential rather than incidental to the measure. See eg, Case C-42/97 *Parliament v Council* [1999] ECR I-869, paras 43–57.

of Parliament required) to adopt framework decisions to approximate the laws of the Member States. Arguably, therefore, the procedure mandated for the adoption of measures on human trafficking pushes the EU towards a more conservative approach. These legal bases require EU measures to have their centre of gravity in the definition of crimes in the area of human trafficking, and the related criminal procedures.

The new legal bases under the TFEU are somewhat less restrictive. Article 82(2) TFEU allows the European Parliament and Council to adopt directives under the ordinary procedure to establish minimum rules on police and judicial cooperation in criminal matters concerning criminal procedure, specifically including the rights of victims of crime. Article 83(1) allows directives to be adopted concerning definitions of serious crimes with a cross-border dimension, including 'trafficking in human beings and sexual exploitation of women and children'. Unlike Article 29 EC, the objective of safety of EU citizens is not linked to the need to fight cross-border crime, which strengthened the orientation of measures combating human trafficking under Articles 29 and following on to crime control rather than victim protection. The text of the relevant legal bases, particularly before Lisbon, therefore pushed the EU much more in the direction of the Palermo Protocol rather than the Council of Europe Convention. However, the TFEU does liberalise matters somewhat, both substantively, and procedurally, by bringing in the Parliament and allowing the Council to act by qualified majority.[62]

It is worth noting, however, that the centre of gravity theory of appropriate legal base does not preclude the inclusion of other matters which are incidental to the overall scheme of the measure. This in practice gives the EU quite a bit of scope to include victim protection measures within any new directive on human trafficking, and explains the inclusion of some limited such measures in the 2002 Framework Decision. The Court of Justice has been reluctant to reject the legal bases provided by the EU unless there are reasons to suspect that the EU might be pushing its competence or trying to manipulate the legislative process through the choice of legal base. The UK challenge to the Working Time Directive presents a good example of how a directive can go quite far beyond the obvious content permitted by a Treaty provision.[63] The Working Time Directive,[64] based on Article 138 (ex 118a) EC, sought to regulate working hours, including breaks, minimum holidays and maximum weekly working hours, under a provision which allowed the EU to harmonise minimum standards in health and safety

[62] Art 82(3) and Art 83(3) provide that where a Member State 'considers that a draft directive … would affect fundamental aspects of its criminal justice system, it may require that the draft directive be referred to the European Council. In that case, the ordinary legislative procedure shall be suspended.' The draft directive may, within four months, be referred back to the Council for resumption of the ordinary procedure, or at least nine Member States may decide to pursue the draft directive as an instance of enhanced cooperation.

[63] Case C-84/94 *United Kingdom v Council* [1996] ECR I-5755.

[64] Directive 93/104/EC, [1993] OJ L307/20.

within the working environment.[65] The Court of Justice found that the legal basis was sufficient to justify all the contents of the Working Time Directive except the provision which stated that in principle the weekly day off should be Sunday. This was found to relate to cultural and religious norms rather than the regulation of the working environment. By way of analogy, it appears that much of the victim protection in the Council of Europe Convention could be included in a directive concerning human trafficking, although probably many of the preventative measures would be seen as falling outside Articles 82 and 83 TFEU.

In addition to the Framework Decision on human trafficking, current EU measures include a Directive on temporary residence permits for trafficking victims, but this only covers those who cooperate with criminal justice procedures.[66] The Directive is similar to the Council of Europe Convention in requiring states to provide a period of reflection and support during that time.[67] However, the application of the Directive to children is optional.[68] Further, it is seen primarily as an immigration control measure rather than a victim support/human rights measure.[69]

Staiger argues that one major reason for the failure of the 2002 Framework Decision to have much impact on the problem of human trafficking is the fact that such measures have only a limited legal effect.[70] Framework Decisions do not create direct effects, although since the *Pupino* decision of the Court of Justice, it is clear that there is an obligation on national courts to ensure that national law is interpreted, as far as possible, in line with the terms of a Framework Decision.[71] In addition, as Staiger notes, preliminary references were less available than in relation to matters under the First Pillar of the pre-Lisbon system. As a result, individuals are less able to enforce rights under a Framework Decision than they would be under a similarly worded Directive.[72] If Staiger is correct, future measures adopted under Articles 82 and 83 TFEU will have a greater impact as they will be directives, which do have direct effect. A further indication of the inconsistent application of the Framework Decision appears from the ILO's 2009 review of national action against forced labour, which notes that European states

[65] H Cullen and A Charlesworth, 'Diplomacy by Other Means: the Use of Legal Basis Litigation as a Political Strategy by the European Parliament and Member States' (1999) 36 *CML Rev* 1243, 1258–60.

[66] Council Directive 2004/81/EC on the residence permit issued to third-country nationals who are victims of trafficking in human beings or who have been the subject of an action to facilitate illegal immigration, who cooperate with the competent authorities [2004] OJ L261/19. See Gallagher, 'Recent Legal Developments in the Field of Human Trafficking' (n 1 above) 167–70.

[67] ibid, Arts 6–7.

[68] ibid, Arts 3(3) and 10.

[69] Gallagher, 'Recent Legal Developments in the Field of Human Trafficking' (n 1 above) 169.

[70] Staiger, 'Trafficking in Children' (n 24 above) 622–23.

[71] Case C-105/03 *Criminal Proceedings Against Maria Pupino* [2005] ECR-I 5285.

[72] Berman and Friesendorf, 'EU Foreign Policy and the Fight Against Human Trafficking' (n 42 above) 197, similarly argue that the legal basis limits accountability through judicial or European Parliament action.

have taken different approaches to criminalising human trafficking. Some emphasise working conditions contrary to human dignity, whereas others emphasise slavery-like conditions such as debt bondage.[73]

Despite the fact that human trafficking is prohibited in Article 5(3) of the EU Charter of Fundamental Rights, current EU measures to combat human trafficking are based on a criminal justice rather than human rights approach, and in fact marginalise human rights. The Council of Europe Convention sets out a much more comprehensive human rights approach. With a significant number of EU Member States having ratified the Convention, and more having signed it, by 2009 the time was ripe for a revamp of EU policy.

V DEVELOPING A BROADER APPROACH TO ANTI-TRAFFICKING POLICY

While the Framework Decision focuses on harmonisation of criminal law and procedure in the area of human trafficking, the EU has recently moved to the use of other methods to broaden its approach. In 2005, the Commission adopted the EU Plan on best practices, standards and procedures for combating and preventing trafficking in human beings.[74] In its evaluation report of 2008, the Commission listed the following activities: funding of research on causes/prevention of trafficking; seminar on victim protection; requests for Member State best practice on deterring trafficking; Europol Information System material on trafficking; prioritising trafficking within Organised Crime Threat Assessment; increased number of trafficking cases recorded with Eurojust; questionnaire sent by Finnish Presidency on victim services.[75]

The Commission has also established an expert group on human trafficking, which provides opinions on various aspects of policy. In 2008, a new expert group was appointed, with more expertise on labour exploitation, thus reflecting the view that trafficking is not solely for the purposes of prostitution.[76]

VI NEW PROPOSALS IN 2009 AND 2010

The 2008 review of the implementation of the EU Plan on best practices, standards and procedures for combating and preventing trafficking in human beings indicated that while investigations of human trafficking have been steadily

[73] ILO, *The Cost of Coercion* (n 15 above) para 155.

[74] [2005] OJ C311/1.

[75] Commission, 'Evaluation and monitoring of the implementation of the EU Plan on best practices, standards and procedures for combating and preventing trafficking in human beings' (Working Document) COM (2008) 657 final, 7.

[76] ibid.

increasing since the adoption of the Framework Decision, the level of prosecutions did not reflect the seriousness of the crime.[77] On victim support, Member States had mostly adopted the necessary legislative measures, including on the residence permit provided for in the 2004 Directive, but the Commission found that information on provision of protection programmes in practice was insufficient.[78] As a result, the Commission concluded that there was a gap between the situation with respect to legislation and implementation in practice. Perhaps in order to encourage Member States, or perhaps simply to pave the way for its upcoming proposal, the Commission noted that where victim protection was more available in practice, there were more prosecutions.[79]

The Commission proposed a total revamping of its policies in the area of human trafficking. The first proposal, adopted in March 2009,[80] seemed designed to address the concern that previous policies were too focused on criminal justice issues, paid insufficient attention to the needs of victims, particularly children, and were not in keeping with the Council of Europe Convention and the approach developed by the Council of Europe. The aim of bringing EU policies into line with the Council of Europe Convention is indicated in the Explanatory Memorandum. As the Framework Decision was not adopted before the Lisbon Treaty came into force, a new proposal under the TFEU was adopted in March 2010 and is currently before the Parliament and Council.[81] It is this latter proposal which will be the focus of my analysis. The key changes from the 2002 Framework Decision are:

— Some definitional changes; elaboration of aggravating circumstances and penalties; non-application of sanctions to the victim.
— Broader and more binding extraterritorial jurisdiction; coordination of prosecution; investigative tools.
— Prevention of secondary victimisation; protection on basis of risk assessment; compensation.
— Identification and assistance of victims;[82] broader range of assistance (including medical and psychological).

[77] ibid, 3.

[78] ibid, 3–4.

[79] ibid, 5.

[80] Commission, 'Proposal for a Framework Decision on preventing and combating trafficking in human beings and protecting victims, replacing the Framework Decision 2002/629/JHA' COM (2009) 136.

[81] Commission, 'Proposal for a Directive of the European Parliament and of the Council on preventing and combating trafficking in human beings, and protecting victims, repealing Framework Decision 2002/629/JHA' COM (2010) 95.

[82] On the importance of identification of trafficking victims, and the need for law enforcement agencies and courts to be trained in such identification, see J Elliot, '(Mis)Identification of Victims of Human Trafficking: The Case of *R v. O*' (2009) 21 *International Journal of Refugee Law* 727. Elliot notes the strong obligations in the Council of Europe Convention in this area.

— Policies for preventing trafficking; training; criminalisation of users of services of trafficked persons.[83]
— Monitoring mechanisms.[84]

However, in most areas the proposal is somewhat less detailed than the Council of Europe Convention, containing 21 articles, compared with 47 in the Convention.[85]

In the recitals, the proposal lays great emphasis on human rights, prevention of trafficking and the protection of victims.[86] There is an acknowledgement that existing EU measures on victims' rights in criminal proceedings do not address the specific needs of trafficked people.[87] Further, the proposal asserts that victims' rights are diverse, and include assistance, rights of residence and special protection for children.[88] The proposal does not seek to address the conditions for residence rights of trafficking victims, leaving the situation as it was with the 2004 Directive.[89]

One interesting development in the proposal is that the definition of trafficking is further clarified. The phrase 'position of vulnerability' used in the Palermo Protocol and the Council of Europe Convention is defined in Article 2(2) of the proposal as occurring 'when the person has no real or acceptable alternative but to submit to the abuse involved'. The application of the definition to children is the same as in the earlier definitions, although the phrasing has been simplified.

The 2010 proposal provides greater detail even than the 2009 proposal in setting out victims' rights, particularly in the criminal justice process. Article 10 of the proposal, concerning protection of victims, provides a more detailed version of Article 28 of the Council of Europe Convention. It guarantees assistance and support before, during and after criminal proceedings. Article 11 emphasises that its protections are additional to those provided in Framework Decision 2001/220/JHA,[90] and guarantees independent legal representation for trafficking victims. Article 11 also specifically calls on member states to prevent

[83] Note that advocates for the rights of sex workers have opposed these measures; see eg E Pisani, 'A bad bill for sex workers', guardian.co.uk, 21 October 2009.

[84] The Council of Europe Convention (n 1 above) in Art 29, is the first binding international instrument on human trafficking to call on states to establish national rapporteurs, although the idea had appeared in other European, but not international, documents as early as 1997: see MY Mattar, 'Comparative Models of Reporting on the Status of Trafficking in Human Beings' (2008) 41 *Vanderbilt Journal of Transnational Law* 1355, 1360–64.

[85] The final few articles of the Convention, Arts 42–47, of course deal with matters pertaining to the particular nature of the Convention as an international treaty (signature, ratification, accession, entry in to force, reservations, denunciation, notifications).

[86] COM (2010) 95 (n 81 above) para 3 of recitals.

[87] ibid, para 12, referring to the Council Framework Decision of 15 March 2001 on the standing of victims in criminal proceedings (2001/220/JHA), [2001] OJ L82/1.

[88] ibid, paras 11–14 of the recitals.

[89] ibid, para 10 of the recitals.

[90] [2001] OJ L82/1.

secondary victimisation (Article 11(5)), and to provide individual risk assessments for victims (Article 11(4)). However, unlike Article 28(1)(d) of the Council of Europe Convention, it does not provide protection for victims' families.

Paragraphs (4) and (5) of Article 10 provide for assistance and support beyond the criminal justice system. Paragraph (4) calls on Member States to take necessary measures to ensure early identification, assistance and support for victims, in cooperation with relevant support organisations. Paragraph (5) sets minimum standards for assistance and support measures:

> Assistance and support measures ... shall include at least standard of living capable of ensuring victims' subsistence through measures such as appropriate and safe accommodation and material assistance as well as necessary medical treatment including psychological assistance, counselling and information in a language they can understand, translation and interpretation services where appropriate, and access to education for children.

This language is close to that of Article 12(1) of the Council of Europe Convention. It is therefore an improvement over the 2009 proposal, which was much less detailed on the rights of victims outside the criminal process.

Articles 12–14 of the proposal call on Member States to apply the special protective measures for children. This is a clear improvement over the 2009 proposal in at least a structural sense. The 2009 proposal cross-referred to a parallel proposal on combating sexual abuse and sexual exploitation of children for protective measures,[91] whereas the 2010 proposal is now a complete guide to trafficking victims' rights. Article 12 calls on Member States to treat child victims of trafficking in accordance with the best interests principle, and requires them to presume a victim is a child, in cases of uncertainty. Article 13 deals with general protection of child victims and Article 14 provides for protection within the criminal justice system. Article 13 requires states to take 'specific actions to assist and support child victims ... in the short and long term, in their physical and psycho-social recovery' following an individual assessment of the victim's needs. Member States must also provide assistance and support to victims' families. Although Article 13(3) provides that these rights of general assistance and support are additional to the rights provided in Article 10, it is unclear how the scope of these two rights differ, other than the fact that rights under Article 10 do not extend to the victim's family.

The key right in Article 14 is the appointment of a special representative for any child victim, where the child is unaccompanied by anyone exercising parental authority or where the interests of the child are in conflict with those of the

[91] Proposal for a Council Framework Decision on combating the sexual abuse, sexual exploitation or children and child pornography, repealing Framework Decision 2004/68/JHA, COM (2009) 135, referred to in Art 11 of the 2009 proposal on human trafficking. As with the human trafficking proposal, part of the impetus is to bring EU policies in line with Council of Europe standards, here the Convention against Child Sexual Exploitation and Abuse: CETS no 201, opened for signature 25 October 2007, not yet entered into force; as at 20 April there were two states parties.

person exercising parental authority. Some of the rights in this Article, however, repeat the general rights set out in Article 11, particularly the right to legal representation. Nonetheless, Article 14(3) and (4) sets out detailed protection for child victims in the context of police interviews, and Article 14(5) requires Member States to provide for the possibility of in camera hearings for trafficking trials involving child victims, or at least the giving of evidence from outside the court using a video link or other appropriate technologies.

While Article 15 of the proposal does call on states to introduce policies to prevent trafficking, in this area, the proposal is far less detailed than the Council of Europe Convention.[92] Article 15 includes four provisions. Article 15(1) is a general call on Member States to seek to discourage demand which fosters exploitation. If this is interpreted in light of Article 6 of the Council of Europe Convention, it could include a wide range of research, educational and possibly directly protective measures. Article 15(2) obliges Member States to act to raise awareness of trafficking in order to reduce the risk of victimisation, particularly of children. Article 15(3) requires Member States to 'promote' (not to 'provide') regular training for officials likely to encounter situations of trafficking, to enable them to identify victims. This is an extrapolation from the more general and diffuse obligations in relation to training in Article 5(2) of the Council of Europe Convention. Article 15(4) calls on states to consider introducing a criminal offence of the use of services resulting from exploitation of trafficked persons. While such an offence would arguably be linked to the goal of reducing the demand for the services of trafficked persons, the inclusion of an additional criminal offence in this part of the proposal seems odd. It departs from the approach to prevention in the Council of Europe Convention which does not call for criminal law measures in attacking the demand for services of trafficked persons, but includes this provision in its criminal law provisions.[93] The Council of Europe Convention, in addition to calling for research, education and general protective measures, more controversially calls on states to establish legal forms of migration to discourage people from turning to traffickers.[94] On children, Article 5(5) calls on states parties to 'take specific measures to reduce children's vulnerability to trafficking', notably by creating a protective environment for them.

An important innovation in both the 2009 and 2010 draft measures, which again follows the Council of Europe Convention, is the inclusion of a monitoring mechanism in Article 16, where Member States are required to establish national rapporteurs (or equivalents) to monitor implementation of the Framework

[92] Lack of attention to the prevention of human trafficking is a common criticism of EU action in this area: see Obokata, 'Trafficking in Human Beings' (n 53 above) 934.

[93] Art 25.

[94] Art 5(4).

Decision.[95] Article 16 states that the national rapporteurs' tasks shall 'include the carrying out of assessments on trafficking in human beings trends, the measuring of results of anti-trafficking actions and reporting to the relevant local authorities.' The use of the term 'include' suggests that the national rapporteurs could be given a broader role in some Member States. The proposal actually goes further than Article 29 of the Council of Europe Convention in making the appointment of national rapporteurs obligatory. This network of rapporteurs could be important in linking the EU's system with that of the Council of Europe Convention, which establishes an expert committee to monitor implementation, and with the United Nations, which has a Special Rapporteur on trafficking in persons, especially women and children.[96] As Yattar argues, the role of national rapporteur should be to 'research, report, review and recommend'—to build on the weak information base we currently have in the area of human trafficking and to push governments towards improving their protection of trafficking victims.[97] It is worth noting that Article 16 of the proposal uses language which mirrors Yattar's to a large extent.

VII CONCLUSION

Ironically, while the coming into force of the Lisbon Treaty has delayed the adoption of a new EU measure on human trafficking, the updated proposal adopted in March 2010 and currently in front of the Parliament and Council is a significant improvement over the proposals discussed in 2009. Assuming that the final version of the directive remains fairly close to the proposal, EU law will be brought substantially into line with the Council of Europe Convention. In particular, the EU is moving much more strongly in the direction of a human rights approach to human trafficking. The proposed directive will be far more protective of the rights of trafficking victims, both in and out of the criminal justice system, than current EU measures are. The EU appears to have gone as far as it can within its competence in shifting away from a criminal justice approach to human trafficking.

The Council of Europe Convention will remain the highest standard amongst legally binding international instruments, although as Gallagher notes, the UN Principles and Guidelines on Human Rights and Human Trafficking, which are non-binding, are more protective still.[98] The Convention imposes stronger obligations on states to take measures to prevent trafficking than does the EU's proposal. The EU appears reluctant to go beyond its 2004 directive in granting

[95] The Netherlands has already established such an office: see ILO, *The Cost of Coercion* (n 15 above) para 161.

[96] For the Special Rapporteur's mandate, see: www2.ohchr.org/english/issues/trafficking/index.htm.

[97] Yattar, 'Comparative Models of Reporting (n 84 above) 1409–13.

[98] Gallagher, 'Recent Legal Developments in the Field of Human Trafficking' (n 1 above) 187.

residence rights for trafficking victims, particularly disadvantaging those from outside the EU. The United Nations High Commissioner for Refugees has identified the weakness of migration rights as the main flaw of the current proposals, and suggested that using Article 79(2)(d) TFEU as a further legal base would allow the EU to address migration issues in a more satisfactory way.[99]

While there are grounds for considering human trafficking a global emergency, it is more important to have an appropriate, comprehensive response, with a human rights focus, than to introduce faulty measures quickly. The extra time for consideration brought by the need to re-introduce the human trafficking proposal will likely bring about a better result than the 2009 proposal adopted quickly would have.

[99] United Nations High Commissioner for Refugees, Bureau for Europe, 'Comments on the proposal for a Directive of the European Parliament and of the Council on preventing and combating trafficking in human beings, and protecting victims' (COM (2010) 95): www.unhcr.org/refworld/docid/4c0fa7092.html.

Part III

The European Union and Global Emergencies: The Perspective of the Institutions

12

Common Security and Defence Policy Crisis Management Missions: an Effective Tool for EU Response to Emergencies

GILLES MARHIC*

I INTRODUCTION

I ARRIVED AT the Council Legal Service in 2001, and at that time no crisis management mission had been launched, established or even planned under the, at that time, European Security and Defence Policy (ESDP). Representatives of Member States sitting in the Council preparatory body dealing with civilian crisis management were working on setting up the 'crisis management procedures',[1] which constitute the practical rules regarding the planning and conduct of crisis management missions.

One important element in these crisis management procedures, is that there is a continuity between the assessment of a situation somewhere in the world, constituting a potential threat to the interests of the Union, and the subsequent possible decision to establish a crisis management mission under the, nowadays, Common Security and Defence Policy (CSDP).[2] EU practice shows that the CSDP is actually an integral part of the Common Foreign and Security Policy (CFSP), which in turn is consistent with other EU external actions, in particular in the area of development.

Ensuring such a consistency is of course not so easy, and as stated in the Report on the implementation of the European Security Strategy approved by the Council in December 2008, 'We must strengthen our own coherence, through

* The views expressed in this chapter are personal to the author: they do not bind the Council or its Legal Service, and are based on the speech delivered by him on the occasion of the Durham University conference on the EU and global emergencies organised on 8 May 2009.

[1] Document 11127/03, available on the Council's website.

[2] The Lisbon Treaty entered into force on 1 December 2009. See Art 42(1) of the Treaty on European Union (TEU): 'The common security and defence policy shall be an integral part of the common foreign and security policy.'

better institutional co-ordination and more strategic decision-making'.[3] Indeed, the EU has faced many institutional challenges in addressing emergencies by means of ESDP, now CSDP, missions.

This chapter will first address three issues linked to the CSDP architecture: the staffing, chain of command and financing of civilian CSDP missions; association of third parties to CSDP missions; and EU–UN cooperation in crisis management. It will then concentrate on the entry into force of the Lisbon Treaty, which both provides for a new institutional framework for EU crisis management and offers new tools for the common security and defence policy.

II STAFFING, CHAIN OF COMMAND AND FINANCING OF CIVILIAN CSDP MISSIONS

When the first ESDP missions were established in 2003, it was necessary for the staff from the General Secretariat of the Council and from the Commission services to learn how to work together in the so-called Crisis Response Coordination Teams (CRCT) in charge of preparing Crisis Management Concepts, the initial planning document for a given CSDP mission.

It was then necessary to establish the appropriate procedures to determine how EU actors should organise, finance and lead fact-finding missions to gather information crucial for the planning of a possible future civilian CSDP mission. And, at the other side of the process, it was necessary to make the arrangements for the termination, extension or refocusing of a civilian CSDP mission; and establish the procedures for having recourse to the 'preparatory measures' budget line within the CFSP budget.[4] On all these aspects, and a few others, the General Secretariat and the Commission have managed to put together concepts and procedures which the relevant Council preparatory bodies have endorsed and use on a routine basis.

But work is still needed, in particular regarding the way civilian CSDP missions are equipped and manned: procurement is key, and with the help of the Commission services, work is being performed to explore solutions in terms of framework contracts and other kinds of accelerated procedures. Force-generation processes are equally key, and significant efforts are being made by Member States, in the framework of the civilian Headline Goal 2010, to foster the development of national strategies aimed at facilitating the deployment of civilian personnel.[5] In addition, the development of Civilian Response Teams

[3] See Document S407/08: report approved by the European Council on 11 and 12 December 2008.

[4] See Document 10238/07, available on the Council website.

[5] See for instance Documents 15253/08 (Civilian Headline Goal 2010: progress report 2008 on civilian ESDP preparedness) and 5602/09 (Civilian Headline Goal 2010: Civilian capability improvement plan 2009), both available on the Council website.

(CRT) composed of pre-identified personnel in Member States' relevant administrations represents an interesting tool for ensuring that specialised personnel are available to the EU.[6] The same kind of arrangement has been made regarding security sector reform experts.[7]

Another kind of institutional challenge relates to the way the chain of command for each civilian CSDP mission is organised and functions. The abovementioned report on the implementation of the European Security Strategy states in this regard that 'Appropriate and effective command structures and headquarters capability are key'. In relation to civilian CSDP missions, a Civilian Planning and Conduct Capability (CPCC) has been set up in the General Secretariat of the Council and is now at the disposal of the High Representative of the Union for Foreign Affairs and Security Policy. In principle, the CPCC Director is the Civilian Operation Commander for each civilian CSDP mission, and this is laid down in the relevant Council Decision establishing the mission.[8]

The Civilian Operation Commander exercises command and control over civilian CSDP missions at the strategic level. This means that the Civilian Operation Commander ensures effective and proper implementation of the Council's decisions regarding the mission, and in particular that he or she may issue instructions to the Head of mission.

The Head of mission exercises command and control on the civilian CSDP mission at theatre level, meaning in the territory where the mission is deployed. Formally, a Member State or third state seconding personnel to the mission transfers operational control to the Civilian Operation Commander, who in turn assigns the Head of mission with corresponding responsibilities. The Head of mission also receives administrative and logistic responsibility including over assets, resources and information put at the disposal of the mission.

This is quite a sophisticated articulation of tasks and duties, but as civilian CSDP missions develop more and more, it is clear that such a reliable system of chain of command is needed, both in terms of efficiency and accountability.

Established and launched pursuant to the provisions of Articles 28 and 43 of the Treaty on European Union (TEU), CSDP missions therefore constitute operational actions 'by the Union'. They should not be seen, at any price, as some sort of 'fire and forget' objects launched in the international landscape. In particular, it follows from Article 38, second subparagraph, of the TEU that the Political and Security Committee (PSC) exercises the political control and strategic direction of crisis management operations referred to in Article 43 of the TEU. The situation of CSDP missions is therefore regularly put on the agenda of PSC meetings. In this context, the representatives of the Member States are in

[6] See Document 15371/09, available on the Council website.

[7] See Document 13246/09, available on the Council website.

[8] See eg Council Decision 2009/906/CFSP on the European Union Police Mission (EUPM) in Bosnia and Herzegovina [2009] OJ L322/22, Art 5(1).

a position to assess the achievements of each CSDP mission, debate on the evolution of the local political situation and give strategic direction to the mission for the future.

In parallel, a permanent structure within the European External Action Service (EEAS)[9] is able to follow and instruct the civilian CSDP mission and to react to any difficulty in the operational, technical, logistical and administrative aspects of the conduct of the mission. The Civilian Planning and Conduct Capability (CPCC) constitutes a precious added-value for addressing emergencies in a timely manner and ensuring consistency between the objectives and tasks defined for each civilian CSDP mission in the relevant legal act and planning documents, on the one hand, and actions delivered on the spot, on the other hand.

Furthermore, for the sake of completeness, it should be mentioned that the Head of mission is responsible for the implementation of the civilian CSDP mission's budget, and signs a contract with the Commission to that effect. In practice, this is how Article 41(2) of the TEU is implemented in the context of civilian CSDP missions, which operating expenditure is in principle charged to the Union budget. This is also consistent with the role of the Commission regarding the execution of the Union budget pursuant to Article 317 of the Treaty on the Functioning of the European Union (TFEU) and with Article 54 of the Financial Regulation regarding methods of implementation of the Union budget.[10]

The Head of mission therefore reports to the Commission on expenditure incurred and is supervised by it on the activities (implying expenditure) undertaken in the framework of his/her contract. Owing to the very fruitful relationship built during the past years between the General Secretariat of the Council and the Commission services, these arrangements have proven very valuable, especially when a particularly rapid deployment of a mission is needed. This has for instance been the case for the EU monitoring mission in Georgia (EUMM Georgia), where within a timescale of two weeks the EU planned the mission and deployed more than 200 monitors from 22 Member States.[11] This is an appropriate answer to an emergency. In these particular circumstances, this was possible thanks to the outstanding efforts made by the Member States in ensuring the availability of their personnel seconded to the mission.

[9] Pending the entry into force of the Council Decision on the functioning and the organisation of the European External Action Service foreseen in Art 27(3) of the TEU, the CPCC has been put at the disposal of the High Representative of the Union for Foreign Affairs and Security Policy (see Document 16866/09, available on the Council website). It is now part of the EEAS.

[10] Council Regulation (EC, Euratom) 1605/2002 on the Financial Regulation applicable to the general budget of European Communities [2002] OJ L248/1.

[11] See Council Joint Action 2008/736/CFSP on EUMM Georgia [2008] OJ L248/26.

III ASSOCIATION OF THIRD PARTIES TO CIVILIAN COMMON SECURITY AND DEFENCE POLICY MISSIONS

Institutional challenges also have had to be faced concerning the relationship between the EU and third states and international organisations in the context of civilian CSDP missions. Third states may be invited to participate in civilian CSDP missions: it is a case-by-case decision by the Council, in accordance with the principle of autonomy of decision-making of the EU. This choice is, where relevant, reflected in the provisions of the Decision establishing the mission pursuant to Articles 28 and 43(2) of the TEU. Such Decisions provide that the third states concerned conclude an agreement with the Union to determine the conditions of their participation, thereby associating themselves with the provisions of the Decision.[12]

Furthermore, in relation to some third states, it was deemed appropriate for the EU to conclude Framework Participation Agreements, the effect of which is not to allow for an automatic participation of the concerned third state to each and every civilian CSDP mission, but to provide a permanent legal framework for such participation, should the Council so decide.[13] This, of course, reduces the administrative burden on both sides and constitutes a facilitating element for diminishing the delays in deployment.

In certain cases, agreements on the status of the mission and their staff are concluded with the host state or a state on which territory the personnel of the mission will transit. In order to avoid having to obtain a new mandate from Council for each negotiation, it has been decided to draft model status of mission agreements (SOMAs), which constitute standing templates. This practice allows the EU to act faster in order to deploy the personnel of the mission with adequate guarantees regarding their status.

The third category of agreements concluded by the Council pursuant to Article 37 of the TEU and Article 218 of the TFEU, which are relevant in the context of civilian CSDP missions, regards the security procedures for the exchange of classified information between the EU and third states or international organisations. The fact that such agreements are in force at the time a civilian CSDP mission is decided, planned and eventually launched allows for an early exchange of relevant planning documents, which are classified.

IV EU–UN COOPERATION IN CRISIS MANAGEMENT

Regarding the relationship between the EU and international organisations in the context of CSDP missions, the case of the United Nations (UN) is particularly interesting. In September 2003, a Joint Declaration on EU and UN cooperation

[12] See eg Council Decision 2009/906/CFSP (n 8 above) Art 11.

[13] See eg the Agreement between the EU and Ukraine [2005] OJ L182/29.

in crisis management[14] was signed by the President of the Council of the EU and the UN Secretary-General, focusing on the establishment of a joint consultative mechanism at the working level, in the areas of planning, training, communication and best practices.

Then in June 2007, a Joint Statement[15] was issued in which 'The United Nations recognise the considerable contribution of human and material resources on the part of the European Union in crisis management'. This statement also recalled the places where the EU and the UN work together, at that time in the Democratic Republic of Congo, in Darfur, Afghanistan and Georgia. The aim of this statement was also to enhance mutual cooperation and coordination, in particular by establishing mechanisms for crisis situations where the UN and the EU are both engaged. In Kosovo, in Georgia, as well as in the Democratic Republic of Congo, in Chad and in the Central African Republic, such cooperation in the field actually materialised.

In addition, the EU has been playing a key role in the setting up and the functioning of the UN Peace Building Commission (PBC), which has been created by two identical Resolutions of the UN General Assembly (A/RES/60/180) and the UN Security Council (S/RES/1645 (2005)).[16] The rules of procedure of the PBC also contain interesting language regarding non-state actors.[17]

Finally, the military CSDP mission EUNAVFOR, also known as operation ATALANTA, was launched in December 2008, in support of UN Security Council Resolutions 1814, 1816, 1838 and 1846 of 2008, in order to contribute to the protection of vessels of the World Food Programme delivering food aid to displaced persons in Somalia, as well as to contribute to the protection of vulnerable vessels cruising off the Somali coast, and the deterrence, prevention and repression of acts of piracy and armed robbery off the Somali coast.[18] The military CSDP mission so far has played an important role, in particular in escorting the World Food Programme ships. It also established cooperation with third states having deployed ships in the region, like China, Russia, India, Malaysia and others.

This military CSDP mission has to be seen in the context of the EU's global and comprehensive approach to the crisis. There is a political process to restore

[14] Document 12510/03, available on the Council website.

[15] Document 10310/07, available on the Council website.

[16] Para 19 of both Resolutions reads: 'Notes the importance of participation of regional and local actors, and stresses the importance of adopting flexible working methods, including use of videoconferencing, meetings outside of New York and other modalities, in order to provide for the active participation of those most relevant to the deliberations of the Commission'.

[17] On 23 June 2006, the Organisational Committee of the PBC adopted its rules of procedure (see Document PBC/1/OC/3, available on the UN website), a two-page document providing that 'Mindful of the intergovernmental character of the Peace Building Commission, members of the Commission as well as participants in accordance with OP 7, 8 and 9 of resolutions A/RES/60/180 and S/RES/1645 (2005) shall be given opportunity to participate fully and equally in the discussions of the Commission in a flexible and interactive manner'.

[18] See Joint Action 2008/851/CFSP [2008] L301/33.

peace in Somalia (the Djibouti peace process) and the Union supports the role of the special representative of the UN Secretary-General in this process. The EU and its Member States also support the African Union military mission in Somalia (AMISOM) both financially and in terms of planning capacity. The Joint Strategy paper for Somalia for the years 2008–13 also provides a European Development Fund (EDF) allocation of more than €200 million to address governance, education and the productive sectors, particularly rural development.

V THE LISBON TREATY: A NEW INSTITUTIONAL SETTING FOR EU CRISIS MANAGEMENT

The entry into force of the Lisbon Treaty on 1 December 2009 marks the beginning of a new institutional setting for EU crisis management. Only the actual implementation of the new provisions in the Treaties will allow for an assessment of their impact on the functioning of CSDP missions. It seems, however, necessary to briefly comment on these provisions in order to highlight their main characteristics.

The limits of Union competences are governed by the principle of conferral. The Union has only the competences conferred by the Member States in the Treaties, and this situation has not changed with the entry into force of the Treaty of Lisbon. The TEU, as amended by the Treaty of Lisbon, contains provisions to the effect that:

— the Member States confer competences to the Union (Article 1);
— competences not conferred upon the Union in the Treaties remain with the Member States (Article 4); and
— the limits of Union competences are governed by the principle of conferral (Article 5).

The Union competences laid down in the TEU for CFSP are very wide and cover potentially any question dealing with foreign policy and the Union's security. For the CSDP, they are laid down in Articles 42 and 43.

That said, the CSDP area has been the subject of specific discussions before the European Council of June 2009. The Decision of the Heads of State or Government meeting within the European Council of 19 June 2009, which entered into force on 1 December 2009,[19] states in particular that the Treaty of Lisbon does not provide for the creation of a European army or for the conscription to any military formation, and that it does not affect the right of any Member State to determine the nature and volume of its defence and security expenditure and the

[19] See Annex 1 to Document 11225/2/09 REV 2, p 17 (available on the Council website).

nature of its defence capabilities. This decision also states that the CSDP does not prejudice the security and defence policy, or the obligations, of any Member State.

At the informal meeting on 19 November 2009, EU Heads of State or Government agreed on the appointment of Baroness Ashton as the High Representative.[20] Her appointment, together with that of the President of the Commission and its other members, has been subject to a vote of consent by the European Parliament.

According to Articles 18 and 27 of the TEU, as amended by the Lisbon Treaty, the High Representative:

— conducts the Union's common foreign and security policy;
— contributes by her proposals to the development of that policy, which she will carry out as mandated by the Council, and ensures implementation of the decisions adopted in this field;
— presides over the Foreign Affairs Council;
— is one of the Vice-Presidents of the Commission, ensuring the consistency of the Union's external action and being responsible within the Commission for duties incumbent on it in external relations and for coordinating other aspects of the Union's external actions;
— represents the Union for matters relating to the common foreign and security policy, conducting political dialogue with third parties on the Union's behalf and expressing the Union's position in international organisations and at international conferences;
— exercises authority over the European External Action Service and over the Union delegations in third countries and at international organisations.

Article 27(3) TEU constitutes the legal basis for the Council decision on the organisation and functioning of the European External Action Service (the EEAS):

> In fulfilling his mandate, the High Representative shall be assisted by a European External Action Service. This service shall work in cooperation with the diplomatic services of the Member States and shall comprise officials from relevant departments of the General Secretariat of the Council and of the Commission as well as staff seconded from national diplomatic services of the member states. The organisation and functioning of the European External Action Service shall be established by a decision of the Council. The Council shall act on a proposal from the High Representative after consulting the European Parliament and after obtaining the consent of the Commission.[21]

[20] She was then formally appointed by written procedure on 1 December 2009; see European Council Decision 2009/880/EU [2009] OJ L315/49.

[21] The EEAS was established by Council Decision 2010/427/EU of 26 July 2010 establishing the organisation and functioning of the European External Action Service [2010] OJ L201/30.

The report to the European Council on the European External Action Service[22] which has been submitted by the Presidency to the European Council of 30 October 2009 can be summarised as follows. The High Representative has been invited to present a proposal for the organisation and functioning of the EEAS as soon as possible after the entry into force of the Lisbon Treaty, with a view to its adoption by the Council at the latest by the end of April 2010. According to the report, the EEAS will be a single service under the authority of the High Representative. The EEAS should be a service of a sui generis nature, separate from the Commission and the Council Secretariat. It should have autonomy in terms of administrative budget and management of staff. The EEAS will have its own section in the EU budget, to which the usual budgetary and control rules will apply. The High Representative will propose and implement the EEAS budget.

The EEAS will help the High Representative ensure the consistency and coordination of the Union's external action as well as prepare policy proposals and implement them after their approval by the Council. It will also assist the President of the European Council and the President as well as the Members of the Commission in their respective functions in the area of external relations and will ensure close cooperation with the Member States. The EEAS should be composed of single geographical (covering all regions and countries) and thematic desks, which will continue to perform under the authority of the High Representative the tasks currently executed by the relevant parts of the Commission and the Council Secretariat.

The EU's crisis management structures, including the Civilian Planning and Conduct Capability (CPCC), should be part of the EEAS while taking full account of their specificities. These structures will form an entity placed under the direct authority and responsibility of the High Representative.

EEAS staff will be appointed by the High Representative and drawn from three sources: relevant departments of the General Secretariat of the Council, of the Commission and of national diplomatic services of the Member States. Recruitment will be based on merit, with the objective of securing the services of staff of the highest standard of ability, efficiency and integrity, while ensuring adequate geographical balance.

The Commission's delegations became Union delegations under the authority of the High Representative and will be part of the EEAS structure. Delegations will contain both regular EEAS staff (including Heads of Delegation) and staff from relevant Commission services. All staff should work under the authority of the Head of Delegation. EU delegations will work in close cooperation with diplomatic services of the Member States. They should play a supporting role as regards diplomatic and consular protection of Union citizens in third countries.

[22] Document 14930/09, available on the Council website. Council Decision 2010/427/EU (see footnote 21) has confirmed these orientations.

Beside those developments specific to CFSP and in particular to CSDP, very important changes occurred regarding the decisions to be adopted by the Council. With the Lisbon Treaty, the Union has at its disposal five legal instruments—regulations, directives, decisions, recommendations and opinions— instead of the previous 15 ones (Article 288 TFEU). This simplification is of particular relevance in CFSP matters: the former Article 12 of the TEU provided that the Union pursued its CFSP objectives by deciding on common strategies, adopting joint actions and common positions. In addition, former Article 13(3) provided that 'The Council shall take the decisions necessary for defining and implementing the common foreign and security policy on the basis of the general guidelines defined by the European Council.'

By contrast, Article 25 of the TEU as amended by the Lisbon Treaty provides that the Union shall conduct the CFSP in particular by adopting decisions defining actions to be undertaken by the Union, positions to be taken by the Union, and arrangements for the implementation of the decisions defining such actions or positions. In turn, Article 26(1) of the TEU provides that the European Council shall adopt the necessary decisions.

Article 28 of the TEU as amended by the Lisbon Treaty corresponds to former Article 14 on Joint Actions. Article 29 of the TEU as amended by the Lisbon Treaty corresponds to former Article 15 on Common Positions. Both mention Decisions to be taken by the Council. Regarding the conclusion of international agreements by the Union, Article 24 of the TEU used to be the basis on which such agreements were negotiated and concluded. It provided all the necessary procedural steps to achieve such a result. With the entry into force of the Lisbon Treaty, Article 37 of the TEU merely provides that 'The Union may conclude agreements with one or more States or international organisations in areas covered by this Chapter'. The relevant procedural provisions may be found in Article 218 of TFEU. Of most relevance is paragraph 3 of this Article, which provides that:

> The Commission, or the High Representative of the Union for Foreign Affairs and Security Policy where the agreement envisaged relates exclusively or principally to the common foreign and security policy, shall submit recommendations to the Council, which shall adopt a decision authorising the opening of negotiations and, depending on the subject of the agreement envisaged, nominating the Union negotiator or the head of the Union's negotiating team.

In turn, paragraph 6 of Article 218 provides that 'Except where agreements relate exclusively to the common foreign and security policy, the Council shall adopt the decision concluding the agreement' after obtaining the consent of the European Parliament in certain cases or after consulting it in other cases. Pursuant to paragraph 10 of Article 218, 'The European Parliament shall be immediately and fully informed at all stages of the procedure'.

Of course, it remains to be seen how this new institutional setting will function in the area of crisis management. When the time is ripe for lessons to be learned, it will be of particular interest to focus on the implementation of certain tools introduced by the Lisbon Treaty.

VI NEW TOOLS FOR THE COMMON SECURITY AND DEFENCE POLICY

In line with the objective developed in the European Security Strategy of making the EU external action (including the ESDP, now CSDP) more effective, the Lisbon Treaty introduced several new tools at the disposal of the Council.

A Enhanced Cooperation

This cooperation is, under the Lisbon Treaty, possible in the CSDP area, and even for actions with military and defence implications. One may remember that former Article 27(b) of the TEU provided that 'Enhanced cooperation pursuant to this title shall relate to implementation of a Joint Action or a common position. It shall not relate to matters having military or defence implications.'

Currently, Article 329(2) of the TFEU reads:

> The request of the Member States which wish to establish enhanced cooperation between themselves within the framework of the common foreign and security policy shall be addressed to the Council. It shall be forwarded to the High Representative, who shall give an opinion on whether the enhanced cooperation proposed is consistent with the Union's common foreign and security policy, and to the Commission, which shall give its opinion, in particular on whether the enhanced cooperation proposed is consistent with other Union policies. It shall also be forwarded to the European Parliament for information.

The scope of enhanced cooperation within CFSP is no longer subject to restrictions: there is no mention of the implementation of a decision (previously a Joint Action or a Common Position) in Article 329(2) of the TFEU, by contrast with former Article 27(b) of the TEU, and there is no exclusion of matters having military or defence implications.

B Capabilities

Article 42(3) of the TEU, as amended by the Lisbon Treaty, provides that:

> Member States shall make civilian and military capabilities available to the Union for the implementation of the common security and defence policy, to contribute to the objectives defined by the Council. Those Member States which together establish multinational forces may also make them available to the common security and defence policy.

While processes on capabilities were launched several years ago, first in the military context and then in the civilian one,[23] no provision existed in the TEU in that respect. The Treaty of Lisbon therefore introduces new language on this question.

C Permanent Structured Cooperation

Article 42(6) of the TEU as amended by the Lisbon Treaty provides that:

> Those Member States whose military capabilities fulfil higher criteria and which have made more binding commitments to one another in this area with a view to the most demanding missions shall establish permanent structured cooperation within the Union framework.

Article 1 of Protocol 10 provides that 'The permanent structured cooperation shall be open to any Member State which undertakes, from the date of entry into force of the Treaty of Lisbon …':

- to proceed more intensively to develop its defence capabilities;
- to have the capacity to supply, by 2010 at the latest, certain targeted combat units.

Article 46 of the TEU as amended by the Lisbon Treaty defines the procedure for joining the Permanent Structured Cooperation:

- either initially, at the beginning of the process in accordance with the criteria and commitments defined in Protocol 10 (Article 46(2) of the TEU);
- or later for those Member States which fulfil those criteria and make those commitments (Article 46(3) of the TEU).

It can be observed that the Council decision adopting the list of the Member States participating in the Permanent Structured Cooperation is to be taken by a qualified majority vote. By contrast, the adoption by the Council of a decision to launch an enhanced cooperation in the area of CFSP, including CSDP, would require unanimity.

D Execution of a task by a group of Member States

Article 42(5) of the TEU as amended by the Lisbon Treaty provides that 'The Council may entrust the execution of a task, within the Union framework, to a group of Member States in order to protect the Union's values and serve its interests.' Article 44 TEU as amended by the Lisbon Treaty further provides that this possibility takes place 'within the framework of the decisions adopted in

[23] See for instance Documents 13931/00 and 15255/08, respectively dealing with military and civilian headline goals, both available on the Council website.

accordance with Article 43', meaning the crisis management operations. The High Representative is associated to the definition of the conditions for the management of the task. Any need for modification of the objective, scope and conditions determined for the task in the decisions already taken in accordance with Article 43(2) TEU should be referred to the Council, which will adopt the necessary decisions.

Together with the Permanent Structured Cooperation, this new possibility for the Council to entrust the execution of a task to a group of Member States is another example of how the Lisbon Treaty creates new possibilities for certain Member States, able and willing to do so, to act in the CFSP area.

E Financial provisions

Article 41(2) of the TEU as amended by the Lisbon Treaty provides that:

> Operating expenditure to which the implementation of this Chapter gives rise shall also be charged to the Union budget, except for such expenditure arising from operations having military or defence implications and cases where the Council acting unanimously decides otherwise.

While this language mirrors former Article 28(3) of the TEU, two provisions are new in Article 41:

— First, the Treaty of Lisbon provides for the establishment by a Council decision of specific procedures for guaranteeing rapid access to appropriations in the Union budget for urgent financing of initiatives in the framework of the CFSP, and in particular for preparatory activities for the tasks referred to in Article 42(1) and 43, meaning the CSDC tasks.

— Second, the Treaty of Lisbon also provides that preparatory activities not charged to the Union budget will be financed by a start-up fund made up of Member States' contributions, following Council decisions establishing the procedures for setting up the fund and administering it. The fund may also be used for implementing a task (and not only regarding the associated preparatory activities), upon authorisation by the Council.

VII CONCLUSION

The Decision on the organisation and functioning of the European External Action Service has recently been adopted by the Council, after consultation of the European Parliament and after obtaining the consent of the Commission.[24]

[24] Council Decision 2010/427/EU [2010] L 201/30.

From the implementation of this decision will emerge a key character, in particular for the planning and conduct of CSDP missions and for their ability to continue to address emergencies in the most efficient way.

13

The Constitutional Apparatus of the European Union: the Perspective of the European Commission

ERIC WHITE*

I INTRODUCTION

THE EUROPEAN COMMUNITY, now called the European Union,[1] was not originally designed to deal with global emergencies. But as a political project intended to bring about ever-closer union among the peoples of Europe, it was inevitable that it would come to play a role in dealing with a number of different kinds of emergencies and it has developed a number of disparate mechanisms for its action. This chapter will briefly review:

— safeguard action;
— Union action in response to global emergencies and in particular the funding of crisis management and civil defence;
— food safety and environmental emergencies in the light of the precautionary principle;
— climate change;
— the financial and economic crisis.

II SAFEGUARD ACTION

The original European Economic Community was initially predominantly about trade, and the oldest form of emergency action provided by the Treaty is safeguard action. In this connection we normally think of action taken to protect

* All views expressed are personal to the author.

[1] Since the entry into force of the Lisbon Treaty on 1 December 2009, the European Community has merged with the European Union and is called the 'European Union', and the EC Treaty has become the Treaty on the Functioning of the European Union. Although this paper was prepared and delivered in April 2009, the terms 'European Community' and 'Community' are only used in it with the meanings that were attributed to them before 1 December 2009, when the new terms would change the meaning.

against the imminent threat of serious injury caused by surges in imports due to unforeseen circumstances (as defined in Article XIX GATT and the WTO Agreement on Safeguards).

However, the TFEU still contains provisions allowing Member States to take urgent measures in case of balance of payments crises (Article 144 TFEU, ex Article 120 TEC). When provisions were included in the Treaty to provide for Community action to protect the environment, the Member States took care to write into the Treaty a provision (Article 174(2) TEC, now Article 191(2) TFEU) providing that 'harmonisation measures answering environmental protection requirements shall include, where appropriate, a safeguard clause allowing Member States to take provisional measures, for non-economic environmental reasons, subject to a procedure of inspection by the Union'.

In the case of classical trade safeguard action against third countries, action could originally be taken very quickly, in a matter of days (although usually by the Member States rather than the Commission).[2] The current Basic Safeguard Regulation[3] is more elaborate and provides for proper investigations to be carried out prior to action being taken. As required by the WTO,[4] there must be:

— serious injury (or imminent threat thereof);
— caused by surges in imports;
— due to unforeseen circumstances.

It is noteworthy that in order to allow the Union to act as speedily as possible, it is provided that the Commission may act alone after consulting the Member States, rather than having to follow a legislative procedure.[5]

III ACTION IN RESPONSE TO GLOBAL EMERGENCIES

A The evolution of European political cooperation to CFSP and EDSP

The Common Foreign and Security Policy and the European Defence and Security Policy evolved from what was called European Political Cooperation, which developed as a complement to Community actions and was first codified in the Single European Act 1986.[6] These are the bases for the most important actions by the Union in response to global emergencies. Since the activities of the Union in this domain are described in detail in the previous chapter, the present chapter will concentrate on the role of that part of the Union which falls under

[2] See eg Arts 12(1), 17(2) and 20(4) of Council Regulation 288/82/EEC on common rules for imports [1982] OJ L35/1.

[3] Council Regulation 260/2009/EC on the common rules for imports [2009] OJ L84/1.

[4] See Art XIX GATT and the WTO Agreement on Safeguards.

[5] See Art 7(3) of Regulation 260/2009 (n 3 above).

[6] Art 30 of the Single European Act on European cooperation in the sphere of foreign policy.

the TFEU rather than the Part V of the TEU (in other words, action that has developed through the use of classical Community methods).

B Funding of European Union Crisis Management—The Instrument for Stability[7]

Before the merger of the European Union and the European Community, it was necessary for the latter to provide the funds for the action decided by the former. The Community developed various instruments for providing funds to deal with emergencies according to need over the years, and there was often confusion about what funds and what procedures could be applied in a given situation. To simplify and render reaction to emergency situations more efficient and rapid, the Community replaced a number of legal instruments in 2006 by Regulation 1717/2006/EC (known as the 'Instrument for Stability').[8]

The Instrument for Stability provides the means to deliver, within a single legal instrument, an effective, immediate and integrated response to situations of crisis and instability in third countries. It built on the added value already demonstrated by the Rapid Reaction Mechanism and on the emergency provisions already provided for in a number of existing external relations financial instruments. For our purposes, it should be noted that it provides for assistance in response to situations of crisis, or emerging crisis, to be provided by the Commission acting alone—without any need for Comitology. These are called Exceptional Assistance Measures and Interim Response Programmes and cover technical and financial assistance in situations of 'crisis or emerging crisis' where there is a threat to democracy, law and order, the protection of human rights and fundamental freedoms, the security and safety of individuals, or a situation threatening to escalate into armed conflict or to destabilise severely the third country or countries concerned. Such measures may also address situations where the essential elements clauses of international agreements are invoked in order to suspend, partially or totally, cooperation with third countries.

The Instrument for Stability contains a list[9] of 16 areas where the Commission may provide funding in emergency situations. Of particular interest is the provision addressing the destabilising effect of the proliferation of small arms and light weapons. The Regulation was adopted in the midst of the dispute between the Commission and the Council about the scope of the Community's powers in this field that gave rise to the ECOWAS case,[10] discussed in this same volume by both Gauci and Dashwood.

[7] See also the contribution by D Gauci in this volume.

[8] [2006] OJ L327/1.

[9] See Art 3(2) of the Instrument for Stability.

[10] Case C-91/05 *Commission of the European Communities v Council of the European Union* [2008] ECR I-3651.

C Other crisis management actions

A role in crisis management has been recognised at the end of the list of the Community's activities in Article 3.1(u) TEC. It is now expressed to be a support competence in Article 6(f) TFEU, which states that:

> The Union shall have competence to carry out actions to support, coordinate or supplement the actions of the Member States. The areas of such actions shall, at European level, be:
>
> ...
>
> (f) civil protection

The Commission undertakes a vast array of activities which can be considered to be responding to global emergencies beyond managing the Instrument for Stability (DG Relex). For example, its Directorates-General for Health, Development, Agriculture, Justice and Home Affairs and even Transport, Industry, Internal Market, Information Society and Regional Policy all have activities in this area related to their areas of operation. The most important are the Secretariat General, which runs crisis coordination departments referred to as Argus and the Crisis Coordination Committee and DG Environment.[11]

Deserving of special note is the activity of coordinating civil defence action managed by DG Environment. In the 1990s, civil protection cooperation was intergovernmental and limited to exchange of information and monitoring of major disasters. This was intensified in 1998 with a specific action programme and in 2001 with the adoption of Council Decision 2007/779/EC, Euratom establishing the Community Civil Protection Mechanism ('the Mechanism').[12] Major progress was made in 2007 with the revision of the Mechanism Decision and the adoption of the Civil Protection Financial Instrument.[13] Community cooperation in civil protection was deepened and the Commission's role was significantly enhanced. All Member States and the three EEA countries participate in the Mechanism.[14] The Mechanism promotes European solidarity towards Member States and third countries hit by major disasters. Its core missions are (1) coordinating the civil protection assistance provided by the participating states to countries affected by major disasters, and (2) enhancing Union's

[11] A detailed 'Inventory of Crisis Management Capacities in the European Commission and in Community Agencies' was published by the Commission as a Commission Staff Working Paper on 31 July 2009 and available at www.cc.cec/home/dgserv/sg/i/crisis_management/docs/inventory_crisis_manag_capac_commission_agencies_31072009.pdf.

[12] Council Decision 2007/779/EC, Euratom establishing a Community Civil Protection Mechanism (recast) [2007] OJ L314/9.

[13] Council Decision 2007/162/EC, Euratom establishing a Civil Protection Financial Instrument [2007] OJ L71/9.

[14] Croatia will soon become the 31st participating state.

preparedness for facing major disasters. The latter target national civil protection services, and include a training programme, full-scale field exercises and exchanges of experts.

As regards responses to emergencies, DG Environment plays a major role for disasters affecting third countries: it manages contacts with the affected country and involved players (Commission Delegation, UN, etc); it conducts needs assessments; it advises participating states on the required assistance, and ensures operational coordination. Within the Union, these tasks are fulfilled by the national authorities.

The main response tools established for responding to disasters are:

— the 24/7 duty system and the operations room (the Monitoring and Information Centre ('MIC'));
— the pool of national experts that may be contracted by the Commission for assessment and coordination missions at the site of disasters—32 experts and 10 DG Environment liaison officers were deployed in third countries in 2008;
— co-funding the transport of assistance to the site of disasters.

D Conclusion

The involvement of the European Commission in responding to global emergencies is very wide-ranging. It has evolved over the years in response to varied perceived needs as an adjunct to other activities of the Community and now the Union rather than as a coherent field of action in itself.

IV FOOD SAFETY AND ENVIRONMENTAL EMERGENCIES IN THE LIGHT OF THE PRECAUTIONARY PRINCIPLE[15]

Europeans evidently care a lot about the quality and safety of the food they eat and the environment—more, perhaps, than many other peoples, if recent legal history and the disputes it has spawned are a reliable indicator. In this respect, one defining moment was the discovery in the UK that bovine spongiform encephalopathy ('BSE') had been passing from cattle, where it was known to have been present for some time, to humans, causing what was called New Variant Creutzfeldt-Jakob disease. The UK government had solemnly reassured the public that this would not happen and that British beef was safe. The disaster for public confidence was aggravated by the fact that this emergency was the

[15] For a general examination of the precautionary principle, see T Christoforou, 'The Precautionary Principle in European Community Law and Science', in JA Tucker (ed) *Environmental Science and Preventive Public Policy* (Washington DC, Island Press, 2003); N de Sadeleer, 'The Precautionary Principle Applied to Food Safety—Lessons from the EC Courts' (2009) 1 *European Consumer Law Journal* 149.

result of intensive feeding policies designed to promote growth, involving the recycling of waste animal meat into cattle feed—and the failure to sterilise the product sufficiently.

The first case to reach the Court of Justice of the European Union in relation to the BSE crisis resulted from a challenge by UK agricultural interests against the emergency measures taken by the Community to combat the spread of the disease.[16] This appears to be the first case that recognised the applicability of the precautionary principle to food safety. Whilst it did not mention the principle by name, the Court of Justice famously stated that:

> Where there is uncertainty as to the existence or extent of risks to human health, the institutions may take protective measures without having to wait until the reality and seriousness of those risks become fully apparent.[17]

It then backed this up with reference to environmental policy, where the precautionary principle has applied since the amendments introduced into the EC Treaty by the Treaty of Maastricht in 1992.[18] The new Article 130r(2) on the environment (which was Article 174(2) under the TEC and is now Article 191(2) TFEU) stated that:

> Community policy on the environment shall aim at a *high level of protection* taking into account the diversity of situations in the various regions of the Community. It shall be based on the *precautionary principle* and on the principles that *preventive action* should be taken, that environmental damage should as a priority be *rectified at source* and that the *polluter should pay.*[19].

Perhaps because the notion was too recent or revolutionary, the Court of Justice did not dare to mention the precautionary principle by name. It referred to Article 130(r) in the following terms:

> That approach is borne out by Article 130r(1) of the EC Treaty, according to which Community policy on the environment is to pursue the objective inter alia of protecting human health. Article 130r(2) provides that that policy is to aim at a high level of protection and is to be based in particular on the principles that preventive action

[16] Case C-157/96 *National Farmers' Union* [1998] ECR I-2211.

[17] Para 63 of the judgment.

[18] It is noteworthy that there is no elaboration of what is meant by the Precautionary Principle in the Treaty of Maastricht. However the start of a definition can be found in Principle 15 of the Rio Declaration on Environment and Development, adopted some four months later on 14 June 1992 (available at www.unep.org/Documents.Multilingual/Default.asp?documentid=78&articleid=1163). This states that: 'In order to protect the environment, the precautionary approach shall be widely applied by States according to their capabilities. Where there are threats of serious or irreversible damage, lack of full scientific certainty shall not be used as a reason for postponing cost-effective measures to prevent environmental degradation'.

[19] (Emphasis added.) The possible need for 'emergency'-type measures in this area is underlined by the second sub-paragraph of this provision which states that 'harmonisation measures answering environmental protection requirements shall include, where appropriate, a safeguard clause'.

> should be taken and that environmental protection requirements must be integrated into the definition and implementation of other Community policies.[20]

(The words 'precautionary principle' in the Treaty are replaced by the words 'in particular'.)

The late 1990s were of course also the time when the Union was battling in the WTO to defend its ban on the use of growth hormones in the production of beef and introduced its 'moratorium' on the further approval of GMOs—both manifestly precautionary measures.

The precautionary principle seems to have fallen on fertile ground in the Union and has become, as we shall show, virtually a general principle of law. On one level, Europeans are expressing basic human reflexes: that it is better to be safe than sorry; that prevention is better than cure. But the precautionary principle takes these reflexes further and asserts: 'We do not care if prevention costs more than cure; we want prevention, not emergencies'. In 2000 the Commission formalised the general applicability of the precautionary principle beyond the field of the environment with its Communication on the precautionary principle.[21] It states, in particular that:

> The precautionary principle is not defined in the Treaty, which prescribes it only once—to protect the environment. But *in practice*, its scope is much wider, and specifically [it applies also] where preliminary objective scientific evaluation, indicates that there are reasonable grounds for concern that the potentially dangerous effects on the *environment, human, animal or plant health* may be inconsistent with the high level of protection chosen for the Community.[22]

That Communication also gives substance to the principle by setting out the conditions to be satisfied for the application of the precautionary principle, which have subsequently been recognised by the Court of Justice of the European Union:

— the potential negative effects must be *identified;*[23]
— there must be a *scientific evaluation* of those negative effects;[24]
— that evaluation must indicate the existence of *uncertainty.*[25]

[20] Para 64 of the judgment.

[21] Communication from the Commission of 2 February 2000, COM (2000) 1 final—not published in the Official Journal but available electronically at http://eurlex.europa.eu/smartapi/cgi/sga_doc?smartapi!celexplus!prod!DocNumber&lg=en&type_doc=COMfinal&an_doc=2000&nu_doc=1 or at http://europa.eu/legislation_summaries/consumers/consumer_safety/l32042_en.htm.

[22] See para 3 of the summary.

[23] Case C-132/03 *Ministero della Salute* [2005] ECR I-4167, para 61; Case T-392/02 *Solvay Pharmaceuticals BV* [2003] ECR II-4555, paras 121, 122; COM (2000) 1 final (n 21 above), point 5.1.1.

[24] Case T-392/02 *Solvay Pharmaceuticals BV* [2003] ECR II-4555, paras 129, 135; Case C-236/01 *Monsanto Agricoltura Italia SpA et al* [2003] ECR I-8105, paras 111, 114; COM (2000) 1 final (n 21 above), point 5.1.2.

[25] Case T-392/02 (n 24 above), paras 129, 135; Case C-236/01 (n 24 above), paras 111, 114; COM (2000) 1 final (n 21 above), point 5.1.3.

There is also a fourth condition which derives from the very nature of precautionary measures that needs to be taken into account once it is established that precautionary measures are warranted, that is, that a *review* of the precautionary measures must be envisaged or possible. The principle is only implicit in the Communication and the case-law but is explicit in Article 5(7) of the WTO Agreement on Sanitary and Phytosanitary Measures.

The precautionary principle is being expressed in new legislation; for example, Article 7 of Regulation 178/2002/EC laying down the general principles and requirements of food law[26] provides that the precautionary principle may be invoked where a food might have harmful effects on health in order to be able to react quickly and take appropriate measures. Similarly, the first subparagraphs of Article 8(2) of Directive 2001/95 on general product safety states:

> When the competent authorities of the Member States take measures such as those provided for in paragraph 1, in particular those referred to in (d) to (f), they shall act in accordance with the Treaty, and in particular Articles 28 and 30 thereof, in such a way as to implement the measures in a manner proportional to the seriousness of the risk, and *taking due account of the precautionary principle.*[27]

Having been given the green light by other Union institutions, the Court of Justice of the European Union is no longer shy of referring to the precautionary principle in the area of public health.[28]

Of particular interest, however, are those cases that suggest an even wider applicability of the principle so that the precautionary principle may have become a general principle of law of wide application. In that way it would not only constitute a defence against an allegation that the Union may have taken disproportionately restrictive measures in the fields of environment and public health, as the first cases may be taken to suggest, but would constitute a principle that Member States and the Union have an obligation to respect in these areas and others. There are a number of interesting judgments in this regard, the most explicit of which is perhaps the judgment of the General Court in *Artegodan*,[29] where a number of pharmaceutical and cosmetics companies contested the withdrawing of marketing authorisations for slimming products and the General Court held that:

[26] Regulation 178/2002/EC laying down the general principles and requirements of food law, establishing the European Food Safety Authority and laying down procedures in matters of food safety [2002] OJ L31/1.

[27] Directive 2001/95/EC on general product safety [2002] OJ L11/4 (emphasis added).

[28] See, in particular, Case C-236/01 *Monsanto Agricoltura Italia SpA and Others v Presidenza del Consiglio dei Ministri and Others* [2003] ECR I-8105 and Case T-13/99 *Pfizer Animal Health SA v Council of the European Union* [2002] ECR II-3305.

[29] Joined Cases T-74/00, T-76/00, T-83/00 to T-85/00, T-132/00, T-137/00 and T-141/00 *Artegodan GmbH, Bruno Farmaceutici SpA, Essential Nutrition Ltd, Hoechst Marion Roussel Ltd, Hoechst Marion Roussel SA, Marion Merell SA, Marion Merell SA, Sanova Pharma GmbH, Temmler Pharma GmbH & Co. KG, Schuck GmbH, Laboratórios Roussel Lda, Laboratoires Roussel Diamant SARL, Roussel Iberica SA, Gerot Pharmazeutika GmbH, Cambridge Healthcare Supplies Ltd, Laboratoires pharmaceutiques Trenker SA v Commission of the European Communities* [2002] ECR II-4945.

> the precautionary principle can be defined as a general principle of Community law requiring the competent authorities to take appropriate measures to prevent specific potential risks to public health, safety and the environment, by giving precedence to the requirements related to the protection of those interests over economic interests,[30]

although it did endeavour to found this conclusion on provisions of the EC Treaty.[31]

In the *Red Bull* case[32] the Commission brought an infringement action against France for not allowing the sale of the drink 'Red Bull'. The Commission considered that this ban infringed Article 28 TEC (now Article 34 TFEU), there being no applicable Community legislation at the time. In its consideration of the justification under Article 30 TEC (now Article 36 TFEU), the Court of Justice accepted that, where scientific uncertainty exists 'a *Member State* may, in accordance with the precautionary principle, take protective measures without having to wait until the existence and gravity of those risks are fully demonstrated'.[33]

Subsequently in the *Codacons* case[34] (concerning the absence of a requirement to label infant foods to indicate the presence of GMOs) the Court of Justice accepted to examine the argument that the application by a Member State of the provisions of a directive that did not mention the precautionary principle at all (Council Directive 79/112/EEC on the labelling of foodstuffs)[35] could be examined for consistency with the precautionary principle.[36]

In both those cases, the application of the precautionary principle was not determinative of the result but they do seem to show that the precautionary principle can be used as a defence by Member States and that it is a principle that they must respect when applying Union law, even where there is no direct legislative or Treaty basis for its application.

V CLIMATE CHANGE

The precautionary principle is not normally invoked to justify the far-reaching action being adopted and considered by the Union and elsewhere in the world to address climate change, but it does seem to be relevant to explain the action being taken to address this rising emergency.

Even if the fact of climate change is fairly well established (and can be measured), the potential effects are inevitably speculative and give rise to intense

[30] Para. 184 of the judgment.

[31] Arts 3(p), 6, 152(1), 53, 174 ECT, now Arts 6(a), 168(1), 60, 191 TFEU. See paras 182–83 of the judgment.

[32] Case C-24/00 *Commission of the European Communities v French Republic* [2004] ECR I-1277.

[33] Para 56 of the judgment (emphasis added).

[34] Judgment of the Court (Second Chamber) of 26 May 2005, Case C-132/03, *Ministero della Salute v Coordinamento delle associazioni per la difesa dell'ambiente e dei diritti degli utenti e dei consumatori (Codacons) and Federconsumatori,* [2005] ECR I-4167.

[35] [1979] OJ L33/1.

[36] See paras 56 et seq of the judgment.

controversy. For many environmental NGOs, disaster seems a certainty unless humanity changes its evil ways and ceases to consume the planet's limited resources without regard to the future. For others, often on the right of the political spectrum and well represented and in the United States, consumption and development appear to be natural rights to be vigorously defended against the designs of power-hungry bureaucrats exploiting the latest excuse to tax and regulate the long-suffering peoples of the world.

What can be said with somewhat more certainty is that if the *possible* consequences of climate change were to become reality, the cost of the disruption to life (or attempting to remedy it once it had happened) would be even greater than the cost of taking preventive action now.[37] Is this not a classic case for the application of the precautionary principle?

In any event, the Union is active on many fronts to confront this danger. It has adopted some of the strictest targets in the world[38] for reducing greenhouse gas emissions and has developed the extremely far-reaching legislation in order to attain those goals.[39] Recognising the global nature of the problem and the fact that its efforts alone cannot provide a solution, the Union is also vigorously pursuing the conclusion of a wide-ranging international agreement within the framework of the United Nations Framework Convention on Climate Change to ensure that other countries contribute to this effort. Furthermore, since some climate change appears to be inevitable, the Union is not only pursuing mitigation action but is also developing policies to promote adaptation to climate change both within the Union and in the wider world.[40]

[37] See *Stern Review on the Economics of Climate Change* (2006), Sir Nicholas Stern, Head of the UK Government Economic Service and Adviser to the Government on the economics of climate change and development, available at http://webarchive.nationalarchives.gov.uk/+/http://www.hm-treasury.gov.uk/Independent_Reviews/stern_review_economics_climate_change/sternreview_index.cfm.

[38] The European Council adopted on 8–9 March 2007 and has reaffirmed many times since, the target of a 20 % reduction in greenhouse gas emissions by 2020 compared to 1995 and committed to increasing this reduction to 30 % within the framework of an ambitious and comprehensive global agreement in Copenhagen on climate change for the period after 2012 on condition that the other developed countries undertake to achieve comparable emission reductions and that the economically more advanced developing countries make a contribution commensurate with their respective responsibilities and capabilities. (Available at www.consilium.europa.eu/ueDocs/cms_Data/docs/pressData/en/ec/93135.pdf.)

[39] Directive 2003/87/EC establishing a scheme for greenhouse gas emission allowance trading within the Community and amending Council Directive 96/61/EC, [1996] L257/26 (amended several times, see the consolidated version at http://eur-lex.europa.eu/LexUriServ/LexUriServ.do?uri=CONSLEG:2003L0087:20090625:EN:PDF) and Decision 406/2009/EC of the European Parliament and of the Council on the effort of Member States to reduce their greenhouse gas emissions to meet the Community's greenhouse gas emission reduction commitments up to 2020, [2009] OJ L140/136.

[40] Commission, White Paper on adaptation to Climate Change COM (2009) 147.

VI THE FINANCIAL AND ECONOMIC CRISIS

The latest global emergency is the financial and economic crisis. Here again the Union has played an important, even if primarily a coordinating, role. The Union has acted together with the Member States to inject a vast amount of money into the economy to stimulate activity and mitigate the expected downturn (the European Economic Recovery Plan). The Union contribution to the actual increased spending was relatively modest—due to its small overall budget and its inability to borrow—but still amounted to €5 billion.[41]

Of greater importance, however, is the *facilitative* role of the Union in dealing with the crisis. In particular, the Commission greatly eased its approach to the approval of state aid, first to allow the massive injections of emergency financial assistance for the banking sector and then to temporarily allow more state aid for industry. The Commission Communication setting out a 'Temporary Community framework for State aid measures to support access to finance in the current financial and economic crisis'[42] was adopted as part of the European Economic Recovery Plan and is a remarkably user-friendly document, listing all the ways in which state aid may be given.

Arguably the greatest contribution that the Union can make to dealing with the financial and economic crisis will be to develop common solutions to identify and avoid repetition of the events causing the crisis. Commission President, José Manuel Barroso conferred a mandate on Jacques de Larosière in October 2008 to chair an 'outstanding group of people' to give advice on the future of European financial regulation and supervision. The de Larosière report[43] was published on 25 February 2009 and is leading to extensive changes to financial regulation and supervision in the Union.

VII CONCLUSION

The Union may not have been created for the purpose of dealing with global emergencies, but it has inevitably come to play a major role in doing so. It normally does not have the resources or the power to act by itself, but even where it cannot, it plays an invaluable role in coordinating and facilitating the action of Member States.

The most important—one might even say 'constitutional'—features of the Union apparatus for dealing with emergencies are the precautionary principle and allowing Member States to act through the provision of possibilities for

[41] €3.98 billion was allocated to energy projects by Regulation 663/2009/EC establishing a programme to aid economic recovery by granting Community financial assistance to projects in the field of energy [2009] OJ L200/31. A further €1.02 billion has been allocated to rural development and the installation of broadband.

[42] [2009] OJ C83/1.

[43] Available at http://ec.europa.eu/internal_market/finances/docs/de_larosiere_report_en.pdf.

taking safeguard action. Another, is the Union's ability to find common solutions to emergencies that have occurred and in doing so to advance the cause for which it was created—the 'ever closer union among the peoples of Europe'.

It is problems and even emergencies that provide the impetus for the Union to advance. They provide a need for action, while the spirit of solidarity that the Union has fostered and the inventiveness arising from the Union's rich diversity provide the apparatus to find the new ways for the Member States of the Union to act together more effectively. In one sense it is emergencies that are part of the constitutional apparatus of the Union.

14

The European Parliament and EU External Aid: Measures of Response to Emergency Situations

DANIELA GAUCI

I INTRODUCTION

THE EUROPEAN PARLIAMENT has played an important part in the shaping of EU external aid, especially through its role as co-decider in the field of development cooperation. This chapter aims at analysing the role played by the Parliament with regard to the shaping of external aid measures, in particular those which provide a legal basis for response in emergency situations. Parliament's legislative powers, coupled with scrutiny of programming and implementation, provide an element of visibility and scrutiny which is required if the European Union's external aid is to continue to be supported by EU citizens.

The first part of this chapter provides a background to the external cooperation instruments covering the period 2007–13, in particular with regard to how these external cooperation instruments provide a legal basis for response in crisis situations. The focus is on the Instrument for Stability[1] and the Food Facility.[2] The analysis of the negotiations leading to the adoption of the Instrument for Stability highlights the difficulties which arise when one aims at drawing a rigid line between security and development measures. It is argued that the notion of the development of a country as being only its 'economic and social' development is not justified. A country's development is also related to its being able to provide a stable and secure environment for its citizens. This chapter also examines the implications of this on the institutional balance, especially since the European Parliament acts as co-decider when such measures are considered to be development measures, but is only informed when the measures are considered to fall under security policy.

[1] Regulation 1717/2006/EC establishing an instrument for stability [2006] OJ L327/1.

[2] Regulation 1337/2008/EC establishing a facility for rapid response to soaring food prices in developing countries [2008] OJ L354/62.

The negotiations on the Food Facility did not raise major legal concerns. It is however interesting as a novel instrument which seeks to respond to an international crisis where the existing instruments, in particular the Humanitarian Aid Regulation[3] and the Development Cooperation Instrument[4] were deemed insufficient or inappropriate in providing an adequate response. Before the coming into force of the Treaty of Lisbon, Article 179 EC provided the legal basis for this instrument. It meant that such an emergency response required a legislative act to be adopted through the co-decision procedure. The Treaty of Lisbon now provides a new legal basis, Article 213 TFEU, for urgent assistance whereby decisions can be adopted by Council without Parliament's co-decision or even consultation.

In the second part, the role of Article 213 TFEU is examined. That provision breaks away from the general rule established in the Treaty that for the adoption of measures defining the framework for external cooperation with third countries (which now includes both developing and non-developing countries), the ordinary legislative procedure applies. For this reason, it can only be used exceptionally, in cases of unavoidable urgency. In this regard, we will consider the specific case whereby various macro-financial assistance measures are adopted in relation to third countries with balance-of-payment problems, since this is one example where recourse to Article 213 TFEU may be deemed necessary. It is argued that this can be avoided by adopting a framework regulation through the ordinary legislative procedure and under the legal basis for cooperation with developing countries and other third countries. That regulation could then empower the Commission to adopt specific measures responding to specific requests for assistance from third countries on the basis of the objectives and principles established therein.

II THE EC EXTERNAL RELATIONS INSTRUMENTS: 2007–13: PROVISION FOR URGENCY MEASURES

In 2006, after two years of debate and negotiations among Parliament, Council and the Commission, a new package of external aid instruments was adopted. It includes seven instruments, namely: the Development Cooperation Instrument (DCI)[5] based on Article 179 EC; the Instrument for Cooperation with Industrialised and other High-Income Countries (ICI)[6] based on Article 181a EC; the

[3] Council Regulation 1257/96/EC concerning humanitarian aid [1996] OJ L163/1, as amended.

[4] Regulation 1905/2006/EC establishing a financing instrument for development cooperation [2006] OJ L378/41.

[5] Regulation 1905/2006/EC (n 4 above).

[6] Council Regulation 1934/2006/EC establishing a financing instrument for cooperation with industrialised and other high-income countries and territories [2006] OJ L405/41.

European Neighbourhood and Partnership Instrument (ENPI)[7] based on Articles 179 EC and 181a EC; the Instrument for Pre-Accession Assistance (IPA)[8] based on Article 181a EC; the Instrument for the Promotion of Democracy and Human Rights Worldwide (EIDHR)[9] based on Articles 179 EC and 181a EC; the Instrument for Stability[10] based on Articles 179 EC and 181a EC; and the Instrument for Nuclear Safety Cooperation[11] based on Article 203 Euratom. Parliament was co-decider on most of the instruments due to the development legal basis.[12]

Each of those instruments has a seven-year duration, reflecting the seven-year duration of the financial framework 2007–13.[13] What is of interest is that all the instruments, while in the main being instruments which provide long-term assistance, include provisions for response to urgent needs. Article 23 of the Development Cooperation Instrument holds that:

> in the event of unforeseen and duly justified needs or circumstances related to natural disasters, civil strife or crises, and which cannot be funded under Regulation (EC) No 1717/ 2006[14] or Regulation (EC) No 1257/96,[15] the Commission shall adopt special measures not provided for in the strategy papers or multiannual indicative programmes (hereinafter referred to as 'special measures'). Special measures may also be used to fund measures to ease the transition from emergency aid to long-term development operations, including those to better prepare people to deal with recurring crises.

The ENPI has a similar provision and its Article 13 provides for special measures to fund activities to ease the transition from emergency aid to long-term development activities, including activities intended to ensure that the public is better prepared to deal with recurring crises. Article 7 of the EIDHR also provides for special measures to be adopted in the event of unforeseen and duly justified needs or exceptional circumstances not covered in the Strategy Papers and Article 9 provides for small grants on an ad hoc basis to human rights defenders responding to urgent protection needs.

[7] Regulation 1638/2006/EC laying down general provisions establishing a European neighbourhood and partnership instrument [2006] OJ L310/1.

[8] Council Regulation 1085/2006/EC establishing an instrument for pre-accession assistance (IPA) [2006] OJ L210/82.

[9] Regulation 1889/2006/EC establishing a financing instrument for the promotion of democracy and human rights worldwide [2006] OJ L386/1.

[10] Regulation 1717/2006/EC (n 1 above).

[11] Council Regulation (Euratom) 300/2007 establishing an instrument for nuclear safety cooperation [2007] OJ L81/1.

[12] Namely the DCI, the ENPI, the IfS and the EIDHR.

[13] For a detailed analysis about the external relations instruments and the negotiations leading to their adoption, see generally S Bartelt, 'The legislative architecture of EU external assistance and development cooperation' (2008) 2 *Europarecht* 9.

[14] The Instrument for Stability.

[15] Council Regulation 1257/96/EC concerning humanitarian aid [1996] OJ L163/1, as amended.

Parliament's role in the adoption of these short-term emergency response measures under these instruments is limited. Under the Development Cooperation Instrument, such short-term measures are adopted by the Commission. If the measure exceeds €10 million, the management procedure[16] is followed. This means that Parliament may, if it deems appropriate, express its views and adopt a resolution holding that the measure is ultra vires the Development Cooperation Instrument provisions[17] but the Commission, while obliged to provide reasons, is under no obligation to adapt the measure to respond to Parliament's concerns. The same procedure applies for the special measures under the ENPI and the EIDHR. The small grants to human rights defenders responding to urgent protection needs are allocated by the Commission, with a duty to inform Parliament and the Member States of the measures carried out.[18] However, these instruments are, in their main, long term instruments. It is only the Instrument for Stability which is specifically aimed at responding to urgent needs.

The Humanitarian Aid Regulation,[19] adopted in 1996, continues to apply to humanitarian aid which comprises assistance, relief and protection operations to help victims of natural disasters, man-made crises, such as wars and outbreaks of fighting, or exceptional situations or circumstances comparable to natural or man-made disasters. That assistance is granted for the time needed to meet the humanitarian requirements resulting from these different situations. Such aid

[16] Since the Development Cooperation Instrument was adopted before the Treaty of Lisbon came into force, the Comitology Decision, Council Decision 1999/468/EC laying down the procedures for the exercise of implementing powers conferred on the Commission [1999] OJ L184/23, as amended by Council Decision 2006/512/EC amending Decision 1999/468/EC laying down the procedures for the exercise of implementing powers conferred on the Commission [2006] OJ L200/11, applies to the measures delegated to the Commission. According to Art 4 of that Decision, the Commission adopts the relevant measures. However, the Commission is assisted by a management committee composed of the representatives of the Member States. The Commission submits a draft of the measures to be taken. The committee gives an opinion and the Commission adopts the measures. However, if these measures are not in accordance with the opinion of the committee, they shall be communicated by the Commission to the Council. The Council, acting by qualified majority, may take a different decision. This procedure changes with the coming into force of the Treaty of Lisbon. Art 202 EC is repealed. Instead, the new Treaty provides, under specific and different conditions, the possibility of adopting non-legislative acts, ie delegated acts or implementing acts, under arts 290 and 291 TFEU. However, provisions concerning comitology in existing legislation continue to apply, unless and only until amended. See more detail in this regard in section IIA, below.

[17] In accordance with Art 7 of the Comitology Decision referred to above, the Commission must inform Parliament of the committee proceedings on a regular basis by sending agendas for committee meetings, a copy of the draft measures submitted to the committees for the implementation of instruments adopted by co-decision, and the results of voting and summary records of the meetings. Art 8 of the same Decision holds that Parliament may indicate in a Resolution that the draft implementing measures exceed the implementing powers provided for in the basic instrument. In that case, the Commission is obliged to re-examine the draft measures but may decide to continue with the procedure. Parliament adopted various such resolutions but not in relation to special measures.

[18] Regulation1889/2006/EC of the European Parliament and of the Council of 20 December 2006 on establishing a financing instrument for the promotion of democracy and human rights worldwide [2006] OJ L386/1, Art 9.

[19] Council Regulation 1257/96/EC concerning humanitarian aid [1996] OJ L163/1.

also comprises operations to prepare for risks or prevent disasters or comparable exceptional circumstances. In other words, humanitarian assistance covers the very early period during conflicts or natural disasters and the immediate aftermath. It is a measure of immediate 'relief', in particular to save and preserve life during emergencies and their immediate aftermath; to provide the necessary assistance and relief to people affected by longer-lasting crises arising, in particular, from outbreaks of fighting or wars; to carry out short-term rehabilitation and reconstruction work, especially on infrastructure and equipment, in close association with local structures, with a view to facilitating the arrival of relief; and to prevent the impact of the crisis from worsening and starting to help those affected regain a minimum level of self-sufficiency. On the political level, the role of the EU in the provision of humanitarian aid worldwide was the subject of a 'Consensus' among the three European institutions, namely the Parliament, Council and the Commission in 2007.[20]

A The Instrument for Stability

Unlike the above-mentioned instruments for the period 2007–13, the main aim of the Instrument for Stability is to provide for short-term response to emergency situations. The aim of the proposal from the Commission was to provide an instrument to 'finance measures to promote peace and stability and assure the safety and security of the civilian population in third countries and territories'.[21] The instrument would provide complementary assistance to what is otherwise

[20] European Parliament resolution of 29 November 2007 on the proclamation of a European Consensus on Humanitarian Aid, P6_TA(2007)0571. Part I, on the EU vision for humanitarian aid, focuses on coherence between Union and Member State action in the humanitarian field and establishes the principles for humanitarian aid and how the Member States and the Community should work, establishing the principles and objectives. Part II focuses on the Union aspect of humanitarian aid. It holds that the Union will seek in the medium term to carry out a special role, including strengthening humanitarian advocacy; facilitating the participation of all Member States in their provision of humanitarian aid through sharing of accumulated experience and offering specific guidance and work with others, including the UN, the Red Cross/Red Crescent Movement and humanitarian NGOs, on ensuring better needs analysis and on identifying continuing response gaps.

[21] Commission, 'Proposal for a Regulation of the Council establishing an Instrument for Stability' COM (2004) 630 final, Art 1. The Instrument for Stability is not the first instrument to create this link between security and cooperation with third countries. The link is made clear in the Consensus on Development Aid. Joint statement by the European Parliament, the Council and the representatives of the governments of the Member States meeting within the Council, and the Commission on European Union Development Policy: The European Consensus [2006] OJ C46/1. Moreover, the Instrument for Stability itself repealed various Regulations which dealt with response to crises situations and which had this link with security issues. In particular, the European Parliament and Council Regulation 1724/2001/EC, concerning action against anti-personnel landmines in developing countries, adopted on the basis of Art 179 EC [2001] OJ L234/1 and Council Regulation 381/2001/EC creating a rapid-reaction mechanism [2001] OJ L57/5.

provided for under the other instruments of cooperation.[22] The Commission justified the proposal by holding that implementation of programmes of assistance in times of crisis and political instability require specific measures to ensure flexibility in decision-making and budget allocation. That proposal, while generally welcome by both Council and Parliament, received various criticisms and was eventually adapted to meet the issues raised by Council and Parliament relating, in particular, to the legal basis, the content, and the structure.

i Legal basis

The original proposal from the Commission based the Instrument for Stability on Articles 308 EC and 230 Euratom. The Commission, in the explanatory memorandum, justified the choice of legal basis as follows:

> the Euratom legal base is required in order to cover the nuclear safety aspects of the proposal. The civilian aspects of crisis response would normally come within the scope of articles 179 and 181a of the EC Treaty. However the provisions relating to the financing of peace keeping, in particular, while clearly contributing to the objectives of Article 179 and 181a, clearly justify a legal basis in Article 308 of the Treaty. Moreover, Articles 179 and 181a are not legally compatible with Article 203 of the Euratom Treaty.[23]

However, Parliament strongly disagreed with this choice of legal basis, calling for a split of the instrument: keeping the main part as an instrument for stability based on Articles 179 and 181a EC and having a separate instrument for the nuclear safety aspects of the proposal. For Parliament, Articles 179 EC and 181a EC constituted more specific legal bases and corresponded to the aim and objective pursued by the proposed regulation, excluding only the nuclear safety aspects of the proposal which could be dealt with in a separate instrument based on Article 203 Euratom. From the aim and content of the proposal, it was considered that the nuclear objectives were secondary. Parliament argued that a separate instrument was more adequate than the actual removal of parliamentary power for the whole Instrument for Stability. This issue was very important for Parliament. Article 308 EC meant that the instrument would be adopted by unanimity in Council, with only the consultation of Parliament.[24]

[22] It must be noted that the instrument is distinct from humanitarian aid. The latter provides humanitarian assistance to victims of man-made and natural disasters, essentially through the provision of goods (food, shelter, etc). It is focused on the individual, it is politically neutral and it is aimed exclusively at alleviating human suffering. The Instrument for Stability aims at providing resources for urgent operations of crisis management and conflict prevention linked to the overall foreign and security policy of the Union.

[23] Commission, 'Proposal for a Regulation of the Council establishing an Instrument for Stability' (Explanatory Memorandum) COM (2004) 630 final, second paragraph.

[24] See the Opinion on the legal basis of the Committee on Legal Affairs to the Committee on Foreign Affairs, dated 13 July 2005, attached to the draft European Parliament Resolution on the proposal for a regulation of the European Parliament and of the Council establishing an Instrument

For the Parliament, the other aspects fell squarely under the dual legal basis of Articles 179 and 181a EC, the former in relation to cooperation which concerned developing countries and the latter for cooperation concerning developed countries since the Instrument for Stability does not have a limited geographic coverage. Article 177 EC was construed in very broad terms providing for three general objectives of development cooperation, namely the sustainable economic and social development of the developing countries, and more particularly the most disadvantaged among them; the smooth and gradual integration of developing countries into the world economy; and the campaign against poverty in developing countries. This in addition to the reference to Community policy in this area contributing to the general objective of developing and consolidating democracy and the rule of law, and to that of respecting human rights and fundamental freedoms. The scope of measures in order to fulfil those objectives must be wide. For this reason, Parliament considered that the inclusion of Article 308 EC was not necessary as a legal basis for the measures included in the proposed Instrument for Stability (excluding the nuclear safety aspects). Council supported Parliament's view and the instrument is based on Articles 179 and 181a EC.[25,26]

At this point, it may be noted that interpreting Article 177 EC broadly was in line with Parliament's position in the then pending *ECOWAS* case[27] (also known as the small and light weapons case). The Commission had sought the annulment of Council Decision 2004/833/CFSP, implementing Joint Action 2002/589/CFSP of 12 July 2002 in relation to the European Union contribution to ECOWAS in the framework of the Moratorium on Small Arms and Light Weapons.[28] Parliament intervened in support of the position of the Commission. The ECOWAS

for Stability as adopted by the Committee on Foreign Affairs on 2 May 2006, A6–0157/2006. In this regard, see generally, F Hoffmeister, 'The relation between development policy and Common Foreign and Security Policy—The case of the Instrument for Stability' (2008) 2 *Europarecht* 9.

[25] The nuclear safety cooperation elements were included in a separate instrument, namely Council Regulation (Euratom) 300/2007 establishing an Instrument for Nuclear Safety Cooperation [2007] OJ L81/1.

[26] At this point, it must be mentioned that within Parliament itself there are also diverging views as to the definition of development cooperation. The Development Committee takes a narrower view, holding that with a broad definition of development, cooperation funds which could otherwise focus on health and development may be lost to issues concerning security, which tend to require higher amounts of funding. In fact, the Development Committee has called for, eg, the inclusion of the DAC-ability criteria in the Development Cooperation Instrument (Art 2(4)) (ie that all measures must be considered as official development assistance by the OECD) in order to ensure that all measures adopted on the basis of that instrument could be eligible as official development assistance, ensuring also that more funding is focused on poverty eradication measures, and in particular health and education.

[27] Case C-91/05 *Commission of the European Communities v Council of the European Union* [2008] ECR I-03651.

[28] Council Joint Action of 12 July 2002 on the European Union's contribution to combating the destabilising accumulation and spread of small arms and light weapons and repealing Joint Action 1999/34/CFSP, OJ L191/1.

judgment has already been amply discussed in literature[29] and it is not the purpose of this chapter to delve into the detail of the judgment. It suffices to briefly mention the two main reasons behind Parliament's intervention in this case.[30]

First of all, Parliament emphasised the role of Article 47 TEU as a provision whose aim is to protect the *acquis communautaire*. It sought to ensure that no measures adopted in the context of the Second (or Third) Pillar of the TEU affect the competences of the Community under the EC Treaty. The relationship between the CFSP and development policy is not only a problem of overlapping and consistency between instruments adopted under the two policies. In reality, it is also a question of separation between two different policies for which the balance of powers among the institutions is different. Secondly, Parliament also sought to clarify the scope of development policy, underlining its view on the importance of stable political conditions and security for the creation of sustainable development, using the same reasoning as it did throughout the negotiations on the Instrument for Stability.[31] Both arguments were eventually accepted by the Court.

With regard to this second argument, a brief examination of instruments such as the Instrument for Stability shows that the line to be drawn between security and development is a very fine one indeed. In fact, the mere presence of an objective of removing an obstacle to the pursuance of development in a third country can be considered sufficient to bring a measure within the scope of development cooperation. The development of a country is not only related to its 'economic' development, it also includes the creation of a safe environment for citizens and a secure state where economic and social development can take place. Moreover, the concept of development evolves and changes in time and is

[29] See generally, J Heliskoski, 'Small arms and light weapons within the Union's pillar structure: An analysis of Art 47 of the EU Treaty' (2008) 6 *European Law Review* 898.

[30] The intervention of Parliament in support of the Commission was decided by the Legal Affairs Committee of the Parliament on 6 June 2005.

[31] While ensuring that development cooperation measures were adopted under the EC Treaty and according to the relevant procedures (ie, co-decision), Parliament also recognised that the evolution of development cooperation was to be decided by virtue of legislation in the field. It sought to do this in two ways: first of all, Parliament played an active role in the reshaping of external aid instruments in the pre-new financial framework period (2004–06); and secondly Parliament sought to ensure that the scope of development cooperation was determined by itself and the Council in co-decided legislation. It has argued that it is not for the Commission to give a broad scope to development cooperation legislation. In fact, in Case C-403/05 *European Parliament v Commission (Philippines Border Management Project)* [2007] ECR I-9045, Parliament challenged a decision adopted by the Commission approving a project on the security of borders in the Philippines. Parliament sought to clarify that even if the definition of Art 177 EC has developed both through legislation and case law, that does not mean that legislation adopted on the basis of Art 179 EC could be given a broad interpretation by the Commission which goes beyond the legislators' intention for that particular 'mother' Act, and the Court supported that line of reasoning. See generally, M Cremona, Annotation (2008) 45 *CML Rev* 1727.

relative to the countries in question and the people concerned. For this reason, an element of flexibility in interpreting what is development cooperation is necessary.

With regard to Article 47, it may be noted that under the Treaty of Lisbon, this article is replaced by Article 40 TEU which creates a two-way approach. It holds that the implementation of the CFSP shall not affect the application of the procedures and extent of the powers of the institutions by the Treaties for the exercise of the Union competences referred to in Articles 3 to 6 of the TFEU. However, it adds that, similarly, the implementation of the policies listed in those articles shall not affect the application of the procedures and the extent of the powers of the institutions laid down by the Treaties for the exercise of the Union competences under the CFSP Chapter. This two-way approach seems to negate the raison d'être behind this article, in the sense that the second subparagraph denies any useful purpose for the first, and vice-versa. However, one must consider that the scope of the CFSP is very broad and could, in fact, be used in every field of the Union's external action. Article 24 TEU holds that 'The Union's competence in matters of foreign and security policy shall cover all areas of foreign policy'. On the other hand, the provisions on cooperation with third countries in the non-CFSP competence are more specific. In this way, one could argue that the latter should be given priority because they provide for specific procedures, including a co-deciding role for the European Parliament, for the particular fields such as development cooperation and humanitarian aid to which they apply.[32]

ii Content: Peace-keeping and peace-support

A second related issue of concern in the original proposal was the inclusion of measures relating to peace-keeping and peace-support. For Parliament, these could contribute to the objective of developing and consolidating democracy and the rule of law. The wording of Articles 179 and 181a EC Treaty did not exclude the financing of peace-keeping and peace-support in order to fulfil their objectives. The proposal only aimed at the security and safety of the civilian population in the third countries, since Article 13 of the proposed regulation explicitly excluded that Community assistance could be used for the financing of military training for combat operations, and for the costs relating to the deployment of the military forces of the Member States. Indeed regional instruments of

[32] See especially, J Heliskoski, 'Small arms and light weapons within the Union's pillar structure: An analysis of Art 47 of the EU Treaty' (2008) 6 *European Law Review* 911. For a different view, see Alan Dashwood's contribution in this volume, 'Conflicts Of Competence In Responding To Global Emergencies'.

development cooperation had already permitted the Community to contribute to actions in the fields of both administrative and institutional reform and democracy; and of conflict prevention and resolution.[33]

Commission, Parliament and Council had divergent views about the measures related to peace-keeping and peace-support. In its proposal, the Commission included:

> support for ... military monitoring and peace-keeping or peace-support operations (including those with a civilian component) conducted by regional and sub-regional organisations and other coalitions of states operating with United Nations endorsement; measures to build the capacity of such organisations and their participating members to plan, execute and ensure effective political control over such operations[34]

providing detailed provisions to ensure consistency with CFSP measures and UN decisions. In Article 6, the Commission recognised the particular political sensitivity of peace support operations and the need to ensure that decisions are taken which are consistent with the political orientations developed in the Council. Moreover, in order to promote close linkages between Community peace-support operations and the military and civilian capacities that could be mobilised under Title V of the Treaty on European Union, the Commission proposed a requirement on the Commission to draw to the attention of the Council any complementary measures that it may consider useful for adoption under the CFSP. As under the Africa Peace Facility,[35] UN endorsement in broad terms would be needed before launching any such operation, operations would be based on an agreement with a regional organisation and the country of operation and no direct financing of EU military activity would be permitted.[36]

Parliament did not oppose this inclusion and the Foreign Affairs committee included in its draft report, in first reading, technical and financial support for peace-keeping and peace-support operations conducted by regional and sub-regional organisations operating with United Nations endorsement and support for measures to address the effects on the civilian population of landmines, unexploded ordnance or other explosive devices and other harmful remnants of war, including the clearance and destruction of stockpiles and risk-awareness

[33] Council Regulation 1726/2000EC on development cooperation with South Africa [2000] OJ L198/1, Art 2(2); Council Regulation 381/2001/EC creating a rapid-reaction mechanism [2001] OJ L57/5. It is true that this regulation was based on Art 308 EC. However, that regulation was adopted before the entry into force of the Nice Treaty by which Art 181a EC was introduced. Art 308 EC would have been required since the mechanism covered both developing countries and other third countries.

[34] Proposal for a Regulation of the Council establishing an Instrument for Stability, COM (2004) 630 final, Art 2(a), second indent.

[35] See Decision no 3/2003 of the ACP-EC Council of Ministers of 11 December 2003 on the use of resources from the long-term development envelope of the ninth EDF for the creation of a Peace Facility for Africa [2003] OJ L345/108.

[36] Art 13(2) of the proposal.

programmes.[37] However, Council did not agree, since it did not consider that Articles 179 and 181a EC, or other articles in the EC Treaty, provided an appropriate legal basis for such measures. In fact the Instrument for Stability, as adopted on 15 November 2006, does not include any reference to peace-keeping and peace-support operations and specifically excludes 'support for measures to combat the proliferation of arms'.[38]

iii Structure of the instrument and its relevance to parliamentary scrutiny

In its proposal, the Commission included all measures under one article, albeit under different sub-articles. As adopted, the Instrument for Stability creates two distinct articles: Article 3 deals specifically with assistance in response to crises or emerging crises (the larger part of the funding under the instrument would be used for such measures);[39] and Article 4 deals with assistance in the context of stable conditions for cooperation. In the framework of its long-term component, the Instrument for Stability enables the EU to help build international, regional and national capacity to address pervasive transregional and global threats affecting every single country and people whose vulnerability is increasing in a context of globalisation. In addition, it allows the EU to help strengthen international organisations, state and non-state actors' capacities in the field of conflict prevention and post-conflict peace-building. The instrument is used as a capacity-building tool with a three-pronged objective: addressing threats to law and order; contributing to risk mitigation; and preparedness relating to chemical, biological, radiological and nuclear (CBRN) materials or agents.

These three objectives are addressed in the Strategy Paper which was adopted by the Commission following the management procedure which, as explained above, leaves narrow powers to the Parliament. The Strategy Paper (2007–13) is accompanied by a multi-annual indicative programme (2007–10) which was also adopted following the management procedure. On the other hand, the actions in a crisis situation provided for under Article 3 (short-term component) are by their very nature unforeseeable and non-programmable and therefore not included in the strategy paper. In this case, exceptional assistance measures and interim response programmes are adopted by the Commission. For exceptional assistance measures costing less than €20 million, the Commission adopts the measures which may have a duration of up to 18 months. However, when the measure costs more, the management comitology procedure has to be followed.

[37] Draft report, adopted by AFET on 2 May 2006, amendment 21, PE 362.697v04–00. It may be noted that this view was not supported by the Development Committee of Parliament. In its opinion to the EP Foreign Affairs Committee the EP Committee on Development opposed the inclusion of peace-support operations and of any support for military or paramilitary operations holding that Art 179 EC was not an appropriate legal basis for such measures.

[38] Instrument for Stability, Art 3(2)(i).

[39] Art 23 holds that no more than 27 % of the funds would be used for measures falling under Art 4, ie measures in the context of stable conditions.

Considering the policy area, the regulation provides that the Council must be 'regularly informed' and the Commission should take account of the relevant policy approach of the Council both in its planning and subsequent implementation of the measures. No mention is made as to a duty to inform Parliament at this stage; however it must be kept in mind that for all measures requiring comitology, Parliament has a right to be informed.[40] Moreover, Article 6(6) provides that 'at as early a stage as possible, following the adoption of exceptional assistance measures, the Commission shall report to Parliament and Council by giving an overview of existing and planned Community response measures'.[41]

iv Revision of the Instrument for Stability

As in the case of all the other external aid instruments, the Instrument for Stability provides for its review in Article 25 which holds that the Commission 'shall submit to the European Parliament and the Council, by 31 December 2010, a report evaluating the implementation of this Regulation in the first three years, if appropriate with a proposal introducing the modifications to the regulation'. In fact, the Commission published its report, accompanied by a legislative proposal to revise the Instrument for Stability Regulation, on 21 April 2009.[42]

When the Instrument for Stability Regulation was adopted on 15 November 2006, the Council and the Commission issued a joint statement in which they agreed that:

> nothing in this Regulation shall be construed as prejudging positions taken in Case 91/05 [*ECOWAS*]. Until such time as the Court of Justice rules on that case the Commission will not seek to take measures under Article 3(2)(i). The Council and Commission agree that in the context of the review of the Regulation establishing an instrument for stability provided for in Article 25 of that Regulation, the scope of Article 3(2)(i) will be revised as necessary, on the basis of a Commission proposal, in the light of the judgment of the Court of Justice in Case C-91/05 (*Commission v. Council*).[43]

[40] Council Decision 1999/468/EC (the Comitology Decision) (n 16 above) Art 7.

[41] Politically, the implementation of such actions is also subject to specific consultation procedures set out in a Joint Council/Commission Declaration adopted alongside the Regulation and which is attached to the Strategy Paper, Instrument for Stability, 2007–11, Annex I. In the Declaration, the Council and Commission declare that particular attention shall be given by the Council and the Commission to ensuring consistency of measures adopted or envisaged under Title V and Title VI TEU and under the Instrument for Stability respectively. The Council and the Commission agree further to enhance their cooperation at the planning stage of measures coming under their respective competencies and responsibilities, in view of the need to ensure a comprehensive EU approach to situations of crisis or emerging crisis. This political coordination and consultation takes place in the relevant instances of the Council, without parliamentary involvement, except for informal exchanges with the Commission.

[42] Commission, 'Proposal for a Regulation of the European Parliament and of the Council amending Regulation 1717/2006/EC establishing an instrument for stability' COM (2009) 0195 final.

[43] Council document 14010/06 ADD 1, 27.10.2006.

Considering the outcome of the *ECOWAS* case, as described above, the Commission has now proposed a revision of Article 3(2)(i) in order to bring it in line with the case law of the Court. For the same reason, the Commission proposes that Article 4(1)(a) on action in support of the fight against illicit trafficking be revised in order to refer explicitly to strengthening the capacity of law enforcement and judicial and civil authorities involved in the fight against small arms and light weapons in the same way as in the case of the fight against terrorism and organised crime. Another significant amendment being proposed concerns Article 24 of the Regulation. The Commission holds that the share of the financial envelope intended for measures under Article 4(1)—law and order, security and safety of individuals, which includes the fight against terrorism and organised crime—has proven to be inadequate and needs to be increased from 7 to 10 per cent.

At the time of writing, Parliament, Council and Commission are in negotiations about the revision of the instrument. The negotiations focus on two aspects: substantive elements and procedure. With regard to the substantive elements, the Parliament adopted its first reading position on 21 October 2010 wherein it agrees with the inclusion of provisions relevant to the fight against the spread of small arms and light weapons. It also agreed with the proposed financial increase for measures concerning the fight against terrorism and organised crime, but calls for this increase to be in line with the current review of the EU Peace-building Partnership and internal resources. Parliament's first reading position also refers to measures relating to pre- and post-crisis capacity-building 'to be implemented, if appropriate, by means of the EU Peace-building Partnership', which will most likely be one main element of contention in negotiations with the Council. Moreover, further support for civil society is called for.

With regard to the procedure, Parliament has taken a horizontal issue up in the ongoing negotiations on the revision of the external relations instruments, including the Instrument for Stability. In particular, Parliament holds that Article 290 TFEU on delegated acts should apply to the adoption of the strategy papers and multi-annual programmes. Each of the external relations instruments establishes the main objectives and principles, but leaves it up to the Commission to adopt measures, such as the multi-country strategy papers, thematic strategy papers and multi-annual indicative programmes under Article 7 of the Instrument for Stability, to determine the framework and priorities for the relevant country, region or theme. To date, these measures and annual action programmes are all adopted following the management procedure—Article 4 of the Comitology Decision[44]—which excludes Parliament's power to veto the measures. In the case of the Instrument for Stability, this would only apply to the strategy papers and multi-annual indicative programmes for the long-term

[44] Council Decision 1999/468/EC (n 16 above).

measures under Article 4 on assistance in the context of stable conditions for cooperation, but not to the Exceptional Assistance Measures and Interim Response Programmes.

This issue is an interesting one. It is debatable whether such strategy papers and multi-annual programmes are to be considered as mere implementing measures, or whether when adopting them the Commission exercises a quasi-legislative role. The very name of the instruments suggests that they are programming instruments—they establish a strategy for a specific theme or country or region, and then funds are programmed according to the needs which result from that strategy. If one followed this reasoning, then it would be for the Commission to adopt such measures, and ex post democratic control of the measures taken would be sufficient. In actual fact, there would not even be a need for the measures to be adopted following the management procedure, which gives Council the power to veto the measures.

However, if one delves beyond the names, strategy papers and multi-annual programmes in fact establish the priorities, expected results and financial contribution for the specific countries, regions or themes. While the discussion on the strategy to be taken and the economic and social analysis of the country, region or theme which form the basis for strategy papers are important elements in the programming process, the choice of priorities, the amount of financial contribution and the decision as to which country, region or theme is funded provides the Commission with a broad discretion and a political choice which should not be underestimated. That discretion calls for an element of ex ante democratic control, especially in the case of instruments such as the Development Cooperation Instrument which have very broad objectives and which cover cooperation for a good number of third countries.

Striking the right balance between the flexibility which the Commission needs to implement the external instruments and the need for effective democratic scrutiny is pertinent. On the one hand, efficiency calls for the Commission[45] to have a certain level of flexibility in the programming of funds. However, EU funds—as is the case with all public funding—require closer political and democratic scrutiny. One could possibly consider, especially in view of the new instruments for the period post-2013,[46] that the elements which have greater political and financial implications and which are now included in strategy papers and multi-annual indicative programmes, could be adopted in a way which provides for Parliamentary scrutiny. This could be done in various ways. For example, one could consider including these elements as Annexes to the Regulations establishing the different instruments and provide for their amendment through the ordinary legislative procedure or through delegated acts.

[45] This would also apply to the European External Action Service when it is established and starts to play its role in the programming of the external relations instruments.

[46] The external relations instruments which were adopted in 2006 have a seven-year period duration and expire in 2013.

Another, more practical option, is to adopt such elements as delegated acts under Article 290 TFEU. The programming would then be done on the basis of these delegated acts by the Commission. This would allow flexibility, while providing for the required ex ante democratic scrutiny.

Before concluding, it is worth mentioning the newly established European External Action Service. The Council Decision establishing the organisation and functioning of the European External Action Service was adopted on 26 July 2010.[47] Article 9 of the Decision holds that: 'The management of EU external cooperation programmes is under the responsibility of the Commission without prejudice to role of the Commission and of the EEAS in programming as set out in the following paragraphs'. With regard to the Instrument for Stability, while the programming will be done by the EEAS for the whole instrument, there is a distinction between Article 4, namely assistance in the context of stable conditions, and the remaining part of the instrument, namely assistance in response to situations of crisis or emerging crises. While in the case of the former, the EEAS shall contribute to the programming and management cycle, and has the responsibility for preparing Commission Decisions regarding the multi-annual programming,[48] the latter shall fall directly under the responsibility of the High Representative/EEAS and the Commission would only be responsible for their financial implementation. Moreover, the relevant Commission department responsible for this implementation shall be co-located with the EEAS.[49]

It will be interesting to note how this will affect a future proposal, if any, to replace the Instrument for Stability, which expires in 2013. The dilemma as to whether the content of such an instrument should rather be considered development cooperation under the now Article 208 TFEU or CFSP will be back for discussion, but this time within a service which is equally responsible for CFSP as it is for other external action policies. This will be relevant, even if at the end of the day the proposal for an instrument will be a Commission proposal. The above discussion on Article 40 TEU will be pertinent in deciding which measures should come within the scope of such an instrument.

B The Food Facility

The Food Facility is a specific instrument that aimed at reacting to the 2007–08 food crises in developing countries. Based on Article 179 EC, it provided a response to such crises through a facility of €1 billion targeted towards addressing the period between emergency aid (which is financed through the Humanitarian Aid Regulation) and the medium- to long-term development cooperation

[47] Council Decision 2010/427/EU establishing the organisation and functioning of the European External Action Services [2010] OJ L201/30.

[48] Ibid, Art 9(3).

[49] Ibid, Art 9(6).

(financed under the Development Cooperation Instrument). The aim of the facility was to provide instant help, mainly for farmers in developing countries, helping them produce food for the local populations; but it also provided relief to people who fell into the hunger trap due to the increase in food prices.

The Development Cooperation Instrument provides specifically for a thematic programme on food security.[50] Its aim is to improve food security in favour of the poorest people and to contribute to achieving the Millennium Development Goal (MDG) on poverty and hunger. The Development Cooperation Instrument, in Article 15, holds that this is to be done through a set of actions which ensure overall coherence, complementarities and continuity of interventions, including in the area of the transition from relief to development.

However, whilst Article 15 provides a legal basis for long-term support in the field of food security, it is not backed by the necessary financial package to tackle emergencies such as the food crises which resulted from high fuel prices in 2007–08. In a Resolution adopted on 22 May 2008,[51] Parliament stressed the fundamental nature of the right to food and the need to improve access for all people at all times to enough food for an active, healthy life. Parliament called on the Council to step up its commitments to the Millenium Development Goals by reaffirming funding commitments and adopting an EU MDG agenda for action at the June European Council. Parliament called on the Commission to carry out a food security impact assessment of EU policies relating to the Common Agriculture Policy, of renewable energy targets, of development aid and of international trade agreements, in order to improve global food security and called on Member States and the international community to meet the extraordinary emergency appeal of the WFP as a matter of urgency. The European Council of 19–20 June 2008 reaffirmed that high food prices were severely affecting the situation of the world's poorest populations and putting at risk progress towards all MDGs. The Council concluded that, from a development and humanitarian assistance perspective, EU action was required.[52]

Reflecting that political will, the Commission proposed, in July 2008, a Food Facility based on Article 179 EC, since it targeted developing countries, to provide short-term response to soaring food prices.[53] The primary objective of this

[50] Council Regulation 1905/2006/EC establishing a financing instrument for development cooperation [2006] OJ L378/41, Art 15.

[51] European Parliament resolution of 22 May 2008 on rising food prices in the EU and the developing countries, T6–0229/2008.

[52] Presidency Conclusions, Brussels, 19/20 June 2008, paras 32–36.

[53] Commission, 'Proposal for a Regulation of the European Parliament and of the Council establishing a facility for rapid response to soaring food prices in developing countries' COM (2008) 0450 final, 2. The proposal followed a Communication 'Tackling the challenge of rising food prices—Directions for EU action', on 20 May 2008, COM (2008) 321 final. This Communication sets out elements for an EU response to the food price challenges, proposing actions internal to the EU, and actions to address the effects of the crisis at international level.

proposal was to encourage a positive supply response of farmers in developing countries in the short to medium term, in the context of sustainable development. The Facility would also support activities to respond rapidly and directly to mitigate the negative effects of high food prices in line with food security objectives. The expected results of the assistance were, among others: (i) an increase in agricultural production and food security in assisted countries, (ii) reduced malnutrition rates, especially among vulnerable groups, and (iii) reduced food price inflation. This would be done through measures to improve access to agricultural inputs and services, including fertilisers and seeds, and safety net measures aiming at maintaining or improving the agricultural productive capacity, and at addressing the basic food needs of the most vulnerable populations.

The idea of such a facility was strongly welcomed in Parliament, in particular by the Committee on Development, but both Parliament and Council outlined various issues of concern in the proposal of the Commission.

i Eligible bodies

First of all, the Commission's proposal aimed to direct the funds under the facility through regional and international organisations such as the FAO (Food and Agriculture Organisation), the WFP (World Food Programme) or the World Bank, which it considered to be better placed to implement the necessary projects. Parliament opposed this and called for widening the eligibility of bodies through which the funds could be distributed to include governments, local authorities, NGOs, etc. While this modality could be useful to ensure rapid implementation, it was also considered necessary to be flexible especially since conditions vary widely from one country to another, including the degrees of expertise, specialisation and effectiveness of different types of organisations which may be used to implement assistance.

Parliament proposed, therefore, to widen the choice of bodies which may be selected by the Commission to implement measures under the Regulation, on the basis of the list already used for the Development Cooperation Instrument. It justified its amendment holding that in order to assist small farmers in particular and lay a stable foundation for sustainable food production, it is necessary to strengthen and support the local and regional grassroot organisations. As a result, the adopted Food Facility included a list of eligible entities in its Article 4. The list included: (a) partner countries and regions, and their institutions; (b) decentralised bodies in the partner countries; (c) joint bodies set up by the partner countries and regions with the Community; (d) international organisations, including regional organisations, UN bodies, departments an missions, international and regional financial institutions and development banks; and (e) entities and bodies of the Member States, partner countries and regions and any other third country.

The Regulation itself did not establish how the funds will be distributed. For Parliament, an appropriate balance should be applied in the allocation of resources between international organisations and other eligible entities, but no figure was mentioned by Parliament in the text nor was it included in the final regulation.

ii Transparency and implementation

Regulations allowing for the implementation of the budget normally set up a system for subsidiary decisions, of a technical nature, to be taken by the Commission following a comitology procedure, as with the external relations instruments described above.[54] At the time, the rules for such committees were laid down in the Comitology Decision,[55] which also enshrines Parliament's right to scrutinise the measures presented to the Committee.[56] However, the proposal from the Commission, due to its focus on rapid implementation, did not establish a comitology procedure. Article 3 foresaw that assistance and cooperation under the Facility should be implemented through a set of decisions to finance supporting measures, adopted by the Commission. The Commission considered the timing required for comitology procedures would hinder the immediate disbursement of funds. However, amendments were tabled to introduce the standard comitology structure for this type of legislation—a management Committee.[57] For the Parliament, this was most important as it was deemed more transparent. The Council and Parliament should, in this way, be informed of the decisions to be taken by the Commission before they are adopted, even if the comitology procedure proposed did not give the Parliament the power to veto these decisions before they are adopted. In this way, Parliament and Council were also informed about the distribution of funds through intergovernmental organisations and other eligible entities. In order to respond to the problem concerning urgency, Parliament and Council agreed, in a separate declaration, that the deadlines required by the comitology decision giving time for Council and Parliament to react would be reduced to the minimum.

The interest in this facility is that the decision-making process for its adoption proved that even under urgent circumstances, Parliament, Council and Commission could work at a fast pace, even if the requirements of the co-decision procedure had to be fulfilled.

[54] See, eg, Arts 21 and 35 of the Development Cooperation Instrument.

[55] Council Decision 1999/468/EC (n 16 above).

[56] In particular ibid, Arts 5a, 7 and 8.

[57] ibid, Art 4. As explained above, if such a Regulation were to be adopted now, Arts 290 and 291 TFEU would apply.

III PARLIAMENT'S ROLE UNDER THE TREATY OF LISBON: COOPERATION WITH THIRD COUNTRIES AND HUMANITARIAN AID

While maintaining the thrust of the provisions under the Treaty of Nice, the Treaty of Lisbon restructures the provisions and adapts the procedures on cooperation with third countries and humanitarian aid. Part V of the Treaty on the Functioning of the European Union (TFEU) has as its opening Article 205, holding that:

> The Union's action on the international scene, pursuant to the this Part, shall be guided by the principles, pursue the objectives and be conducted in accordance with the general provisions laid down in Chapter 1 of the Title V of the Treaty on the European Union,

thereby placing the EU's external cooperation provisions within the broader framework of the Union's external actions. Title III of Part V focuses on cooperation with third countries (developing and non-developing) and humanitarian aid. While Parliament will now be co-decider for both development cooperation and economic, financial and technical cooperation with third countries other than developing countries, a new provision providing for urgent financial assistance to any third country excludes it from any decision-making power. This new balance of power will be examined in this section, with special reference to the scope of new Article 213 TFEU on urgent financial assistance.

A Parliament as co-decider for cooperation instruments with all third countries

The ordinary legislative procedure applies to all instruments of cooperation with third countries, be they developing countries or not. This removes the anomaly in the previous treaties, where Parliament was a co-decider for instruments of development cooperation (Article 179 EC) but not for other cooperation instruments with third countries (Article 181a EC).[58] The new provisions, Article 209 TFEU on cooperation with developing countries and Article 212(2) TFEU on cooperation with third countries other than developing countries, both provide that measures necessary for the implementation of these policies shall be adopted by the ordinary legislative procedure.

[58] That anomaly gave rise to various discussions among the institutions on when Arts 179 EC and 181a EC were the appropriate legal basis. See especially Case C-155/07 *European Parliament v Council of the European Union* [2008] ECR I-8103.

The substance of the articles is also adapted. Article 208 TFEU replaces ex-Article 177 EC and holds that 'Union development cooperation policy shall have as its primary objective the reduction and, in the long term, the eradication of poverty'. This objective appears, at first hand, to have limited the scope of development cooperation. Ex-Article 177 EC seemed to have a broader scope within its list of three objectives, namely: the sustainable economic and social development of the developing countries, and more particularly the most disadvantaged among them; the smooth and gradual integration of developing countries into the world economy; the campaign against poverty in developing countries. These were in addition to the reference to Community policy in this area contributing to the general objective of developing and consolidating democracy and the rule of law, and to that of respecting human rights and fundamental freedoms.

The issue as to whether development cooperation should now be given a narrower interpretation is important when one considers the adoption of future instruments similar to the Instrument for Stability. In this regard, a reading of Article 208 within the broader picture of external action in the Treaty of Lisbon is necessary. The opening sentence of Article 208 TFEU holds specifically that 'Union policy in the field of development cooperation shall be conducted within the framework of the principles and objectives of the Union's external action'. Article 21(2) TEU, in fact, includes the objective to consolidate and support democracy, the rule of law, human rights and the principles of international law; to foster the sustainable economic, social and environmental development of developing countries, with the primary aim of eradicating poverty and to encourage the integration of all countries into the world economy, including through the progressive abolition of restrictions on international trade,[59] and various other common policies.

In practical terms, while the adaptation of words calls for more focus on poverty eradication, there is nothing to suggest that the aim of the new wording is to narrow down the scope of development cooperation. After all, a large variety of policies and action can lead to poverty eradication. Such a reading is in line with the general provisions on the Union's external action in Title V of the TEU in the Treaty of Lisbon which include that 'The Union shall ensure *consistency* between the different areas of its external action'.[60] One thing the wording does seem to change is that the emphasis is on the needs of the people in developing countries. This should avoid development cooperation from being used as an instrument of the foreign and security policy of the Union, rather than for the benefit of the developing countries themselves and their people.[61]

[59] Art 21(2) (b), (d) and (e).

[60] Treaty of Lisbon, Art 21(3), second subpara, TEU, emphasis added.

[61] See JF Brakeland, 'Politique commerciale et aide humanitaire' in G Amato, H Bribosia, B De Witte (eds), *Genesis and Destiny of the European Constitutional* (Brussels, Bruylant, 2007) 870.

Another interesting element for Parliament is that the Treaty of Lisbon does away with Article 179(3) EC, which held that 'the provisions of this article shall not affect cooperation with the African, Caribbean and Pacific countries in the framework of the ACP-EC Convention'. What are the implications of this amendment? The deletion of Article 179(3) EC follows a recommendation of the European Convention, in Working Group VII on External Action, which held that:

> There was a high degree of support in favour of the integration of the European Development Fund (EDF) into the Community budget and thus making it subject to the same procedures as other areas of Community financial assistance. Such an integration must be accompanied by improvements in the effectiveness and poverty focus of EC development programmes. It was also pointed out by some that such integration into the budget should be organised in a way which in no case leads to reducing the volume of aid directed towards ACP countries.[62]

The amendment brought about by the Treaty of Lisbon can, therefore, be considered as a first step towards the expression of the political will of the Member States to bring the EDF within the Union budget. Such a move towards the budgetisation of the EDF would not only bring more coherence in the EU's action in the field of development cooperation but it would also provide a parliamentary dimension to all cooperation of the EU with developing countries.

Development cooperation continues to be an area of shared competence where the exercise of Union competence cannot result in Member States being prevented from exercising their own.[63] This means that the Court judgment in *Parliament v Council*,[64] on development aid under the Fourth Lomé Convention, continues to apply, as codified by Article 4(4) TFEU. The Court held that 'Since the Community' s competence in the field of development aid is not exclusive,

[62] Document CONV 459/02, 16.12.2002, para 56.

[63] Art 4(4) TFEU explicitly includes development cooperation within the list of areas falling under 'shared competence'. Having said that, it must be noted that while both the Union and the Member States are competent to act in the field, the Treaty of Lisbon holds that 'The Union's development cooperation and that of the Member States complement and *reinforce* each other' (Art 208 (1), first subpara, TFEU). Moreover, Art 210 TFEU emphasises the need for coordination. It provides that 'In order to promote the complementarity and efficiency of their action, the Union and the Member States shall coordinate their policies on development cooperation and shall consult each other on their aid programmes, including in international organisations and during international conferences. They may undertake joint action. Member States shall contribute if necessary to the implementation of Union aid programmes'. According to the same provision the Commission may take any useful initiative to promote such coordination. Thus, Union development cooperation is meant to be on an equal footing to that of the Member States, and the Union is not just another donor. While this is clearly an area where Member States are competent to act, they are legally obliged to coordinate with the Union and to contribute, where necessary, to the implementation of Union aid programmes. It can here be noted that the political will of the Member States and the EU to coordinate has been expressed, in particular, through the Joint Statement by the Council and the representatives of the Governments of the Member States meeting within the Council, the European Parliament and the Commission on European Union Development Policy: 'The European Consensus on Development', B6–0653/2005, P6_TA(2005)0528.

[64] Case C-316/91 *European Parliament v Council of the European Union* [1994] ECR I-625.

the Member States are entitled to enter into commitments themselves vis-à-vis non-member States, either collectively or individually, or even jointly with the Community.'[65] Therefore, while the Treaty of Lisbon clearly does not hinder the inclusion of the EDF in the Union budget, the decision remains essentially one to be made by the Member States.

The Treaty of Lisbon also introduces a new chapter on humanitarian aid. The current humanitarian aid regulation is based on Article 179 EC, ie, the legal basis for development cooperation. Under the Treaty of Lisbon, legal acts concerning humanitarian aid have a new legal basis. Article 214(2) TFEU holds that humanitarian aid shall be conducted 'in compliance with principles of international law and with the principles of impartiality, neutrality and non-discrimination'. The importance of this subparagraph cannot be underestimated when one considers the necessity of ensuring that humanitarian aid is not mingled with other foreign policies, in particular defence and security. The Humanitarian Aid Consensus agreed upon by Parliament, Council and the Commission on 29 November 2007[66] emphasised these principles. It can be noted that such assistance is not restricted to developing countries, but extends to relief and protection for people in third countries who are victims of natural or man-made disasters, without distinction as to the third country they are in. Furthermore, the main objective is providing assistance, relief and protection to victims, rather than long-term poverty alleviation as is the case with development cooperation.

The procedures, the competences and the requirement of coordination (among the Union and the Member States and also with international organisations and bodies) are the same as those applying to development cooperation. In particular, Parliament is also a co-legislator, and its assent is required for the conclusion of international agreements concluded with third countries or international organisations helping to achieve the objectives of humanitarian aid. If a new regulation on humanitarian aid were to be adopted, the ordinary legislative procedure would apply. The Treaty of Lisbon also provides a legal basis for the establishment of European Voluntary Humanitarian Aid Corps (Article 214 (5) TFEU). Parliament had called for the establishment of such a 'Peace Corps' in various resolutions.[67] The rules and procedures for its establishment will also be adopted by Parliament and Council according to the ordinary legislative

[65] Case C-316/91 *European Parliament v Council of the European Union* [1994] ECR I-625, paras 26 and 34. See, generally, P Eeckhout, *External Relations of the European Union, Legal and Constitutional Foundations* (Oxford, Oxford University Press, 2005) 107, 108.

[66] European Parliament resolution of 29 November 2007 on the proclamation of a European Consensus on Humanitarian Aid, B6–0484/2007. See, in particular, European Parliament resolution of 14 November 2007 on a European Consensus on Humanitarian Aid, A6–0372/2007, in particular its para 8.

[67] See European Parliament recommendation on the establishment of a European Civil Peace Corps, A4–0047/99 [1999] OJ C150/153. Parliament had recommended that Council 'make minimum, flexible arrangements for the sole purpose of reviewing and mobilising both the resources of NGOs and those made available by states, and possibly participating in their coordination' (para 3).

procedure. At the time of writing, Parliament has just started discussing a Communication from the Commission on how to express EU citizen's solidarity through volunteering.[68] This should lead to a legislative proposal from the Commission by end 2012.

B Article 213 TFEU—special procedure for measures of urgent financial assistance

The Treaty of Lisbon also provides for a specific legal basis for emergencies. Article 213 TFEU provides that 'when the situation in a third country requires urgent financial assistance from the Union, the Council shall adopt the necessary decisions on a proposal from the Commission'. This article, while welcome for providing a legal basis for urgent needs, gives rise to various questions. This is an exception to the general rule that legislative acts in the field of external relations be adopted by the ordinary legislative procedure and since it therefore upsets the balance of powers among the institutions, it can only be applied exceptionally, and only in instances where the urgency of the measure does not allow for use of the ordinary legislative procedure.

In this regard, it is interesting to consider what could fall under this article. As explained above, the Lisbon Treaty provides a specific legal basis for humanitarian aid. Article 214 TFEU supplements the EU's powers under Articles 208–11 TFEU (development cooperation) and Article 212 TFEU (cooperation with non-developing countries) by adding a specific legal basis for humanitarian aid, which is not restricted to developing countries. Under Article 214 TFEU, Parliament and Council can adopt framework regulations in order to equip the EU with a legal basis for humanitarian aid. Such a regulation would provide the legal framework for the EU to act in urgent humanitarian catastrophes such as the recent earthquakes in Haiti and Pakistan. This illustrates that with regard to humanitarian catastrophes (natural or manmade), Article 213 TFEU is not, generally, required. Moreover, as explained above, most external relations instruments provide for special measures in cases of emergency.

Another example of emergency aid to date is macro-financial assistance (MFA) granted to third countries, in most cases countries neighbouring the EU, but not necessarily so. MFA is a policy-based financial instrument of untied and undesignated balance-of-payments support to partner third countries. It generally takes the form of medium/long-term loans or grants, or a combination of these. From past examples, it can be noted that MFA is exceptional in nature and is mobilised on a case-by-case basis with a view to assisting the beneficiary countries in dealing with serious, but generally short-term, balance-of-payments

[68] Commission, Communication to the European Parliament and the Council on how to express EU citizen's solidarity through volunteering: First reflections on a European Voluntary Humanitarian Aid Corps, COM(2010)683 final.

or budget difficulties. It is released on the basis of the fulfilment of economic and financial policy conditions set out in the Memorandum of Understanding agreed between the Commission and the authorities of the recipient country. Recent examples include macro-financial assistance granted to Armenia, Georgia, Serbia and Moldova.[69]

All the Council Decisions providing this type of assistance under the Treaty of Nice were based on Article 308 EC, thereby requiring unanimity in Council.[70] The reason for using Article 308 EC and not Article 181a EC is that under Declaration no 10 attached to the Treaty of Nice, balance of payments aid fell outside the scope of Article 181a EC on economic, financial and technical cooperation with third countries.[71] One could also argue that in some cases Article 179 TFEU (development cooperation) could have been used when the third country concerned was a developing country. However, at this point, it should be noted that the definition of developing countries depends on that given to them by the Union. Neither previous treaties nor the Treaty of Lisbon contain a specific definition or a list of the countries which are to be considered as 'developing'. Guidance may be sought from the work of international organisations such as the OECD, which have attempted to define the term 'developing country' by categorising countries according to various criteria, in particular gross national income (GNI) per capita.[72] However, it is finally up to the European institutions to define which countries they specifically regard as

[69] Council Decision 2009/890/EC providing macro-financial assistance to Armenia [2009] OJ L320/3;Council Decision 2009/889/EC providing macro-financial assistance to Georgia [2009] OJ L320/1; Council Decision 2009/892/EC providing macro-financial assistance to Serbia [2009] OJ L320/9. Decision 2010/938/EU of the European Parliament and of Council providing MFA to the Republic of Moldova [2010] OJ L277/1.

[70] See FX Priollaud and D Siritzky, *Le Traité de Lisbonne, Commentaire, article par article, des nouveaux traités européens (TUE et TFEU)* (Paris, La Documentation Française, 2008) 311.

[71] Declaration on Art 181a of the Treaty establishing the European Community: 'The Conference confirms that, without prejudice to other provisions of the Treaty establishing the European Community, balance-of-payments aid to third countries falls outside the scope of Art 181a'. In this regard, the European Parliament adopted a resolution on the implementation of macro-financial assistance to third countries on 3 June 2003. In that resolution Parliament referred to Art 308 as inadequate (especially after enlargement) and regretted the decision to include Declaration 10 in the Nice Treaty and avoid the use of Art 181a EC for the balance of payments (P5_TA(2003)0233, para C).

[72] The World Bank classifies countries in income groups according to GNP per capita. The Development Assistance Committee (DAC) of the OECD maintains a list of developing countries based essentially on aid flows; the DAC treats the transition economies as a group separate from developing countries. The United Nations Conference on Trade and Development (UNCTAD) maintains a list of least-developed countries (LDC) including currently 49 countries. See B Martenczuk, 'Cooperation with Developing and Other Third Countries: Elements of a Common Foreign Policy', in S Griller and B Weidel (eds), *External Economic Relations and Foreign Policy in the European Union* (New York, SpringerWien, Research Institute for European Affairs Publication Series, vol 20, 2002) 389.

developing countries. For example, some of the recent examples of macro-financial assistance decisions relate to countries falling under the Instrument for Pre-Accession (IPA), such as Montenegro[73] and Bosnia and Herzegovina.[74] Countries which aspire to join the EU may be considered as potential candidate states, rather than 'developing countries', by the Union, even if the OECD[75] defines them as developing countries. Other examples relate to countries which fall under the European Neighbourhood Policy Instrument (ENPI), such as the MFA decision for Lebanon.[76] When determining which legal basis applies, such considerations would have to be kept in mind.

The question arises as to which is the appropriate legal basis for the adoption of MFA regulations under the Treaty of Lisbon. The choice between Articles 209(1) and 212(2) TFEU will depend on the beneficiary country in question. If it is a developing country, Article 209(1) TFEU will be the appropriate legal basis—such measures can be considered to be means of reducing poverty if they are required in developing countries. Article 212(2) TFEU would be the appropriate legal basis when the beneficiaries are other third countries.

On the other hand, considering that they respond to short-term urgent needs, it may be argued that Article 213 TFEU may be used as a legal basis. This would imply that decisions are taken by the Council, excluding Parliament's involvement. But there are arguments against this position. Practice shows that macro-financial assistance is disbursed on the basis of separate instalments over a period of two years or more.[77] While the first instalment may fall under the category of 'urgent financial assistance from the Union', the other instalments do not. Moreover, before 1 November 2010, the Council had acted on the basis of Article 308 EC, which equally requires a certain amount of time due to consultation of Parliament. The requirement that such Decisions be adopted by the ordinary legislative procedure will not necessarily lengthen the time required for the procedure in Parliament.[78] This explains why, in principle, decisions to grant MFA should be based on Article 209 or 212 TFEU, rather than Article 213 TFEU. The Council and Commission have recognised this. In fact, Decisions granting MFA to Moldova and Ukraine adopted in 2010[79] were based on Article 212 TFEU

[73] Council Decision 2008/784/EC establishing a separate liability of Montenegro and reducing proportionately the liability of Serbia with regard to the long-term loans granted by the Community to the State Union of Serbia and Montenegro (formerly the Federal Republic of Yugoslavia) pursuant to Decisions 2001/549/EC and 2002/882/EC [2008] OJ L269/8.

[74] Council Decision 2004/861/EC amending Council Decision 2002/883/EC providing further macro-financial assistance to Bosnia and Herzegovina [2004] OJ L370/80.

[75] Organization for Economic Cooperation and Development.

[76] Council Decision 2007/860/EC providing Community macro-financial assistance to Lebanon [2007] OJ L337/111.

[77] See, eg, ibid, Art 3.

[78] eg, the Food Facility was proposed on 18 July 2008 and adopted on 16 December 2008.

[79] Decision 2010/938/EU of the European Parliament and of the Council providing Macro-financial Assistance to the Republic of Moldova [2010] OJ L277/1 and Decision 388/2010/EU of the European Parliament and of the Council providing Macro-financial Assistance to Ukraine [2010] OJ L179/1.

and were thereby adopted by Parliament and Council following the Ordinary Legislative Procedure. Parliament applied the simplified procedures available in its internal rules in order to ensure that unnecessary delays are avoided and first reading agreements were reached. This ensures that the MFA reaches the relevant third countries without delay .

In trying to find a balance between the requirement to respond to the needs of third countries in due time, while at the same time ensuring its involvement in policy-shaping for MFA, Parliament has lately considered the idea of having a framework regulation for macro-financial assistance.[80] Such a framework regulation, adopted on the basis of Articles 209 and 212 TFEU by ordinary legislative procedure, would provide a basis for the Commission to be in a position to adopt measures granting macro-financial assistance to third countries in the shape of delegated acts. Such a system would, in practice, reduce the powers of Parliament in terms of negotiating the specific instruments of macro-financial assistance individually. However, a framework regulation could be welcome for at least two reasons: (a) Parliament and Council would be in a position to negotiate the type of criteria they want to see applied in all macro-financial assistance measures without being under pressure of time; and (b) when there is a true urgency, the Commission would be in a position to respect basic criteria, established beforehand by ordinary legislative procedure and still act immediately.

For this reason, it remains to be seen under what circumstances Article 213 TFEU will be used. Could Article 213 TFEU be used for an instrument similar to the food facility? One could argue that considering that the food crises required an urgent response, Article 213 TFEU would be appropriate for similar situations. But this is debatable. First of all, one could argue that the actual emergency would only be acceptable for the first commitments and disbursements, and thereby Article 213 TFEU could only possibly be justified for one part (the very urgent initial response) of the instrument. Secondly, such an instrument requires a substantial budgetary manoeuvre for which Parliament would in any case have to be involved on the budgetary level if not the legislative one.

[80] In the explanatory memoranda of the reports on Parliament's opinion on the proposals for Council decisions referred to in n 57 above, the rapporteur stated that 'in line with previous Parliament resolutions … such a substantial instrument as MFA cannot be simply regarded as "exceptional". It is therefore unjustifiable that such an instrument lacks a regular legal basis and continues to be based on ad hoc Council decisions for each operation. A co-decided framework regulation on MFA is necessary in order to enhance transparency, accountability, monitoring and reporting systems. In this respect it must be stressed that after the entry into force of the Treaty of Lisbon, the appropriate legal basis for a Decision granting MFA will be Art 209(1) and 212(2) of the Treaty on the Functioning of the European Union (TFEU), depending on whether the beneficiary country is classified as developing country or not by the Union institutions. In both cases, the ordinary legislative procedure applies. Art 213 TFEU should not apply to Decisions granting MFA.'

IV CONCLUSION

The need for scrutiny and visibility in external aid cannot be denied. Parliamentary legislative powers, coupled with scrutiny of programming and implementation, are required if the European Union is to continue to have external aid policies which are recognised and supported by European citizens. In this regard, the broadening of Parliament's co-decision powers in the Treaty of Lisbon to cooperation with all third countries, be they developing countries or other third countries, is welcome. The Treaty also opens the door for cooperation with ACP partners to be brought within the EU budget. This would create a simplified approach in terms of policy and bring this substantial part of development cooperation within Parliamentary control.

On the other hand, Article 213 TFEU leaves an option for urgent measures to be adopted without delay, with Council acting by qualified majority and without requiring the opinion or co-decision of Parliament. As it derogates from the general rule that the ordinary legislative procedure applies to EU cooperation measures with third countries, this provision must be interpreted narrowly and should be restricted only to very urgent measures.

In this regard, framework regulations which provide principles, objectives and criteria to be established by the legislator, while allowing for the Commission to adopt the required measures in urgent situations, should be explored in all instances in order to avoid the need for resorting to the derogation. As explained above, this already happens in the vast majority of emergency situations through special provisions in the external relations instruments, and more expressly through special instruments focused on emergency assistance such as the humanitarian aid regulation, the Instrument for Stability and the Food Facility. Such a structure could be further developed in the case of macro-financial assistance which, from the above examples, is generally granted in comparable situations with a view to assisting the beneficiary countries in dealing with serious, but generally short-term, balance-of-payments or budget difficulties. The objectives and criteria could, in practice, be defined in a framework regulation. Such a system provides a good balance in the sense that the essential elements, in particular objectives, principles and other criteria are determined by Parliament and Council jointly, while the actual response in cases of emergency would be carried out by the Commission, subject to Parliamentary scrutiny but without the time concerns related to the adoption of legislative acts.

Index